Rashi, Biblical Interpretation, and Latin Learning in Medieval Europe

In this volume, Mordechai Cohen explores the interpretive methods of Rashi of Troyes (1040–1105), the most influential Jewish Bible commentator of all time. By elucidating the "plain sense" (*peshat*) of Scripture, together with critically selected midrashic interpretations, Rashi created an approach that was revolutionary in the talmudically oriented Ashkenazic milieu. Cohen contextualizes Rashi's commentaries by examining influences from other centers of Jewish learning in Muslim Spain and Byzantine lands. He also opens new scholarly paths by comparing Rashi's methods with trends in Latin learning reflected in the Psalms commentary of his older contemporary, Saint Bruno the Carthusian (1030–1101). Drawing upon the Latin tradition of *enarratio poetarum* ("interpreting the poets"), Bruno applied a grammatical interpretive method and incorporated patristic commentary selectively, a parallel that Cohen uses to illuminate Rashi's exegetical values. Cohen thereby brings to light the novel literary conceptions manifested by Rashi and his key students, Joseph Qara and Rashbam.

Mordechai Z. Cohen is Professor of Bible and Associate Dean of the Bernard Revel Graduate School of Jewish Studies, Yeshiva University. He is the author of *Three Approaches to Biblical Metaphor* (2003), *Opening the Gates of Interpretation* (2011), and *The Rule of Peshat* (2020) and a recognized expert on Jewish Bible interpretation in its Muslim and Christian cultural contexts. He has taught at universities in the USA, Israel, Europe, and China.

Rashi, Biblical Interpretation, and Latin Learning in Medieval Europe

A New Perspective on an Exegetical Revolution

MORDECHAI Z. COHEN
Yeshiva University, New York

CAMBRIDGE
UNIVERSITY PRESS

CAMBRIDGE
UNIVERSITY PRESS

University Printing House, Cambridge CB2 8BS, United Kingdom

One Liberty Plaza, 20th Floor, New York, NY 10006, USA

477 Williamstown Road, Port Melbourne, VIC 3207, Australia

314–321, 3rd Floor, Plot 3, Splendor Forum, Jasola District Centre,
New Delhi – 110025, India

79 Anson Road, #06–04/06, Singapore 079906

Cambridge University Press is part of the University of Cambridge.

It furthers the University's mission by disseminating knowledge in the pursuit of education, learning, and research at the highest international levels of excellence.

www.cambridge.org
Information on this title: www.cambridge.org/9781108470292
DOI: 10.1017/9781108556538

First published 2021

A catalogue record for this publication is available from the British Library.

ISBN 978-1-108-47029-2 Hardback

In memory of Nehama Leibowitz (1905–1997)
Who dedicated her life to the study and teaching of the Bible
with Rashi's commentaries

Contents

Acknowledgments *page* x
List of Abbreviations xiii

Introduction 1
Key Challenges in Rashi Scholarship 5
Understanding Rashi in Light of St. Bruno 19
Outline of this Study 22

1 A New Program of *Peshat* ("Plain Sense" Exegesis) 26
Rashi and his *Peshat* School 28
The Text of Rashi's Commentaries 33
Three Paradigms that Privilege "the *Peshat* of Scripture" 36
Rashi's Key Exegetical Concepts and Terminology 52

2 "Settling" the Words of Scripture Using Midrash 55
Midrashic Rendering of the Biblical Narrative 56
Typological Reading 59
Halakhic Reading 61
Disregarding the Talmudic *Peshat* Maxim 66
Rashi's Dual Interpretive Goal 69

3 St. Bruno on Psalms: Precedent for Rashi? 79
Grammatical Interpretive Method 80
The Historical/Literal Sense 83
Continuity and Sequence 84
Authorial Intention 87
Bruno and Rashi: Assessing Parallels and Possible Influence 90

4 Comparison to the Andalusian Exegetical School 102
Ties to Judeo-Arabic Scholarship 102
Samuel ben Hofni's Construction of *Peshat* 104

Ibn Janah's Construction of *Peshat* 113
Further Development of the *Peshat* Maxim in the Andalusian Tradition 121
Andalusian Conceptions of *Peshat* vs. Christian *Sensus Litteralis* 129

5 Comparison to the Byzantine Exegetical School 134
Reuel and the Scholia on the Pentateuch 136
A Possible Source for Rashi? 146
"The *Peshat* of Scripture" in *Leqaḥ Ṭov* 150
Peshat in Tobiah ben Eliezer's Song of Songs Commentary 157

6 Rashi's Literary Sensibilities and Latin *Grammatica* 164
Critical Selection of Traditional (Midrashic, Patristic) Commentaries 166
Prologue Format and "the Holy Spirit" 167
Literary Structure: *Ordo Artificialis* vs. *Ordo Naturalis* 177

7 Rashi's Notion of "the Poet" (*ha-Meshorer*) in the Latin Context 187
The "Poet's" Structural Intentions 189
Shifts in Perspective, Addressee, and Theme 192
The "Poet" vs. the Biblical Editor 196
"Writer of the Book (*Kotev ha-Sefer*)" 198
Rashi's Literary Conceptions and Possible Latin Parallels 199

8 Joseph Qara and Rashbam: *Peshat* Legacy in Northern France 207
Biographic and Bibliographic Background 210
Attitudes toward Contemporary Modes of Bible Interpretation 215
New Methods of *Peshat* 221

9 Literary Sensibilities of *Peshat* within a Latin Context 238
Hermeneutics: Status of *Peshat* in Relation to Midrash 239
Peshat vs. Halakhah 243
Conceptions of the Biblical Narrator-Editor 248
Reflections of Rashi's Notion of "the Poet" (*ha-Meshorer*) in Rashbam 256
Innovation in a Traditional Framework: *Peshat* and Human Literary Agency 261
"Mosaic" Authorship of the Pentateuch 266
From Rashi to Rashbam: *Peshat* and the Literary Dimensions of Scripture 270

Bibliography 272
Manuscripts 272

Acknowledgments

As with many scholarly endeavors, especially interdisciplinary ones, this study reflects valuable input by colleagues in a variety of fields. The origins of this volume can be traced to fruitful scholarly exchanges in 2010–2011 in the semester-long international research group "Encountering Scripture in Overlapping Cultures: Early Jewish, Christian and Muslim Strategies of Reading and their Contemporary Implications," which I was privileged to direct, together with Meir Bar-Asher, at the Israel Institute for Advanced Studies in Jerusalem. Each of the fourteen group members submitted a chapter to the volume *Interpreting Scriptures in Judaism, Christianity and Islam: Overlapping Inquiries* (Cambridge University Press, 2016), which I edited with Adele Berlin, with assistance from Meir Bar-Asher, Rita Copeland, and Jon Whitman. The chapters of that volume, which run from antiquity to the twentieth century, attest to the depth of the underlying comparative project, in the spirit of which this volume was written.

Early in the project I discussed Rashi and his Latin intellectual context with Rita Copeland, Jon Whitman, and Alastair Minnis (who counts the renowned Beryl Smalley among his mentors). Our discussions in Jerusalem turned to the eleventh-century cathedral master Bruno the Carthusian, whose Psalms commentary has been the subject of groundbreaking studies by Andrew Kraebel, then completing his PhD with Alastair Minnis at Yale and who subsequently joined our group in Jerusalem. Andrew and I sat for weeks studying Rashi and Bruno side by side and were struck by the methodological parallels between them, notwithstanding everything that would naturally separate medieval Jewish and Christian readers of the Bible. The initial fruits of that discovery were published in an essay entitled "A New Perspective on Rashi of Troyes in Light of Bruno the Carthusian:

Exploring Jewish and Christian Bible Interpretation in Eleventh-Century Northern France" that appeared in *Viator* 48:1 (2017): 39–86.

It soon became clear that the implications of that study for understanding the *peshat* revolution pioneered by Rashi in northern France required further treatment in a full-length monograph – a desideratum fulfilled by the current volume. In its preparation, I benefited from further discussions with learned colleagues. In particular, Rita Copeland continually provided invaluable expert advice on the Western Christian interpretive tradition within the larger context of medieval Latin learning – and the possible parallels within the commentaries of Rashi and his successors in the northern French *peshat* tradition. I am grateful to Lisa Fredman for sharing with me her wisdom regarding the text of Rashi's commentaries in light of the medieval manuscripts and early printed editions.

An earlier draft of Chapter 7 was recently published in the *Internet Journal of Jewish Studies* 18 (2020): 1–42. Special thanks to Baruch Alster, Yitzhak Berger, Jonathan Jacobs, and Eran Viezel for their review of that study of Rashi's conception of the biblical narrator, which is essential not only to Chapter 7, but to this volume as a whole.

My teacher Haym Soloveitchik helped refine the arguments in Chapter 8 regarding the complex Ashkenazic intellectual milieu of Rashi's school as it developed in the twelfth century. The discussion of *piyyut* commentary in that chapter benefited from the wisdom of Elisabeth Hollender.

Deserving special mention is David Berger, (now former) dean of the Bernard Revel Graduate School of Jewish Studies at Yeshiva University, with whom I have been privileged to work closely as associate dean since 2008. David made insightful comments regarding Rashi's possible reactions to Christian interpretation, an issue that permeates this study. David deserves immense credit for ably steering our graduate school through often turbulent waters to uphold its quality and ensure support for faculty research. As anyone who knows him will affirm, David's very intellectual presence inspires awe, matched only by his integrity – both scholarly and personal.

I am grateful to other key administrators at Yeshiva University, my cherished home institution. President Ari Berman has been a close friend for over three decades. Having recently assumed leadership of YU, he has already made clear the importance of quality research and collaborative, interdisciplinary studies in the twenty-first century. These values are skillfully fostered and implemented by our provost, Selma Botman, and her senior advisor Stu Halpern. I am likewise grateful to Karen Bacon, dean of the undergraduate faculty of arts and sciences, and to Ephraim Kanarfogel, now former chairman of the Rebecca Ivry Judaic Studies

Department at Stern College for Women, as well as Deena Rabinovich, who recently filled that critical administrative position, for creating an academic atmosphere congenial to genuine scholarship.

Rochel Hirsch deserves a great deal of credit for helping prepare this volume for publication. She reviewed and copyedited the entire manuscript, enhancing its logic and readability. She also composed the indexes, with the assistance of Borong Zhang. Zvi Erenyi, Mary Ann Linahan, and Moshe Schapiro of the Yeshiva University Library helped locate the necessary volumes for my research.

I am grateful to Beatrice Rehl, Publishing Director for Humanities and Social Sciences at Cambridge University Press, for inviting me to submit this work for publication, and to Eilidh Burett, editorial assistant at Cambridge, for patiently guiding it through the manuscript stages. Rebecca Granger, content manager at Cambridge, provided essential guidance in formatting the manuscript clearly. Finally, I owe special thanks to the highly expert copyeditor Mary Starkey, who meticulously reviewed the text, notes, bibliography, and indexes of this volume to ensure their accuracy and consistency. It was a special treat to learn that Mary had once been a student of the late Professor Sarah Kamin of Jerusalem, whose writings are cited throughout this work.

This volume is dedicated to the memory of Nehama Leibowitz (1905–1997), who devoted her life to teaching the Bible and its commentaries, with pride of place given to Rashi. Nehama, as she was affectionately known by thousands of students over the course of a teaching career that spanned nearly seven decades, applied her keen literary sensibilities and masterful pedagogic skills to illuminate the depth and complexity of Rashi's exegesis.

My wife, Suzanne, has provided essential emotional support as I devoted many hours, days, weeks, and months to this project. Herself an ardent student and teacher of the Bible, Suzanne values Rashi's commentaries, which we have discussed together at length over the years. It was an honor to introduce Suzanne to Nehama Leibowitz in 1990 when we were engaged to be married. Nehama's blessing to us – as two young Bible teachers – was that we never grow tired of learning and dedication to our students. In memory of Nahama Leibowitz our third daughter was named Gila Nehama when she was born in 2002. All of our children, Yaffa, Shai, Miri, Gila, and Elisha, deserve honorable mention for their patience with a mom and dad enamored with the study of old books. As they have matured, these magnificent kids offer important perspectives that enrich our scholarship – and our lives, of course.

Abbreviations

AJS	Association for Jewish Studies
Ar.	Arabic
b.	Babylonian Talmud
HBOT	*Hebrew Bible/Old Testament: The History of its Interpretation*, ed. Magne Sæbø, Menahem Haran, and Chris Brekelmans. Göttingen: Vandenhoeck & Ruprecht. Vol. I/1, *Antiquity*, 1996; vol. I/2, *The Middle Ages*, 2000.
Heb.	Hebrew
HUCA	*Hebrew Union College Annual*
j.	Jerusalem Talmud
JJS	*Journal of Jewish Studies*
JQR	*Jewish Quarterly Review*
JSIJ	*Jewish Studies Internet Journal*
JSQ	*Jewish Studies Quarterly*
JTS	Jewish Theological Seminary of America
m.	Mishnah
MS	manuscript
MT	Masoretic Text
PEPP	Greene, Roland, and Stephen Cushman, eds. *The Princeton Encyclopedia of Poetry and Poetics*. 4th ed. Princeton: Princeton University Press, 2012.

PL	*Patrologia Latina* (*Patrologia Cursus Completus: Series Latina*), ed. Jaques Paul Migne, 221 vols. Paris: Migne, 1844–1864. (References given by volume and column.)
REJ	*Revue des études juives*
s.v.	*sub verbo*
t.	Tosefta

Introduction

Rabbi Solomon Yitzhaqi (1040–1105), known as Rashi, is perhaps the most influential Jewish Bible interpreter of all time. A native of Troyes in the French county of Champagne, Rashi traveled in his youth to study for a decade in the Rhineland talmudic academies (*yeshivot*) of Mainz and Worms, then the intellectual center of the Ashkenazic (Franco-German) Jewish world.[1] He returned to Troyes around 1070 and established a vibrant school of Jewish learning that ultimately drew from the best and brightest students of the Ashkenazic community, who would, in turn, become its leading rabbinic figures in the twelfth century.[2] Rashi's literary output centers on two major works: his Talmud commentary and his Bible commentary, each monumental in its own right.[3] Drawing upon his training in the Rhineland academies by the disciples of the renowned Rabbenu ("our rabbi/master") Gershom ben Judah (c. 960–1028), known as the "luminary of the diaspora," Rashi composed a line-by-line commentary on virtually the entire Talmud, the central rabbinic work that embodies the halakhah (Jewish law). Continually perfected throughout his lifetime, Rashi's Talmud commentary is comprised of lemmas and gloss type notes that elucidate this highly complex and cryptic multi-volume rabbinic legal work. Though innovative in quality and style, its lineage can be traced to earlier exegetical work in the Rhineland

[1] On Rashi's early life, see Grossman, *Rashi*, 12–19. On the Rhineland talmudic academies, see Kanarfogel, *Intellectual History and Rabbinic Culture*, 37–53, 96–97.

[2] On Rashi's later life and the school he founded, see Grossman, *Rashi*, 19–70.

[3] Rashi also composed liturgical poetry (*piyyutim*), wrote commentaries on earlier liturgical poetry, and issued *responsa*, mostly on halakhic matters. See Grossman, *Rashi*, 149–161; Gruber, *Rashi on Psalms*, 29–37, 75–105.

academies, from which would emanate the Talmud commentary of "the sages of Mainz," a collective work rooted in the teachings of Rabbenu Gershom that was in the process of formation in Rashi's day, reaching its final form in the twelfth century.[4]

Rashi's Bible commentary, on the other hand, was unprecedented in Ashkenazic learning, in which the standard accompaniment to the biblical text was midrash (also referred to as *derash*), the creative and at times fanciful rabbinic genre of interpretation. Rashi, on the other hand, pioneered a model of *peshat*, or plain-sense Bible exegesis, which he used as a standard for evaluating rabbinic midrashic interpretations.[5] Displaying philological and grammatical acumen as well as keen methodological awareness, the rabbinic master of Troyes regularly noted his departures from midrashic readings that, as he put it, are not "settled upon" (*mityashevim 'al*), i.e., do not sit well with, "the language of Scripture" (*leshon ha-miqra*) and its "sequence" (*seder*) – values that became his exegetical touchstones. Rashi's commentaries were copied widely and spread quickly. The *peshat* method was refined and brought to new heights by his close students Joseph Qara (c. 1055–c.1125) and Rashbam (Rashi's grandson Samuel ben Meir, c. 1080–c. 1160), and their students throughout the twelfth century.[6] With the advent of printing, Rashi's popularity

[4] On Rashi's Talmud commentary and its relation to earlier Rhineland works, see Grossman, *Rashi*, 133–148; Ta-Shma, *Talmudic Commentary I*, 32–56; Soloveitchik, *Collected Essays II*, 32–35, 62–64; Gruber, *Rashi on Psalms*, 38–52.

[5] The scholarly literature on Rashi's Bible exegesis is vast and will be introduced throughout this study as relevant. For a helpful introductory overview, see Grossman, *Rashi*, 73–132; Gruber, *Rashi on Psalms*, 52–75. The precise definition of *peshat*, as will be seen in this study, is a complex matter – debated through the centuries as well as in modern scholarship. As an initial working definition, the Hebrew/Aramaic term *peshat* can be rendered *the plain sense* or *plain sense exegesis*, though the correspondence is not exact, and this translation does not reflect the fact that various key *pashtanim* (practitioners of *peshat*) in the formative medieval period worked with somewhat different conceptions of *peshat*. See Cohen, "Emergence"; Cohen, *Rule of Peshat*. In any case, the common translation of *peshat* as *the literal sense*, while workable in many cases, is problematic because *peshat* readings are at times figurative, in accordance with contextual factors. (The term *mashma'*, on the other hand, can be said to connote *the literal sense*, and Rashi does at times acknowledge its correlation with *peshat*, as discussed in Chapter 1.) Midrash or *derash*, which characterizes virtually all rabbinic Bible interpretation, connotes a reading that departs from the plain sense or *peshat*. Working with the assumption that the biblical text is written as a sort of cipher that hints to its hidden "true" meaning, midrash often violates the rules of grammar and philology, as well as historical-scientific sensibility – all of which guided medieval *peshat* exegesis.

[6] The extensive scholarly literature on the exegetical work of these two key students of Rashi and their students will be introduced in this study as relevant. For a helpful overview, see Grossman, "Literal Exegesis," 346–371. The years of the birth and death of Qara and

increased even further. His Talmud commentary became a standard accompaniment of the Talmud, and his Bible commentary, which displaced midrash as a standard accompaniment of Hebrew Scripture, became a central pillar of the highly influential Rabbinic Bible (*Miqra'ot Gedolot*) – both appearing in publications reprinted and used widely to this day.[7]

Even within certain Christian interpretive schools Rashi's Bible commentary would become a key exegetical resource. Christianity traditionally considered the Jews blind to the true, inner, "spiritual" sense of the Law, as they stubbornly adhered to its "letter" and the "carnal" or literal sense of Scripture. Yet a movement emerged in medieval Latin learning that increasingly privileged the literal sense (*sensus litteralis*), prompting scholars to consult Jewish sources to an extent unprecedented in Christian tradition since Jerome.[8] Most notably, Nicholas of Lyra (d. 1349), considered by many to have been the best-equipped Latin Bible scholar of the Middle Ages, cites Rashi often.[9] Nicholas was following a trend set by earlier medieval Christian Bible scholars, as Rashi's interpretations were evidently utilized extensively by Andrew of St. Victor (c. 1110–1175)[10] and Herbert of Bosham (1120–1194);[11] and they may have even been known to Hugh of St. Victor (c. 1096–1141).[12] By the time of the Renaissance, Christian Hebraists would regularly turn to Rashi's Bible commentary, which became readily accessible in the printed Rabbinic Bible.[13]

So sharp and sudden was Rashi's introduction of *peshat* exegesis that within a mere two generations – from the Troyes master to his grandson Rashbam – the Ashkenazic scholarly community moved from the "pious meditations" of midrash (to borrow a term used by Beryl Smalley[14]) to

Rashbam are not known precisely. On the range of possibilities raised in modern scholarship, see Grossman, *Franco*, 254–258; Liss, *Fictional Worlds*, 57–58.

7 See Stern, *Jewish Bible*, 142–157; Heller, *Printing the Talmud*.

8 See Dahan, *Les Intellectuels chrétiens*, 289–322; Dahan, "Connaissance"; Klepper, *Insight of Unbelievers*, 13–31.

9 See Klepper, *Insight of Unbelievers*, 32–57; see also Geiger, "Student and Opponent"; Geiger, "Commentary"; Hailperin, *Rashi and the Christian Scholars*.

10 See van Liere, "Andrew of St. Victor"; Leyra Curiá, *In Hebreo*; Smalley, *Study of the Bible*, 149–156; van 't Spijker, "Literal and Spiritual."

11 See Goodwin, *Herbert*; Smalley, "*Hebraica*"; de Visscher, *Reading the Rabbis*.

12 See Smalley, *Study of the Bible*, 102–105, 364–366; Hailperin, *Rashi and the Christian Scholars*, 105–110; Leyra Curiá, *In Hebreo*.

13 See Burnett, "Strange Career"; Burnett, *Christian Hebraism*, 99–102.

14 Smalley, *Study of the Bible*, 2. Smalley's characterization will be discussed more fully later in this chapter.

producing an analytic mode that anticipates many aspects of modern philological Bible scholarship. As Moshe Greenberg, for example, has remarked: "In principle, nothing has changed in the definition of ... *peshat* interpretation of the Bible from Rashbam's day till today ... We can still participate in the excitement of these exegetical pioneers who witnessed the remarkably rapid development of a clearly formulated exegetical method in [Rashi's] lifetime."[15] To be sure, Rashbam emphasized the incomplete nature of his grandfather's *peshat* project, which did not preclude frequent adoption of midrashic interpretation. In a revealing passage that will be discussed later in this chapter, Rashbam records that Rashi himself acknowledged the "*peshat* interpretations that newly emerge (*ha-mitḥaddeshim*) every day,"[16] on the basis of which more "pure" *peshat* commentaries on various books of the Bible would be composed by Rashbam and his circle. And yet, Rashbam credited Rashi with the revolutionary endeavor to interpret "the *peshat* of Scripture" in the first place.

Given the powerful influence Rashi ultimately exerted on the later tradition of Bible interpretation, it is understandable that modern scholarship has largely viewed his accomplishments in light of the subsequent development of the concept of *peshat* – and, in parallel, the concept of the "literal sense" in Christian interpretation. The aim of this study, on the other hand, is to explore Rashi against the backdrop on his eleventh-century intellectual setting, taking into consideration developments in Latin learning and Bible interpretation in northern France just prior to what has been termed the "twelfth-century renaissance." The central argument it puts forth is that a comparative study of Rashi and contemporaneous trends in Christian interpretation – as represented most clearly by Bruno of Cologne (c. 1030–1101), master at the cathedral school of Rheims (66 miles from Troyes) from the mid-1050s until around 1080 (after which he would go on to found the Carthusian order, and accordingly he would come to be known as St. Bruno the Carthusian)[17] – can offer a fresh account of Rashi's innovative exegetical program and conception of *peshat* by revealing common features of how Jews and

[15] Greenberg, "Relationship," 567 (my translation from Hebrew).

[16] Rashbam on Gen 37:2, Rosin ed., 49.

[17] See Levy, "Bruno the Carthusian," 5; Mews, "Scholastic Culture," 49. Bruno left Rheims c. 1077 to become a hermit, initially in the forest of Colan. By 1084 he had moved to La Grande Chartreuse, where he established the Carthusian order of cloistered monastics. On Bruno's substantial influence on Christian learning in northern France in the second half of the eleventh century, see Steckel, "*Doctor doctorum*" and the discussion below.

Christians encountered sacred Scripture in the second half of the eleventh century in northern France. This comparative analysis, in turn, offers a powerful tool for a reassessment of the further developments within the northern French *peshat* school by Qara, Rashbam, and their circle, against the backdrop of new conceptions of Bible interpretation that emerged in twelfth-century Latin learning in the school of St. Victor and elsewhere in the cathedral schools of northern France.

KEY CHALLENGES IN RASHI SCHOLARSHIP

Given his Ashkenazic rabbinic background, it is hardly surprising that Rashi turned to the Talmud as a source of authority for emphasizing the importance of "the *peshat* of Scripture" (*peshuto shel miqra*). The maxim that "a biblical verse does not leave the realm of its *peshat*" – cited three times in the Talmud – is the touchstone of Rashi's Bible commentaries.[18] Yet this talmudic lineage must not obscure the innovative nature of Rashi's *peshat* program, for in the Talmud the *peshat* maxim is actually quite marginal, and rabbinic exegesis, as a rule, is midrashic.[19] In privileging "the *peshat* of Scripture" Rashi reconfigured the hermeneutical landscape in the Ashkenazic community.[20] As an essential part of his *peshat* program, Rashi engaged extensively in grammatical and philological analysis of the biblical text, aided by the Aramaic Targums, glossaries that rendered difficult biblical words into Old French, as well as the lexicographic works of Menahem ben Saruq (a dictionary entitled the *Maḥberet*) and Dunash ben Labrat (extensive critical notes on Menahem's *Maḥberet*), two tenth-century lexicographers who lived and worked in al-Andalus (Muslim Spain).[21] Harnessing these sources, which he combined in a powerful new way, Rashi often challenged traditional midrashic interpretation.

And yet, Rashi's exegetical practice as a whole does not seem consistent with his programmatic statements regarding the importance of "the *peshat* of Scripture." Notwithstanding the remarkably clear applications of philological contextual interpretation he offers regularly, the bulk of Rashi's Bible commentaries are actually drawn from rabbinic midrashic interpretation and seem to violate the rules of *peshat* that he himself exemplifies adeptly elsewhere. This disparity was noted acerbically by

[18] See Gelles, *Rashi*, 1–14. The *peshat* maxim appears in b.*Shabbat* 63a; b.*Yevamot* 11b, 24a.

[19] See Weiss Halivni, *Peshat & Derash*, 53–79.

[20] See Kamin, *Categorization*, 57–59.

[21] See Chapter 1.

Abraham Ibn Ezra (Spain, Italy, France, England; 1089–1164), a staunch *pashtan* (practitioner of *peshat*) who epitomized the philological-contextual interpretive tradition that had developed separately among Jews in Muslim lands in the tenth and eleventh centuries, powered by substantial advances in Hebrew grammar and philology inspired by developments in Arabic linguistics.

Already in the early tenth century, Saadia ben Joseph al-Fayyumi (882–942, Fustat, Baghdad), known as Saadia Gaon, and regarded by Ibn Ezra as "the first speaker in all areas," had pioneered a rational, philological-contextual method of Bible interpretation that privileged the literal sense of Scripture.[22] Saadia penned extensive Bible commentaries and translated a number of biblical books into Arabic, most notably the Pentateuch, a translation that came to be known as the *Tafsīr*.[23] Saadia's model was followed by virtually all Rabbanite Bible commentators in Muslim lands.[24] (In parallel, a vibrant Karaite tradition of Bible interpretation emerged in the Muslim East beginning in the late ninth century; but it is beyond the purview of this study to explore in detail.[25]) Saadia's exegetical methods were

[22] For further details, see Chapter 4. The broad gamut of Saadia's achievements has been discussed extensively in modern scholarship and surveyed in a recent monograph by Robert Brody. See Brody, *Sa'adyah Gaon*. For an in-depth view of Saadia's work within the broader geonic context, see Brody, *Geonim*, 235–332.

[23] See Brody, *Sa'adyah Gaon*, 58–78.

[24] The term "Rabbanite," used both as a substantive noun ("a Rabbanite") and as an adjective ("a Rabbanite author"), should be distinguished from the term "rabbinic" (used only as an adjective), which, when used to describe a scholar, connotes proficiency in the midrashic style of learning and interpretive methods of the Rabbis. Ibn Ezra (like many of his Andalusian predecessors), for example, was a staunch Rabbanite, but was not a rabbinic scholar, as he was not an expert in Talmud, and he distanced himself from rabbinic interpretive methods (as discussed below). Saadia, on the other hand, might well be termed a rabbinic scholar, since he was an expert in Talmud. Moreover, despite the novelty of his philological exegetical methods, he was prone, at times, to incorporate midrashic material into his Bible commentaries. See Ben-Shammai, *Leader's Project*, 10–14, 336–373. The terms "rabbinic Judaism" and "Rabbanite Judaism" are much closer to one another, as both connote Judaism in accordance with the teachings of the Rabbis (i.e., not following the Bible alone). The term Rabbanite Judaism, though, is used especially to connote opposition to Karaite Judaism.

[25] The Karaites rejected the authority of talmudic interpretation, which, in their view, distorted the true intention of the Bible. Notwithstanding the popular view of Karaite interpreters as strict literalists, the truth is that early Karaite (or proto-Karaite) interpretation was not completely literal, and, indeed, displayed many of the same characteristics of the rabbinic interpretative mode of Late Antiquity. The Karaite philological-contextual method emerged toward the end of the ninth century, and was developed fully in the tenth, especially by younger contemporaries of Saadia in what has come to be known as the Karaite "Jerusalem school." For further references, see Frank, *Search Scripture*; Polliack, "Major Trends."

developed further by Samuel ben Hofni Gaon (d. 1013) and transplanted to al-Andalus a generation later.[26] As a scion of the Andalusian exegetical school, Ibn Ezra was familiar not only with the lexicographic works of Menahem and Dunash – which were composed in Hebrew and therefore accessible to Rashi – but also with the highly influential grammatical, philological, and exegetical works by subsequent Andalusian scholars, who all wrote in Judeo-Arabic (as did Saadia), a language Rashi did not read.[27]

Within the Andalusian school, the lexicographic achievements of Menahem and Dunash had been superseded by Judah Hayyuj (c. 945–c. 1000, born in Fez, settled in Cordoba in 960), who revolutionized the study of Hebrew grammar through his discovery of the principle of the triliteral verb-root, i.e., that every Hebrew root is composed of at least three radicals (root letters), though some of them "disappear" in various verbal conjugations of the "weak" and "geminate" roots.[28] That discovery put Andalusian biblical exegesis on a methodologically sound footing by endowing it with a precise template for philological analysis. Jonah Ibn Janah (late tenth to early eleventh century; Lucena, Cordoba, and Saragossa) codified Hayyuj's linguistic revolution in his influential grammar (*Kitāb al-Luma'*) and dictionary (*Kitāb al-Uṣūl*), which would serve as the foundation for subsequent Andalusian Bible exegesis, particularly the influential commentaries of the eleventh-century exegetes Moses Ibn Chiquitilla and Judah Ibn Bal'am.[29] Those Andalusian authorities informed the exegetical outlook of Ibn Ezra, to whom the grammatical conceptions in Rashi's commentary, which he probably first encountered when he arrived in Italy in 1140, appeared rudimentary. As Ibn Ezra's younger Andalusian contemporary Joseph Kimhi (c. 1105–1170) noted, the linguistic horizon of Ashknenazic scholars was limited, as they knew only the lexicographic works of Menahem and Dunash, which had long been outmoded among Arabophone Jewish scholars.[30] Even more egregious for Ibn Ezra was Rashi's frequent reliance on midrash notwithstanding his claim to adhere to the talmudic *peshat* maxim, a disparity that prompted Ibn Ezra to remark:

Our early [Sages] . . . interpreted sections, verses, words and even letters by way of *derash* (i.e., midrashically) in the Mishnah, Talmud and Baraitas. Now there is no doubt that they knew the straight path as it is and therefore expressed the rule: "A

[26] See Ibn Ezra, *Sefer Moznayim*, Jimenez Paton and Sáenz-Badillos ed., 4*–6*; Brody, *Geonim*, 300–316.
[27] See Chapter 4. [28] See Maman, "Linguistic School," 263–267.
[29] See Maman, "Linguistic School," 267–281.
[30] Joseph Kimhi, *Sefer ha-Galui*, Mathews ed., 3.

biblical verse does not leave the realm of its *peshat*," whereas *derash* is [merely] an added idea. But the later generations made *derash* essential and fundamental. For example, Rabbi Solomon (=Rashi) of blessed memory, who interpreted Scripture by way of *derash*. He thought that it is by way of *peshat*; but the *peshat* in his books is less than one in a thousand. Yet the sages of our generation celebrate these books.[31]

Coming from an Andalusian perspective, Ibn Ezra distinguished sharply between the typically midrashic interpretations of the Rabbis in the Talmud and "the *peshat* of Scripture" – something Rashi does not seem to do, as he most often engages in midrashic interpretation.

A number of modern scholars echo Ibn Ezra's critique. In his systematic study of Rashi's conceptions of *peshat* and *derash*, Benjamin Gelles, for example, concludes that Rashi "had not yet reached the modern finality of evaluation which allocates to each sense a realm of its own."[32] This outlook, however, was challenged by Moshe Greenberg, who remarked: "The concept of *peshat* was considered so self-evident that scholars of Rashi saw no need to discern precisely how he understood it, and regarded his work as missing the mark rather than asking if he had set a different target than they imagined."[33] In other words, instead of measuring Rashi according to the standard of Ibn Ezra's *peshat* ideal, it is necessary to assess the eleventh-century northern French exegete in his own terms and clarify his distinctive exegetical objectives. This challenge was taken up by Greenberg's student Sarah Kamin in her seminal book *Rashi's Exegetical Categorization in Respect to the Distinction between Peshat and Derash*, published in Jerusalem in 1986. As Kamin shows, composing a pure *peshat* commentary was not actually Rashi's objective. Rather, Rashi aimed to produce a commentary that "settles" the words of Scripture properly by respecting its "language" (*lashon*) and "sequence" (*seder*), a goal he often fulfilled through a selective deployment of midrashic interpretations. In Kamin's view, *peshat* was a central value for Rashi, but not his exclusive exegetical aim.

According to Kamin, by contrast with Gelles' understanding, Rashi was fully capable of discerning "the *peshat* of Scripture" consistently, but deliberately chose not to do so, preferring instead to compose a critically selected midrashic commentary.[34] But this raises the question: If Rashi indeed knew how to discern "the *peshat* of Scripture," why didn't he apply that method consistently rather than relying so heavily on the

[31] Ibn Ezra, *Safah Berurah*, Wilensky ed., 288. [32] Gelles, *Rashi*, 33.

[33] Greenberg, "Relationship," 561.

[34] Building on Kamin's perspective, subsequent scholars have explored Rashi's goals in producing such a midrashic commentary. See, e.g., Marcus, "Rashi's Choice"; Viezel, "Secret."

older rabbinic midrashic mode of reading? As Moshe Ahrend remarked, by Kamin's account, "Rashi ... resembles a craftsman who perfected a new and original technique, but set it aside to display to his audience a haphazard collection of works by his predecessors."[35] Why, then, did Rashi not compose a "pure" *peshat* commentary – as his grandson Rashbam would do – and thereby display his own powerful new exegetical method exclusively?

The answer to this question, as we aim to demonstrate in this study, is dependent on a proper assessment of the cultural-intellectual background of Rashi's exegetical program. Offering a valuable contemporary perspective on Rashi's trailblazing role within Ashkenazic learning, Rashbam makes the following foundational programmatic remarks:

Our Rabbis taught us that "a biblical verse does not leave the realm of its *peshat*," even though the essence (*'iqqar*) of the Torah comes to teach and inform us the *haggadot* (traditions, lore), *halakhot* (laws), and *dinim* (regulations) through the hints of (*remizat*) the *peshat* by way of redundant language, and through the thirty-two hermeneutical rules (*middot*) of Rabbi Eliezer ... and the thirteen hermeneutical rules (*middot*) of Rabbi Ishmael. Now the early generations, because of their piety, tended to delve into the *derashot*, since they are fundamental (*'iqqar*), and therefore they were not accustomed to the deep *peshat* of Scripture ... Now our Master, Rabbi Solomon (=Rashi), the father of my mother, luminary of the Diaspora, who interpreted the Torah, Prophets and Writings, endeavored to interpret the *peshat* of Scripture. And I, Samuel, son of his son-in-law Meir (of blessed memory), debated with him personally, and he admitted to me that if he had the opportunity, he would have to write new commentaries according to the *peshat* interpretations that newly emerge (*ha-mitḥaddeshim*) every day.[36]

Although he prominently cites the talmudic *peshat* maxim, Rashbam also explains why "the *peshat* of Scripture" was effectively ignored in the Talmud. As an accomplished talmudist, Rashbam knew full well that the laws and creed of rabbinic Judaism are not based on contextual-philological analysis of Scripture, but rather on talmudic scrutiny of the "hints of the *peshat*," using the rules of midrashic derivation (known as *middot*) codified in lists ascribed to the ancient Sages Rabbi Eliezer and Rabbi Ishmael.[37] By Rashbam's account, this was the exclusive focus of Jewish Bible interpreters – the pious "early generations" – prior to Rashi,

35 Ahrend, "Concept," 245–246.

36 Rashbam on Gen 37:2, Rosin ed., 49. This passage is discussed more fully in Chapter 9.

37 On these lists see Elon, *Principles of Jewish Law*, 57–67; Kahana, "Halakhic Midrashim," 13–16; Yadin, *Scripture as Logos*, 97–121; Enelow, "Thirty-Two Rules."

who was the first to privilege "the *peshat* of Scripture." Rashbam goes on to record that Rashi himself acknowledged – and approved of – the further development of the *peshat* method he had initiated.[38]

Rashbam's words underscore the revolutionary nature of Rashi's exegetical program, which prompts the following question: Why, in fact, did Rashi choose to focus attention on "the *peshat* of Scripture" in a way that was unprecedented in Ashkenazic tradition? In other words, what could have motivated Rashi to embark on his innovative exegetical program in the first place? Four theories, broadly speaking, have been advanced in modern scholarship to answer this question.

In the mid-twentieth century some scholars argued that it was Rashi's intensive activity as a Talmud commentator that prompted him to engage in philological-contextual analysis of the Bible, as he did in analyzing the Talmud line by line.[39] To be sure, Rashi's substantial skills in Talmud exegesis, imbued in him from his early studies in the Rhineland academies, would have proved invaluable in his endeavor to ascertain "the *peshat* of Scripture." But Avraham Grossman points out that this factor, by itself, does not suffice to explain Rashi's motivation for engaging in *peshat* exegesis in the first place. At least two generations of intensive Talmud exegesis preceded Rashi in the Rhineland academies, as reflected in the surviving fragments of the Talmud commentary of "the sages of Mainz." Yet there is no evidence that actual *peshat* commentaries on Scripture were produced within that school.[40] If the endeavor to elucidate "the *peshat* of Scripture" were a natural result of this sort of commentarial activity, Grossman reasons, it should have emerged in the Rhineland before Rashi's time.[41]

Avraham Grossman regards Rashi's exposure to Jewish Bible exegesis in Muslim lands – particularly in al-Andalus – as a key impetus for his *peshat* program. As already mentioned, it is well known that Rashi drew upon the lexicographic works of the Andalusian linguists Menahem and Dunash,

[38] The post-Rashi development of the *peshat* method is discussed in Chapters 8 and 9.

[39] See Grossman, *France*, 458–459.

[40] Interestingly, Grossman himself argues elsewhere that a tendency to analyze the biblical text philologically (rather than exclusively midrashically) can be detected, albeit sporadically, in the Rhineland academies in the eleventh century – and that this may have inspired Rashi's *peshat* program. See Grossman, *France*, 462–466. Grossman's evidence, however, is meager. See Berger, "Ashkenazic Rabbinate," 484, n. 7. More importantly, even according to Grossman, the few philological glosses attested in the writings produced in the Rhineland academies hardly amount to *peshat* commentaries anywhere near the scale of Rashi's work.

[41] Grossman, *France*, 459.

which evidently had become available in the Ashkenazic orbit in the eleventh century. But Grossman goes a step further, making the following argument: "It is inconceivable that the French scholars [i.e., Rashi and his students] could have been so conversant with the linguistic research of Spanish-Jewish scholars without being influenced by their approach to scriptural interpretation."[42] Grossman argues that Rashi and his students were inspired by the substantial exegetical achievements of the Andalusian school in the generations following Menahem and Dunash, i.e., by Hayyuj, Ibn Janah, Ibn Chiquitilla, and Ibn Bal'am – which would be epitomized in the *peshat* commentary of Abraham Ibn Ezra in the third quarter of the twelfth century.[43] German Jewish scholars, Grossman notes, were generally closed to outside streams of Jewish learning, whereas Rashi – following a trend of earlier Jewish scholars in France – displayed a remarkable openness in this regard and avidly sought to learn about developments in other centers of Jewish learning.[44] Eleazar Touitou, however, raised the following objection to Grossman's theory: Rashi did not read Judeo-Arabic, the language of all Andalusian linguistic and exegetical works, apart from those of Menahem and Dunash.[45] While Grossman does argue that Rashi could have had access to Judeo-Arabic writings translated for him by traveling scholars and even merchants from Muslim lands,[46] Touitou's critique should give us pause and prompt us to consider other factors that could have motivated Rashi to engage in his *peshat* program.

In 1996 Nicholas de Lange published a commentary on Ezekiel and the Minor Prophets originating in Byzantine lands that manifests a strikingly independent philological method.[47] This commentary, written by a certain Reuel in Hebrew with occasional Greek glosses (the language of the Byzantine empire), has been dated to around 1000 – at least two generations before Rashi was active in the third quarter of the eleventh century.[48] Another, more fragmentary, commentary on Genesis

[42] Grossman, "Literal Exegesis," 327. [43] Grossman, *France*, 471–472.

[44] Grossman, *France*, 472–473.

[45] Touitou, *Exegesis*, 46–47. The role of Menahem and Dunash in Rashi's exegetical project will be discussed in Chapter 1. See also p. 136. Recently, Hananel Mack has argued that Rashi's *peshat* program can be traced to the influence of R. Moses ha-Darshan of Narbonne (early eleventh century, Provence), whose teachings he cites occasionally. But that claim seems tenuous to me, as discussed in Chapter 1, on p. 30.

[46] Grossman, *France*, 561. [47] De Lange, *Greek Jewish Texts*, 165–294.

[48] See Brin, *Reuel*; Ta-Shma, "Hebrew-Byzantine Exegesis." It is evident that Reuel was a Rabbanite and not a Karaite. See Steiner, "Byzantine Biblical Commentaries." It has long been known that Karaite Bible commentaries were penned in Byzantium from the eleventh century onward, beginning with the project of Tobiah ben Moses, who himself

and Exodus from the same general era and locale was published by de Lange.[49] Although that commentary (unlike Reuel's) draws heavily upon midrash, it does manifest a linguistic orientation and thus suggests that Reuel's commentary was not a unicum, but rather the product of a Byzantine school of exegesis. Evidence for the continued vibrancy of the Byzantine school can be brought from the work of Tobiah ben Eliezer, who lived in the Balkans and composed commentaries on the Pentateuch and Five Scrolls at the very end of the eleventh century, which bear linguistic and exegetical affinities to the earlier Byzantine commentaries.[50] Tobiah's commentaries are predominantly midrashic, but he manifests awareness of a philological *peshat* approach, perhaps due to his exposure, directly or indirectly, to commentaries in Reuel's style.[51]

Based on the discovery of Reuel's commentary, Israel M. Ta-Shma boldly put forth the theory that Rashi became aware of the Byzantine tradition of philological Bible interpretation and that it inspired his *peshat* program.[52] Since the Byzantine commentaries are in Hebrew, Rashi theoretically would have been able to read them (unlike those penned in Muslim lands in Judeo-Arabic); but there is virtually no evidence that Reuel's commentaries or any others of Byzantine provenance were actually known to him.[53] Indeed, Rashbam's testimony that Rashi was the first interpreter to advance a *peshat* program would suggest that neither he nor his grandfather were aware of any earlier *peshat* traditions – in Byzantine lands or in al-Andalus. After all, had either Rashi or Rashbam known of such interpretive traditions, they should have cited them to bolster the authority of their otherwise unprecedented *peshat* program.

studied in the Jerusalem Karaite school, to translate from Arabic the great exegetical works of the Karaite "Golden Age." See Ankori, *Karaites in Byzantium*, 415–452. The possible impact of that tradition will be addressed briefly in Chapter 5.

49 De Lange, *Greek Jewish Texts*, 85–116.

50 Tobiah's work has long been known, though it was only in the twentieth century that scholars definitively placed him within the Byzantine orbit. Some earlier scholars, for example, had assumed his provenance to be Ashkenazic. See Buber, *Leqaḥ Ṭov*, 12–22. See also Steiner, "Byzantine Biblical Commentaries."

51 See Chapter 5. 52 Ta-Shma, "Hebrew-Byzantine Exegesis," 253–256.

53 It is conceivable that the Byzantine commentaries may have been brought to the Rhineland area via traders from Byzantium. See Soloveitchik, *Collected Essays II*, 127–141. Others suggest that Shemaiah, Rashi's close secretary and amanuensis (see Chapter 1, p. 32), was either of Italian origin or spent time in the Byzantine sector of Italy, where he could have been exposed to the Byzantine exegetical tradition and informed Rashi of it. See Steiner, *Stockmen*, 24.

A completely different theory regarding the impetus for Rashi's *peshat* program was advanced by Eleazar Touitou.[54] It had long been assumed that Rashi, like other Ashkenazic scholars, lived, worked, and thought in intellectual isolation from the currents of his Latin milieu, quite unlike Jewish scholars in Muslim lands, who avidly embraced Arabic learning. In recent decades, though, scholars have increasingly discerned in Rashi and his students awareness of Christian doctrines and conceptions of Bible interpretation.[55] In this spirit, Touitou argued that Rashi became aware of an increasing Christian interest in the literal sense of Scripture – which would emerge in northern France during the "twelfth-century renaissance" – and this could have inspired him to develop a Jewish plain-sense reading of the Bible, for which he recruited – and effectively refitted – the otherwise marginal talmudic *peshat* maxim. Touitou's theory has been widely accepted by scholars of Jewish Bible interpretation, most notably by Sarah Kamin; and it is even accepted by Grossman as a supplementary factor contributing to Rashi's novel exegetical program.[56]

As opposed to Rashi's Andalusian and Byzantine coreligionists, Christian authorities would understandably not be cited by Rashi, nor credited by him for having developed a suitable methodology of interpreting the Bible, much less one superior to traditional Jewish interpretation. The suggestion of Christian influence on Rashi's interpretive program is more subtle: it posits a subconscious absorption of ideas from a general *Zeitgeist*, rather than direct borrowing. And so, the lack of explicit acknowledgment of Christian Bible interpreters in Rashi's commentary does not contradict this theory of the source of his *peshat* program. There is, however, a problem with Touitou's theory that comes to light when we consider the modern scholarship of medieval Christian interpretation upon which he relied. Since this matter relates directly to the subject of the current study, we shall discuss it here in detail.

[54] See Touitou, *Exegesis*, 15–33.

[55] Rashi's awareness of Christian doctrines and Bible interpretation is usually manifested in polemical contexts. See Berger, "Mission," 195–196. This led some earlier scholars to suppose that Rashi's *peshat* program was polemically motivated, i.e., to show the strength of Jewish interpretation in response to the increasing anti-Jewish polemics in his day that asserted the superiority of the Christian reading of Scripture. See Baer, "Historical Reality"; Grabois, "*Hebraica Veritas*." Touitou incorporates this approach into his more comprehensive theory that Rashi formulated his exegetical program as part of his engagement with currents in his Latin intellectual milieu. See Touitou, "Rashi on Genesis"; also Grossman, "Literal Exegesis," 329–330.

[56] See Kamin, "Affinities"; Grossman, "Literal Exegesis," 327–329.

In her influential work *The Study of the Bible in the Middle Ages* (first published in 1941 and republished in several later editions until 1983), Beryl Smalley valorized the emerging interest in the "literal sense" of Scripture in the school of St. Victor near Paris. Smalley highlighted the work of Hugh of St. Victor, followed by his successor (and possibly his student) Andrew of St. Victor, and the new value they placed on the *sensus litteralis* in what Smalley regarded as "scientific study" of the Bible historically and philologically.[57] These Victorines began a process that reached fuller definition in St. Thomas Aquinas (c. 1225–1274).[58] Prior Christian interpretation focused on the Bible's "spiritual senses," prompting medieval readers to "not look at the text, but through it."[59] "Spiritual exposition," as characterized by Smalley, "generally consists of pious meditations or religious teaching for which the text is used merely as a convenient starting-point."[60] Touitou, in a study published in 1982, followed by Kamin in a 1988 study, relied heavily on Smalley's characterization of the trajectory of medieval Christian interpretation and argued that the emergence of the northern French *peshat* school can be attributed to the new spirit of learning in the "twelfth-century renaissance."[61] However, developments over the last three decades in the study of the history of Christian interpretation call for an adjustment of their theory.

To begin with, it would seem that Touitou and Kamin are guided by what Stephen Jaeger has termed "the logic of looking for something where there is light even when you have lost it in the dark."[62] Rashi lived in the eleventh century, not the twelfth – and it is questionable how much one can illuminate his exegetical endeavor by comparison with the more pronounced interest in the "literal sense" in the school of St. Victor.[63]

[57] Smalley, *Study of the Bible*, 41, 83–106, 112–196; Smalley, "Andrew." On the possibility that Andrew was Hugh's student, see Leyra Curiá, *In Hebreo*, 34.

[58] Smalley, *Study of the Bible*, 300–302.

[59] Smalley, *Study of the Bible*, 2.

[60] Smalley, *Study of the Bible*, 2.

[61] Touitou, "Exegetical System"; Kamin, "Affinities."

[62] Jaeger, *Envy of Angels*, 1.

[63] To be sure, neither Touitou nor Kamin made their claims based on a direct line of influence from Hugh to any particular Jewish interpreter, even, say, on Rashbam, who does fit the chronological timeframe. Their claim, rather, was that the intellectual environment of the "twelfth-century renaissance" that fostered the new Christian interest in the literal sense was shared by Jewish interpreters. See Kamin, "Affinities," xxxiv; Touitou, "Exegetical System," 62. It is possible that Hugh could have influenced Rashbam (or vice versa), who is known to have spent some time in Paris (see his commentary on Gen 11:35), especially since his commentary seems to have been written late in his life, between 1150 and 1160. See Kislev, "Short Commentary of Ibn Ezra." Smalley, *Study of the Bible*, 104, remarks that a conversation between the two exegetes, historically speaking, is not implausible. See also Basch, "Comparative Examination."

Additionally, the very notion of the "renaissance" of the twelfth century has been called into question in recent scholarship, which emphasizes the continuous vitality of Latin learning in the tenth and eleventh centuries.[64] And, perhaps most importantly, Smalley's "grand narrative" of the triumph of the literal sense has been challenged in recent scholarship, which charts a more gradual and nuanced picture of the increasing valuation of the literal sense in medieval Christian learning.[65]

The distinction between the literal (sometimes called "historical") and "spiritual" (sometimes called "mystical," i.e., hidden, mysterious) senses was a well-established one in Christianity, discussed at length by early Church Fathers such as Origen (185–254), Jerome (347–420), and Augustine (354–430).[66] To be sure, those authorities privileged the spiritual senses, which they subdivided further into more specific categories. Augustine, for example, highlighted *allegoria*, aiming to demonstrate how the Old Testament narrative foreshadows that of the New Testament.[67] The importance of the literal sense would be emphasized occasionally, for example, in the *Moralia in Job* by Gregory the Great; but it was generally marginalized, with the preponderance of attention directed toward the spiritual sense.[68] Gregory himself adopted a threefold pattern in which the literal-historical sense was a first step, leading to the allegorical sense, and ultimately to the third and highest level of understanding, the moral sense, which serves as a guide to the practice of a Christian life.[69] Elaborating on Gregory's model, Hugh of St. Victor argued that the historical sense was the "foundation" upon which the allegorical and moral (also called "tropological") senses were to be constructed.[70] By the early thirteenth century, a theory of "the four senses of Scripture" became widely accepted, as delineated, for example, by Stephen Langton (1150–1228).[71] Aquinas followed this trend in delineating three spiritual senses – allegorical, moral (or tropological), and anagogical – all of which are "founded" or "based upon" the literal

64 See Jaeger, "Pessimism," and, more broadly, Benson and Constable, eds., *Renaissance and Renewal.*
65 See Minnis, "Figuring the Letter."
66 See Paget, "Alexandrian Tradition," 521–526; Wright, "Augustine," 704–707, 722–727.
67 See Fredrickson, "Allegory and Reading God's Book," 139–149.
68 See Smalley, *Study of the Bible*, 33–35; Minnis, *Authorship*, 37–38.
69 See Kessler, "Gregory the Great," 140–142 and the citation from Gregory in Chapter 4, on page 131.
70 This will be discussed in Chapter 4.
71 See Dahan, "Aquinas," 50–51; Dahan "Langton"; Smalley, "Langton and the Four Senses."

or "historical sense."[72] In practice, though, Latin Bible exegesis in the twelfth and thirteenth centuries continued to be dominated by the spiritual senses rather than the literal sense, a trend Smalley has been criticized for failing to acknowledge adequately.[73]

Alastair Minnis argues that the growing Christian interest in the literal sense, albeit as a minor note, manifested itself largely in a renewed focus on the literary intentions of the human authors of Scripture.[74] This conception was sharply formulated by Aquinas, for whom "the literal sense is that which the author intends,"[75] though it had been adumbrated by Hugh of St. Victor.[76] The emphasis on authorial intention put pressure on a long-existing tension between two attitudes: (i) the Bible is a *sui generis* divine work unlike secular literary works, which therefore requires a different mode of analysis that aims to uncover its recondite spiritual senses, as expounded by the Church Fathers; (ii) the Bible is an essentially literary work, penned by human authors (divinely inspired, of course), and therefore subject to the sort of analysis typical of other literary works. The introduction of the Aristotelian conception of causality – specifically the notion of the "twofold efficient cause" (*duplex causa efficiens*) – into Latin learning in the thirteenth century helped diffuse this tension by allowing these two perspectives to coexist. God was deemed the first *auctor* of the Bible, its "primary efficient cause," whereas its human authors were considered "instrumental efficient causes."[77] This allowed the medieval schoolmen to focus attention on the individual human *auctor* and his intended meaning, i.e., the "literal sense." The spiritual or "mystical" senses of Scripture, on the other hand, were attributed to the Holy Spirit.[78] The implications of these distinctions would emerge in Aquinas' interpretive theory and practice, and would be more fully realized in the literal expositions of Nicholas of Lyra[79] – trends that postdate Rashi by one to two centuries.

[72] Aquinas, *Summa theologiae*, I.9–10. See Minnis and Scott, *Literary Theory*, 239–243; Dahan, "Aquinas," 51–70.

[73] See de Lubac, *Exégèse médiéval*, II/1.238–262, II/2.334–367. See also Harkins, *Reading and the Work of Restoration*, 188–189; Minnis, "Figuring the Letter."

[74] This is the general argument made in Minnis, *Authorship*. See also Allen, *Friar as Critic*. For a different view, see Ocker, *Biblical Poetics*.

[75] *Quia vero sensus litteralis est, quem auctor intendit* (*Summa theologiae* I.9). See Whitman, "Redefinition," 140–142.

[76] See Smalley, *Study of the Bible*, 101; Minnis and Scott, *Literary Theory*, 67.

[77] Minnis, *Authorship*, 79. [78] Minnis, *Authorship*, 81–85.

[79] Minnis, *Authorship*, 86–90. See also Copeland, "Rhetoric and the Literal Sense"; Kennedy, "Aquinas and the Literal Sense"; Klepper, *Insight of Unbelievers*.

Despite the relative paucity of the literary output of the cathedral schools of the eleventh century (a subject of Jaeger's monograph *The Envy of Angels*), it is evident that Bible interpretation played an important role in their courses of study. It is to this period that we can trace the roots of the *Glossa Ordinaria*, for which Anselm of Laon (d. 1117), master of the cathedral school of Laon from around 1080 and a "founding figure" of the scholastic exegetical tradition,[80] seems to have been largely responsible. Assembled after Anselm's death by his students, the *Gloss* marks a new mode of learning, presenting discrete patristic and earlier medieval interpretations in a readily accessible, easily referenced way.[81] Though the *Gloss* was produced in the twelfth century, it reflects the exegetical activity of Anselm and probably also that of his teachers[82] – scholarly figures of the mid-eleventh century, and slightly older contemporaries of Rashi. As Cédric Giraud notes in his recent monograph, the search for the influences on Master Anselm proves them elusive. A tradition that Anselm studied at the abbey of Bec under Anselm of Bec (1033–1109, later archbishop of Canterbury) and under the inspiration of Lanfranc of Bec (1005/10–1089), proves to have little basis.[83] Evidence is likewise lacking for the theory that Anselm of Laon was a student of Manegold of Lautenbach (1030–1103).[84] Drawing upon earlier scholars, Giraud places Anselm at the cathedral school of Rheims in the 1070s, where he would have studied under Bruno of Cologne.[85]

This exercise has yielded the names of prominent Christian Bible interpreters in Rashi's time and geographic vicinity: Lanfranc of Bec, Anselm of Canterbury, Manegold of Lautenbach (who seems to have worked in the Rhineland), and Bruno of Cologne, who came to be known as "the Carthusian." For the first three of these figures we do not have actual Bible commentaries that can be readily be compared with Rashi's empirically.[86]

80 Giraud, *Per verba magistri*, 8.

81 For recent scholarship on the *Gloss*, see Smith, *Glossa Ordinaria*. For a critique of that work, see Andrée, "Laon Revisited."

82 See Evans, *Language and Logic*, 38.

83 Giraud, *Per verba magistri*, 40–42.

84 Giraud, *Per verba magistri*, 42–47.

85 Giraud, *Per verba magistri*, 47–49, citing Williams, "Cathedral School," 669. See also Andrée, "Laon Revisited," 260.

86 Lanfranc composed a commentary on the Pauline Epistles that draws substantially upon the arts of the *trivium*, especially dialectic and rhetoric. See Gibson, "Lanfranc's Commentary"; Collins, *Teacher in Faith*. (A doubt about the attribution of the commentary has been raised: see Hoffmann, *Die Würzburger Paulinenkommentare*.) But it is difficult to compare that commentary with those of Rashi on the Hebrew Bible. Some believe that Lanfranc composed a Psalms commentary, but it is not known to have

Bruno, however, composed a commentary on the Psalms – "the book of the Old Testament most beloved by patristic and medieval exegetes" because it was understood "as a guide to the Christian life and as a prophecy of Christ and his church."[87] The commentary survives in a single manuscript, from La Grande Chartreuse, now Grenoble, Bibliothèque municipale, 341 (240), copied in the first third of the twelfth century.[88] Yet the interpretive method it embodies occupies a pivotal place in a tradition of Christian interpretation that linked the study of the liberal arts and the Bible.[89] Andrew Kraebel and Constant Mews have shown that Bruno applied a grammatical-literary approach in his interpretation of the Psalms, using methods typically applied to pagan poetry, in *enarratio poetarum* (interpreting, lit. "narrating out," the poets).[90] In doing so, Bruno refined a trend that can be traced to Remigius of Auxerre (d. 908), Carolingian-era master at Rheims expert in *grammatica* and its application to Bible exegesis, whose teachings remained influential there well into the eleventh century.[91] Bruno's methods, in turn, influenced the later Bible commentators Roscellinus of Compiègne (d. c. 1125), John of Rheims (d. c. 1125), Gilbertus Universalis (d. 1134) – and perhaps Anselm of Laon.[92]

survived. See Collins, *Teacher in Faith*, 25. Anselm of Canterbury seems to have devoted attention to questions of interpretive theory; but he did not write commentaries per se. See Châtillon, "Anselm et l'écriture"; Leclercq, "Monastic Commentary," 41–42; Sweeney, *Anselm*, 175–181; Evans, *Language and Logic*, 17–24. (A similar observation can be made about Anselm's younger colleague Gilbert Crispin; see Evans, *Language and Logic*, 25–26. See also Abulafia and Evans, *Crispin*, xxxiii–xxxv.) On the controversies surrounding the Bible commentaries attributed to Manegold (in any event mostly not extant), see Ziomkowski, *Manegold*.

87 Colish, "*Psalterium*," 531. Bruno also composed a commentary on the Pauline Epistles, as noted in Chapter 3.

88 The commentary was published in 1611 and reprinted in *PL* 152. Though its attribution to Bruno was questioned in the 1950s, his authorship has been reconfirmed by recent scholarship. See Williams, "Cathedral School," 668; Kraebel, "*Grammatica*"; Mews, "Scholastic Culture," 52; Levy, "Bruno the Carthusian," 13–16 (also addressing questions raised regarding the authenticity of the commentary on the Pauline Epistles). A French translation of Bruno's commentaries on Psalms 119–133 (Psalms 120–134 in the Masoretic text) was published in 2006: see Pradié, *Psaumes des montées*. The entire Psalms commentary was translated into French by André Aniorté and published in 2017.

89 On that tradition in Western Christian learning, see Copeland and Sluiter, *Medieval Grammar and Rhetoric*.

90 See Kraebel, "Place of Allegory"; Kraebel, "Prophecy and Poetry"; Kraebel, "*Grammatica*"; Mews, "Scholastic Culture."

91 See Kraebel, "Poetry and Commentary." See also Mews, "Scholastic Culture," 56.

92 See Williams, "Cathedral School," 668–669; Kraebel, "John of Rheims"; Kraebel, "*Grammatica*," 84–85; Mews, "Bruno and Roscelin"; Levy, "Bruno the Carthusian," 14 (citing Smalley). The possibility that Anselm of Laon studied under Bruno was discussed earlier in this chapter. See also Mews, "Scholastic Culture," 80.

UNDERSTANDING RASHI IN LIGHT OF ST. BRUNO

Bruno represents an important moment in eleventh-century Latin learning – heralding a trend to critically evaluate the interpretations of the Church Fathers based upon the philological and literary sensibilities fostered by the study of classical grammar and rhetoric. As Constant Mews remarks:

> Bruno was heir to the renewal of classical learning promoted in late tenth-century Reims ... While only a single copy is known today of his commentary on the Psalms ... the work was innovative in its approach ... At Reims, Bruno had access to the great commentaries on both the liberal arts and on the Bible by predecessors like Remigius of Auxerre, who came to Reims ... in the late ninth century. Bruno was able to tap into that tradition, and take it into a new direction. Bruno's commentary may not have been widely copied, but it did have an influence on certain teachers of the next generation.[93]

Furthermore:

> The originality of Bruno's commentary is evident when it is compared to that of another Bruno, bishop of Wurzburg (1005–1045). This latter commentary provides relevant extracts from the Fathers on the Psalms (in particular Cassiodorus, Augustine and Jerome), in an essentially derivative compilation, derived from a Carolingian pattern. Bruno's commentary is based on a similar range of sources, but provides sustained argument in favour of a historical reading of the Psalms, often rejecting the allegorical interpretations of particular passages proposed by Augustine. Bruno certainly followed the core teaching of these patristic authors that the Psalms illuminated Christian teaching, but interprets them in such a way as to emphasize their 'literal' sense and the meaning of individual words.[94]

Bruno's tendency to utilize his grammatical expertise to critically evaluate patristic interpretive traditions bears a striking resemblance to Rashi's pioneering exegetical program that likewise invokes grammar, philology, and literary sequence – key elements of what he termed "the *peshat* of Scripture" (*peshuto shel miqra*) – to critically evaluate midrashic interpretive traditions.

There is also a striking biographic parallel between Bruno and Rashi. Initially educated in his native Cologne, Bruno's thought was shaped within a still-vibrant Carolingian intellectual milieu that combined Christian and classical ideals under imperial patronage.[95] He moved to Rheims in the late 1040s – when he was just under the age of twenty – likely attracted by the strong tradition of classical learning in the cathedral

[93] Mews, "Scholastic Culture," 79. [94] Mews, "Scholastic Culture," 71.
[95] Mews, "Scholastic Culture," 52–53.

school there, especially in grammar, rhetoric, and dialectic.[96] Bruno would ultimately reinvigorate learning at the Rheims cathedral school, achieving renown as a teacher of the liberal arts and the Psalms.[97] Like Bruno, Rashi left a vibrant intellectual center in Germany – the Rhineland talmudic academies, where he studied in the 1060s – to launch his intellectual career in France, with his school at Troyes ultimately rivaling the academies of Mainz and Worms (which were also devastated during the First Crusade). It is not implausible that Rashi's bold *peshat* program, which directly engages the biblical text, reflects an endeavor, whether conscious or unconscious, to advance a unique and novel agenda in his Troyes academy, differentiating it from the more established Rhineland academies.

There are, on the other hand, significant differences between the biographic trajectories of the two scholars. Achieving scholarly renown, Bruno reanimated learning within the well-established cathedral school at Rheims, which was already centuries old by his time; but it was Rashi who put the Troyes academy on the intellectual map of Ashkenazic Jewry, transforming the small Jewish community into a great center of rabbinic learning. Until his death, Rashi remained active as a master and communal leader in Troyes and would exert enormous influence in subsequent Jewish tradition. Bruno, on the other hand, departed from Rheims after a dispute with Archbishop Manassas I in 1080 or 1081 to live as a hermit, initially in the forest of Colan. By 1084 he had moved to La Grande Chartreuse, where he established the Carthusian order of cloistered monastics. He was summoned to Rome in 1090 by his former student Pope Urban II (1088–1099) to become archbishop of Reggio in Calabria. Bruno declined the invitation and instead established a hermitage at La Torre, where he stayed until his death in 1101.[98] It seems that Bruno's withdrawal from academic life as a cathedral master limited the direct influence he exerted upon later Latin learning. Unlike Rashi within Jewish tradition, Bruno's name did not feature widely in the canon of authorities for Christian Bible interpreters in later centuries, as would the name of Anselm of Laon, for example.[99]

Yet in his own time Bruno seems to have achieved renown as a teacher of the liberal arts and interpreter of the Psalms. When he died, monks from

96 Mews, "Scholastic Culture," 53–57.
97 See the discussion of Bruno's mortuary roll later in this chapter.
98 See Levy, "Bruno the Carthusian," 5; Mews, "Scholastic Culture," 49, 60–62.
99 See Mews, "Scholastic Culture," 79–81.

his hermitage in Calabria traveled widely in Western Europe to collect testimonies about Bruno. The resulting mortuary roll features nearly 180 eulogy entries from religious communities throughout France, Italy, Germany, and England attesting to his reputation as a great teacher.[100] We must, of course, allow for exaggeration within this celebratory genre.[101] Yet Bruno is recalled vividly as "the teacher of many grammarians," "learned psalmist, most clear and sophistic" who "embodied the knowledge and prudence of the liberal arts … [and was the] supreme teacher of the Church of Rheims, most clear in the Psalter and in other sciences."[102] Even though Bruno's Psalms commentary does not seem to have been copied much, and he is best known in later tradition as the founder of the Carthusian monastic order rather than a Bible interpreter, these descriptions suggest that during his lifetime Bruno's teachings on the Psalms informed by grammatical learning made an impact upon his devoted students.

Capitalizing on the clearer picture of Bruno's interpretive work and its place within Christian learning that recent scholarship offers, this study will advance the following three interrelated arguments regarding Rashi within his eleventh-century Latin intellectual milieu:

1. There are significant methodological parallels between Rashi and Bruno.
2. These raise the possibility that Rashi was influenced (consciously or unconsciously) by Bruno to draw upon his Jewish sources in a new way that privileges grammatical analysis of Scripture.
3. Independent of the question of influence, an understanding of the strategy of reading Bruno applied to the Psalms and the dynamics it represents in Christian tradition sheds valuable new light on (i) Rashi's novel exegetical program within the context of Ashkenazic learning; (ii) its relation to other Jewish interpretive streams in the Muslim and Byzantine orbits; and (iii) its later development among his students in northern France in the twelfth century.

A few words are in order about the relationship among these three arguments, as they will be carried out in this study.

[100] An annotated edition of the mortuary roll with English and German is now available: see Beyer, Signori, and Steckel, eds., *Bruno and his Mortuary Roll.*

[101] See Steckel, "*Doctor doctorum*," 88–89.

[102] See Steckel, "*Doctor doctorum*," 89–116; Mews, "Scholastic Culture," 50–51; Williams, "Cathedral School," 667–668; Kraebel, "*Grammatica*," 66–68.

- Whereas the first argument is based on an empirical comparison of interpretive methods, the second entails a more speculative historical investigation, as there is no evidence that Rashi knew of Bruno. Yet the possibility should not be discounted. Rashi's writings reveal familiarity with Christian interpretation and it is not impossible for him to have met the cathedral master of Rheims himself, especially since both traveled between Champagne and the Rhineland in the 1160s and 1170s. Rashi could have also learned of Bruno's interpretations from one of his students – and three entries in Bruno's mortuary roll from Troyes and its environs suggest that his teachings were known there.[103]
- The third argument would seem most meaningful if Rashi knew Bruno's work. Yet this investigation is, in fact, valuable independently, as a clearer understanding of contemporaneous Latin Bible exegesis, particularly at Rheims, offers new insight into the distinctive northern French *peshat* school Rashi pioneered, by contrast with other Jewish exegetical schools. An exploration of the shared assumptions of Jewish and Christian encounters with Scripture within the *Zeitgeist* of eleventh-century northern France leads to new solutions to key unanswered questions posed in modern Rashi scholarship.

OUTLINE OF THIS STUDY

This study is divided into nine chapters that present Rashi's innovative exegetical program (Chapters 1, 2) and its further development by his students (Chapters 8, 9), by comparison with parallel trends in Christian interpretation (Chapters 3, 6, 7) and precedents in the Geonic-Andalusian and Byzantine Jewish interpretive traditions (Chapters 4, 5).

Chapter 1 outlines Rashi's revolutionary *peshat* program, both in his theoretical pronouncements and exegetical practice. It illustrates Rashi's philological and grammatical sensibilities, and shows how they enabled him to devise interpretations that depart from traditional midrashic rabbinic readings.

[103] One entry is from Saint-Pierre Cathedral of Troyes, another from the nearby Benedictine monastery at Montier la-Celle, and a third from the nearby Benedictine monastery of Saint-Pierre at Montiéramey. See Beyer, Signori, and Steckel, eds., *Bruno and his Mortuary Roll*, 171–172.

Chapter 2 turns to the pronounced midrashic tendencies in Rashi's Bible commentary notwithstanding his stated *peshat* program. Rashi offers typological, halakhic, and otherwise non-literal readings of Scripture side by side with his *peshat* interpretations. Following Kamin, whose view was mentioned above, this chapter demonstrates that Rashi aimed to create a commentary in which "the *peshat* of Scripture" serves as a baseline for a critical selection of midrashic interpretations that "settle" or "are settled upon" (*mityashevim 'al*) the language (*lashon*) and sequence (*seder*) of the biblical verses.

Chapter 3 outlines how Bruno, adapting a model devised by Remigius at Rheims, draws upon tools from *ars grammatica* to analyze the Psalms philologically, just as classical grammarians glossed Virgil. Bruno manifests concern for the literary coherence and "order" (*ordo*) of the verses in each psalm. Although he drew from patristic authorities such as Augustine, Jerome, and Cassiodorus (485–585), Bruno expressed reservations about their readings that do not accord with the "sequence" (*sequentia*) of the verses, and thus do not reflect David's authorial intention (*intentio auctoris*). The chapter considers the methodological parallels between Rashi and Bruno, showing how both developed criteria for selecting from among the interpretations offered by their respective traditions (the Church Fathers, the Rabbis) in a new critical way based on grammatical and literary criteria. It also raises the possibility that Rashi could have been inspired by Bruno's model to develop a Jewish reading of Hebrew Scripture that applies grammatical-literary criteria to ascertain the prophetic intentions of its authors through the Holy Spirit, which Rashi believed to be embodied in midrashic tradition.

In order to properly assess this hypothesis, the next two chapters address the competing theories that trace the inspiration for Rashi's innovative *peshat* program to the Geonic-Andalusian interpretive tradition or the Byzantine exegetical school.

Chapter 4 explores the evidence that Rashi could have drawn his conception of *peshat* from Judeo-Arabic Bible interpretation, beginning in the Muslim East with the work of Saadia and Samuel ben Hofni, who seems to have been the first to make the talmudic *peshat* maxim a guiding principle of his exegetical work. Tracing further development of the "rule of *peshat*" that emerged in al-Andalus, the chapter highlights in particular a striking parallel between Rashi's programmatic formulation of his *peshat* program and that of Ibn Janah. Apart from assessing the historical plausibility of a scenario in which Rashi came to know Ibn Janah's work (for example, from a traveling scholar from Muslim Spain), this chapter considers how Rashi's model of *peshat* actually compares with its Andalusian manifestation. Ironically, Rashi's conception of *peshat* and its relation to midrash seems to more closely resemble Christian conceptions of the "literal sense" in relation to the "spiritual senses" of Scripture. As this chapter shows, even if Rashi had access to the earlier Jewish *peshat* interpretation in the Geonic-Andalusian tradition, it is evident that he incorporated it into a hermeneutical framework relevant to his eleventh-century northern French interpretive outlook – shared by Jews and Christians in their encounter with sacred Scripture.

Chapter 5 explores the possibility that Rashi had access to, and was influenced by, the Byzantine philological tradition, of which there is now only fragmentary evidence. This chapter assesses some of the striking methodological and stylistic parallels between Rashi and the extant late tenth- and early eleventh-century Byzantine commentaries. It also compares Rashi's conception of "the *peshat* of Scripture" with that of his Balkan contemporary Tobiah ben Eliezer. Although it is unlikely that Tobiah's *Leqaḥ Ṭov* commentary itself (composed no earlier than the very end of the eleventh century) could have influenced Rashi, it seems to draw upon earlier Byzantine exegetical traditions that could have conceivably come to Rashi's attention.

Moving beyond the question of the inspiration for Rashi's *peshat* program, Chapter 6 underscores the benefit of casting the Troyes master against the backdrop of contemporaneous Latin learning, rather than other streams of Jewish interpretation. It shows how some of Rashi's novel interpretive strategies and the literary concepts underlying them are uniquely illuminated by trends in Christian Bible interpretation, which may have come to Rashi's attention. In any case, even where Rashi uses terminology drawn from traditional Jewish sources, he endows it with meanings that resonate with conceptions developed in Latin learning.

Chapter 7 explores a particularly striking example of this resonance by showing how Rashi's conception of an implied author-narrator in the Bible is uniquely illuminated by analogous concepts in Latin poetics current in his time. The Biblical Hebrew term *meshorer* (lit. "singer") appears in Rashi's commentaries on the Psalms and Song of Songs connoting *the poet*, a term he uses to refer to the literary agency of King David and King Solomon in composing those texts. To be sure, the term *meshorer* was also used to connote *a poet* in the Andalusian school; but that usage was informed by the rich tradition of Arabic poetics, which was unknown to the Troyes master. Rashi's usage, it would seem, is better illuminated by the conceptions of *enarratio poetarum* and *grammatica* applied by Bruno and other Christian authors in their interpretations of the Psalms.

Chapter 8 takes a broader view of the development of the post-Rashi northern French *peshat* school by exploring how the trajectory of Latin learning in the twelfth century can shed light on the hermeneutical conceptions of Joseph Qara and Rashbam. To be sure, previous scholars have pointed to the increasingly privileged status of the "literal sense" as a parallel to the sharpened focus on *peshat* represented in the exegetical program of these close students of Rashi. But, in light of the parallels between the traditions epitomized by Bruno and Rashi, this chapter will offer new ways of assessing the further development of Rashi's *peshat* project by Qara and Rashbam.

Chapter 9 expands the discussion of Rashi's exegetical heirs by examining their view of *peshat* relative to the traditional midrashic mode of reading Scripture. Rashbam, in particular, advanced Rashi's dual hermeneutic by offering radical *peshat* interpretations while preserving the normative authority of halakhic midrash. Drawing parallels to Latin learning, this chapter also explores how Joseph Qara, Rashbam, and their students conceived the role of the human authors responsible for the literary format of the Bible.

1

A New Program of *Peshat* ("Plain Sense" Exegesis)

The foundations of Rashi's scholarly career were established during his years in the Rhineland around 1060–1070. He first came to Mainz to study under R. Jacob ben Yaqar (c. 990–1064), a key disciple of Rabbenu Gershom, who is generally regarded as the fountainhead of Ashkenazic rabbinic learning.[1] R. Jacob, renowned for his piety and humility, was credited by Rashi as the most formative influence on his scholarship, analytic abilities, and religious persona.[2] After R. Jacob's death, Rashi continued at the Mainz academy, then headed by R. Isaac ben Judah (c. 1010–c. 1090), who played a key role in consolidating Rabbenu Gershom's talmudic interpretations.[3] A year or two later, Rashi transferred to the more recently established Worms academy, to study under R. Isaac ben Eliezer ha-Levi (c. 1000–c. 1080), another disciple of Rabbenu Gershom who was also deeply involved in communal affairs as the spiritual leader of the Worms community – a model Rashi would later emulate in Troyes.[4]

Rabbinic literature, chiefly the Babylonian Talmud, was the primary subject of study in the Rhineland academies. Indeed, the ambitious, wide-ranging Talmud commentary attributed to "the sages of Mainz," based on the teachings of Rabbenu Gershom, was composed by his students and

[1] See Grossman, *France*, 126, disputing the earlier view that Rashi first studied with R. Jacob in Worms. On Rabbenu Gershom and his enormous influence on the Ashkenazic Jewish community, see Grossman, *Ashkenaz*, 106–174.

[2] See Grossman, *France*, 127–128; Grossman, *Ashkenaz*, 233–257. Rashi referred to R. Jacob as his "teacher in Talmud and Scripture." See Rashi on b.*Pesaḥim* 111a, s.v., חיק קבל and Rashbam ad loc., s.v., מתקטלין בחיק קבל.

[3] See Grossman, *France*, 128; Grossman, *Ashkenaz*, 298–321.

[4] See Grossman, *France*, 128–129; Grossman, *Ashkenaz*, 266–292.

their students – with a notable role in this project played by Rashi's teacher R. Isaac ben Judah.[5] Their project stood in contrast to the commentary traditions of Rabbenu Hananel ben Hushiel (c. 990–1053) and Rabbi Isaac Alfasi (1013–1103), who worked in Muslim lands. Of Italian origin, Hananel (referred to as "R. Hananel of Rome" by later Ashkenazic authors of the Tosafist school) was educated in the Qayrawan rabbinic academy (*yeshiva*) in North Africa, where he absorbed Geonic traditions and maintained contact with the Geonic center of learning in Baghdad.[6] Alfasi, himself of North African origin, was Hananel's student in Qayrawan but went to on establish a rabbinic academy in Lucena, where he made a substantial impact on Talmud study throughout al-Andalus (Muslim Spain).[7]

Rabbenu Hananel penned commentaries that summarize the Talmud; Rabbi Isaac Alfasi composed an abridgement of the Talmud. Both focused on its passages that bear directly on the halakhah as it is to be practiced.[8] The followers of Rabbenu Gershom in the Rhineland talmudic academies, on the other hand, labored in their line-by-line commentary-glosses to explicate the entire text of the Talmud, including its theoretical discussions, anecdotes, and tales (sometimes referred to as *aggadeta*).[9] The revolutionary aim of their exegetical project was to "grasp ... [the Talmudic text] in its entirety," powered by a presumption that its "every nook and cranny ... had to be illuminated; every thought and interpretation, however briefly entertained ... had to be understood in all its detail."[10] This Rhineland commentary project was still in the process of being formed when Rashi studied at Mainz and Worms, and his exegetical mindset was undoubtedly shaped by the massive collective interpretive undertaking he witnessed. Educated in this intellectual workshop, Rashi returned to Troyes around 1070 as an accomplished talmudist. Always acknowledging the importance of his education in the Rhineland, Rashi continued to correspond with his teachers there from Troyes. There is an extant series of twelve queries by Rashi to R. Isaac ben Judah on Talmud exegesis, as well as the latter's responses.[11] And Rashi returned to Worms at least once (c. 1075) to visit R. Isaac ben Eliezer.[12]

5 See Soloveitchik, *Collected Essays II*, 42–43, 50; Grossman, *Ashkenaz*, 316–318.
6 Ta-Shma, *Talmudic Commentary I*, 122–124.
7 Ta-Shma, *Talmudic Commentary I*, 146–148.
8 See Ta-Shma, *Talmudic Commentary I*, 118–154.
9 See Ta-Shma, *Talmudic Commentary I*, 35–40; see also Soloveitchik, *Collected Essays II*, 159, cited in Chapter 3.
10 Soloveitchik, *Collected Essays II*, 159, 63.
11 See Soloveitchik, *Collected Essays II*, 50.
12 See Grossman, *France*, 129.

Yet Rashi forged his own path both as an intellectual pioneer and communal leader.[13] In matters of Talmud interpretation and halakhah, he boldly disagreed at times with his Rhineland teachers. In fact, he records that, at one meeting during his return visit to Worms, R. Isaac ben Eliezer conceded that Rashi was correct in a halakhic matter the two had debated.[14] Most importantly, the Troyes master composed his own monumental line-by-line commentary on virtually the entire Talmud, which distilled and refined the best features of the commentary project underway in his time based on the teachings of Rabbenu Gershom. In fact, the Rhineland commentaries were eventually largely lost (now surviving on only a few tractates), as they were ultimately eclipsed by Rashi's work, which became a standard accompaniment of the talmudic text unrivaled until the modern period. At Troyes, Rashi's academy would draw the best and brightest students from France and even Germany, who became the leading Ashkenazic Talmud scholars of the twelfth century.[15] They and their students were the founders of the illustrious Tosafist movement, which revolutionized Talmud study by developing a new and robust dialectic method and applying it to the corpus of Jewish law embodied in the vast and ancient rabbinic text. (The name of this movement is derived from the Hebrew term *tosafot* ["additions"], i.e., explanatory notes on the legal discussions in the Talmud.[16]) Rashbam contributed to Tosafist learning; but the towering figure of this school was his younger brother Jacob (c. 1100–1171), known as Rabbenu Tam, who resided in Ramerupt (about 20 miles from Troyes).[17]

RASHI AND HIS PESHAT SCHOOL

Apart from advancing Talmud scholarship, the Troyes master pioneered an entirely new discipline in the Ashkenazic world: Departing from the older rabbinic midrashic modes of reading Scripture still dominant in his Franco-German intellectual milieu, Rashi developed a revolutionary brand of *peshat*, or plain-sense Bible exegesis. Rashi's Bible commentary

[13] See Grossman, *Rashi*, 25–27, 149–158, 289–296. [14] See Grossman, *France*, 129.

[15] See Grossman, *France*, 166–174.

[16] On the development and contours of the Tosafist school, see Kanarfogel, *Intellectual History and Rabbinic Culture*.

[17] See Friedman, "Tosafot"; Reiner, "Rabbenu Tam and his Contemporaries"; Reiner, "From Rabbeinu Tam to R. Isaac of Vienna"; Ta-Shma, *Talmudic Commentary I*, 58–92, 111–112.

quickly spread throughout the Ashkenazic world, though its penetration among Jews in Muslim lands would be more gradual.[18]

Rashi manifested interest in biblical grammar and philology unprecedented in Ashkenazic circles. For this purpose, he drew upon the works of the tenth-century Andalusian Hebraists Menahem ben Saruq and Dunash ben Labrat,[19] the ancient Aramaic Targums (Bible translations), the masoretic notes and separate works that illuminate morphological subtleties in the biblical text, and medieval glosses known as *le'azim* (sing. *la'az*) – composed by so-called *poterim* (interpreters, translators) – that render biblical words and phrases in Old French.[20] Yet Rashi's novel exegetical program went beyond philological analysis of individual words. Aiming to account for the sequence and arrangement of the biblical text, Rashi exhibited interest in its literary dimensions and the ancient historical events its narrative conveys.[21] Perhaps most important, as discussed in the current chapter, Rashi regularly manifests methodological awareness in establishing the importance of *peshat*, and differentiating it from midrashic interpretation.

Crucial building blocks of Rashi's Bible exegesis were undoubtedly acquired during his years in the Rhineland. The Aramaic Targums and masoretic notes and works were standard accompaniments to the Bible in rabbinic circles, and would have been part of the curriculum at Mainz and Worms. It is even conceivable that Rashi first encountered the linguistic works of Menahem and Dunash in the Rhineland, where international trade brought literature from the far ends of the Jewish world in the tenth and eleventh centuries.[22] Yet if those works were available in the Rhineland academies it is not clear how much they were actually utilized to interpret the Bible before Rashi chose to do so. Avraham Grossman has gathered a number of examples of philological interpretations of specific

[18] See Grossman, *Rashi*, 42–49. See also Gross, "Spanish Jewry and Rashi's Commentary", Lawee, "Rashi's *Commentary* in Spain."

[19] See Pereira-Mendoza, *Rashi as Philologist*; Haas, "Rashi's Criticism"; Zohory, *Grammarians*; Mirsky, "Topics," 100–108.

[20] On Rashi's use of the Targums, see Viezel, "Examination of Rashi concerning Onkelos"; Viezel, "Onkelos in Rashi's consciousness." On Rashi's use of Masorah, see Himmelfarb, "Rashi's Use of Masorah"; Himmelfarb, "Jewish–Christian Polemic and Masorah in Rashi." On the Old French glosses, see Banitt, "*Les Poterim*"; Fudeman, *Vernacular Voices*, 103–104; Liss, *Fictional Worlds*, 21–22. There were also Old French glosses on the Talmud that seem to have predated Rashi. See Brandin, *Les gloses françaises*.

[21] See Signer, "Restoring the Narrative." These aspects of Rashi's commentary will also be discussed at length in this chapter.

[22] See Soloveitchik, *Collected Essays II*, 127–141.

biblical expressions by R. Jacob ben Yaqar and other eleventh-century Rhineland scholars recorded by Rashi.[23] Particularly revealing is his interpretation of a difficult talmudic locution through an Old French gloss and a parallel in Ezek 26:9, which Rashi attributes to R. Jacob ben Yaqar, his "teacher in Talmud and Scripture," who himself conveyed this interpretation in the name of his Master, Rabbenu Gershom.[24] However, there is no evidence that interpretations like these were actually part of a comprehensive program comparable to Rashi's ambitious and innovative Bible commentary project.

In his Bible commentaries, Rashi regularly draws upon the teachings of Rabbi Moses ha-Darshan ("the preacher, master of homiletics") of Narbonne (Provence, early eleventh century). While most of the interpretations Rashi cites in his name are midrashic, some are used in service of his *peshat* exegesis, including a handful of philological notes based on comparisons with Arabic.[25] Hananel Mack has argued that R. Moses' interpretive work should be viewed as a key source of inspiration for Rashi's *peshat* program.[26] But this seems tenuous to me, since the extant fragments of R. Moses' commentaries do not manifest the hallmarks of Rashi's philologically sensitive *peshat* exegesis (as discussed in the current chapter) with any degree of consistency. Furthermore, whereas Rashi established *peshat* as an exegetical value and differentiated it from midrash, there is scant evidence that R. Moses delineated the two categories, nor that he even used the term *peshat* itself. The same observations apply to R. Menahem bar Helbo (c. 1015–c. 1085), an Ashkenazic scholar who seems to have studied in Provence with R. Judah ha-Darshan, son of Moses ha-Darshan, in Toulouse.[27] Rashi occasionally cites R. Menahem's interpretations, usually transmitted through the latter's nephew, Joseph Qara. The extant fragments of R. Menahem's commentaries at times reflect a nascent contextual-philological method; but he, too, most often adopts a midrashic interpretive style and never speaks explicitly of *peshat* exegesis as such.

Evidently animated by his mission to establish a revolutionary exegetical standard, Rashi composed commentaries on virtually the entire Hebrew Bible: the five books of the Torah (Pentateuch), all of the

[23] See Grossman, *France*, 462–466. Grossman's argument that these interpretations represent a trend in the Rhineland academies to interpret the Bible philologically – and thus can be considered a precedent for Rashi's *peshat* project – is questionable. See Berger, "Ashkenazic Rabbinate," 484 n. 7.

[24] See note 2. [25] See Mack, *Mystery*, 75–76, 133–141.

[26] See Mack, "Bifurcated Legacy."

[27] See Poznanski, *Fragments*, 13–17; Grossman, *France*, 340–346.

Former and Later Prophets, and most of the books of the Writings, with the exception of Ezra–Nehemiah, Chronicles, and the final chapters of Job. Apart from composing his own Bible commentaries, Rashi trained others to independently apply his methodology – which developed further during his lifetime and beyond, yielding a remarkable number of *peshat* commentaries by exegetes such as Joseph Qara, Rashbam, and their students throughout the twelfth century.[28] The above-mentioned lacunae in Rashi's commentaries on the Writings could thus readily be filled by later scribes and printers seeking a full commentary on the entire Bible in the spirit of Rashi's exegetical method. Rashi's Job commentary was thus "completed" by copyist-scribes from the thirteenth century onward with commentaries on Job 40:26–42:12 by other northern French exegetes, and the one ultimately printed in the Rabbinic Bible is evidently from that of Rashbam.[29] The commentaries appearing in Rashi's name on Ezra–Nehemiah and Chronicles in the Rabbinic Bible (so-called Pseudo-Rashi on Ezra–Nehemiah and Chronicles) were probably composed in the mid-twelfth century by exegetes from the circles of Qara and Rashbam.[30]

Whereas the language Rashi uses in his Talmud commentary reflects dependence on Rhineland interpretive traditions, the language of his Bible commentaries reflects a spirit of independence, as he often differentiates his *peshat* interpretations from midrashic ones with formulations such as " . . . but I have come [to say]," " . . . but I wish to explain," " . . . but I wish to say."[31] This spirit of independence continued to animate the northern-French *peshat* school, as suggested by the following remark by his grandson Rashbam:

> Now our Master, Rabbi Solomon (Rashi), the father of my mother, luminary of the Diaspora, who interpreted the Torah, Prophets and Writings, endeavored to interpret the *peshat* of Scripture. And I, Samuel, son of his son-in-law Meir (of blessed memory), debated with him personally, and he admitted to me that if he had the opportunity, he would have to write new commentaries according to the *peshat* interpretations that newly emerge (*ha-mitḥaddeshim*) every day.[32]

Rashbam attests that Rashi was well aware of the continuous development of the exegetical method he had pioneered, and even acknowledged the superiority of some interpretations formulated by other *pashtanim*.

[28] For an overview of the northern French *peshat* school – from Rashi through the next two generations of Bible exegetes – see Grossman, "Literal Exegesis."

[29] See Japhet, *Rashbam on Job*, 13–36; Penkower, "Rashi on Job."

[30] See Viezel, *Commentary on Chronicles*; Viezel, "Ezra–Nehemiah."

[31] See Gelles, *Rashi*, 13–14.

[32] Rashbam on Gen 37:2, Rosin ed., 49. This passage was cited earlier and will be discussed more fully in Chapter 9.

The expression Rashbam uses, "the *peshat* interpretations that newly emerge (*ha-mitḥaddeshim*) every day," suggests intensive engagement with an exciting and new methodology by multiple student-scholars in Rashi's school, each regularly proposing novel *peshat* readings in the course of their study. Furthermore, in recording that he "debated" with the master himself, Rashbam attests to the intellectually open atmosphere in Rashi's school, in which students were encouraged to think for themselves and engage in a dialogic style of learning – otherwise known to be characteristic of the *disputatio* in eleventh- and twelfth-century Latin learning in the cathedral schools of northern France.[33] Most of the newly proposed *peshat* interpretations to which Rashbam refers were undoubtedly formulated orally and have been lost; but some were recorded in marginal gloss-type notes on manuscripts of Rashi's commentaries. Usually, these notes simply offer alternatives to Rashi's interpretations, some with attribution (e.g., to Joseph Qara, to Rashbam, or other scholars in their circle), but most without.[34] At times these marginal notes also record Rashi's approval of the alternatives raised by his students.[35]

We have, for example, *peshat* interpretations in glosses appended to the margins of Rashi's Pentateuch commentary by Joseph Qara, accompanied by notations such as: "But I Joseph son of Simon say," or "but according to the *peshat* . . ., " and in one particularly revealing instance, "Thus I, Joseph son of Simon interpreted, and Rashi acknowledged that my view is correct."[36] This confirms Rashbam's report that his grandfather valued "the *peshat* interpretations that newly emerge every day."[37] In fact, there is evidence that Rashi actually did revise at least some of his commentaries accordingly.[38] In a *responsum* to the rabbis of Auxerre, Rashi remarks with respect to the original version of his commentary on Ezek 42:10: " . . . in any event, I erred in that commentary . . . and now I have studied it with our brother Shemaiah and I have corrected it."[39] Shemaiah (c. 1060–1130), Rashi's close

33 See Novikoff, *Medieval Culture of Disputation*, 68–70.

34 See Berliner, *Pletath soferim*.

35 See Grossman, "Literal Exegesis," 333–334, 342–343.

36 See Poznanski, "Introduction," XXV.

37 See Grossman, *Rashi*, 27–32, for further evidence that Rashi was willing to accept the views of his students contrary to his own initial positions.

38 See Grossman, *France*, 184–193, 359–366; Penkower, "Rashi's Commentary on Ezekiel"; Penkower, "Corrections on the Pentateuch"; Penkower, "Corrections on the Prophets."

39 Citation in Grossman, *France*, 211–212; Penkower, "Textual Transmission," 223.

student and amanuensis, helped the master transcribe – and revise – his writings late in his life.[40]

THE TEXT OF RASHI'S COMMENTARIES

The dynamic nature of the development of the *peshat* method through the give and take between Rashi and his students has important implications for addressing a key challenge raised in modern scholarship regarding the very text of his Bible commentaries, a matter that is obviously critical for any assessment of his exegetical methodology. Already in the nineteenth century, scholars noted the substantial variations among the manuscripts and printed editions of Rashi's commentaries on the Bible. The manuscript evidence indicates, for example, that the text of Rashi's supremely influential Pentateuch commentary published in the Rabbinic Bible had been altered from its original form – primarily by additions, but also by omissions in some cases. Getting at the original text of Rashi's Bible commentaries is especially challenging because there is no extant autograph of this work and the earliest manuscripts date from the second third of the thirteenth century, over one hundred years after Rashi's death. In the nineteenth century, Abraham Berliner took a major step to address this challenge. He published a critical edition of Rashi's Pentateuch commentary (first edition 1866; revised second edition 1905) based on manuscripts and on the 1475 Reggio di Calabria printed edition, the earliest dated printed edition of the commentary.[41] This enabled Berliner to identify many passages that were not part of Rashi's original work, but were added based on what had once been marginal gloss-notes that eventually were incorporated into what we now have as Rashi's commentaries.[42] Pointing to evidence from the medieval manuscripts, Berliner observes that such additions were often first introduced with a sign (perhaps a single letter, Hebrew *taw*) indicating "an addition" (*tosefet*). Subsequent scribes dropped that mark as well,

[40] See Grossman, *France*, 348–366. Shemaiah wrote extensive *piyyut* commentaries and perhaps some Talmud commentaries. It is unclear if he wrote independent Bible commentaries.

[41] On the Reggio di Calabria edition, see www.library.upenn.edu/exhibits/cajs/revealed/revealed-med-det13.html.

[42] In some cases, the name of the original author of the gloss was preserved; see, e.g., the commentaries of Rashi (drawn from Joseph Qara) on Prov 5:14, 6:23, 18:22 in the printed edition of the *Miqra'ot Gedolot*.

yielding the multiple interpretations within Rashi's commentaries that are all presented as his.[43]

Notwithstanding the substantial further scholarship on the text of Rashi's Pentateuch commentary throughout the twentieth century, Berliner's 1905 second edition is generally regarded as the closest we now have to a published "critical" text.[44] A challenge was raised, though, in a provocative study published in 1987 by Eleazar Touitou, who argues that the *majority* of the printed text of Rashi's Pentateuch commentary, even in Berliner's edition, is not the work of the master himself; rather, it consists of interpretations by subsequent commentators added by scribes into their manuscripts of Rashi's commentary.[45] An especially common feature of Rashi's Pentateuch commentary is the presentation of multiple interpretations of a single verse or phrase, usually with some dividing marker between, such as "and another interpretation is ... " or "this is its midrashic interpretation; but its *peshat* is . . . ." Berliner already noted that in some cases all but one interpretation is missing in some manuscripts – a list that Touitou demonstrated could be enlarged manifold by examining additional medieval manuscripts unavailable to Berliner. Touitou reasoned that scribes would never knowingly omit an interpretation by Rashi, and therefore concluded that an interpretation missing from virtually any single manuscript must be an addition, leaving only the "least common denominator" among the medieval manuscripts as original to Rashi. Furthermore, Touitou argued that any interpretation appearing both in the commentaries of Rashi and Rashbam must not have appeared originally in Rashi's commentary, since Rashbam's goal was to offer new *peshat* interpretations and he would not have ever simply repeated those already given by his grandfather.[46] Touitou thus posits that in such cases Rashbam's gloss had been incorporated into Rashi's commentary by a later copyist. A similar argument has been made with respect to the identical interpretations appearing in the commentaries of Rashi and Qara on Samuel and Kings, i.e., that these were added from Qara's commentary by later copyists.[47]

Naturally, Touitou's theory has far-reaching implications for any attempt to study Rashi's methodology systematically, as it calls into question the authenticity of most of the interpretations appearing in the printed editions of Rashi's Bible commentaries – especially where more

[43] Berliner, *Raschi*, ix–xiv. [44] See the useful summary in Kearney, *Rashi*, 22–24.

[45] See Touitou, "Original Version."

[46] See Touitou, *Exegesis*, 229–237, based on a study published in 1990.

[47] See Eppenstein, *Qara*, 18–20; cf. Ahrend, *Qara on Job*, 23–25.

than one interpretation appears.[48] However, Touitou's theory has been challenged by Avraham Grossman, primarily on the basis of evidence from MS Leipzig 1 (Universitätsbibliothek Leipzig B.H. 1), which contains Rashi's commentaries on the Pentateuch and other sections of the Bible read in the synagogue. This manuscript was transcribed by a scribe named Makhir in the thirteenth century from a manuscript that seems to have been penned by Rashi's close student Shemaiah himself, and thus can reasonably be identified as a close replica of Rashi's original commentary. Based on his examination of MS Leipzig 1, Grossman rejects Touitou's argument that "much of the printed edition of Rashi's commentary is not his" and concludes "that the proportion of extraneous material is much smaller, not exceeding ten percent."[49] To be sure, even MS Leipzig 1 reflects the susceptibility of Rashi's commentaries to revision, since Makhir notes at times that he is including additions and corrections that Shemaiah made, in some cases at Rashi's request.[50]

The last case is particularly illuminating, because it suggests that Rashi himself instructed Shemaiah to augment or otherwise alter his original commentary. Indeed, in a number of important studies, based on an extensive investigation of Rashi manuscripts, Jordan Penkower has traced quite a number of Rashi's corrections of his various Bible commentaries.[51] Given Rashi's expressed wish, recorded by Rashbam, to revise his commentaries "according to the *peshat* interpretations that newly emerge every day," it is conceivable that interpretations originally proposed by Rashi's students were endorsed by the master himself and incorporated into his commentaries – either by his own hand, or Shemaiah's at his instruction. This process seems to be behind Rashi's commentary on Isa 64:3, which contains two interpretations, the second of which, appearing only in some manuscripts, has the following note appended: "Thus I heard from Rabbi Joseph, and it pleased me."[52]

[48] In such cases Touitou posits that Rashi originally offered only a single interpretation, which was later augmented by others. On this basis, Touitou challenged the conclusions of Sarah Kamin based on the "double commentary" format discussed below. See Touitou, "Review of Kamin" and note 80 below.

[49] See Grossman, "Literal Exegesis," 333–334 (quotation from p. 334); Grossman, *France*, 187–193.

[50] See Grossman, *France*, 360–362. On the use of MS Leipzig 1 judiciously to establish an accurate text of Rashi's commentary, see Eisenstat, "Text(s) of Rashi's Commentary."

[51] See Penkower, "Rashi's Commentary on Ezekiel"; Penkower, "Corrections on the Pentateuch"; Penkower, "Corrections on the Prophets."

[52] This comment is not attested in all manuscripts and is therefore presented in brackets in *Miqra'ot Gedolot ha-Keter* (see the following note). It is conceivable that this was a late

The conclusion that we draw from the manuscript evidence adduced by scholars who have studied the state of the text of Rashi is twofold. (1) Naturally, in the course of our investigation of Rashi's methodology it is necessary to check the best available editions of Rashi's Bible commentaries as well as medieval manuscripts such as MS Leipzig 1 where feasible.[53] This investigation has been made possible by important new online resources, including digitized versions of a number of important medieval manuscripts.[54] Accordingly, we will use caution in citing interpretations absent in some Rashi manuscripts, which may not be original to the master himself, but rather were proposed by another interpreter and added to Rashi's commentary by a later hand. As we shall see, though, some such interpretations closely resemble Rashi's style – a reflection of the influence of Rashi's methodology in his time. (2) But the complexity of the development of Rashi's work over his own lifetime requires that we also consider the possibility of a different explanation for the variation among the manuscripts, namely that Rashi himself (or Shemaiah upon his instructions) may have changed or augmented his commentary based on proposals by his students, what Rashbam refers to as "*peshat* interpretations that newly emerge every day." What is certain is (a) that Rashi pioneered a concept of *peshuto shel miqra*, (b) that his students refined it, (c) that Rashi himself endorsed this development, and (d) that he even revised his commentaries accordingly.

THREE PARADIGMS THAT PRIVILEGE "THE PESHAT OF SCRIPTURE"

A key feature of Rashi's Bible commentary is the attention he devotes to methodological pronouncements and exegetical criteria that set his *peshat*

addition to Rashi's commentary. Rashi also cites Qara (who transmitted to him the interpretation of Menahem bar Helbo) on Isa 10:24.

[53] In addition to using Berliner's edition of Rashi's Pentateuch commentary and the other critical editions listed in the bibliography, we have consulted *Miqra'ot Gedolot ha-Keter*, a modern version of the Rabbinic Bible that was edited based on early Rashi manuscripts. A list of the manuscripts of Rashi's Bible commentaries consulted for this study appears in the Bibliography.

[54] The website of *Miqra'ot Gedolot ha-Keter* features links to digitized versions of the manuscripts used by their editorial team. See www.mgketer.org/home/manuscripts. An online version of Rashi's Pentateuch commentary is being edited by Hillel Novetsky. It includes copious notes regarding variations among the medieval manuscripts – but it is incomplete to date. See https://rashi.alhatorah.org/. A full list of the manuscripts and editions Novetsky utilizes can be found at https://alhatorah.org/Commentators:R._Shelomo_Yitzchaki_(Rashi)/ManuscriptsandEditions.

interpretations apart from earlier, traditional midrashic ones. Furthermore, the Troyes master invests his comments about the *peshat* with personal urgency, in prefaces such as " . . . but I have come [to say]," " . . . but I wish to explain," " . . . but I wish to say," that differentiate his interpretations from midrashic ones.[55] In other words, Rashi does not simply engage in *peshat* interpretation; he makes a point of labeling it as such, and also explaining how it differs from midrashic interpretation. These features of Rashi's commentary must not be taken for granted, as there were other, earlier Jewish authors who engaged in philological interpretation of the Bible without characterizing it as *peshat* and without contrasting it to midrashic interpretation. The commentary of Reuel from the Byzantine orbit is an excellent case in point, as will be discussed in Chapter 5. More pertinent to Rashi, these features are lacking in the lexicographic works of Menahem and Dunash, which Rashi used as basic building blocks of his *peshat* exegesis. Those Andalusian authors engaged in philological analysis unselfconsciously, a model that would be followed in al-Andalus by the great commentators Ibn Chiquitilla and Ibn Bal'am.[56] By contrast, Rashi, immersed in Ashkenazic rabbinic culture, could do so only by dint of the talmudic maxim that "a biblical verse does not leave the realm of its *peshat*" and within the framework of the *peshat–derash* opposition that it implies.

As James Kugel illustrates, the Rabbis of Late Antiquity, like the Church Fathers, assumed that Scripture is a "book of instruction" fundamentally relevant to faithful readers in every generation, and not merely a historical record of the past, as might appear from the text.[57] In this vein, Paul said regarding the history of the Israelites in the desert recounted in Scripture, "Now these things happened to them as a warning, but they were written down for our instruction" (1 Cor 10:11). That axiom, in turn, was based on the underlying assumption that the Bible is a cryptic document, a sort of cipher, in which the surface meaning hints at its truer, deeper meaning.[58] For the Church Fathers, the Hebrew Bible's inner, "spiritual" meaning is Christological: Although, on its surface, the Old Testament (as Christians referred to it) is an ancient Israelite narrative, its higher value lay in foreshadowing the life, death, and resurrection of Jesus

[55] See Gelles, *Rashi*, 13.

[56] See Cohen, *Gates*, 66. Ibn Janah, on the other hand, does invoke the talmudic *peshat* maxim to create a niche for *peshat* exegesis by contrast with midrash – much as Rashi would do. See Chapter 4, where the possibility that Rashi could have been aware of Ibn Janah's model is also discussed.

[57] Kugel, *Bible as it Was*, 19–20. [58] Kugel, *Bible as it Was*, 18, 21.

Christ and his gospel, much as Jesus himself prescribed a "spiritual" understanding of the details of the Law – which the Jews adhered to in a literal way.

The Rabbis, of course, did take many details of the Law literally. Yet many of the laws and practices of rabbinic Judaism are dependent on readings of the biblical text that depart substantially from its straightforward literal sense. Analogously, while the Rabbis naturally rejected Christological readings of the Bible, they engaged in similar typological, theological, and other non-literal modes of reading that made Scripture relevant to the contemporary Jewish faith and experience. Indeed, the Rabbis – not unlike the Church Fathers – generally seemed uninterested in the "plain sense" of Scripture, i.e., philological, grammatical-literary analysis of the various books of the Bible that reflects their original ancient Near Eastern historical setting. Mining the Bible for eternal moral, religious, and legal (i.e., halakhic) guidance, they engaged in midrashic interpretation, taking the Bible's surface text as a jumping-off point for aggadic and halakhic investigation (*derash*) through the midrashic hermeneutical principles (*middot*), as enumerated, for example, in lists compiled by R. Eliezer and R. Ishmael.[59] The Rabbis, like the Church Fathers, adhered to what Kugel characterizes as "the doctrine of omnisignificance," i.e., that "nothing in Scripture is said in vain or for rhetorical flourish: every detail is important, everything is intended to some teaching ... Apparently insignificant details in the Bible – an unusual word or grammatical form, any repetition ... – all were read as potentially significant."[60] Accordingly, the Rabbis used the midrashic hermeneutical rules to read between the lines of Scripture, scrutinizing words and turns of phrase, making connections between different formulations, to discover hints to miraculous events in the past, which hold promise to the Jewish people for the future.[61]

As a rabbinic scholar, Rashi was well aware of these characteristics of midrashic exegesis. This makes his departure from them in his *peshat* exegesis – which looks "at the text" and not "through it," to borrow Beryl Smalley's expression[62] – all the more striking. Indeed, it is most often in the course of probing and challenging midrashic interpretation

[59] See Elon, *Principles of Jewish Law*, 57–67; Kahana, "Halakhic Midrashim," 13–16; Yadin, *Scripture as Logos*, 97–121; Enelow, "Thirty-Two Rules."

[60] Kugel, *Bible as it Was*, 20–21.

[61] See Kugel, *Bible as it Was*, 18. Cf. Rashbam's characterization of midrashic interpretation in his commentary on Gen 37:2, cited in the Introduction.

[62] See Smalley, *Study of the Bible*, 2.

that Rashi defines his criteria of *peshat*. Three paradigms of this sort, to which we now turn, can be delineated within his Bible commentary.

Peshat as the Exclusive Option, Without Citing Midrash

In a small but noticeable number of instances, Rashi will state his own adherence to "the *peshat* of Scripture," and either explicitly or implicitly exclude the midrashic commentary altogether. For example, he makes a point of differentiating his *peshat* interpretation from what was an evidently well-known midrashic interpretation in his gloss on the word *lahaṭ* in Gen 3:24, "He drove the man out, and stationed east of the garden of Eden the cherubim and the *lahaṭ* of the ever-turning sword to guard the way to the tree of life":

The ever-turning sword – and it had a *lahaṭ* to threaten Adam so as not to enter the Garden again. The Aramaic Targum of *lahaṭ* is *shenan* (=blade) ... and in the vernacular (*la'az*; i.e., Old French): *lame* (=blade). And there are aggadic *midrashim*, but I relate only the *peshat* of [Scripture] (*peshuto*).[63]

The aggadic midrash to which Rashi refers here can be seen in *Genesis Rabbah*, his primary midrashic source on this biblical book:

And the lahaṭ – like "his ministers are a fire that burns (*loheṭ*)" (Ps 104:4) .... "And the *lahaṭ* of the ever-turning sword" – like "And the day that comes shall burn (*liheṭ*) them up" (Mal 3:19).[64]

This midrashic reading was evidently influential in Rashi's time, as it is cited in the *Leqaḥ Ṭov* commentary of his contemporary Tobiah ben Eliezer.[65] According to the midrashic interpretation, "the *lahaṭ* of the sword" means *a flaming sword*, an ancient interpretation attested in the Vulgate rendering of this verse (*et conlocavit ante paradisum ... flammeum gladium*, i.e., " ... a flaming sword"). Rashi, on the other hand, built his *peshat* interpretation on an independent line of philological analysis, based on the Aramaic Targum, rendering *lahaṭ* as *blade* (and thus "the blade of the sword" in Gen 3:24), not as *a flame*. For the Rabbis, who typically emphasized the supernatural in the biblical narrative, this

63 Rashi on Gen 3:24, Berliner ed., 9. For a detailed analysis of this passage, see Kamin, *Categorization*, 75–77.

64 *Genesis Rabbah* 21:9, Theodor–Albeck ed., 203–204.

65 *Leqaḥ Ṭov* on Gen 3:24, Buber ed., I:28. A product of the Byzantine school of exegesis (discussed at length in Chapter 5), Tobiah typically relied on midrashic sources, even though he expresses a personal voice (unlike earlier midrashic compilations, which tend to be anonymous) and reworks the midrash selectively.

was a miraculous flaming sword, whereas Rashi's *peshat* reading renders it in a more naturalistic, mundane way. Rashi built his *peshat* interpretation on an independent line of philological analysis, based on the Aramaic Targum, for which he provided an Old French equivalent.[66] This sort of example, in which Rashi's philological *peshat* interpretation entirely displaces the traditional midrashic interpretation, which is not even cited, would seem to illustrate Rashi's adherence to "the *peshat* of Scripture" most dramatically.[67]

Peshat as the Exclusive Option; with an Explanation for the Exclusion of Midrash

In a slightly different paradigm, more common in his commentary, Rashi actually cites the midrashic interpretation he disqualifies exegetically. For example, on Gen 35:16 (" ... they set out from Bethel; and there was a *kevarah* of land [*kivrat ereṣ*] on the way to Efrat, and Rachel was in childbirth ... "), Rashi offers the following explanation of the difficult Hebrew word *kevarah*:

> Menahem explained that it is derived from the word *kabir*, meaning *much*, *a great distance*. But the *aggadah* explains: "when the ground is riddled like a sieve [*kevarah*], when plowed fields abound, when the winter has passed, and the heat has not yet come." This, however, is not the *peshat* of the verse, since we find concerning Naaman, "and he traveled some distance (*kivrat ereṣ*) from him" (2 Kgs 5:19). Now I say that it is the name of a land measure, like the distance of a parasang or more. Just as one says [in measuring an area], "acres [lit., yokes] of a vineyard" (Isa 5:10), "a plot [lit., division] of a field" (Gen 33:19), so too with a man's journey it gives the measure "a *kevarah* of land."[68]

This comment nicely illustrates the profound methodological influence Menahem ben Saruq exerted on Rashi's thinking. The midrash, in its

[66] Menahem Banitt has argued that when Rashi offers an Old French term, his intention is to negate an earlier Old French rendering. It is thus conceivable that an older Old French rendering here followed the midrashic reading and perhaps the Vulgate. See Banitt, *Rashi*, 6–7. Old French could have been a meeting ground for Rashi and Christian interpreters. On Christian vernacular glosses on the Bible, see Vaciago, *Glossae Biblicae*. On Jewish Old French glosses on the Bible and Talmud, see Banitt, "*Les Poterim*"; Fudeman, *Vernacular Voices*, 103–104; Liss, *Fictional Worlds*, 21–22; Brandin, *Gloses françaises*.

[67] For other examples, see Gelles, *Rashi*, 9–14, including, most famously, Rashi's programmatic statement on Gen 3:8, cited later in this chapter. See also Rashi on Ps 51:7, cited in Chapter 6.

[68] Rashi on Gen 35:16, Berliner ed., 72. The midrash is from *Genesis Rabbah* 82:7, Theodor–Albeck ed., 983.

typical associative fashion, interprets the word *kevarah* in this verse based on its common Rabbinic Hebrew usage in the sense of *a sieve*. Although this sense is attested once in the Bible (in Amos 9:9), it yields a rather forced rendering of the expression "a *kevarah* of land" in Gen 35:16. Menahem, on the other hand, applies a more systematic philological analysis based on other biblical occurrences and his recognition that Rabbinic Hebrew and Biblical Hebrew must not automatically be equated. He thus discerns that the Biblical Hebrew root *k-b-r* means *much*, *great* (a sense also attested in Arabic), a sense that can readily be applied to this context (a *kevarah* of land) to yield *a great distance*.[69] Rashi disqualifies the midrashic construal as being inconsistent with "the *peshat* of the verse," since it cannot be applied to the other attested case of the expression *kivrat ereṣ* in 2 Kgs 5:19. In other words, "the *peshat* of Scripture" must be based on a systematic philological study of Biblical Hebrew usage – as Rashi learned from the meticulous lexicographic work of Menahem. Now in this case Rashi goes on to offer his own philological analysis that differs from Menahem's based on an analogy to other verses that speak of measurements of land. This is hardly an isolated instance, as Rashi often cites Menahem but then proceeds to offer his own philological analysis of the expression in question.[70] This tendency of independence notwithstanding, it is the philological mode of analyzing Biblical Hebrew – which Rashi first learned from Menahem – that guides his *peshat* exegesis.

Menahem's example also provided Rashi an alternative to the midrashic interpretation of a difficult word in the heading of Psalm 5, "To the chief Musician upon *neḥiloth*, a psalm of David":

Upon neḥiloth – Menahem explained that all of the terms *neḥiloth*, *'alamoth* (Ps 46:1), *gittith* (Ps 8:1, 84:1), and *jeduthun* (Ps 39:1; 62:1; 77:1) are names of musical instruments and that the melody for the Psalm was made appropriate to the music characteristic of the particular instrument named in the title of the particular psalm.[71] An aggadic midrash on this book interprets *neḥiloth* as

[69] See *Maḥberet*, s.v., כבר, which refers to other examples of this root in Biblical Hebrew, e.g., in Job 36:5, Isa 25:2. It is not unlikely that Menahem was also influenced by the Arabic meaning of the term *kabir* (=*great, big*), even though, in principle, he seems to have denied the validity of deriving the sense of Biblical Hebrew words by comparison with Arabic cognates. On this matter, see Maman, *Comparative Philology*, 14–15, 276–288.

[70] See Haas, "Rashi's Criticism."

[71] See *Maḥberet*, s.v., גת, עלם. Interestingly, this sort of interpretation is not given by Menahem for the root *n-ḥ-l* itself. Perhaps Rashi misremembered what he had read in the *Maḥberet*. In any case, this is a reasonable extension of Menahem's approach to such unknown terms in the Psalms superscriptions.

a synonym of *naḥalath* (inheritance).[72] But this is not the plain meaning of the word (*mashma'ut ha-tevah*). Moreover, the subject matter (*'inyan*) of the psalm does not refer to inheritance.[73]

Rashi here confronts the midrashic interpretation that the term *neḥiloth* in the heading of this psalm connotes inheritance, an aphilological, associative reading well entrenched in Jewish and Christian Psalms interpretation.[74] Rashi justifies his rejection of this midrashic interpretation on two counts: (a) it is not based on the "plain meaning" (*mashma'ut*) of the word, i.e., its normal usage in Biblical Hebrew, as determined through philological analysis; (b) it does not suit the context (*'inyan*), i.e., the body of this psalm, which is a supplication to God for protection against "murderous deceitful men" (v. 7). As an alternative to the midrash, Rashi presents the approach offered by Menahem that some of the difficult Hebrew terms appearing in the headings of the Psalms were names of musical instruments or melodies in biblical times that are now unknown.[75]

The values of philologically sound analysis of the Bible's language and consideration of the immediate literary context are frequently reflected in the challenges Rashi poses to midrashic interpretation. These values are illustrated quite clearly in his commentary on Exod 6:2–9, a passage that follows Moses' initial failed confrontation with Pharaoh:

God spoke to Moses and said to him, "I am the Lord. I appeared to Abraham, Isaac, and Jacob as El Shaddai, but I did not make Myself known to them by My name Jehovah. I also established My covenant with them, to give them the land of Canaan, the land in which they lived as sojourners. I have now heard the

[72] *Midrash Tehillim* on Ps 5:1, Buber ed., 49–51.

[73] Rashi on Ps 5:1, Gruber ed., 812 (Heb.), 188 (Eng.). Citations of Rashi on Psalms in this study are based on the Gruber edition (itself based MS Vienna 220), the Maarsen edition, *Parshandatha*, vol. III (based on MS Bodleiana 186 [Oppenheim 34]), and *Miqra'ot Gedolot ha-Keter* (based primarily on MS De Rossi 181, with adjustments based on other manuscripts). For a list of the major manuscripts consulted in this study (and their provenance), see the Bibliography. Our English translations follow Gruber, with slight adjustments. On the complexity of the Hebrew text of Rashi on Psalms based on the extant medieval manuscripts and early printed editions, see Gruber, *Rashi on Psalms*, 158–164.

[74] It is reflected, e.g., in the Vulgate (where the superscription reads *victori pro hereditatibus canticum David*), and is therefore explicated in the highly influential commentaries of the early Church Fathers Augustine and Cassiodorus on this verse. Some scholars suggest that Rashi was aware of Christian Bible exegesis, particularly in the Psalms. See Shereshevsky, "Rashi's and Christian Interpretations"; Grabois, "*Hebraica Veritas*," 632–633. For a more cautious view, see Berger, "Mission," 196n.

[75] Rashi goes on to offer his own suggestion as to the meaning of this heading, as discussed in Chapter 7.

moaning of the Israelites because the Egyptians are holding them in bondage, and I have remembered My covenant. Say, therefore, to the Israelite people: I am the Lord. I will free you from the labors of the Egyptians and deliver you from their bondage. I will redeem you with an outstretched arm and through extraordinary chastisements. And I will take you to be My people, and I will be your God. And you shall know that I, the Lord, am your God who freed you from the labors of the Egyptians. I will bring you into the land which I swore to give to Abraham, Isaac, and Jacob, and I will give it to you for a possession, I am the Lord."

After offering his interpretation of these verses, Rashi goes on to record a midrashic reading that construes God's words in verses 2–4 as a rebuke to Moses for questioning his mission (Exod 5:22) and for asking God His name (Exod 3:13). The forefathers, on the other hand, had perfect faith: they never questioned God's covenant "to give them the land of Canaan," even though they always remained "sojourners" there (v. 4); nor did they ever ask God His name, even when He identified himself to them simply as El Shaddai ("God Almighty," v. 3). However, Rashi registers the following objection: "But this midrashic exposition is not 'settled' upon the verse for several reasons." He notes, firstly, that it does not correspond to the language of the biblical text: "It does not say 'They did not ask me My name,'" rather, God is recorded as saying "I did not make Myself known to them by My name Jehovah." Furthermore, the midrashic reading is acontextual; as Rashi remarks: "How does the sequence follow (*ha-semikhah nismekhet*) in the words with which it continues?" In other words, verses 2–4 would seem to serve as a preface to the following verses (5–9) which record God's recollection of His covenant, prompting Him to send Moses to free the Israelites from their bondage in Egypt and bring them to the Promised Land. Having cited these exegetical considerations, Rashi concludes:

Let the verse be settled (*yityashev ha-miqra*) according to its *peshat* (*peshuto*), though the midrashic reading can be expounded as such (*ha-derashah tiddaresh*), as it is said: "Behold, My word is like fire – declares the Lord – and like a hammer that shatters rock" – it splits into many sparks (see b.*Sanhedrin* 34a).[76]

For Rashi, this verse can be "settled," i.e., interpreted philologically within its context, only "according to its *peshat*." By this standard, the

[76] Rashi on Exod 6:9, Berliner ed., 112. For an analysis of this comment, see Schwartz, "Rashi's Commentary on Exodus 6." This interpretation is absent in MS Leipzig 1. But it appears in Berliner's edition and in *Miqra'ot Gedolot ha-Keter*. It also appears in MS London 26917 and MS Berlin 514.

midrashic reading is excluded, though Rashi allows for its legitimacy qua midrash.[77]

Rashi's exegetical criteria and the terminology he used to express them are well illustrated in his commentary on Isa 26:11, where he remarks:

> I have seen a number of midrashic expositions of the verses of this entire biblical section (lit., "above and below"), but they are not "settled" (*meyushavim*) upon the precision of the language (*diqduq ha-lashon*) or the sequence of the verses (*seder ha-miqra'ot*). I, however, am compelled to interpret it according to its sequence (*seder*).[78]

Rashi goes on to cite some such midrashic readings and to explain why they do not respect the rules of Biblical Hebrew nor adhere to the sequence of the biblical text.[79]

"Double Commentary": *Peshat* Interpretation Differentiated from Midrash

At times Rashi's commentary juxtaposes a philological-contextual *peshat* interpretation with a midrashic interpretation that he does not disqualify. Distinctive of this paradigm, which Sarah Kamin has dubbed "the double commentary," is Rashi's use of methodological labels ("this is its *peshat*" [*zehu peshuto*] and/or "this is its *derash*" [*zehu midrasho*]) to distinguish between the two methods that he juxtaposed in his commentary.[80] A fine

[77] On this evaluation of midrash within Rashi's system, see Gelles, *Rashi*, 66, 141.

[78] Rashi on Isa 26:11, *Miqra'ot Gedolot ha-Keter*, 170. Compare Rashi's use of the term *diqduq ha-lashon* – to connote *precisely what the language means* (i.e., without further inferences) – in his gloss on b.*Ketubbot* 83b, s.v., רב אשי אמר.

[79] This example is characteristic of the exegetical criteria Rashi mentions elsewhere. In his introduction to the Song of Songs, discussed in Chapter 2, Rashi criticizes the midrashic commentaries "that are not settled upon the language of Scripture (*leshon ha-miqra*) and the sequence of the verses (*seder ha-miqra'ot*)." Rashi's concern for conformity to the rules of Biblical Hebrew is also evident, for example, in his commentary on Ps 68:36. Likewise, in a number of places, Rashi criticizes Onkelos because "he was not meticulous to translate according to the language of the verse/to interpret according to the Hebrew language" (*lo diqdeq letargem aḥar leshon ha-miqra/lefaresh aḥar leshon ha-'ivri*). See Rashi on Gen 42:7, 43:3; Exod 15:13. Additional examples in which Rashi employs the term *seder* to express the value of interpreting the biblical text sequentially are discussed in Chapter 3.

[80] See Kamin, *Categorization*, 158–208; Shapira, "Dualistic Approach." In accordance with his overall theory regarding the printed text of Rashi, Touitou argues that in many cases this double commentary format resulted from interpolations by students or later copyists. In light of Grossman's critique of Touitou's conclusion, however, it seems to me that the double commentary format can legitimately be ascribed to Rashi himself. For the debate between Grossman and Touitou, see nn. 45, 46, 48, 49, earlier in this chapter.

example of this paradigm is Rashi's commentary on the "covenant between the parts" (*berit bein ha-betarim*) recounted in Genesis 15, in which Abraham was told by God to gather three large animals (a heifer, a goat, and a ram) and two birds (a turtledove and a pigeon). Abraham then cut the large animals in half to confirm his covenant with God. To explain this curious ritual, Rashi cites the typological midrashic interpretation according to which these animals symbolize the animal sacrifices that the people of Israel would later offer to God in the Temple in Jerusalem or, alternatively, to prophetically foretell how various nations will oppress and exile Israel but will ultimately be destroyed ("cut to pieces"), whereas Israel herself (represented by the two birds) will survive eternally (therefore "he did not cut up the birds," v. 10).[81] Tobiah ben Eliezer, likewise, offers symbolic midrashic interpretations in this vein.[82] Rashi, however, added the following remark that puts a spotlight on "the *peshat* of Scripture":

> But the biblical verse does not leave the realm of its *peshat*. Since God was making a covenant with him to keep His promise to give the land to his progeny, as it says, "On that day the Lord made a covenant with Abraham saying" and so on (Gen 15:18), and the typical manner of those who made covenants (*derekh koretei berit*) in biblical times was to split an animal and to pass between its parts, as it says elsewhere: "those who passed between the parts of the calf" (Jer 34:19). So too here: "A smoking oven and a flaming torch which passed between those pieces" (Gen 15:17) – that was the agent of the divine presence, which is fire.[83]

Invoking the talmudic *peshat* maxim, Rashi elucidates "the *peshat* of Scripture" by accounting for these events within their historical context, citing Jer 34:19 as evidence that the cutting of animals was a normal way of making a covenant in biblical times. *Peshat* here entails a historical sensibility that we find in later Jewish and Christian twelfth-century literal sense exegesis, and even more so in Lyra's in the thirteenth.[84] In this spirit, Rashi here and elsewhere seeks to explain occurrences in the biblical narrative based on what he surmises were the norms and conventions of biblical times, based in part on his observations from his own time. For this purpose he often uses the expression "this is the typical manner of...

[81] See Rashi on Gen 15:10, Berliner ed., 27, drawing upon *Genesis Rabbah* 44:9, Theodor–Albeck ed., 437.

[82] *Leqaḥ Ṭov* on Gen 15:9–10, Buber ed., I:69–70.

[83] Rashi on Gen 15:10, Berliner ed., 27.

[84] For other examples of this paradigm in Rashi, see Gelles, *Rashi*, 20–26. On Lyra's historical sensibilities, see Signer, "Vision and History."

(*ken derekh* ...)."[85] Whereas midrashic interpretation typically reads the Bible in a miraculous, supernatural way, Rashi offers an alternative *peshat* approach based on empirical observation. This tendency would be refined by Rashbam and his students in the twelfth century, using terminology similar to Rashi's.[86]

The double commentaries are especially valuable because they highlight the methodological differences between the *peshat* and midrashic methods, revealing Rashi's clear understanding of both. An illustrative example is Rashi's interpretation of the awkward locution "the night was divided for (or: upon) them" (ויחלק עליהם לילה; Gen 14:15) in the description of the military campaign of Abraham and his servants against "the four kings." Rashi here cites the traditional rabbinic interpretation:

> The aggadic midrash expounds that the night was divided: during its first half a miracle was done for him, and the second half was kept for the midnight of the exodus in Egypt.[87]

The midrash reads the expression in question most literally, and, in typical fashion, looks beyond the story at hand and takes it as an allusion to an unrelated biblical episode – making a connection that highlights the miraculous nature of both. This midrashic interpretation was evidently well known as it is paraphrased by Tobiah ben Eliezer in *Leqaḥ Ṭov*.[88] But Rashi proposes a solution of his own that treats the locution in the wider context of the verse:

> According to its *peshat*, you must invert the order of the verse (*sares ha-miqra*): "*He and his servants* divided *themselves* against them at night" as is the typical manner (*derekh*) of those who divide up to pursue enemies fleeing in different directions.[89]

The way in which Rashi resolves the difficulties of interpreting this locution reflects a number of characteristic features of the *peshat* method. Instead of adhering to a literal, word-for-word reading of this clause in isolation, as the midrash did, Rashi interprets it within the context of the verse as a whole. Recognizing the syntactic flexibility of Biblical Hebrew and invoking the rabbinic notion of *miqra mesoras* ("an inverted verse"),

[85] See, e.g., Rashi on Gen 14:15 (cited later in this chapter), 14:18, 43:30; Exod 16:20 (cited in Chapter 4); Deut 28:7; 1 Kgs 9:8; Isa 5:30, 28:25, 34:13; Ezek 34:12; Nah 3:17; Ps 10:10, 35:8; Job 2:4, 38:40.

[86] See Chapter 8.

[87] Rashi on Gen 14:15, Berliner ed., 26. Rashi's source is *Genesis Rabbah* 43:3, Theodor–Albeck ed., 417, which is also reflected in *Leqaḥ Ṭov*, Buber ed., I:65.

[88] *Leqaḥ Ṭov* on Gen 14:14, Buber ed., I:65.

[89] Rashi on Gen 14:15, Berliner ed., 26.

Rashi argues that it is grammatically legitimate to "correct" the "inversion" and posit that "he and his servants" (and not "the night") is the subject of the verb *divided* (ויחלק), with night (לילה) being an adverb, i.e., *at night*.[90] And, to explain why Abraham and his servants "divided," i.e., split in different directions, he cites "the manner of those who pursue," i.e., a common battle practice he would have known from his own time. Instead of relating this verse to divine miraculous interventions in other epochs, the *peshat* reading views the event in mundane terms in its own historical context. This realistic – rather than fantastic or miraculous – way of reading Scripture is evident elsewhere in Rashi's *peshat* interpretations, and it would be applied systematically by Rashbam, who termed it *derekh ereṣ* (lit., "the way of the world").[91]

The previous example shows how Rashi's sensitivity to syntactic structure played a key role in his *peshat* method. Elsewhere, his *peshat* interpretations are predicated on his ability to discern a complex literary structure in the biblical narrative. For example, he describes a structural feature of Exodus 6 in the course of addressing a difficulty in verse 13 in that chapter, "So the Lord spoke to both Moses and Aaron in regard to the Israelites and Pharaoh king of Egypt, instructing them to deliver the Israelites from the land of Egypt." The verse spells out the "command" regarding the Israelites – to deliver them from Egypt; but the nature of the command concerning Pharaoh remains enigmatic, especially since the following verses move on to a different topic, providing the genealogical background of Moses and Aaron. Rashi offers two answers to this dilemma, distinguished by methodological markers:

> ... *in regard to* ... *Pharaoh king of Egypt* – that they should show respect to him in all that they spoke. That is its midrashic interpretation. But its *peshat* interpretation is: He commanded them with regard to Israel and with regard to his mission on which he had sent them to Pharaoh. And the purport of this command is explained in the section after this one (vv. 29–31), after the order of genealogy (vv. 14–28). But because it mentioned Moses and Aaron it interrupts the account, "These are the heads of their father's houses" (v. 14ff.), to inform us

[90] On *miqra mesoras* in midrashic tradition, see Melammed, *Bible Commentators*, 64–67. This notion is applied by Rashi elsewhere in his Bible commentaries as part of his *peshat* program. For example, on 2 Sam 22:42, "They turned, but there is no savior, to the Lord, but he did not answer them," Rashi writes: "This is an inverted verse (*miqra mesoras*) [in which the proper order would be]: 'They turned to the Lord, but He did not answer them, and there is no savior'" (*Miqra'ot Gedolot ha-Keter*, 264). See also Shereshevsky, "Inversions."

[91] See Chapter 8.

how Moses and Aaron were born, and with whom they are connected by descent.[92]

Whereas the midrash fills in the gap of information in this verse by fabricating an otherwise unstated "command" to Moses with respect to Pharaoh, the *peshat* interpretation does so by pointing to a command to Moses mentioned explicitly later in this chapter: "And the Lord said to Moses, 'I am the Lord; speak to Pharaoh king of Egypt all that I will tell you'" (v. 29).

Rashi's *peshat* reading of Exod 6:13 is based on a nuanced analysis of the arrangement of Exodus 6. As he sees it, the account in verses 12–13 is interrupted by the genealogy of verses 14–27 and resumes in verses 29–30. There, God's instruction to Moses to issue an order to Pharaoh evokes the following response: "Moses appealed to the Lord, saying: 'See, I am of impeded speech; how then should Pharaoh heed me!'" (v. 30). On that verse, we find in Rashi's commentary what can be regarded as the completion of his *peshat* interpretation of verse 13:

> *And Moses said before the Lord* ... – This is the statement that was said above (v. 12), "The Israelites would not listen to me; [how then will Pharaoh heed me, a man of impeded speech?]" Scripture (*ha-katuv*) repeated it here because it had interrupted the account (lit., matter). And this is typical [of biblical] style (*shiṭṭah*), as a person might say, "Let's go back and review from the beginning (*naḥazor 'al ha-rishonot*)."[93]

This interpretation renders verses 29–30 a case of "resumptive repetition,"[94] i.e., the biblical narrator reorients the reader by repeating

[92] Rashi on Exod 6:13, Berliner ed., 112–113. Rashi's midrashic interpretation is found in *Tanḥuma Bo* §7. The words "And the purport of this command is explained ... " are missing in the Reggio di Calabria edition and in some early manuscripts of Rashi's commentary (e.g., De Rossi 181, Vienna 220). On this basis, Touitou argues that these words are not original to Rashi but were added by a later hand, perhaps a student in his circle. See Touitou, "Original Version," 225. However, this interpretation does appear in MS Leipzig 1, and on that basis we believe it is likely to have originated from the teachings of Rashi himself.

[93] Rashi on Exod 6:30, Berliner ed., 113. This comment is absent in the Reggio di Calabria edition of Rashi and in some early manuscripts (Leipzig 1, De Rossi 181, Vienna 220) as noted by Touitou, "Original Version," 225. Here Touitou adds another consideration: The same observation can be found in Rashbam's commentary on this verse (cited in Chapter 6), which, in his opinion, suggests that it was added into Rashi from there. It should be noted, however, that this comment is cited in Rashi's name by Nahmanides on Exod 6:12–13, and it also appears in MS De Rossi 175 (Spanish, dated 1305).

[94] The term "resumptive repetition" was coined by modern scholars of biblical narrative. See Berlin, *Biblical Narrative*, 126–128. See also Harris, "Literary Hermeneutic," 191–201.

information that was already given earlier. Support for this bold claim is given by noting that resumptive repetition can be regarded as a normal stylistic convention,[95] the way that any narrative might work. This comment on verse 30 is missing in a number of early Rashi manuscripts including MS Leipzig 1, which raises the possibility that it is not original to Rashi, but rather was added by a later hand.[96] Yet the language of this comment closely resembles the language found in Rashi's commentaries elsewhere.[97] This suggests that it could have been written by Rashi himself, though it is conceivable that a student who closely followed his *peshat* style added it – in the spirit of the master's commentary on Exod 6:13.

The gradual development of the literary *peshat* strategy – in opposition to the older midrashic reading – within Rashi's school comes to light in the interpretation found in Rashi's commentary on Exod 15:6, "Your right hand, O Lord, glorious in power, Your right hand, O Lord, shatters the foe," which offers no less than three explanations for the redundant phrase "Your right hand, O Lord":

> *Your right hand ... Your right hand* – Why is it said twice? Because when Israel performs the will of the Omnipresent, the left hand (symbolizing punishment) becomes a right hand (symbolizing reward). "Your right hand, O Lord, glorious in power" – to deliver Israel; and "Your second right hand shatters the foe."
>
> But to me it appears more fitting to explain that the very same right hand shatters the foe, something which is impossible for a human being – to do two things with one hand.
>
> But the *peshat* of Scripture is: "Your right hand, O Lord, glorious in power" – what does it do? "Your right hand, O Lord, shatters the foe." There are many scriptural verses exactly in this form, for example, "For behold your enemies, O Lord, [for behold your enemies will perish]" (Ps 92:10).[98]

The first explanation, drawn from the midrash (*Mekhilta*), is typical of the rabbinic endeavor to seek meaning in an apparent redundancy in the biblical text. According to the midrashic reading, the repeated phrase "your right hand" actually refers to God's *left hand*, i.e., the attribute of

[95] This is suggested by the use of the term *shiṭṭah*. On this usage in Rashi, see Chapter 3, note 64. The term is also used in a similar way by Eliezer of Beaugency. See Harris, "Literary Hermeneutic," 190.

[96] See the discussion in note 93.

[97] Rashi uses similar terminology ("it returns to the earlier subject" [*ḥozer la-ʿinyan ha-rishon*]) to note a case of "resumptive repetition" in his commentary on Gen 39:1, Berliner ed., 79 (text corrected based on MS Leipzig 1). See Gottlieb, *Order*, 109. See also Rashi on Song of Songs 2:8 (discussed in Chapter 6) and on Ps 68:29 (discussed in Chapter 7).

[98] Rashi on Exod 15:6, Berliner ed., 133.

judgment, whereas God's right hand itself represents the attribute of mercy. This midrashic interpretation derives a theological lesson from the redundancy: When Israel performs God's will, they prompt Him to use His anger for merciful purposes, i.e., to rescue Israel from her enemies – by striking them. Not surprisingly, this interpretation is also given in Tobiah's *Leqaḥ Ṭov* commentary.[99] In Rashi, however, there are two additional interpretations in the spirit of the *peshat* method that explain away the redundancy in linguistic or stylistic terms without deriving a theological message from it. The second interpretation still shares the syntactic assumption of the midrash that the repeated "Your right hand, O Lord" is a grammatically necessary component of this verse, which comprises two separate sentences ([1] "Your right hand, O Lord, [is] glorious in power"; [2] "Your right hand, O Lord, shatters the foe"). The third reading, specifically labeled "the *peshat* of Scripture," severs the midrashic link altogether by analyzing this verse as a single sentence, in which the repeated "Your right hand, O Lord" is employed purely for stylistic purposes, and, grammatically speaking, could have been omitted. In other words, the verse could have been written more concisely: "Your right hand, O Lord, [which is] glorious in power, shatters the foe." The poetic logic of this biblical convention is spelled out more clearly in Rashbam's commentary here:

> This verse is like "The ocean sounds, O Lord, the ocean sounds its thunder" (Ps 93:3), "How long shall the wicked, O Lord, how long shall the wicked exult" (Ps 94:3), "Surely your enemies, O Lord, surely your enemies perish" (Ps 92:10). The first half does not finish the statement until the second half comes and repeats a phrase and then completes the statement. But the first half mentions about whom it speaks.[100]

Rashbam, who does not bother citing the midrashic interpretation (nor does he mention the second interpretation in Rashi), accounts for the redundant phrase as a biblical stylistic convention, the structure of which he describes is a remarkably clear way that foreshadows what modern scholars would refer to as "staircase parallelism."[101]

Although this would seem to be a fine example of a double commentary that juxtaposes Rashi's *peshat* alternatives with the older midrashic

[99] *Leqaḥ Ṭov*, Buber ed., I:94–95. [100] Rashbam on Exod 15:6, Rosin ed., 102.

[101] Indeed, a key element of Rashbam's *peshat* methodology is to identify biblical stylistic tendencies, what he refers to elsewhere as *derekh ha-miqra'ot* ("the typical style of the biblical verses"), as we shall see below. See also Touitou, *Exegesis*, 126–134. According to Japhet (*Rashbam on Job*, 170), "Parallelismus membrorum is the central subject in the area of [biblical] style that Rashbam investigated."

reading, the manuscript evidence points to a complex history of this passage. The midrashic interpretation alone appears in Rashi's commentary in the 1475 Reggio di Calabria printed edition, in MS Leipzig 1, and in other medieval manuscripts.[102] Moreover, Berliner notes the stylistic "markers" – the "seams" conjoining the three commentaries – that suggest that the second and third interpretations are later additions to Rashi's commentary by other hands.[103] He attributes the second reading to Qara, who characteristically prefaced his marginal glosses on Rashi's commentary with the phrase "But to me it appears." Berliner traces the third reading to Rashbam, since it is introduced by the formula "But the *peshat* of the verse is" characteristic of Rashbam, whose commentary here actually features a similar reading.

Yet there is evidence suggesting that Rashi himself ultimately accepted Rashbam's interpretation. The phenomenon of staircase parallelism – based on the verses cited by Rashbam on Exod 15:6 – is described clearly in a gloss on Rashi's commentary on Gen 49:22, to which the following remark is appended:

> All of this is from the written work (*yesod*) of Rabbi Samuel (=Rashbam), and when Rabbi Solomon (=Rashi) his grandfather came to these verses he called them "Samuel's verses" in his name.[104]

This anecdote – recorded by a third party – concurs with Rashbam's version of the exchange with his grandfather, who acknowledged that he considered updating his commentaries according to the new *peshat* interpretations devised by others. This precious moment of self-reflection in the northern French *peshat* school reveals that Rashi did not regard his commentary as the final word. Quite the contrary, as Rashbam portrays it, his grandfather was well aware of having taken only the first steps in a project that would ultimately be completed by his successors. In light of the evidence mentioned above that Rashi revised his commentaries over his lifetime, in part with the assistance of Shemaiah, we can consider the possibility that the master himself incorporated interpretations originally

102 The second and third interpretations do appear in some medieval manuscripts, e.g., MSS Bodleiana 2440, London 26917, Berlin 514. But they are absent in MSS Berlin 1221, Bodleiana 186 (=Oppenheim 34), De Rossi 181, and Leipzig 1. Accordingly, they appear in brackets in *Miqra'ot Gedolot ha-Keter*.

103 See Berliner, *Raschi*, ix–x.

104 MS Vienna Nationalbibliothek Cod. Hebr. 32, 75r. See Poznanski, "Introduction," XLV. The distinctive medieval Ashkenazic usage of the Hebrew root *y-s-d* in the sense of *writing* or *a written work* is discussed in Chapter 2.

suggested by Qara and Rashbam – and this could explain the duplications and "seams" in Rashi's commentaries. In this spirit, Berliner posits that Rashi himself added the third reading to his commentary on Exod 15:6 based on his grandson's insight.[105]

RASHI'S KEY EXEGETICAL CONCEPTS AND TERMINOLOGY

The discussion above provides insight into the key components of Rashi's *peshat* method, which he used both to evaluate midrashic readings and to interpret the biblical text independently of rabbinic tradition. Perhaps Rashi's most fundamental *peshat* value is the systematic philological analysis of the language of Scripture. Whereas midrashic tradition interprets the Bible's language freely and associatively, Rashi, following the model established by Menahem in his *Maḥberet* and Dunash in his critical notes, seeks to do so based on a systematic philological study of biblical usage and stylistic conventions. Additionally, Rashi seeks to interpret the biblical text contextually, according to its sequence, as opposed to the midrashic tendency to interpret individual verses and even phrases and words in isolation.

As they crystalized in his exegetical consciousness, these *peshat* values came to be associated with special terminology that would become characteristic of Rashi's style, distinguishing his methodologically self-aware commentary from rabbinic midrashic readings of the Bible. Rashi regularly expresses his objective to correctly ascertain the "plain meaning" (*mashma'[ut]*) of the biblical verses, and criticizes midrashic interpretations that violate it.[106] In Rashi's eyes, for a commentary to be legitimate, it must correspond to – or be "settled upon" – the sequence of the verses (*seder ha-miqra'ot*) and the "[precision of] the language of the verse ([*diqduq*] *leshon ha-miqra*)."[107]

Of particular interest is Rashi's use of the term *diqduq*, which in Medieval Hebrew came to connote the discipline of *grammar*, though in

[105] See Berliner, *Raschi*, ix. (Cf. Japhet, *Rashbam on Job*, 172n, who questions this conclusion.) A similar textual development may well be behind Rashi's double commentary on 1 Sam 1:23. The *peshat* commentary there resembles the one given by Qara on 1 Sam 1:17 – and that may well have been Rashi's source. See also Qara's commentary on Gen 24:7 published in Berliner, *Pletath soferim*, 14.

[106] See Rashi on Num 10:21; Deut 16:4; Ps 5:1 (cited earlier in this chapter); Song of Songs, introduction (cited further in this chapter); Esth 1:6. The sense of the term *mashma'(ut)* in Rashi's usage is discussed in Chapter 2.

[107] See, e.g., Rashi on Exod 6:9, Isa 26:11, both cited and discussed earlier in this chapter. See also note 79.

Rabbinic Hebrew it had only the more basic sense of *precision of language*, i.e., reading, speaking, and understanding accurately. This transition seems to have occurred in the Muslim East around the tenth century. The masoretic work *Sefer diqduqei ha-ṭeʿamim* by Aaron ben Asher (early tenth century) documents key morphological patterns in Biblical Hebrew, and thus can be said to provide the foundations for the discipline of Hebrew grammar.[108] However, in that work, and in masoretic literature in general, the term *diqduq* itself is used primarily in the sense of *precision of reading*, which is in line with the chief objective of the masoretes to safeguard the accurate vocalization of the Bible. Stemming from that usage, however, the term eventually developed the specific technical sense of *the discipline of grammar*, as attested, for example, in the work known as *al-Diqduq* by the Karaite author Joseph Ibn Nuḥ (Jerusalem, late tenth century), which lays out rules of Hebrew morphology and phonology.[109] In Menahem ben Saruq the latter technical usage is attested, albeit only rarely.[110]

The rabbinic sense of the term *diqduq* is attested in Rashi's writings, including some of the examples of the expression *diqduq ha-lashon* discussed above. Yet in one case Rashi, perhaps following the precedent he would have known from Menahem ben Saruq, seems to use the term *diqduq ha-lashon* in the sense of *grammar*, i.e., the rules of Biblical Hebrew morphology and phonology. On the narrative describing how Pharaoh's daughter found Moses in the river, Rashi comments on Exod 2:5, "She spied the basket among the reeds and sent her *amah* (*amatah*) to fetch it":

> *Amatah* – means her maidservant. Now our Rabbis interpreted it as "her hand" (b.*Soṭah* 12b). However, according to the grammar of the sacred tongue (*diqduq leshon ha-qodesh*) it would then have to be vocalized *ammatah*, with a *dagesh* in the *mem* (indicating gemmination of the consonant). But they interpreted it to mean "her hand," i.e., that her hand extended many cubits (Heb. *ammot*: lit., hand lengths).[111]

As Rashi records, the Talmud takes *amah* in this verse to mean *a hand*, and, with a play on words typical of midrashic interpretation, describes how Pharaoh's daughter's hand (*ammah*) miraculously extended "many

[108] See Dotan, *Sefer Diḳduḳe ha-ṭeʿamim*, 26–39.

[109] See Khan, *Karaite Grammatical Thought*, 6–11.

[110] See *Maḥberet*, s.v., הג, הי. See also Mirsky, "Linguistic Theory," 166 (my thanks to Aharon Maman for this reference).

[111] Rashi on Exod 2:5, Berliner ed., 104.

cubits" (*ammot*, i.e., handlengths). However, Rashi notes that this interpretation is not consistent with the rules of Biblical Hebrew grammar, since *ammah* in the sense of *a hand*, *handlength*, always appears with a geminated *mem*, whereas the term *amah* with an ungeminated *mem* always connotes *a maidservant*.

The concern with Hebrew grammar intensified among Rashi's students. Particularly noteworthy is the dedicated treatise by Rashbam on this subject entitled *Sefer Dayyaqut* (a variant of the Hebrew term *diqduq*).[112] That work emphasizes the centrality of systematic philological analysis ("to learn the meaning of a word from others similar to it") of Scripture according to the rules of grammar (*diqduq*) for "discerning its true meaning (*la'amod 'al amittatah*)."[113] As a continuation to *Sefer Dayyaqut* Rashbam also composed a dedicated grammatical commentary on the first chapters of Genesis (perhaps an unfinished work) which deals exclusively with matters of morphology and phonology.[114]

[112] See Eldar, "Grammatical Literature," 29–31; Merdler, "Rashbam and Hebrew Grammar." As Merdler (10 n. 4) notes, the correct vocalization of the title is *Dayyakut* (not *Dayykot*), the meaning of which is "the discipline of grammar." According to Eldar (29), this title was given by the copyist, not necessarily by Rashbam himself.

[113] *Sefer Dayyaqut*, Merdler ed., 18.

[114] See Merdler, "Grammatical Commentary." A number of scholars believed *Dayyaqut* to be a late work of Rashbam's, which could explain why the grammatical commentary that followed remained unfinished. But Yosef Ofer argues that *Dayyaqut* was penned early in Rashbam's career. See Ofer, "When Was '*Dayaqot*' Written?"

2

"Settling" the Words of Scripture Using Midrash

The previous chapter illustrated Rashi's abilities as a *pashtan*, manifested by the innovative philological-contextual readings of the biblical text he offers as alternatives to the midrashic readings otherwise current in his Ashkenazic milieu. Indeed, thanks to the continued efforts of Rashi's students and their students throughout the twelfth century the Ashkenazic interpretive landscape had been forever altered – with new *peshat* interpretations competing with the older midrashic interpretive tradition. As Rashbam records, the latter were the province of the "early generations," who, "because of their piety, tended to delve into the *derashot*," which "inform us the *haggadot* (traditions, lore), *halakhot* (laws), and *dinim* (regulations) through the hints of (*remizat*) the *peshat* by way of redundant language, and through the thirty-two hermeneutical rules (*middot*) of R. Eliezer ... and the thirteen hermeneutical rules (*middot*) of R. Ishmael."[1] To use Beryl Smalley's characterization, midrashic interpretation features "pious meditations or religious teaching for which the text is used merely as a convenient starting-point."[2] By contrast, Rashi opened the gates of *peshat* interpretation with his systematic philological interpretations that respect the sequence of the biblical text. And yet, most of Rashi's commentaries are actually drawn from midrashic sources, without being labeled as *derash* or being accompanied by an alternative *peshat* interpretation. In order to arrive at a comprehensive understanding of Rashi's exegetical program, we shall now address the various ways in which the great northern French pioneer of *peshat* advances what appears to be a midrashic agenda.

[1] Rashbam on Gen 37:2, Rosin ed., 49, cited in full in the Introduction, on p. 9.

[2] See Smalley, *Study of the Bible*, 2.

MIDRASHIC RENDERING OF THE BIBLICAL NARRATIVE

The biblical narrative, as rendered by the midrashic "traditions and lore," is not merely a historical account focusing on the ancient People of Israel; it is laden with religiously significant, miraculous accounts that are of timeless significance for people of faith, which the Rabbis expounded through the "hints" of the text, as Rashbam put it. A typical example can be seen in Rashi's commentary on an episode in the family of Abraham (when he still bore his original name, Abram) in Gen 11:28, "And Haran died in front of his father Terah, in his native land, Ur of the Chaldeans." Rashi offers two distinct explanations of the expression "in front of" and two corresponding ones of the expression "Ur of Chaldees":

> *In front of his father Terah* – during his father's lifetime.[3]
>
> But the aggadic midrash says that he died through his father's actions. For Terah complained to Nimrod about his son Abram because he smashed his idols, and Nimrod cast Abram into the fiery furnace. And Haran sat and said in his heart: "If Abram triumphs, I am with him, but if Nimrod triumphs I am with him." And when Abram was saved, they asked Haran, "Whose side are you on?" Haran said to them: "On Abram's side." They cast him into the fiery furnace and he was burnt. And that is "Ur (lit., fire) of the Chaldeans."
>
> But Menahem [ben Saruq] explained: *ur* means *a valley*. And similarly, "Glorify the Lord in the valleys (*urim*)" (Isa 24:15), and like "the den (or: hole; *me'urat*) of a viper" (Isa 11:8). Every hole or deep cleft may be called *ur*.[4]

With *ur* construed to mean *fire*, the reading Rashi identifies as midrashic takes this verse as a reference to a miraculous event – Abram's surviving the fiery furnace – symbolic of the victory of monotheism over idolatry. In typical fashion, the midrash casts this as an example of the power of faith to bring forth God's miracles, which is naturally a crucial eternal religious lesson.[5] On the other hand, the alternative philological analysis drawn from Menahem, implicitly cast as *peshuto shel miqra*, takes *ur* to mean *a valley*, rendering the verse a more ordinary account of a son dying within his father's lifetime – in the valley of the Chaldees. Similarly, Rashi's

[3] This philological observation can be traced to midrashic sources. See, e.g., *Pesikta de-Rav Kahana*, §26, Mandelbaum ed., 328. On the phenomenon of Rashi using midrashic material to construct his own philological *peshat* interpretations, at times contrasted with another interpretation explicitly labeled midrashic, see Kamin, *Categorization*, 151–157.

[4] Rashi on Gen 11:28, Berliner ed., 21–22. The midrashic interpretation is from *Genesis Rabbah* 38:13, Theodor–Albeck ed., 361–364. The citation of Menahem is from his *Maḥberet*, s.v., אר.

[5] On this midrashic tendency, see Kugel, *Bible as it Was*, 18, 21.

commentary implies that the same methodological distinction holds between the alternative ways of analyzing the expression "in front of his father": the midrashic reading construes this expression to mean that Haran died *because of his father*, whereas the *peshat* approach (classified thus implicitly) takes it to mean only that Haran died during his father's lifetime.

The midrashic reading of Gen 11:28 was well known and is even reflected in Saadia Gaon's commentary.[6] But the methodological awareness manifested by Rashi is especially evident by comparison with the commentary of Tobiah ben Eliezer here:

> *And Haran died in front of his father Terah* – For until now the son never died before the father. And why did this one die? On account of the incident in Ur of the Chaldees. For Abraham used to smash Terah's idols and people became angry with him and cast him into the fiery furnace. And Haran stood to fuel the fire and a flame consumed him. Thus it says: And Haran died in front of his father Terah.
>
> *In Ur of the Chaldees* – The name of the place.[7]

Tobiah begins his commentary with a philological note resembling Rashi's: "Haran died in front of his father Terah," meaning that he died during his father's lifetime. He likewise notes, in a philological vein, that "*Ur* of the Chaldees" is the name of a place. But Tobiah fuses these linguistic notes with the miraculous midrashic reading, which underscores what is unique about Rashi's endeavor to differentiate between the midrashic reading and the philological one.

In the preceding example Rashi offered a *peshat* alternative to the midrashic reading. But it is more typical for him to rely primarily on a midrashic source, at times blending it with his philological insight. For example, in an early Genesis episode regarding Abraham (when he was still referred to as Abram) we read of the capture of his nephew Lot, which prompts the following reaction on his uncle's part: "When Abram heard that his kinsman had been taken captive, he mustered his trained men, who numbered three hundred and eighteen, and went in pursuit as far as Dan" (Gen 14:14). Rashi here begins with a philological analysis:

> *His trained men* (*ḥanikhayw*) – whom he trained to observe the commandments (*miṣwot*). The Hebrew root *ḥ-n-kh* means to initiate a person or utensil for the skill or function that he/it will have in the future. As in these verses: "Train (*ḥanokh*; i.e., initiate) the lad … " (Prov 22:6), " … initiation (*ḥanukkah*) of the altar"

[6] Saadia on Gen 11:28, Zucker ed., 111 (Ar.), 354–355 (Heb.).

[7] *Leqaḥ Ṭov* on Gen 11:28, Buber ed., I:55.

(Num 7:11), "... initiation (*ḥanukkah*) of the house" (Ps 30:1). In the vernacular (*la'az*; i.e., Old French): *enseigner* (= to instruct).[8]

Based on its other occurrences in Biblical Hebrew, Rashi notes that the root *ḥ-n-kh* means *to initiate a person or object*. As he often does, Rashi provides the equivalent *enseigner* in Old French, the vernacular of his community. Hence, *ḥanikhayw* would mean *the ones he instructed or trained*. Given that Abram was a man of God, not a warrior, Rashi presumes that the "instruction" and "training" he imparted was religious. Rashi goes on to identify who was "trained" by Abraham in this way:

Three hundred and eighteen – Our Rabbis said that it was Eliezer alone, and this [318] is the *gematria* (numerical) value of [the letters that make up] his name.[9]

Relying on a midrashic tradition, Rashi posits that the reference here is to Eliezer, Abram's faithful servant, described in Gen 15:2 as the steward of his household. As midrashic commentaries go, the reading cited here is not unusual: the biblical text is "interpreted" using the numerology referred to as *gematria* to reach a conclusion quite different from what is stated plainly in the text, i.e., that Abram secured his victory with a force of 318 men. The Rabbis transformed this into a miraculous victory by "Eliezer alone," demonstrating how faith overcomes military might.

This midrashic interpretation is mentioned and sharply rejected by Ibn Ezra, who took a dim view of *gematria*, as it opens the door to exegetical anarchy.[10] Not surprisingly, Tobiah takes the midrashic approach and relies on the *gematria* in *Leqaḥ Ṭov* on this verse:

He readied his trained men – [the Hebrew word for "his trained men"] is written [as though it were in the singular] *ḥ-n-kh-w* [to indicate that] it was Eliezer alone, whose name adds up to 318.[11]

[8] Rashi on Gen 14:14, Berliner ed., 25–26. The standard printed edition of Rashi in the *Miqra'ot Gedolot* begins with another comment: "*ḥanikhayw* is written *ḥ-n-kh-w* [i.e., as though it were a noun in the singular] – this is Eliezer." However, as Berliner notes, this comment does not appear in the Reggio di Calabria edition of Rashi. Nor does it appear in Rashi's commentary attested in MSS Berlin 140, De Rossi 181, Leipzig 1. In *Miqra'ot Gedolot ha-Keter* it is omitted, as it would seem to be a late addition to Rashi's commentary.

[9] Rashi on Gen 14:14, Berliner ed., 26. This midrash appears in *Genesis Rabbah* 42:2, Theodor–Albeck ed., 416. Every Hebrew letter has a numerical value. The use of these values for interpretive purposes is a common midrashic endeavor known as *gematria*.

[10] Ibn Ezra on Gen 14:14, Weiser ed., I:55. See Mondschein, "Attitude."

[11] Buber ed., I:65.

Ibn Ezra was even more critical of *Leqaḥ Ṭov* – whose commentary circulated in Italy – than he was of Rashi.[12] The latter, in Ibn Ezra's view, was misguided in his endeavor to correctly construe "the *peshat* of Scripture"; but he casts Tobiah among "the sages in Greek (i.e., Byzantine) and Roman (i.e., western Christian) lands, who pay no attention to grammar (lit., the weights of the scales[13]), but merely follow the way of *derash*."[14] Rashi, it is true, did not rely exclusively upon *gematria*, to which he added a philological analysis of the Hebrew root *ḥ-n-kh*. Yet ultimately even Rashi's reading of the verse is at odds with the *peshat* program of Ibn Ezra, for whom "three hundred and eighteen men" should be taken literally. Ibn Ezra's harsh critique of this midrashic reading was probably sparked by the fact that it was cited not only in *Leqaḥ Ṭov*, but also by Rashi, who purports to adhere to "the *peshat* of Scripture." As Aaron Mondschein has demonstrated, many of Ibn Ezra's interpretations appear to be directed specifically against Rashi's, as if to underscore that the latter "interpreted Scripture by way of *derash* [even though] he thought that it is by way of *peshat*."[15]

TYPOLOGICAL READING

Notwithstanding the historical *peshat* sensibilities he manifests at times, Rashi more frequently follows in the footsteps of the Rabbis, reading into Scripture eternal messages for the Jewish people – especially his downtrodden coreligionists in medieval Christian Europe. For example, Psalm 42 would appear to be the lament of an ancient Israelite in exile, perhaps in Babylonia, grieving over his inability to visit the Holy Temple in Jerusalem – a joyful experience this psalm recalls. Indeed, this was the opinion of Moses Ibn Chiquitilla, cited by Ibn Ezra.[16] For Rashi, however, the psalmist "prophesied about the three kingdoms that will bring the worship in the Temple to an end: Babylonia, Greece and Rome. And Israel cries in anguish [suffering from all three], but will be rescued."[17] Later verses in this psalm read:

O my God, my soul is downcast; therefore I think of You in this land of Jordan and Hermon, in Mount Mizar, where deep calls to deep in the roar of Your cataracts;

[12] For Ibn Ezra's critique of Rashi, see *Safah Berurah*, Wilensky ed., 288, cited in the Introduction.

[13] Heb. *mishqal mo'znayim*. Ibn Ezra's own grammatical work is entitled *Sefer Mo'znayim*.

[14] Standard introduction to the Pentateuch, "The Fourth Way," Weiser ed., I:7.

[15] See *Safah Berurah*, Wilensky ed., 288 and Mondschein, "One in a Thousand."

[16] See Ibn Ezra on Ps 42:1, *Miqra'ot Gedolot ha-Keter*, 132.

[17] Rashi on Ps 42:3, Gruber ed., 825 (Heb.), 336 (Eng.).

all Your breakers and billows have swept over me. By day may the Lord vouchsafe His faithful care, so that at night a song to Him may be with me, a prayer to the God of my life. (Ps 42:7–9)

Ibn Ezra here manifests the historical and literary-contextual sensibilities typical of the Andalusian *peshat* approach:

Deep calls to deep – Within the context of this passage, it would seem that [the psalmist] refers here to streams that descend from the mountains. And the meaning of "Deep calls to deep" is that the water of the streams combines at low points ... [as] he used to enjoy himself when he passed through the mountains in the summer, and the flowing waters – like waves and billows of the sea – flowed over him. But one who interprets this verse about the matter of the exile disconnects it from the context (lit., what comes before and after it).

By day – he recounts traveling with the celebrants by day with the security of God's grace.

And at night – they sang ... [hymns of] prayer.[18]

Taking into consideration the references to the terrain of northern Israel, Ibn Ezra interpreted these words as a wistful recollection of the joyous pilgrimage travels through mountains and streams by day, followed by devotional communal song at night.

The last line of Ibn Ezra's commentary on verse 8 ("But one who interprets ... ") seems to be a response to Rashi, who takes this psalm midrashically as a collective lament said by the "Congregation of Israel."[19] Rashi emphasizes Israel's suffering in exile:

Deep calls to deep – One calamity invites another, pouring suffering upon me like gushing water, and so "all Your waves and billows have swept over me" ...

By day may the Lord vouchsafe His faithful care – i.e., may the light of redemption arrive.

And in the night – in the darkness of exile and suffering ...[20]

For Rashi, the violent water imagery symbolizes calamities, the night exile and suffering, and the day redemption – all for the Jewish people in his time, far removed from the experiences of the ancient psalmist.

[18] Ibn Ezra on Ps 42:1, *Miqra'ot Gedolot ha-Keter*, 135.

[19] Ibn Ezra seems to refer to Rashi in his remark at the opening of this psalm: "Some say that [the psalmist] speaks in the name of the people of the current exile" (comm. on Ps 42:1, *Miqra'ot Gedolot ha-Keter*, 132).

[20] Rashi on Ps. 42:7–9, Gruber ed., 826 (Heb.), 337 (Eng.).

HALAKHIC READING

Rashi's adherence to midrash is particularly evident in the realm of halakhah. Whereas Rashbam would offer strikingly novel *peshat* readings of the halakhic sections of the Pentateuch,[21] Rashi most typically relies on talmudic interpretation, following in the footsteps of "the early generations" who extrapolated the "*halakhot* (laws) and *dinim* (regulations)" midrashically. A prime example appears in Rashi's commentary on the law of levirate marriage:

When brothers dwell together and one of them dies and leaves no son, the wife of the deceased shall not be married to a stranger, outside the family. Her husband's brother shall ... take her ... as his wife ... And it shall be that the firstborn she bears shall succeed to the name of his brother, so that his name may not be blotted out in Israel. (Deut 25:5–6)

The verses seem clear: the child born from the levirate marriage will take the place of the deceased, perhaps by being given his name. But Rashi interprets verse 6 atomistically:

(1) *And it shall be that the firstborn* – the commandment of the levirate marriage devolves upon the surviving elder brother.
(2) *that she bears* – this excludes a woman who is incapable of procreation.
(3) *shall succeed to the name of his brother* – the one who performed the levirate marriage takes the portion of their father's inheritance belonging to the deceased brother.
(4) *so that his name may not be blotted out* – this excludes the wife of a eunuch whose name is already blotted out.[22]

This follows the Talmudic reading:

Our Rabbis expounded:

(1) *And it shall be that the firstborn* – this implies that the commandment of the levirate marriage devolves upon the surviving elder brother.
(2) *that she bears* – this excludes a woman who is incapable of procreation, since she cannot bear children.
(3) *shall succeed to the name of his brother* – with respect to inheritance ...
(4) *so that his name may not be blotted out* – this excludes a eunuch whose name is already blotted out.[23]

[21] See Chapter 9. [22] Rashi on Deut 25:6, Berliner ed., 397. [23] b.*Yevamot* 24a.

Ibn Ezra cites this very example as a classic case of *asmakhta* (i.e., an *ex post facto* link to a scriptural locution to provide "support" for a tradition transmitted orally) which cannot be taken as a genuine interpretation, since "every Jew knows the meaning of the verse, which is according to its plain sense (*mashma'*) and *peshat*."[24] For him, the law "derived" from this verse in the Talmud was actually an oral tradition:

> "And it shall be, that the firstborn she bears" is ... according to its plain sense (*mashma'*). They also had a tradition that the eldest of the brothers must be the one who performs the levirate marriage, and they interpreted this verse midrashically [in that vein] as a reminder (*zekher*) and an *asmakhta*.[25]

This verse is also rendered contextually in Saadia's *Tafsīr*: "And the firstborn they anticipate that she will bear from him ... "[26]

Rashbam here remarks briefly "according to its *peshat*, the son [i.e., and not the levir] will take the place (lit., the name) of his brother."[27] But it is Joseph Bekhor Shor, a student of Rabbenu Tam, who most fully articulates the opposition between the *peshat* and midrashic interpretations:

> (1) *And it shall be that the firstborn* – this implies that the commandment of the levirate marriage devolves upon the [surviving] elder brother.
> (2) *that she bears* – this excludes a woman who is incapable of procreation, since she cannot bear children.
> (3) *so that his name may not be blotted out* – this excludes a eunuch whose name is already blotted out.
> (4) *shall succeed to the name of his brother* – with respect to inheritance, that he takes his portion and the portion of his brother in their father's inheritance, and for this reason he is called the "firstborn," since he takes a two-fold portion (as a firstborn does; see Deut 21:17).
>
> And this verse leaves the realm of its *peshat*. For according to the *peshat* it would have seemed that it means this:
>
> *And it shall be that the firstborn* – the first child that the levirate wife bears

[24] Short commentary on Exod 21:8, Weiser ed., II:291. It is possible that Ibn Ezra used the terms *mashma* and *peshat* together as a hendiadys. Rashi at times used the terms *mashma'* and *peshat* interchangeably. See Gelles, *Rashi*, 119–120; Viezel, "Onkelos in Rashi's Consciousness," 6–7.

[25] Short commentary on Exod 21:8, Weiser ed., II:291–292.

[26] וליכן אלבכר אלד'י ירג'ו אן תלד מנה ... (Derenbourg ed., 290).

[27] Commentary on Deut 25:6, Rosin ed., 221.

shall succeed to the name of his brother – of the lever, i.e., the deceased, meaning that if his name was Simon he shall be named Simon, and if Reuben, he should be named Reuben.[28]

In saying that this verse "leaves the realm of its *peshat*," i.e., that it's an exception to the rule that "a biblical verse does not leave the realm of its *peshat*," Bekhor Shor reveals his talmudic colors, as this reading was actually raised, but ultimately rejected, in the Talmud:

You say, "with respect to inheritance"; perhaps it does not mean that, but rather, "with respect to the name"? For example, if the deceased was Joseph the child shall be called Joseph; if Yohanan he shall be called Yohanan! Not so. For here it states, "He shall succeed in the name (על שם) of his brother" and elsewhere it is stated, "They shall be called after the name (על שם) of their brethren in their inheritance" (Gen 48:6). Just as the "name" mentioned there is inheritance, so too the "name" mentioned here is for inheritance ...

Raba remarked: although normally (lit., in all of the Torah) a biblical verse does not leave the realm of its *peshat*, here the *gezerah shawah* came and removed it from its *peshat* entirely.[29]

The talmudic sage Raba notes that the *gezerah shawah* overrides the *peshat*, by which he seems to mean the straightforward contextual reading.[30] In theory, this would support the claim made by some *pashtanim* that the Rabbis – as a rule – seek to protect the integrity of the philological-contextual sense. But the truth is that the supposed "exception" seems to reflect the rule in the Talmud, which often invokes a *gezerah shawah* or another one of the *middot* to interpret Scripture and forsake the straightforward sense.[31] Furthermore, Rashi, following the Talmud, likewise often offers midrashic halakhic readings without offering a *peshat* alternative.

On occasion, however, Rashi seems to manifest concern for the disparity between his halakhic midrashic interpretation and what might otherwise be

[28] Bekhor Shor on Deut 25:6, Nevo ed., 363. [29] b.*Yevamot* 24a.

[30] As noted by *Tosafot* (ad loc., s.v. או אינו אלא לשם), if it were not for the *gezerah shawah* the Talmud would have read the entire verse as a single unit, i.e., taking "the firstborn" to refer to the child born of the levirate marriage. In other words, it is because of the *gezerah shawah* that the Talmud interpreted the entire verse atomistically; otherwise, it could all be read as a unit in a straightforward way: the firstborn of the levirate marriage shall be given the name of the deceased so that his name will not be blotted out.

[31] To explain this apparent inconsistency, Nahmanides argues that the *peshat* rule does not disqualify midrashic readings that diverge from the straightforward sense, but merely indicates that they do not supplant the straightforward sense (*peshuto shel miqra* according to his definition). See *Hassagot*, Chavel ed., 44–45.

the *peshat* interpretation of a given verse. This concern manifests itself in his tendency to rework his midrashic sources, evidently to better accommodate his *peshat* sensibilities. This would seem to be the case, for example, in his commentary on the pericope that presents the laws of priestly defilement for close relatives in Leviticus 21:

> The Lord said to Moses: Speak to the priests, the sons of Aaron, and say to them: None shall defile himself for any [dead] person among his kin, (2) except for the relatives (*she'er*) that are closest to him: his mother, his father, his son, his daughter, and his brother; (3) also for a virgin sister, close to him because she has not married, for her he may defile himself. (4) A husband (*ba'al*) among his people, he may not be defiled to profane himself. (Lev 21:1–4)

Although a priest is prohibited from becoming "defiled" through contact with a dead body, verses 2–3 make an exception for family relations, assumed in talmudic tradition to include "seven close relatives" for whom a person is obligated to mourn.[32] In addition to the six mentioned explicitly in these two verses, the Talmud states that "his *she'er* means his wife."[33] Verse 4 contradicts this, as it prohibits "a husband" from becoming defiled. The Talmud resolves the contradiction in the following way:

> There is a husband who may defile himself, and there is a husband who may not defile himself. How is this so? He may defile himself for a wife who is "fit" (halakhically permitted); and he may not defile himself for a wife who is "unfit."[34]

Reflecting his Geonic-Andalusian philological background, Ibn Ezra notes that "by way of *peshat*, the wife is never called *she'er*," and he thus posits that the talmudic "interpretation" of this word is merely an *asmakhta*.[35] This

[32] There is a debate whether the obligation to mourn is biblical or rabbinic. Maimonides – following Isaac Alfasi – maintains that there is a biblical obligation to mourn, but only on the single day of death and burial (whereas the week-long mourning period is of rabbinic origin); see *Mishneh Torah, Hilkhot Evel* 1:1, with *Radbaz* and *Kesef Mishneh*. The expression "seven close relatives" (*shiv'ah qerovim*) is not stated explicitly in the Talmud, but it does appear in the early post-talmudic literature, e.g., the *She'iltot* of R. Aha of Sabha and *Halakhot Gedolot*: see Brody, *Textual History*, 160–161.

[33] b.*Yevamot* 22b.

[34] b.*Yevamot* 22b. A priest is not permitted, for example, to take a divorcée as a wife (see Lev 21:7).

[35] Alternate introduction to the Pentateuch, "Fourth Way," Weiser ed., I:141. This follows Saadia's construal of the word *she'er*, which was adopted subsequently in the Andalusian tradition. See Zucker, *Translation*, 387.

understanding would seem to underlie Rashbam's *peshat* interpretation on verse 4:

A husband (ba'al) among his people, he may not be defiled – No husband in the priestly class (lit., in the "nation" of priests) may defile himself for his wife; "to profane himself" – because in doing so he profanes his priesthood.[36]

It is, of course, remarkable that Rashbam formulates a *peshat* interpretation that contradicts the halakhah. But this accords with his programmatic statements elsewhere that "the *peshat* of Scripture" carries no legal implications, as the midrashic reading determines halakhah.[37]

Rashi's interpretation of these verses is bound by the talmudic understanding. On verse 2 he writes:

Except for his kin (she'er) – means his wife.[38]

Then, on verse 4 he writes:

A husband (ba'al) among his people, he may not be defiled – he may not defile himself for an unfit wife, through whom he profanes himself (i.e., with an illicit marriage) by being with her.[39]

Although the talmudic resolution of the contradiction underlies Rashi's analysis, he augments it with a construal of verse 4, arguing that the expression "to profane himself" teaches that the prohibition applies only to an unfit wife. Elijah Mizrahi (Constantinople, 1435–1526), in his supercommentary on Rashi here, comments:

It appears to me that this is neither the midrashic interpretation of the verse nor its *peshat* interpretation, but rather is nothing other than an adjustment of the midrash and its extension in accordance with the plain sense (*mashma'ut*) of the verse and its *peshat*.[40]

In other words, Rashi sought to bring the midrash into line with "the sense" of Scripture that might emerge from a *peshat* reading. It is perhaps this quality of Rashi's commentary that Rashbam had in mind when he offered the following assessment:

36 Rashbam on Lev 21:4, Rosin ed., 163.

37 He thus goes on here to cite the reconciliation of verses 2 and 4 "according to the words of the Sages." On Rashbam's *peshat* interpretations that do not accord with the halakhah, see Chapter 9.

38 Rashi on Lev 21:2, Berliner ed., 257.

39 Rashi on Lev 21:2, Berliner ed., 257.

40 Mizrahi on Rashi on Lev 21:4, Phillip ed., III:413–414. Mizrahi is generally considered to be the most important supercommentary on Rashi. His approach is discussed later in this chapter.

In the explanations of my grandfather, our Master Rabbi Solomon ... most of the *halakhot* and *derashot* are close to the *peshat* of the Scriptures, and all of them can deduced [from the redundancies and anomalies] of the language.[41]

Rashi may not have adhered strictly to *peshat*, as Rashbam would do; but his selection and reworking of midrash is inspired by *peshat* considerations – making his interpretations "close to the *peshat* of the Scriptures."

DISREGARDING THE TALMUDIC PESHAT MAXIM

In his commentary on Deut 25:6 (cited above), Rashi might be forgiven for abdicating his *peshat* sensibilities and interpreting the verse atomistically because the Talmud explicitly identifies this verse as an exception to the rule that "a biblical verse does not leave the realm of its *peshat*." However, we must wonder why Rashi disregarded the clearest application of the talmudic *peshat* maxim, as found in b.*Shabbat* 63a. The subject of that talmudic discussion is the mishnaic dispute between the majority view that "a man must not go out with a sword or bow on the Sabbath," since carrying in the public domain is prohibited, and the dissenting opinion of R. Eliezer, who maintains that this is permitted because "they are ornaments for him" – and one is permitted to wear ornaments, just as one wears clothing. This prompts the inquiry:

What is R. Eliezer's reason ... ? Because it is written, "Gird your sword on your thigh, O brave warrior; it is your glory and your majesty" (Ps 45:4). R. Kahana objected to Mar bar R. Huna: But this refers to the words of the Torah! He replied: "a biblical verse does not leave the realm of its *peshat*."

The verse cited from Psalms indicates that a sword is considered glorious and majestic, which supports R. Eliezer's opinion. R. Kahana evidently had been taught – and accepted – a figurative interpretation of this verse, according to which the "sword" is taken to refer to "the words of Torah." As Rashi explains in his gloss-commentary on this talmudic line:

You must be diligent to review your learning so that it is ready for you when necessary to bring a proof – like the sword on the thigh of a brave warrior that enables him to be victorious in battle – and it is your glory and your majesty.[42]

[41] Introduction to Leviticus, Rosin ed., 144–145. Rosin added the bracketed phrase based on Rashbam's formulations elsewhere.

[42] Rashi, b. *Shabbat* 63a, s.v., בדברי תורה כתיב.

In light of this figurative midrashic interpretation, R. Kahana argues that the verse actually does not refer to weaponry at all. At this point, the Talmud records that Mar bar R. Huna states the rule that "a biblical verse does not leave the realm of its *peshat*." In other words, the figurative reading cannot supplant the literal sense of the verse, i.e., "its *peshat*."

There is no clearer application of the *peshat* maxim in all of the Talmud than the one appearing in b.*Shabbat* 63a.[43] One therefore would have expected Rashi to formulate his interpretation of Ps 45:4 according to "the *peshat* of Scripture," or at least acknowledge it. But Rashi, in fact, seems to have interpreted that entire psalm in accordance with the figurative midrashic reading of that verse. Psalm 45 is described by many modern scholars as a "royal psalm" because it praises the king, i.e., one of the monarchs of ancient Israel.[44] Rashi, however, construes this psalm as a praise of Torah scholars, as is evident in his commentary on the superscription, "[A psalm] for lilies, by the sons of Korah" (v. 1):

> *for lilies* – They composed (*yissedu*)[45] this psalm in honor of Torah scholars, because they are soft as lilies, beautiful as lilies and, like lilies, they make good deeds blossom.[46]

[43] In b.*Yevamot* 24a, as mentioned above, the maxim is cited to say that Deut 24:1 is an exception to the rule, as that verse does, in fact, "leave the realm of its *peshat*." The only other instance in which the *peshat* maxim is invoked in the Talmud, in b.*Yevamot* 11b, involves a discussion over whether the expression "after she was defiled" in Deut 24:4 is also an exception to the rule and "leaves the realm of its *peshat*."

[44] See Gerstenberger, *Psalms 1*, 186–190. Abraham Ibn Ezra (comm. on Ps 45:1), likewise, interpreted this psalm as a praise of King David or his son Solomon, who reigned after him.

[45] The root *y-s-d* in Biblical and Rabbinic Hebrew normally means *to establish*. But in medieval Ashkenazic Hebrew it was used also to connote *writing, composing literature*. See Ben-Yehuda, *Dictionary*, s.v., יסד (both in the *qal* and *pi'el* forms); Viezel, "Examination of Rashi concerning Onkelos," 182 n. 3; Spiegel, *Jewish Book*, 452–454. (My thanks to Simcha Emanuel for the last reference.) From the spelling of this word with a double *yod* (ייסדו) in the Gruber edition and in *Miqra'ot Gedolot ha-Keter*, we may conclude that Rashi used this root here in the *pi'el* form, rather than *qal*, i.e., *yasad*. (In the Maarsen edition, *Parshandatha*, III:43, it appears with a single *yod*, which could be read either in *pi'el* or *qal*). Pseudo-Rashi on Ezra 3:10, s.v., ויסדו (*we-yissedu*), specifically notes the convention to write the *pi'el* form of this verb with double *yod* (even though it appears in that verse in the *pi'el* form with a single *yod* in the MT), the first serving as the imperfect tense prefix, the second being the first radical of the root *y-s-d*. Although Pseudo-Rashi on Ezra (i.e., the commentary attributed to Rashi in the *Miqra'ot Gedolot*) is not actually by Rashi, it does emanate from Rashi's northern French exegetical school. See Viezel, "Ezra–Nehemiah."

[46] Gruber ed., 826 (Heb.), 349 (Eng.).

By highlighting these perceived similarities, Rashi aims to argue that Torah scholars can be referred to metaphorically as "lilies." This typifies Rashi's endeavor to demonstrate that this psalm was composed as a praise of Torah scholars, rather than as praise of a king. Rashi goes on to explain the subject matter of the psalm in his commentary on verse 2:

> *My heart is astir* – Thus the poet (*ha-meshorer*) began his poem: "*My heart* motivated within me *gracious words* in praise of you, Torah scholar."
>
> *I say: "My works for the King"* – i.e., this poem that I composed (*yissadti*)[47] and "made," I address to one who is worthy to be king, as it says, "by virtue of me [i.e., Wisdom] kings shall reign (Prov 8:15)."[48]

Once again, Rashi's interpretation of the term "king" is part of his effort to demonstrate that the language of this psalm can legitimately be construed figuratively as praise of Torah scholars, rather than literally as praise of a king. Rashi applies this understanding to reinterpret praises of the king throughout the psalm, as we see in his commentary on verse 6:

> *Your arrows, sharpened, [pierce] the breast of the King's enemies* – We have found that students are called arrows, for it is stated, "like arrows in the hand of a warrior are sons born to a man in his youth" (Ps 127:4). Moreover, Torah scholars who argue with each other about halakhah are called "enemies" temporarily in accord with what is stated, "They shall not be put to shame when they contend with the enemy in the gate" (Ps 127:5).[49]

It is in line with this interpretation that we can appreciate Rashi's comment on verse 4: "'Gird your sword upon your thigh' – to wage the war of Torah (i.e., to argue points of the law). Now it is 'your splendor and glory'."[50] Rashi adopts the figurative midrashic interpretation of Ps 45:4 in b.*Shabbat* 63a, in which "sword" is interpreted to mean "words of Torah" without even mentioning "the *peshat* of the verse," even though the Talmud applied the principle to this very verse.

One other feature of Rashi's commentary on Psalm 45 is noteworthy for our purposes. The figurative interpretation that Rashi formulates for this entire psalm does not have any clear precedent in rabbinic sources.[51] While it is theoretically possible that Rashi was drawing upon midrashic sources no longer extant, it would seem that in this case he devised his own

[47] In the Gruber edition a double *yod* appears in this word (ייסדתי). This clearly indicates that the root *y-s-d* is in the *pi'el* form. (In *Miqra'ot Gedolot ha-Keter* and in the Maarsen edition, however, it appears with a single *yod*). See the discussion in note 45.

[48] Gruber ed., 826 (Heb.), 349 (Eng.).

[49] Gruber ed., 826–827 (Heb.), 350 (Eng.).

[50] Gruber ed., 826 (Heb.), 350 (Eng.).

[51] See Gruber, *Rashi on Psalms*, 352–353.

midrashic readings, inspired by the figurative interpretation of Ps 45:4 in b.*Shabbat* 63a. But whereas the Talmud interpreted just a single verse in isolation in this vein, Rashi finds it necessary to interpret the entire psalm consistently according to this approach. He does so by marshaling evidence from other biblical verses (and their midrashic interpretations) that every verse can be construed metaphorically to refer to Torah study and Torah scholars – as attested in his commentaries from that psalm cited above.

RASHI'S DUAL INTERPRETIVE GOAL

The question of how to reconcile Rashi's prevailingly midrashic exegetical practice with his stated *peshat* program is an old one. A venerable tradition of supercommentaries on Rashi's Pentateuch commentary diligently endeavored to show how each and every midrashic reading offered by the master of Troyes was motivated by compelling philological-literary considerations and is not simply a whimsical or gratuitous midrashic elaboration. Elijah Mizrahi, who penned the most celebrated of these works, commonly employs this strategy and remarks that Rashi's commentaries are therefore "close to the *peshat* of Scripture."[52] In the twentieth century, this approach was refined by Nehama Leibowitz, who drew upon modern literary analytic methods to show that Rashi engages in what is now called "close reading," which – in Leibowitz's view – can be classified as *peshat*.[53] Yet this approach works in only some cases, whereas in others Rashi seems to exceed the boundaries of "the *peshat* of Scripture" – as exemplified by the very interpretations that Rashi labels as such (as seen in Chapter 1), in which he offers historically sensitive, contextual-philological interpretations.

Benjamin Gelles dealt at length with this incongruity in his systematic study of Rashi's exegesis.[54] His starting point was a remark by Rashi in his commentary on Gen 3:8, which can be regarded as his most definitive programmatic statement:

> There are many midrashic *aggadot* (homilies; sing. *aggadah*) and our Rabbis have already arranged them in their appropriate place in *Genesis Rabbah*. But I relate

[52] Mizrahi's work is known simply as "the Mizrahi commentary." On that and other Rashi supercommentaries, as well as their methodology, see Leibowitz, "Rashi's Method." The expression "close to the *peshat* of Scripture" was already applied to Rashi's commentary by Rashbam. See his introduction to Leviticus, Rosin ed., 144–145 (a passage cited earlier in this chapter).

[53] See Cohen, "Reproduction." [54] Gelles, *Rashi*.

only the *peshat* of Scripture and the *aggadah* that "settles" the words of Scripture [and its sense (*u-shemu'o*)], "each word in its proper place (*'al ofnayw*)" (Prov 25:11).[55]

Gelles concluded that Rashi – throughout his writings (Bible and Talmud commentaries and his *responsa*) – employed both the term *peshuto shel miqra* and the language of "settling" the text (the Hebrew root *y-sh-b* in the *pi'el* form[56]), i.e., making it cohere naturally, interchangeably to connote historically sensitive, philological-contextual analysis. But since most of his interpretations are, in fact, midrashic, Gelles concluded that Rashi "had not yet reached the modern finality of evaluation which allocates to each sense a realm of its own."[57] In other words, "when Rashi composed his commentary on Scripture he had not yet come to a clear recognition of *peshat* and *derash* as belonging to two unconnected realms of interpretation."[58] It seems he basically accepted the assessment of Abraham Ibn Ezra that Rashi intended to compose a *peshat* commentary but naively employed midrashic interpretations believing (erroneously) that they fulfill the criteria of *peshat* interpretation.[59]

Sarah Kamin, however, reopened this question and arrived at a different conclusion, namely that Rashi indeed was capable of distinguishing between *peshat* and midrashic interpretation, but that his notion of "settling" the text is not identical to his conception of *peshat*.[60] When the great northern French exegete promised to limit himself to (a) *peshuto shel miqra* and (b) the sort of *aggadah* that "settles" (*meyashevet*; or: "is settled upon") the language of Scripture "each word in its place," he was actually speaking of two distinct interpretive categories, and two distinct goals. The latter category is not identical to "the *peshat* of Scripture," but rather represents a critical selection of midrashic interpretations, particularly those that "settle," i.e., conform to, the language of Scripture so that each word is accounted for sequentially within its context.[61] In other

[55] Rashi on Gen 3:8, Berliner ed., 8. On this and similar programmatic statements in Rashi's exegesis, see Kamin, *Categorization*, 57–110. The translation here follows the text in Berliner's edition. On the textual complexities of this passage, see Kamin, *Categorization*, 63n. As Kamin notes, the addition *u-shemu'o* ("and its [literal] sense") is found in some medieval manuscripts. It also appears in the Reggio di Calabria edition. See www.library.upenn.edu/exhibits/cajs/revealed/revealed-med-det13.html.

[56] Either with Scripture as the direct object ("to settle the verse") or indirect object prefaced by a preposition ("settled upon the verse," "settled after the verse").

[57] Gelles, *Rashi*, 33. [58] Gelles, *Rashi*, 42. [59] See the citation in the Introduction, p. 7.

[60] Kamin, *Categorization*, 57–157.

[61] Kamin, *Categorization*, 109–110. See also Kamin's review of Gelles' book in *Jews and Christians*, lxxviii–lxxx, and Japhet, *Collected Studies*, 26–27.

words, Rashi's criteria of conformity to ("settling") Scripture are looser than those of strict *peshat* exegesis, though they share some basic features. In Kamin's words:

> The root ["to settle"] in its exegetical use [by Rashi] expresses a conception of sequence, mutual correspondence among the components of the commentary, [and] organization of the details on "their place" within the complete context. Rashi's intention, expressed in [the term] "to settle" ... is the creation of a commentary that manifests internal unity and sequential coherence of its contents that corresponds to the language of Scripture as a syntactic and contextual unit.[62]

According to Kamin, Rashi distinguished between *peshat* and *derash*, but never intended to limit himself to the former exegetical category. His goals were: (1) to preserve the integrity of "the *peshat* of Scripture," and accordingly (2) to select midrashic interpretations that meet methodological criteria that are analogous – but not identical – to the criteria of *peshat* exegesis.

Kamin's theory that Rashi endeavored to compose a midrashic interpretation that "settles" the biblical text by accounting for each word within its sequence seems to be a particularly apt characterization of the examples cited earlier in this chapter. As we have seen, Rashi often reworks his midrashic sources in order to formulate this sort of continuous midrashic commentary. As Mizrahi (cited earlier in this chapter) noted regarding Rashi's commentary on Lev 21:4, his interpretation is neither "the *peshat* of Scripture" nor classical midrashic reading; it is "an adjustment of the midrash and its extension in accordance with the plain sense (*mashma'ut*) of the verse and its *peshat*."[63] Perhaps most strikingly, Rashi on Psalm 45 ignores the reading of verse 4 that the Talmud itself defined as "the *peshat*," and instead interprets it figuratively; but he does so within a comprehensive program of figurative interpretation that applies to that psalm as a whole. Whereas the figurative reading recorded in the Talmud relates to verse 4 in isolation (a phenomenon not uncharacteristic of midrash), Rashi's interpretation is continuous and systematic.[64] That is to say, it respects "the sequence of the verses" (*seder ha-miqra'ot*).

Of particular importance are the instances in which Rashi explicitly disqualifies midrashic interpretations because they do not meet his exegetical

[62] Kamin, *Categorization*, 109.

[63] Mizrahi on Rashi on Lev 21:4, Phillip ed., III:413–414.

[64] A similar observation can be made about Rashi's typological reading of Psalm 42 discussed earlier in this chapter.

criteria. In two such cases discussed in Chapter 1, his commentaries on Exod 6:2–9 and on Isa 26:11, he specifies that the well-known midrashic interpretations are not "settled" upon the language of the verses, i.e., they do not adhere to the rules of Biblical Hebrew, and do not respect the sequence of the biblical text. Rashi is willing to similarly disqualify halakhic midrashic interpretations found in the Talmud. For example, in his commentary on Exod 23:2, which serves as the basis for key judiciary laws in the Talmud, he remarks: "On this verse there are midrashic interpretations by the sages of Israel, but the language of the verse is not properly settled (*meyushav*), "[each word] in its place (*ofnayw*)" through them."[65] Rashi goes on to analyze in detail three separate talmudic halakhic readings of the three sentences that make up this verse. While he endeavors mightily to show how those readings can be extracted from the language of the verse, his presentation also demonstrates that they render the verse a discontinuous expression of three disparate laws of judicial procedure. He then concludes:

> But I say the following in order to "settle" [each word] in its place according to its *peshat* ...[66]

Rashi here brings us into the laboratory of his mind, revealing his typical interpretive process: he would first attempt to identify midrashic interpretations that can legitimately be related to the text and account for each of its words in sequence, and only if he is unable to so would he acknowledge that the *peshat* interpretation alone fulfills these exegetical criteria.[67]

Perhaps the most developed articulation of this endeavor of Rashi's is found in his programmatic introduction to the Song of Songs,[68] in which he carefully discusses the relationship between what he sees as the two layers of scriptural signification. He opens the introduction accordingly:

> *One thing God has spoken; two things have I heard* (Ps 62:12) – "One verse can have (lit., goes out to) a number of meanings" (b.*Sanhedrin* 34a), but in the end a biblical verse does not leave the realm of its plain sense (*mashma*ʿ).

[65] Rashi on Exod 23:2, Berliner ed., 162. [66] Rashi on Exod 23:2, Berliner ed., 162.

[67] See Kamin, *Categorization*, 60–61. Cf. Gelles, *Rashi*, 38–39. According to Gelles, this instance shows that Rashi's ideal of "settling" the text of Scripture is part and parcel of his *peshat* agenda.

[68] The text of the introduction that is cited and analyzed below is from Rashi's Song of Songs commentary, Kamin and Saltman ed., 81 (Hebrew section), which is based on NY JTSA MS Lutzki 778. For further discussion of this passage, including the textual variants, see Cohen, *Gates*, 205; Kamin, *Categorization*, 79–86, 123–124.

Rashi here makes an argument for the dual signification of Scripture – an argument that involves multiple steps. He begins with the verse in Psalms, which states that when "God has spoken" it is possible to hear "two things." Rashi appends to this the talmudic understanding of these words that "one verse can have a number of meanings." Rashi then brings greater specificity to the "two things" one "hears" from the word of God by invoking the talmudic *peshat* maxim in a slightly modified form: "a biblical verse does not leave the realm of its plain sense (*mashma*ʿ)," instead of the usual talmudic formulation "a biblical verse does not leave the realm of its *peshat*."[69] Indeed, it is not unusual in his Bible commentary, particularly on the Song of Songs, for Rashi to employ the terms *mashma*ʿ and *peshat* interchangeably.[70] The implication is that some non-literal sense is assumed, but that the text nonetheless retains its *mashma*ʿ/*peshat*.

The connection between the literal and non-literal senses of Scripture is emphasized by Rashi as he continues in his introduction:

> Although the prophets uttered their words in allegory (*dugma*),[71] one is required to fit (*leyashev*; lit., "settle") the allegorical meaning (*dugma*) on its basis and sequence (*seder*), just as the verses are arranged (*sedurim*) one after the other. Now I have seen many aggadic *midrashim* on this book ... that do not fit ("are not settled upon"; *mityashvim ʿal*) the language of Scripture (*leshon ha-miqra*) and the sequence of the verses (*seder ha-miqra'ot*). I therefore decided to grasp the plain sense (*mashma*ʿ) of the verses, in order to settle their interpretation according to their sequence (*seder*), and the rabbinic *midrashim* I shall set, one by one, each in its place.

By correlating the talmudic statement that "One verse can have a number of meanings" with the talmudic *peshat* maxim, Rashi devised a system in which Scripture conveys two layers of meaning for which he has special terminological labels: the "plain" or "literal" sense (*peshat*/*mashma*ʿ) and the allegorical sense (*dugma*).[72] Furthermore, he argues that the latter must "be settled upon" the former; i.e., the allegorical interpretation must correspond to the literal sense of the verses and their sequence.

[69] The edition of Rashi's commentary printed in the Rabbinic Bible actually reads " ... its *peshat*." But the text in MS Lutzki 778, from which we cite, reads " ... its *mashma*'," a reading found also in MS Leipzig 1.

[70] On Rashi's interchangeable use of the terms *mashma*ʿ and *peshat*, see Gelles, *Rashi*, 119–120; Viezel, "Onkelos in Rashi's Consciousness," 6–7.

[71] Although the term *dugma* appears in rabbinic literature, Rashi endows it with new meaning as a technical term that he uses as the term *exemplum* was used in Latin interpretation. See Kamin, *Jews and Christians*, 69–88.

[72] See Kamin, *Jews and Christians*, xxxii.

In accordance with his programmatic preface, Rashi introduces two major innovations in his commentary on the Song of Songs. (1) To begin with, he devises what in his milieu was a revolutionary contextual-philological analysis of the literal love tale depicted in the Song, which he labels "its *peshat*" (*peshuto*) and "its *mashma*'" (*mashma'o*).[73] (2) Rashi's second innovation relates to the midrashic level of his commentary. Having criticized the haphazard allegorical mode of interpretation of the Song of Songs dominant in his Ashkenazic milieu, Rashi strives to apply consistent criteria for selecting allegorical interpretations from midrashic sources and reworking them in order to formulate a commentary that conforms to ("is settled upon") "the language of Scripture (*leshon ha-miqra*) and the sequence of the verses (*seder ha-miqra'ot*)." Rashi's philological-contextual analysis of the Song of Songs to discern its *peshat/mashma'* is thus a necessary step for its proper allegorical interpretation. His interpretation of the book as a collection of love-songs serves as a baseline upon which he constructs his midrashic reading of the Song as a national allegory reflecting the relationship between God (the lover) and Israel (the beloved).[74]

Rashi's commentary on Song 2:10–13, a description by the beloved of an invitation extended by her lover, offers a fine illustration of this dual hermeneutic involving both *peshat* and critically selected midrash:

> My beloved spoke thus to me: Arise, my darling; My fair one, come away! For now the winter is past, The rains are over and gone. The blossoms have appeared in the land, The time of pruning has come; The song of the turtledove is heard in our land. The green figs form on the fig tree, The vines in blossom give off fragrance. Arise, my darling; My fair one, come away!

Rashi explains each element within this description of the change of seasons from winter to spring, and in conclusion he summarizes:

[73] See, e.g., his commentaries on Song 1:2, 1:4, 2:13 (cited further in this chapter), 5:10.

[74] Living in a very different intellectual climate – in the midst of the nineteenth-century Haskalah, in which *peshat* was certainly privileged – the nineteenth-century rabbinic interpreter Malbim argued that the allegorical reading is indeed the *peshat* of the Song of Songs, since it is the intention of King Solomon, the book's author. On Malbim's interpretation of the Song of Songs, see Alster, "Human Love," 19–20, 39–43. On Malbim as a Bible interpreter, see Cohen, "Malbim." Rashi, on the other hand, specifically classifies the allegorical reading as the midrashic sense of the Song of Songs, and not "its *peshat*." In Rashi's milieu, unlike Malbim's, *peshat* was not the most privileged sense of Scripture – and he therefore did not feel compelled to align it with the "true" sense of Scripture and the intention of King Solomon.

This entire matter, according to its *peshat*, is an expression of loving enticement that a young man uses to gain favor with his betrothed to accompany him.[75]

Rashi first reads this section continuously – on the *peshat* level – as part of the love story within the Song of Songs. After doing so, he returns to the very beginning of these four verses and interprets each one allegorically, as a reference to the exodus from Egypt, which took place in the springtime. As this example illustrates, Rashi's commentary on the Song of Songs comprises largely the "double-commentary" format cited above: a *peshat* interpretation which serves as the basis for the midrashic one.

Rashi's allegorical interpretation of Song 2:10–13 is taken from midrashic sources – as are almost all of his allegorical commentaries on that book.[76] However, in sharp contrast with the midrashic works known to him, Rashi compiled a coherent commentary by selecting among midrashic interpretations those that "fit" or "conform to" (lit., are "settled upon") the language and sequence of the verses in this biblical book, as he expounds them in his analysis of "its *peshat*." Rashi thus excluded from his commentary those "aggadic *midrashim* ... that do not fit ('are not settled upon') the language of Scripture and the sequence of the verses" – as he establishes in his introduction. Indeed, in his commentary on Song 2:7, Rashi makes the following closely related programmatic statement:

There are many midrashic *aggadot*, but they are not settled upon (*mityashevim 'al*) the sequence of the words (*seder ha-devarim*), for I maintain that Solomon prophesied and spoke about the exodus from Egypt, the giving of the Torah, the construction of the Tabernacle, entry into the Land, the Temple, the Babylonian exile, the Second Temple and its destruction.[77]

Here Rashi repeats the criterion of sequence mentioned in the introduction to the Song of Songs, as he maps out the chronology of the allegorical level of interpretation. And, indeed, in his commentary he adheres to this mapping in a sequential reading of the Song, selected from among midrashic sources.

The role of Solomon's prophetic presentation of Israel's history and its connection to the love story Rashi identifies on the *peshat* level becomes clearer in the continuation of his introduction to the Song of Songs:

Now I say that Solomon saw with the Holy Spirit that Israel will be exiled, exile after exile, destruction after destruction, and will mourn in this exile over their

[75] Rashi on the Song of Songs, Kamin and Saltman ed., 85 (Hebrew section).
[76] See Kamin, *Jews and Christians*, 24.
[77] Rashi on the Song of Songs, Kamin and Saltman ed., 85 (Hebrew section).

original glory, and will remember the first love [of God toward them], which made them His chosen among all nations ... and they will recall His kindness and their transgression, and the good things that He promised to bestow upon them at the end of days.

And he [Solomon] composed (*yissad*)[78] this book with the Holy Spirit in the language of a woman stuck in living widowhood, longing for her husband, pining over her lover, recalling to him the love of their youth, and admitting her sin. Likewise, her lover suffers over her pain, and recalls the goodness of her youth and her beauty, and the excellence of her deeds, through which he was tied to her in powerful love, to say to them that ... she is still his wife and he is her husband, who will ultimately return to her.[79]

Following the midrashic tradition, Rashi made this biblical text relevant to the people of Israel for eternity – even in "this exile," by which Rashi meant his own experience in Christian Europe.[80] In fact, Rashi read the Song of Songs as an affirmation that God has not abandoned Israel – as averred by his Christian neighbors. As Kamin argues, Rashi used this biblical text to engage in a polemic with the Christians and to rebut their argument that Israel's prolonged exile is evidence that she has been rejected by God.[81] Yet Rashi found it necessary to delineate the human love story that comprises the *peshat* of this text – an older woman and man recalling their youthful love relationship – which he establishes through contextual-philological analysis of the literary format he attributes to King Solomon, inspired by the Holy Spirit.[82]

Rashi's elaborate introduction to the Song of Songs would suggest that his programmatic statement at Gen 3:8 does not imply an intention to limit his commentary to *peshat*, but rather expresses his endeavor to engage in *peshat* analysis to serve as a baseline for a selective midrashic commentary that "settles" the words of Scripture. While Rashi's claim regarding Scripture's dual signification is attached to the Song of Songs, which he takes to be an allegorical text, and as such might arguably be a special case (since he does not assume the Pentateuch, for example, to be

78 On this distinctive medieval Ashkenazic usage of the root *y-s-d*, see note 45.

79 Rashi on the Song of Songs, Kamin and Saltman ed., 81. For analysis of this text, see Kamin, *Categorization*, 247–249.

80 Nicholas of Lyra would take Rashi's midrashic reading to be the literal sense of the Song of Songs, superseded by the Christological sense. See Dove, "Literal Senses"; Kamin, *Jews and Christians*, 58–68.

81 See Kamin, *Jews and Christians*, 22–57. We return to this matter in Chapter 6.

82 Rashi's investigation of the literary format of the Song independently of its midrashic sense inspired subsequent northern French *pashtanim* to ascribe that literary format entirely to Solomon's own creative spirit, as discussed in Chapter 9.

allegorical), comments of his elsewhere, as well as his "double commentary" style, indicate that he applied this dual signification to all of Scripture. Rashi evidently continued to regard midrash as a reflection of the essential meaning of the Bible, to be discovered beneath its surface;[83] his innovation was in establishing a place for plain sense exegesis – "the *peshat* of Scripture" – as a baseline interpretation of the surface layer of the text.

As presented here, based on Kamin's studies, the great innovation of the sage of Troyes was to create a new sort of midrashic commentary tethered to the *peshat* of Scripture by respecting "the plain sense" and the order of the verses.[84] This account of Rashi's interpretive agenda has been criticized by those who believe that arriving at "the *peshat* of Scripture" was, in fact, Rashi's primary and exclusive goal – even if he did not attain it.[85] Scholars adhering to the latter position forgive Rashi for his inability to devise a consistent *peshat* interpretation, but cannot countenance the possibility that Rashi would knowingly abdicate his *peshat* sensibilities to formulate what even he regarded as a midrashic interpretation. As Moshe Ahrend remarked, by Kamin's account, "Rashi ... resembles a craftsman who perfected a new and original technique, but set it aside to display to his audience a haphazard collection of works by his predecessors."[86] In order to answer this critique, it is necessary to explore the impetus for Rashi's innovative exegetical agenda. As mentioned in the Introduction, a number of theories have been advanced to explain what could have motivated Rashi's *peshat* revolution: (1) his engagement with talmudic interpretation, (2) his exposure to earlier exegetical trends in the Andalusian or Byzantine schools, or (3) his exposure to the increasing attention paid to the literal sense in Christian Bible exegesis. In the following chapter we shall develop a new version of the third theory based on affinities between Rashi's interpretive work and a trend in Latin learning in eleventh-century northern France exemplified by Bruno the Carthusian. In addition to considering the possibility that Rashi was

83 See, in this vein, Marcus, "Rashi's Choice."

84 On the question of how consistent Rashi was in actually adhering to these criteria of selective midrashic commentary is complex and has been discussed at length in recent scholarship, but is beyond the scope of this study. See, e.g., Grossman, "Literal Exegesis," 334–336.

85 See Ahrend, "Concept."

86 Ahrend, "Concept," 245–246. Following the approach of Nehama Leibowitz, Ahrend ("Concept," 248–259) argues that, on the contrary, Rashi reworked midrashic material and transformed it into genuine *peshat* interpretations.

influenced (consciously or unconsciously) by Bruno's distinctive exegetical methods, we shall show how the comparison between the two eleventh-century northern French exegetes can help to explain Rashi's motives for maintaining a dual hermeneutic that introduces *peshat* sensibilities but still privileges midrashic interpretation, on the condition that it is "settled upon" the "sense" and "sequence" of Scripture.

3

St. Bruno on Psalms: Precedent for Rashi?

The techniques of grammar and rhetoric – the language arts of classical learning – had long played an integral role in Christian Bible interpretation and were a central part of the curriculum of the cathedral schools. Grammar, the first of the liberal arts, encompassed a range of reading skills and prominently included *enarratio poetarum* (i.e., interpreting the poets).[1] As the important Carolingian theologian and Bible interpreter Rabanus Maurus (c. 780–856) remarked, "grammar (*grammatica*) is the science of interpreting the poets" and it is "the origin and foundation of the liberal arts."[2] This echoes Quintillian's characterization of the dual purpose of grammar: *recte loquendi scientia* (the science of speaking correctly) and *poetarum enarratio* (the art of interpreting poets), a dual characterization that would be repeated throughout the Middle Ages.[3] (In Hebrew and Arabic learning, by contrast, the discipline of grammar – termed *diqduq*/*dayyaqut* and *al-naḥw*, respectively – was more sharply circumscribed and focused on phonology, morphology, and syntax, all of which might be subsumed under *recte loquendi scientia*.[4]) The language arts of grammar and rhetoric flourished anew in the eleventh century in the cathedral schools of northern France, a wave of learning in which Bruno the Carthusian played a key role.[5]

[1] See Lausberg, *Literary Rhetoric*, 9–15; Murphy, *Rhetoric in the Middle Ages*, 24–29.
[2] *PL* 107:395. English trans. from Levy, "Bruno the Carthusian," 18–19.
[3] See Baswell, *Virgil in Medieval England*, 52–53; Graves, *Jerome's Hebrew Philology*, 74.
[4] See, e.g., Tene, "Hebrew Linguistic Tradition"; Owens, *Arabic Grammatical Theory*.
[5] See Gibson, "*Artes* in the Eleventh Century."

GRAMMATICAL INTERPRETIVE METHOD

Arriving at Rheims from his native Cologne in the 1040s, Bruno studied under Herimann (d. c. 1075), who was a distinguished teacher of grammar and rhetoric and seems to have brought renewed prominence to the Rheims cathedral school.[6] In Bruno's time, the scholarship of the late Carolingian master Remigius of Auxerre still exerted influence at Rheims, as is evident from the copies of his writings produced there, and citations by later authors in the city.[7] Remigius had developed a new "grammatical" analysis of the Psalms by drawing upon his expertise in the liberal arts. Adopting a strategy from commentary on classical poetry, Remigius would occasionally supply a more idiomatic order for the words of Scripture, as he does, for example, on Ps 17:42 (MT [=Masoretic Text] 18:42):

They cried, but there was no one to save them, to the Lord. The order of the words (*ordo verborum*) is: They cried to the Lord, but there was no one to save them.[8]

This was the sort of grammatical commentary commonly applied to Virgil's *Aeneid* by the early fifth-century grammarian Servius (whose commentary dominated medieval Virgil exegesis),[9] whereas earlier patristic Bible commentaries focused instead on the spiritual sense of the Psalms rather than their poetic form.[10] Being well versed in the commentary tradition on the classical poets, chief among which was Virgil as glossed by Servius, Remigius himself wrote commentaries on the grammatical works of Donatus and on Martianus Capella's *On the Marriage of Philology and Mercury*. Commentary on the classical poets entailed a study of the language divided into small units, with a focus on grammatical forms, syntax, literal vs. figurative language, historical and geographic references, all typically prefaced by a biographical study of the author, as well as a general exposition of his intention and the subject matter of his book.[11] Notwithstanding the disparity between the Bible – with its recondite

[6] See Williams, "Cathedral School," 663–666; Levy, "Bruno the Carthusian," 6–7.

[7] See Jeudy, "L'œuvre de Remi d'Auxerre"; Irvine, *Textual Culture*; Kraebel, "Poetry and Commentary."

[8] MS Rheims 132, f. 26rb: "*Clamauerunt, nec erat qui saluos faceret, ad Dominum.* Ordo uerborum est: Clamauerunt ad Dominum, nec erat qui faceret." Cited in Kraebel, "Poetry and Commentary," 232. Rashi on 2 Sam 22:42 (a virtually identical verse) makes a similar observation, invoking the rabbinic notion of *miqra mesoras*. See Chapter 1, note 90.

[9] See Kraebel, "Poetry and Commentary," 232; Baswell, *Virgil in Medieval England*, 49.

[10] Remigius' gloss on Ps 17:42 has no antecedent, e.g., in Cassiodorus's commentary. See Cassiodorus, *Expositio in Psalterium*, Walsh trans., I:165.

[11] See Copeland and Sluiter, *Medieval Grammar and Rhetoric*, 125–147.

spiritual senses – and secular poetry, Remigius employed some of the same grammatical techniques of analysis to the Psalms that he used in glossing the classical poets.[12] By contrast, the early Church Father Jerome, for example, aimed primarily "to make the old text speak authoritatively on matters of faith, to affirm right doctrine and condemn heresy, and to promote good morals and discourage bad,"[13] and this led him, generally speaking, to move away from the more technical, gloss-style of exegesis common among classical grammarians – who otherwise exerted substantial influence on this thought.[14]

Bruno developed Remigius' grammatical interpretive method further,[15] and, in turn, trained students who produced Bible commentaries that circulated in northern France in the last third of the eleventh century.[16] These interpreters analyzed the Psalms as poems, treating their author, David, as a prophetic poet. Considering the Psalms as poetry allowed them to bring the analytical techniques taught in the arts curriculum, especially *grammatica*, to bear on their understanding of the biblical text.[17] In parallel, Bruno's commentaries on the Pauline Epistles, like those of Lanfranc of Bec, utilize principles from the discipline of rhetoric, derived principally from the works of Cicero and the pseudo-Ciceronian work *Ad Herennium*.[18]

To be sure, the Psalms had long been classified as poetry in Christian tradition. Cassiodorus (c. 485–c. 585) and Bede (672/3–735) cited biblical examples in their Psalms commentaries to illustrate the figures and tropes (metaphor, synecdoche, hendiadys, prolepsis, etc.) employed in classical poetry.[19] Yet the Psalms were a source of Christian inspiration for a separate reason: their "mystical," "spiritual" sense was assumed to be about Christ – his passion, resurrection, divinity, etc. – and the Psalms' Christological content was therefore the focus of patristic interpretation.

[12] See Kraebel, "*Grammatica*," 75. [13] Graves, *Jerome's Hebrew Philology*, 74.

[14] Graves, *Jerome's Hebrew Philology*, 72.

[15] Bruno mentions Remigius by name in his commentary on Ps 47:8; but he borrowed from Remigius elsewhere without acknowledgment. See Kraebel, "*Grammatica*," 75–78; Mews, "Scholastic Culture," 72. See also Pradié, *Psaumes des montées*, 38–39.

[16] As discussed in the Introduction.

[17] Kraebel, "Prophecy and Poetry," 418–419; Mews, "Scholastic Culture," 71–76.

[18] See Levy, "Bruno the Carthusian," 19–26. As Levy notes, the application of the discipline of rhetoric to the analysis of the Pauline Epistles appears already in the Epistles commentaries of Lanfranc of Bec, believed to have been written c. 1055–1060, though they may have been written as early as 1042.

[19] See Copeland and Sluiter, *Medieval Grammar and Rhetoric*, 63–64; Kugel, *Idea*, 164–167.

In any case, these two perspectives – the grammatical and the mystical – initially remained largely separate, and authors like Cassiodorus and Bede simply cited examples of poetic techniques in the Psalms as an ancillary part of their commentaries. As Andrew Kraebel has shown, it was Bruno who applied grammatical analysis in a more essential way – to discover King David's Christological intentions in the Psalms.[20]

The *ordo*-style gloss found in Remigius was applied more regularly by Bruno. For example, on Ps 40:3 (MT 41:3), "May the Lord preserve him and give him life," Bruno remarks: "the order is backward" (*praeposterus ordo*), probably because he reasoned that one must first be alive before one's life can be "preserved."[21] Occasionally, Bruno's concern for the logical sequence of the biblical text prompts him to apply this strategy more dramatically. Hence, in his gloss on Ps 67:10 (MT 68:10), he effectively "rearranges" the five preceding verses:

> And all of this, beginning where it says *God in his holy place* (v. 6), is the same (*aequipollens est*) as if it were said in this order (*ordo*): Therefore the people *will be troubled* (v. 5), since *the heavens* (v. 9) will drop *rain* (v. 10), by which *the earth* (v. 9) will be moved, i.e., it will be troubled with a good disturbance, *when you will go forth in the face of your people* (v. 8) and *you will pass through into the desert* (v. 8). And then *you will lead out the bound* (v. 7) and *those who dwell in tombs* (v. 7), and thus *you will make them dwell in a house* (v. 7).[22]

Adopting a strategy typically used by Servius in commenting on Latin poetry, Bruno employs the technical phrase *aequipollens est* (is the same as) to argue that entire sentences of this psalm – composed in poetic form – are out of their more proper prosaic order.[23] While the parallels to Rashi will be discussed more systematically later in this chapter, it is already worth noting the similarity between Bruno's interest in the syntactic arrangement of Scripture as displayed in his *ordo* and *aequipollens* glosses and Rashi's interests when employing the notion of *miqra mesoras*.[24] This similarity, of course, is not distinctive enough by itself to make a case for any sort of influence; but it does indicate that the two eleventh-century northern French interpreters, one Christian, the other Jewish, shared

[20] See Kraebel, "*Grammatica*," 75; Kraebel, "Prophecy and Poetry," 453.

[21] *PL* 152:810A, Aniorté trans., 308. For similar examples, see *PL* 152:734D, 1196D, 1924C.

[22] *PL* 152, 954C–D, Aniorté trans., 507–508.

[23] See Kraebel, "Poetry and Commentary," 239. On the term *aequipollens* and its usage in late eleventh-century Bible commentary and in the liberal arts curriculum, see Gibson, "Lanfranc's Commentary," 104–105 and 105 n. 1.

[24] See note 8 in this chapter.

grammatical-style concerns and developed similar commentarial strategies to address them and arrive at a proper understanding of the logical sequence of the biblical text.

THE HISTORICAL/LITERAL SENSE

Bruno adhered to a traditional Christian distinction among three senses of Scripture – literal/historical, allegorical, and moral – as enumerated, for example, by Gregory the Great.[25] In his commentary on the eightfold alphabetic acrostic Psalm 118 (MT 119), Bruno associates the alphabet, being rudimentary for children's education, with the literal sense, which is a foundation for the moral instruction (*moralis instructio*) that leads to "blessedness" (*beatitudinem*), the topic of this psalm.[26] Bruno offers a conventional definition of allegory in his commentary on Gal 4:24: "some other understanding than what the literal sense here conveys" (*per allegoriam, id est per alium intellectum quam sit litteralis hic habendum*).[27]

Bruno highlights the distinction between the literal/historical and allegorical/mystical senses in his commentary on Psalm 77 (MT 78), which recounts the history of Israel, from the exodus from Egypt to the sojourn in the desert to the selection of Zion as God's holy place. Bruno begins his commentary by explaining the meaning of this psalm's title, "A Psalm of understanding for Asaph":

> *Of understanding* (*intellectus*) ... – in which a mystical understanding is contained ...
>
> *Asaph* – [a teaching] by the perfectly faithful Synagogue [i.e., the Church] to Asaph, [i.e.,] the [synagogue of the Jews, which is] less perfect in faith.[28]

[25] See *PL* 153:126C, 393Cc; Levy, "Bruno the Carthusian," 24. On Gregory's threefold scheme, see p. 15. The famous "four senses of Scripture" enumerated, e.g., by Aquinas, would only become commonplace in Christian learning in the twelfth and thirteenth centuries, as discussed in the Introduction.

[26] *PL* 152:1258B.

[27] *PL* 153:306D. Translation from Levy, "Bruno the Carthusian," 24.

[28] *PL* 152:1029D–1030A, Aniorté trans., 608. The interpretation of Asaph as "synagogue" was common in the patristic tradition upon which Bruno relied. Cassiodorus writes: "Asaph in Hebrew means 'synagogue,' or in Latin *collectio*, i.e., a gathering" (*Expositio in Psalterium*, 709, Walsh trans., II:250). Cassiodorus, in turn, probably relied on Jerome or Augustine. Jerome writes "Asaf – congregans" (*Liber interpretationis hebraicorum nominum*, 118). Cf. Augustine's similar remark in his commentary on Ps 72:1. Although Asaph is a proper name, the Hebrew root *'-s-f* (*asaf*) means "to gather" and can thus be construed as "synagogue" (i.e., a congregation, assembly, a "gathering" of people).

In other words, the heading *intellectus* points specifically to the fact that this psalm has a deeper, "spiritual" sense distinct from its surface meaning – a point already made by Jerome and Augustine, and reiterated by Remigius in their commentaries on this verse.[29] Elaborating on this thought by his two illustrious predecessors, Bruno places a great deal of emphasis on the next lines of this psalm:

Attend, O my people, to my law: incline your ears to the words of my mouth. I will open my mouth in parables: I will utter propositions from the beginning. (77:1–2 [MT 78:1–2])

On these lines, he remarks:

Narrating the former benefits God bestowed upon their fathers in ancient times, the beginning of this psalm adjur[es] the same less perfect Asaph that he attentively and diligently hear the things which are said to him in "parables" and "propositions," i.e., that he understand those benefits mystically, not so much according to the letter, as their incredulous fathers did, who neglected them and, understanding only the letter, perished. Therefore he narrates those benefits to teach them history, in so far as these things happened to an earlier people, and to teach them in figures, in so far as these things likewise come to pass in the Church.[30]

In other words, the opening lines of this psalm reveal how it is to be interpreted: spiritually, rather than purely literally. The distinction Bruno makes here between the mystical and literal ("according to the letter") understanding of the history of ancient Israel was, of course, standard in Christian interpretation.

CONTINUITY AND SEQUENCE

Bruno, however, goes on to make a telling remark about the precise relationship between the two ways of reading the psalm:

[29] Jerome comments on the similar heading of Psalm 73 (MT 74): "The title '*intellectus*' is designated beforehand, because a twofold captivity follows, i.e., literal (carnal) and spiritual" (*Ideo intellectus in titulo praenotatur, quia duplex captivitas sequitur, et carnalis videlicet et spiritalis*: *Commentarioli in Psalmos*, 217). Augustine remarks similarly on the heading of our psalm: "For it is not without reason inscribed, 'Understanding of Asaph': but it is perchance because these words require a reader who does perceive not the voice which the surface utters, but some inward sense" (comm. on Ps 77:1 [MT 78:1], Coxe trans., 730). Compare with the gloss of Remigius on this title: *Sane quod in titulo intellectus praemittitur, innuitur omnia quae iuxta historiam narrantur spiritualiter esse intellegenda* ("Indeed, that which is announced in the title '*intellectus*' indicates that everything that is narrated historically must be understood spiritually": MS Rheims 132, f. 127va, cited in Kraebel, "Place of Allegory," 211n.). Cassiodorus does not interpret the heading *intellectus* in this vein.

[30] *PL* 152:1030A, Aniorté trans., 608.

Although this psalm, which is to be read continuously for its history (*continuatim juxta historiam*), contains within it an allegory (*allegoriam*), it does not everywhere contain an allegory that can be read continuously (*juxta allegoriam continuatim*) ... This psalm, like the rest [of the Psalms], contains prophecy, although not when it is read historically (*ad historiam*).[31]

It is only on the literal level, according to Bruno, that the psalm offers a coherent, "continuous" narrative.[32] Implicitly, then, the allegorical reading is discontinuous. In other words, it can be read into the text of the psalm only sporadically. Tellingly, there is no precedent in Bruno's sources for this limitation that he places here on the allegorical sense.[33]

Indeed, Bruno follows through on this prefatory remark throughout his commentary on this psalm, in a way that departs from earlier Christian commentaries from which he drew, e.g., those of Augustine, Cassiodorus, and Remigius. This long psalm, comprising seventy-two verses, recounts much of the history of ancient Israel – beginning with the exodus from Egypt and the sojourn in the desert – the details of which were traditionally interpreted allegorically by Christian commentators. Bruno certainly highlights the allegorical interpretations of this psalm, but he shows greater respect than his predecessors did for the literal-historical sense. For example, the last phrase of verse 12, "Wonderful things did He do in the sight of their fathers, in the land of Egypt, in the field of Tanis" was interpreted thus by Cassiodorus (who adapted a similar comment by Augustine on this verse):

The expression, *in the field of Tanis*, is not idle, for Tanis means a humble instruction, which Christ when on earth is known to have taught when he said: *Learn of me, for I am meek and humble of heart, and your will find rest for your souls* (Matt 11:29).[34]

This interpretation is given by Bruno as well.[35] However, he first gives a full historical interpretation of this verse within the context of

[31] *PL* 152:1030A–B, Aniorté trans., 608. [32] Kraebel, "Place of Allegory," 212.

[33] Kraebel, "Place of Allegory," 211.

[34] Cassiodorus, *Expositio in Psalterium*, 713–714, Walsh trans., II:256. Augustine writes similarly: "'The plain of Thanis' is the smooth surface of lowly commandment. For lowly commandment is the interpretation of Thanis. In this world, therefore, let us receive the commandment of humility" (*Enarrationes*, 1078, Coxe trans., 739). This interpretation of Tanis seems to be taken from Jerome's *Liber interpretationis hebraicorum nominum* (*Book of the interpretation of Hebrew names*). See Cassiodorus, *Expositio in Psalterium*, Walsh trans., II:487, n. 35.

[35] *PL* 152:1035B, Aniorté trans., 614: "And '*In the field [of] Taneos*' ... i.e., in the plain of the humble precept/commandment ... Since a 'field' is a plain land. Properly, Taphnis means 'humble precept.'"

a contiguous literal reading of verses 9–13, which he takes to be a single literary unit. Only upon conclusion of that literal reading does Bruno turn to allegory, which he prefaces in the following way:

> Thus should all the rest of the benefits, all the way to the end of the psalm, be read according to the letter, and we will expound all of these things continuously (*continue*) according to the letter in their proper place. But since allegories appear to be contained in individual events, it seems best to expound the individual allegorical mysteries one at a time, either to avoid tedium, or because the allegory is difficult, or because it would be impossible to read the psalm continuously according to these allegories. And therefore we will now turn to the allegories contained in what we have just read according to the letter, beginning where it says, *The sons of Ephraim* (v.9) and thus we will continue to expound verses in turn historically and then allegorically.[36]

In accordance with this programmatic statement, Bruno interprets – and marks off as independent literary units – large sections of this psalm historically before turning, after each section, to the allegorical meanings.[37] The notion of dividing this psalm into sections is hardly Bruno's innovation, as it was done by Cassiodorus before him.[38] But it is only Bruno who makes the point that the literary division of the psalm and its sequential reading are features of the literal-historical sense alone.

We will speak at greater length later in this chapter about the parallels between Bruno and Rashi and their significance; but already at this point we should note two important ways in which these eleventh-century northern French exegetes relate similarly to the biblical text, as well as to the commentary traditions they inherited. Rashi, as we have seen in earlier chapters, placed emphasis on the adhering to the "sequence of the words/verses" (*seder ha-devarim/miqra'ot*) and sought to explain their logical arrangement (at times employing the term *miqra mesoras*). Bruno, likewise, manifests a strong concern for the sequence and literary ordering (*ordo*) of the biblical text. As Bruno notes in his commentary on Psalm 77 (MT 78), it is only on the literal level that this biblical text can be read in a sequential way, which he evidently regarded as a literary value. Additionally, just as Rashi on the Song of Songs aims to preserve the

[36] *PL* 152:1034AB, Aniorté trans., 613.

[37] Consider the following comments by Bruno throughout this psalm: "The allegory should be related to that which the letter of these twelve verses investigates … Once the succession of these seventeen verses has been explained on a literal level, the allegorical sense must be rendered … Therefore, once the letter of these fourteen verses has been explained, let us occupy ourselves with the allegory" (*PL* 152:1043B, 1047C, 1054C, Aniorté trans., 623, 629, 637).

[38] See Cassiodorus, *Expositio in Psalterium*, 709, Walsh trans., II:250–251.

literary coherence of the *peshat* reading before moving on to the midrash, Bruno on Psalm 77 systematically expounds the historical sense before moving on to the allegory.

AUTHORIAL INTENTION

Although Bruno's methodological preface and commentary on Psalm 77 demonstrate his ability to read a psalm in its literal-historical sense as distinct from its mystical-Christological one, that demarcation is actually atypical, as Bruno usually offers Christological readings alone. Yet, as Bruno emphasizes, the Christological reading reflects the intentions of King David himself as the author of the Psalms. Since David was a prophetic writer, Bruno's reasoning goes, he was able to incorporate his foreknowledge of the life of Christ into his poetry – and this, then, is his proper intention.[39] However, that intention had to be discovered though grammatical analysis, and Bruno – along with other interpreters emanating from the school of Rheims – therefore interpreted the Psalms using the analytic techniques developed by the well-known commentators on classical works, which were naturally interpreted only "according to the letter." Hence, the grammatical methods that Servius had used to uncover meaning in the works of Virgil were applied by the Remois Psalms exegetes to discover the intentions of David as an author.[40]

This application of grammatical rigor led Bruno to be more selective than his predecessors in adopting the Christological interpretations of the Church Fathers. Bruno pointed out that some allegorical interpretations are not consistent with David's intention as expressed in the language of the Psalms. For example, the superscription of Psalm 50 (MT 51), "A Psalm of David, when Nathan the prophet came unto him, after he had gone in to Bathsheba," was interpreted typologically by Cassiodorus, on the authority of Jerome and Augustine, making David a "type" (i.e., typological symbol) of Christ, and Bathsheba a type of the Church:

> Blessed Jerome among others points out that Bathsheba manifested a type of the church or of human flesh, and says that David bore the mark of Christ; this is

[39] As Kraebel notes, Bruno and his followers in the school of Rheims "include what might otherwise be seen as pertaining to the realm of the spiritual senses within their literal interpretation": see Kraebel, "Prophecy and Poetry," 419, 446. It is important to note, however, that Bruno does not actually regard the Christological sense as part of the literal sense – a move that would be made in the late medieval Latin interpretive tradition. See Whitman, "Redefinition."

[40] Kraebel, "Poetry and Commentary," 229, 246–247.

> clearly apt at many points. Just as Bathsheba when washing herself unclothed in the brook of Cedron delighted David and deserved to attain the Royal embraces, and her husband was slain at the prince's command, so too the church, the assembly of the faithful, once she has cleansed herself of the foulness of sins by the bath of sacred baptism, is known to be joined to Christ the Lord . . . Augustine, in the books which he wrote against the Manichee Faustus, discussed this typology of David and Bathsheba amongst other subjects most carefully.[41]

Remigius added further details to this reading, interpreting Uriah (whose death David had arranged, as described in 2 Samuel 11), as a type of the devil – and he was therefore justly put to death.[42] This patristic reading was too influential to be ignored by exegetes in the eleventh and twelfth centuries.[43] Yet its treatment by Bruno is revealing. He opens his interpretation of the psalm's superscription with a discussion of the historical circumstances to which it refers: Nathan's rebuke of David for his adultery with Bathsheba. Bruno cites the account in 2 Samuel 11, which records how David coveted Bathsheba after watching her bathe from his roof. Upon concluding that discussion, he remarks: "In this history a figure is involved (*continetur*), which, even though it does not appear to pertain to the intention of this psalm, still has something useful to offer to the audience."[44] Although he proceeds to record Remigius' reading in all of its detail, this preface reveals Bruno's reservations about it. Whereas in other psalms Bruno was prepared to accept the traditional typological Christological interpretation, in this case he resists doing so because it is so far from the language of the psalm that it cannot reasonably be construed as David's intention, even though he acknowledges its "usefulness" (Christian inspirational value, presumably) for the audience. This can be compared with Rashi's observation that the traditional midrashic reading of Exod 6:2–9 does not adhere to the language or sequence of Scripture, though he allows for its legitimacy qua midrash.[45]

Bruno's treatment of the heading of Psalm 141 (MT 142), "Of understanding (Hebrew *maskil*; Latin *intellectus*) for David, A prayer when he was in the cave," manifests a similar critical attitude toward earlier Christological interpretation. Cassiodorus writes the following regarding this heading:

[41] Cassiodorus, *Expositio in Psalterium*, 452–453, Walsh trans., I:493.

[42] See Kraebel, "Prophecy and Poetry," 444. [43] See Minnis, *Authorship*, 105.

[44] *PL* 152:860C: *In hac historia figura continetur, quae, tametsi ad huius intentionem psalmi non videtur attinere, non tamen dicenda est audientium utilitate carere*, Aniorté trans., 379. See Kraebel, "Place of Allegory," 210.

[45] This example was discussed in Chapter 1.

The theme of the Psalm is contained in this heading, but an apposite indication of a spiritual meaning is revealed to us through physical parallels. David, the son of Jesse, fled from the Prince Saul, and when he lay hidden in a cave he uttered a prayer which he revealed that the Lord Christ would make in the flesh before his passion. When *understanding* (*intellectus*) prefaces this prayer, the comparison is shown to refer to him (i.e., Jesus Christ) who avoided his persecutors as he prayed and hid himself by moving to various places. This was so that the son of God could fulfill the promise which he had made about himself through the prophets, and revealed the truth of the incarnation which he had assumed; for this psalm includes the words of the Lord Savior when he sought to avoid the most wicked madness of the Jews. So the flight of David was rightly placed in the heading to point to the persecution by the Jews, for David, as we have often said, denotes both that earthly king and the kingdom of heaven.[46]

For Cassiodorus, the historical background of David's flight from Saul is merely a "pointer" indicating the true reference of this heading to the prayer of "the Lord Savior" for God's protection from the persecution of the Jews. Bruno, on the other hand, interprets the heading of this psalm historically (*juxta historiam*), describing the circumstances in which it was uttered: when David was hiding in a cave, which Saul entered but did not see him, as described in 1 Samuel 24.[47] Following this, Bruno does cite an allegorical reading in the spirit of the one preferred by Cassiodorus, but with the following proviso: "The allegory of this history, not altogether worth pursuing, is as follows."[48] Although he dutifully elaborates on the allegorical potential of this psalm to indicate the Passion of Christ and his prayer to God, Bruno clearly has reservations about this reading, evidently because it is not borne out by the language of the psalm, unlike the historical reading, which is well supported by the biblical evidence.

By contrast with earlier patristic commentators, such as Augustine and Cassiodorus, who typically interpreted individual verses of the Psalms separately and atomistically (resembling the midrashic mode of interpretation), Bruno and other Remois commentators following his lead regularly sought to explain how consecutive verses within each psalm fit together, adopting what Kraebel has termed a "coherent, poetic hermeneutic."[49] This interpretive concern, which follows the model of how the grammarians interpreted secular poetry, is attested, for example,

[46] Cassiodorus, *Expositio in Psalterium*, 1268, Walsh trans., III:399–400. On this reading of the term *intellectus* in the patristic tradition, see note 29.

[47] *PL* 152:1380B.

[48] *PL* 152:1380B–C: *Allegoria autem hujus historiae, non usquequaque persequenda, talis est*, Aniorté trans., 1088.

[49] Kraebel, "Prophecy and Poetry," 450.

in Bruno's *ordo*-gloss on Ps 68:5–10 and his concern for the "continuous" reading of Psalm 78, both discussed earlier in this chapter. The value that Bruno placed on literary coherence also motivated him to evaluate allegorical readings critically, as evident in his treatment of Ps 97:3 [MT 98:3]. In Bruno's view, this psalm relates how David prophetically foretells that "all the faithful who will live in the time of God's fullness will sing a new song to God the Father." He goes on to say that the psalm's second and third verses, "He has revealed in the sight of the peoples" (*revelavit in conspectu gentium*) and "all the ends of the earth have seen" (*viderunt omnes termini terrae*) speak of the fulfilled faith of the gentiles, as opposed to the Jews' imperfect faith. But then he cites what he characterizes as an "allegorical" alternative reading: "Or this can be read allegorically [*allegorice legi*]: . . . *the ends of the earth*, that is, all those who restrain their earthly qualities."[50] The characterization of this interpretation as allegorical is probably based on the fact that the Latin term *termini* ("ends") is taken figuratively rather than literally. Bruno, however, remarks that he prefers the first reading: "Yet, according to the letter (*ad litteram*), what follows (*sequentia*) seems to accord better with the earlier meaning (*priori sententiae*)."[51] In other words, the literal reading of verse 3 is to be preferred over the allegorical reading, because it best accords with the "sequence," i.e., the verse that follows. Admittedly, this case is somewhat exceptional, as Bruno does not regularly differentiate between the literal and spiritual senses (a trend more pronounced in the school of St. Victor). Yet he manifests new and consistent interest in the literary construction of the Psalms and their analysis according to the discipline of *grammatica* in order to select the mystical/allegorical readings that best reflect King David's intentions.[52]

BRUNO AND RASHI: ASSESSING PARALLELS AND POSSIBLE INFLUENCE

Based on the parallels between Rashi and Bruno we have noted, it is worth considering (1) whether Rashi could have had access to Bruno's interpretation of the Bible and (2) if that exposure might have had an

[50] *PL* 152:1153C: *Vel potest hoc allegorice legi* ... omnes termini terrae, *id est omnes terminantes in se terrenitate*, Aniorté trans., 776. This allegorical interpretation is cited neither by Augustine nor by Cassiodorus in their Psalms commentaries on this verse.

[51] *PL* 152:1153D: *Caeterum priori sententiae ad litteram melius videntur sequentia concordare*, Aniorté trans., 776. See Kraebel, "Place of Allegory," 215–216.

[52] See Kraebel, "Prophecy and Poetry," 456–459.

impact on his exegetical program. Given the tensions of medieval Jewish–Christian relations, it is problematic to speak of Bruno "influencing" Rashi in the way, for example, that the Andalusian linguist Menahem ben Saruq undeniably did. Though part of a different stream of Jewish learning, Menahem was a coreligionist whom Rashi could comfortably regard as a legitimate exegetical resource. Bruno represented a competing Christian conception of Hebrew Scripture that Rashi rejected; and so, it is difficult to imagine that the sage of Troyes would have respected the Rheims master as an authority on the Bible. However, awareness of Bruno's exegetical method – which seems to have been part of a wave of grammatical Latin Bible interpretation in the eleventh century in northern France – could have stimulated Rashi's exegetical thought in other ways, perhaps unconsciously. Given Rashi's tendency to respond to Christian doctrines and claims about the Bible, it is conceivable that he would have appreciated the importance of learning about Bruno's interpretive program and accordingly felt the need to devise an opposing Jewish one.

The methodological parallels between Bruno and Rashi, each exegete in his own tradition, are striking. Bruno's consistent distinction in Psalm 77 (MT 78) between the literal and mystical senses is comparable to Rashi's distinction between *peshat* and *derash* in his "double commentaries," perhaps most notably his consistent differentiation between the love story (*peshat*) and historical allegory (*midrash, dugma*) in the Song of Songs. But the distinction fades into the background in most cases, where both Rashi and Bruno primarily expound the deeper sense of Scripture (midrashic, mystical/allegorical) within the new theoretical frameworks they constructed. Both Rashi and Bruno inherited traditions of interpretation that they incorporated into their commentaries selectively: Rashi the midrashic readings of the Rabbis, Bruno the allegorical and mystical readings of the earlier Church Fathers. And both Rashi and Bruno challenge the cogency of earlier readings that do not meet their exegetical criteria, namely, adherence to the language and its order, sequence, or "continuity" (Hebrew *seder, semikhah/semikhut*; Latin *ordo, sequentia, continuitas*).

Bruno's exegetical criteria, as we have seen, stemmed from his classical Latin grammatical training, which he applied critically in his Psalms commentary – following a tradition already attested in Remigius. What could have prompted Rashi to engage in a similarly critical selection of midrashic interpretations? Although Rashi did not have exposure to the liberal arts and the Latin grammatical tradition, he developed a literary sense that led him to select only those midrashic interpretations that conform to ("are settled upon") the text of Scripture, "each word in its proper place" (as he remarked in his commentary on Gen 3:8), by which he meant that each midrashic interpretation he incorporated into his commentary is "settled" (1) "on its basis," which, as Kamin demonstrates, refers to a linguistic correspondence, and (2) accords with "the . . . sequence of the verses." Now it is true that Rashi's chief source for the study of Hebrew grammar was Menahem's *Maḥberet* and the critical notes of Dunash ben Labrat. But the question remains: What could have prompted Rashi to turn to those Andalusian works to acquire tools for interpreting the Bible in a manner unprecedented in Ashkenazic learning? It is reasonable to presume that Rashi developed his own grammatical-literary sensibilities through his extensive work in the detailed sort of line-by-line Talmud exegesis that had emerged earlier in the eleventh century as a distinct and rigorous discipline in the Rhineland academies, in which Rashi's intellectual persona was shaped by the disciples of Rabbenu Gershom.[53]

In a recent study, Haym Soloveitchik emphasizes just how innovative this discipline devised by Rabbenu Gershom and his students was:

> They introduced line-by-line exegesis . . . No summary but a phrase-by-phrase explication of all the winding . . . [discussions] of the Talmud with almost no expression left unexplained.
>
> They equally did not distinguish in their exegetical enterprise between halakhah [=law] and aggadah [=lore, tales]. Every line of aggadah had to be explicated in as precise a fashion as the halakhic passages . . . [We must] not blunt our sensitivity to [the] radical originality [of this move] . . . The halakhic portions of the Talmud are strongly formulaic . . . If one knows some thirty or forty idiomatic phrases in Jewish Babylonian Aramaic, most halakhic passages will pose few linguistic problems. (Understanding their legal content is a different matter.) However, the aggadic narratives entail a wide-ranging and detailed knowledge of the Aramaic language – all the terms of different household utensils, farm equipment, agricultural practices, domestic animals, flora and fauna, to mention just a few areas of life that are reflected in the [talmudic] narratives . . . We are talking about a vocabulary of some 10,000 to 12,000 words if not more.[54]

The linguistic prowess of Rabbenu Gershom's school is reflected by the fact that Rashi's Italian contemporary Rabbi Nathan ben Jehiel of Rome (c. 1035–1106) drew heavily upon the "the sages of Magentsa (=Mainz)" in his talmudic lexicon, *Sefer ha-'Arukh*. Haym Soloveitchik notes how remarkable this is, given the fact that Rabbi Nathan had access to the

[53] See Chapter 1. [54] Soloveitchik, *Collected Essays II*, 159.

teachings of Rav Hayya (Hai) Gaon (c. 939–1038), who inherited the living talmudic traditions of Babylonia: "Why this fuss of the interpretations of Magentsa? What tradition could anyone from Mainz possess that would explain gnomic terms and obscure references in the Talmud? How could R. Natan possibly view them as a source of talmudic lexicography on a par with Rav Hai Gaon?"[55] In answering these questions, Soloveitchik advances the bold theory that the forerunners of the Mainz academy were tenth-century immigrants to the Rhineland from Babylonia, where they had participated in the very process of the formulation of the Talmud in an academy other than the two well-known ones of Sura and Pumbedita.[56] In addition to being native Aramaic speakers, these transplanted scholars could thus transmit living interpretive traditions of the Talmud to Rabbenu Gershom's teacher, a certain Rabbi Leontin (about whom precious little is known).[57]

David Berger considers this to be an intriguing but highly speculative suggestion and argues that the phenomena to which Soloveitchik points could be accounted for in other ways. For example, a thorough command of the Aramaic Targums on the twenty-four books of the Hebrew Bible could have enabled the scholars in Rabbenu Gershom's circle to determine the meaning of very many difficult words in the Talmud.[58] This philological analytic approach to the Talmud could have been augmented by an interpretive tradition that did not depend on the survival of Aramaic as a spoken language.[59]

In any case, both Berger and Soloveitchik agree that the sages of the Mainz school displayed a remarkable ambition to engage in a comprehensive philological analysis of the talmudic text, and that they displayed extraordinary linguistic facility in Aramaic in fulfilling that ambition. Unlike the Bible, perceived as an esoteric divine text possessing a hidden "deeper" meaning expounded through ancient midrashic traditions, the Talmud had no "midrashic" commentary tradition. Its interpretation had to be entirely philological and contextual, based exclusively on what is evident from the text itself, just as pagan poetry was glossed by the classical grammarians. This Rhineland tradition of *enarratio talmudae* – analogous to *enarratio*

[55] Soloveitchik, *Collected Essays II*, 161. [56] Soloveitchik, *Collected Essays II*, 157–194.

[57] On Rabbi Leontin, see Grossman, *Ashkenaz*, 80–86.

[58] Soloveitchik, *Collected Essays II*, 207–213.

[59] I am grateful to David Berger for clarifying this point – and his approach to this matter in general – in an email communication. Apart from the summary by Soloveitchik (see the previous note), Berger's response to Soloveitchik's theory is unavailable in published form.

poetarum in the classical discipline of *grammatica* – was the foundation of Rashi's education.

Rashi's innovation, then, was to apply these very same philological skills to the Bible.[60] Indeed, Benjamin Gelles has observed a terminological link between the two projects: in his Talmud commentary Rashi also uses the term "to settle" the text in describing his exegetical goal, i.e., to interpret the language of the Talmud contextually and philologically.[61] As Rashi remarks, for example, regarding a difficult passage of the Talmud: "I have labored since my youth [to understand it], taking into consideration all aspects of the manner (*shiṭṭah*) of the Talmud, to 'settle' it properly in accordance with [my teachers'] words."[62] Rashi endeavored "to settle" the text by adducing evidence from "the manner of the Talmud," i.e., its normally attested linguistic usage and stylistic conventions – what might be termed "grammatical" analysis by the Latin tradition Bruno represents.[63] Rashi, in his Bible commentary, likewise sought to "settle the text" according to "the manner of Scripture,"[64] which naturally led to his focus on *peshat* and his critical assessment of midrashic readings that do not meet these criteria.

The theory that Rashi's *peshat* project grew out of his Talmud commentary was already raised in the 1940s; but it was challenged by Avraham Grossman, who reasoned that if a *peshat* approach to Scripture were a natural result of intensive talmudic exegesis, then it should have already emerged in the Rhineland academies before Rashi's time.[65] Here is where consideration of the Latin intellectual milieu in general, and the proximate school of Rheims in particular, is instructive. As mentioned above, in the twelfth and thirteenth centuries the emerging interest in the literal sense went hand in hand with an increasing focus on the common features of Scripture and human literary works – which had to contend with the traditional uneasiness about equating the Bible, understood to be God's word, and human literary compositions. Bruno

[60] See Gelles, *Rashi*, 136–138. [61] See Gelles, *Rashi*, 17–19.

[62] Rashi on b.*Sukkah* 40a.

[63] Rashi regularly uses the term *shiṭṭah* in this sense in his Talmud commentary. He does not use the term *peshat* in his talmudic exegesis, undoubtedly because there is no counterpart "midrashic" interpretation of the Talmud.

[64] See his commentaries on Ps 16:1 ("the manner [*shiṭṭah*] of Scripture does not accord with this midrash"); Lam 3:20 ("this is its *peshat* according to the sense and manner [*shiṭṭah*] of Scripture"); Qoh 8:14 ("our Rabbis interpreted it midrashically in another way ... and it is not settled for me according to the manner [*shiṭṭah*] of the language"). See also Prebor, "Use of Midrash," 213–221.

[65] See Grossman, *France*, 459.

provides an important precedent for this development in the eleventh century. While there were examples of grammatical commentary on Scripture from much earlier, Bruno represents the blossoming of this trend as a widespread teaching regime across the cathedral schools of northern France. As part of this outlook, Bruno boldly used his grammatical and poetic training to critically evaluate the inherited allegorical interpretations of the Church Fathers.

This phenomenon in Christian learning can help us appreciate Rashi's hermeneutical innovation. The transfer of exegetical tools of analysis from Talmud commentary to Bible commentary would not have been a natural one in Rashi's Ashkenazic milieu. The Talmud, a human literary composition, is not comparable to the Bible, which is divinely authored and therefore subject to a quite different interpretive mode, as embodied in the authoritative tradition of midrashic interpretation, which, as Rashbam attests, was the sole focus of Bible interpretation in the Ashkenazic realm prior to the advent of Rashi's commentary.[66] Rashi's innovative move – analogous to what Bruno does within the Christian interpretive tradition – was to transfer the tools of Talmud commentary to Bible commentary.[67] Mirroring the trend of Christian learning exemplified by Bruno, Rashi used the analytic "grammatical" skills he had perfected for interpreting a human literary composition – the Talmud (as Bruno did with classical literature) – to develop criteria for selecting among the traditional interpretations of the Rabbis (analogous to patristic interpretation), which do not adhere to these same analytic norms. Neither Bruno nor Rashi aimed to supplant the non-literal interpretations of their predecessors. Instead, they sought to select among them those that could reasonably be construed as reflecting the intent of the biblical authors based on some "correspondence" to the language and sequence of the text.

66 As Rashbam remarks: "the early generations, because of their piety, tended to delve into the *derashot*, since they are essential (*'iqqar*), and therefore were not accustomed to the deep *peshat* of Scripture." See the Introduction, p. 9; see also Kamin, *Categorization*, 272–273.

67 The chronology of Rashi's works is not known with certainty. Yet it is reasonable to assume that Talmud commentary was the fruit of his studies in the Rhineland (subject to continuous revision and even rewriting), with the Bible commentaries coming later. See Gelles, *Rashi*, 136–143; Soloveitchik, *Collected Essays I*, 4, 186–189. In other words, Talmud commentary in the mode perfected in the Rhineland academies was part and parcel of Rashi's earliest studies, inherited from his teachers, whereas Bible commentary, in the distinctive mode he would go on to develop independently, represents a subsequent phase in his scholarly career.

Given the striking methodological parallels between Rashi and Bruno, we must consider whether the great Bible exegete-talmudist of Troyes could have actually known about the Bible interpretation of the older cathedral master of Rheims, around 66 miles away. As mentioned in the Introduction, Bruno was an influential teacher of the Bible and the liberal arts at Rheims during Rashi's formative years. Furthermore, Rheims was an important intellectual, cultural center of the Champagne region of France, in which Troyes was a vibrant commercial hub that hosted markets, and perhaps even large fairs, that drew merchants and other travelers from far and wide.[68] Troyes itself had a large Christian clerical population, with the Abbey of Saint-Loup, the Cathedral of Saint-Pierre (where Peter Comestor would serve as dean from 1147 to 1164), and the collegiate Church of Saint-Etienne all in close proximity to one another – and to the Jewish section of the city which housed the synagogue, and presumably Rashi's school.[69] An entry in Bruno's mortuary roll from the Troyes Cathedral of Saint-Pierre suggests that he was known in the city,[70] and it is therefore conceivable that his teachings circulated there as well, especially given the frequency of travel between the two Champenois centers.

The further question we must consider is whether Rashi could or would have availed himself of Bruno's scholarship, even if it circulated among his Christian neighbors.[71] Here we encounter the thorny social-historical problem of Jewish–Christian relations in medieval France, where Jews and Christians, as elsewhere in Europe, regarded one another as religious adversaries. Rashi termed Christians *minim* (sing. *min*: lit. "sectarian," "heretic") and, throughout his writings, emphasized their wickedness and even the danger of conversing with them.[72] Christians, likewise, regarded the Jews as enemies of God, blind to His truth, and guilty for the murder of Christ.[73] In addition, a language barrier divided Jewish and Christian scholars, since the former wrote in Hebrew, the latter in Latin – making

[68] See Holmes and Klenke, *Chrétien*, 9. On the scope of the Troyes fairs in Rashi's time, debated by some scholars, see Taitz, *Medieval France*, 96, 246 n. 82.

[69] See Holmes and Klenke, *Chrétien*, 12–17.

[70] See the Introduction, note 103.

[71] Indeed, the extent of Rashi's knowledge of Christian Bible commentary is debated among modern scholars. See Chapter 1, note 74.

[72] Rosenthal, "Polemic," 105–106; Cohen, "Comparison," 450–461. On b.*Rosh ha-Shanah* 17a Rashi glosses the talmudic term *minim* with the following remark: "*minim* are the students of Jesus the Nazarene, who violated the words of the living God for evil."

[73] The literature on this subject is vast. See, e.g., Dahan, *Les Intellectuels chrétiens*. For a broad review of approaches to medieval Christian anti-Semitic attitudes, see Berger, "Crusades to Blood Libels." On the negative attitudes of Christians toward Jews in and around medieval Troyes, see Holmes and Klenke, *Chrétien*, 71, 120–122.

the works of one religious community effectively inaccessible to the other. Although Rashbam seems to have known some Latin, there is no indication that Rashi did.[74]

On the other hand, Rashi could have learned about Christian Bible interpretation by conversing with Christian scholars in Old French, a language he used extensively in his writings. Evidence for precisely such an intellectual exchange is provided in a remarkable account of collaborative work initiated by Stephen Harding, among the founders of Cîteaux Abbey (just over 100 miles from Troyes) in Burgundy in 1098, and who became Abbot in 1109.[75] That year saw the completion of Stephen's Cîteaux Bible, based on the Vulgate – with corrections in accordance with the original Hebrew and Aramaic.[76] In his introduction to the work, Stephen describes how, in order to access those ancient texts, he "resorted to certain Jews expert in their Scripture, and ... interrogated them most diligently in romance speech (i.e., Old French)." As he recounts, "opening many of their books before us, they explained the Hebrew or Chaldean Scripture to us in romance speech."[77] It is not unlikely that the Jewish Bible experts Stephen consulted were from Rashi's school – and it is conceivable that Stephen had forged a connection a few years earlier with the master himself. The trouble, of course, is that we lack written records of the many other oral exchanges that must have taken place between Jews and Christians in the eleventh and twelfth centuries.

Yet occasionally we can get glimpses of such exchanges from the writings of Rashi and his circle. Rashbam, for example, records debates of his with Christians in his commentaries on Exod 20:13 (where he also notes an error in the Vulgate translation of a biblical term) and Lev 19:19.[78] And a series of three queries about the Bible by "the authorities in Champagne" was answered in detail by Rabbenu Tam: one about Enoch's departure (being "taken" by God) from this world (Gen 5:24), another about the announcement that there will be "leprous plague" in the walls of the houses the Israelites will conquer in the land of Canaan (Lev 14:34), and another about the seemingly unfair divine rejection of King Saul for his relatively minor sins by comparison with King David's much more grievous sins – causing the death of Uriah and taking his wife

[74] See Japhet, "Did Rashbam Know the Vulgate?" [75] Stercal, *Harding*, 1–3, 18–20.
[76] Stercal, *Harding*, 37–50.
[77] Stercal, *Harding*, 54–55. See also Grabois, "*Hebraica Veritas*," 617–618.
[78] See Rashbam on Exod 20:13, Lev 19:19. See also Japhet, "Did Rashbam Know the Vulgate?" 263–267.

Bathsheba.[79] It would appear that the queries were from Henry I ("Henry the Liberal"; 1127–1181), count of Champagne from 1152 until his death. Henry and his wife Marie (daughter of King Louis VII of France and Eleanor of Aquitaine) were avid patrons of learning, with particular interest in the Bible – the subject of Henry's correspondence with John of Salisbury and Herbert of Bosham.[80] Evidently, Henry was also curious to know the opinion of a Jewish scholar about biblical issues that perplexed him, and thus turned to Rabbenu Tam, who seems to have had a political connection to his court.[81]

Apart from these records of exchanges Rashi's grandsons had with their Christian neighbors, a gloss in Rashi's commentary suggests that the Troyes master himself engaged in such conversations, and even acknowledged benefiting from them. An interpretation that can be traced to Jerome appears in Rashi's commentary on Ezek 2:1, with the following comment, presumably added by a student: "This was told to our master [Rashi] by a Christian (*min*) and it pleased him."[82] Rashi's acceptance of a Christian interpretation – though surprising – is perhaps not completely

[79] See Reiner, "Bible and Politics." [80] See Benton, "Court of Champagne."

[81] Reiner, "Bible and Politics," 70–72. Ephraim Kanarfogel cites Rabbenu Tam's exchange with Henry, and Rashbam's discussions with Christians about the Bible within his argument that the Tosafists likely became aware of the dialetic mode of learning prevalent in the Cathedral schools of northern France in their time and that this was an important catalyst in the development of the revolutionary Tosafist dialectic method. See Kanarfogel, "Ashkenazic Talmudic Interpretation."

[82] In Rashi's commentary here we find the following remark: "Given the fact that he gazed upon the heavenly chariot and walked amongst heavenly beings and interacted with angels, Ezekiel is called 'son of man' as if to say, 'there is no one born of woman here except for this one.' This was told to our master [Rashi] by a Christian (*min*) and it pleased him. But to me it seems that he was called 'son of man' so that he would not become arrogant, since he had become accustomed to seeing the divine chariot and the heavenly angels" (Rashi on Ezek 2:1, *Miqra'ot Gedolot ha-Keter*, 10, in brackets, indicating that it is absent in some manuscripts).

It is apparent that at least part of this commentary was added to Rashi's original commentary, and that it is a report by one of Rashi's students, who are otherwise known to have had a hand in the revision of his commentary on Ezekiel. See Penkower, "Rashi's commentary on Ezekiel." On the evidence regarding this note in particular, see Levy, *Rashi on Ezekiel*, 6–7. It would seem that Rashi and his student were told of Jerome's comment on Dan 8:17:

> Inasmuch as Ezekiel and Daniel and Zechariah behold themselves to be often in the company of angels, they were reminded of their frailty, lest they should be lifted up in pride and imagine themselves to partake of the nature or dignity of angels. Therefore they are addressed as sons of men, in order that they might realize that they are but human beings" (*Jerome on Daniel*, Archer trans., 88).

This interpretation underwent some adaptation either in the Christian's oral report to Rashi, or by Rashi himself who recorded it only partially. The interpretation given by his student, on the other hand, comes closer to Jerome's.

out of character. As Grossman has noted, Rashi was always intellectually curious and open to traditions previously unfamiliar to him from other centers of Jewish learning (which may have been brought to his awareness by Jewish travelers to Troyes) to a much greater extent than his more conservative teachers in Germany were.[83]

Yet Rashi's interest in Christian interpretation would not have been motivated only by intellectual curiosity. A key concern of Rashi's, manifested throughout his commentaries, is the need to protect the Jewish community from the enticement of Christian beliefs and doctrines.[84] This seems to have been a realistic concern in Rashi's time and place, as some Jews exposed to Latin learning were swayed by it and ultimately converted to Christianity.[85] A remarkable gloss on a line of liturgical poetry (*piyyuṭ*) thought to be penned by Joseph Qara suggests the attractiveness of Christian "words," perhaps a reference to Latin learning.[86] This would be borne out in the case of Herman the Jew of Cologne (c. 1107–1181), who reports in his autobiography that discussions with Christian clerics, including the renowned Rupert of Deutz (1075–1129), set the stage for his ultimate conversion to Christianity.[87] In an endeavor to bolster Jewish faith under these conditions, Rashi frequently engages in anti-Christian polemics in his Bible commentaries, undercutting Christian doctrines and interpretations of the Bible. These polemical passages (some of which have been removed from the printed editions of Rashi and are found in only some medieval manuscripts) most clearly manifest Rashi's awareness of Christian interpretations and doctrines.

Anti-Christian polemical motifs have been identified in Rashi's commentaries on the Pentateuch, Isaiah, Proverbs, Song of Songs, and Daniel;[88] but his most apparent polemical program emerges in Psalms.[89] On Ps 2:1, for example, Rashi remarks: "Many of the students of Jesus interpreted this passage in reference to the King Messiah. But as a response to (or: refutation of; *teshuvah*) the Christians (*minim*) it would be more

[83] See Grossman, *Rashi*, 56–63. [84] See Touitou, "Rashi on Genesis," 163.
[85] See Berger, "Mission." [86] See Urbach, *Arugat ha-bosem*, II:220.
[87] See Schmitt and Novikoff, *Conversion*, 20, 11–43, 204–211, including deliberations in recent scholarship regarding the historicity of Herman's autobiography.
[88] See Chazan, "Daniel"; Grossman, "Rashi on Isaiah"; Kamin, *Jews and Christians*, 22–57; Touitou, "Rashi on Genesis." Cohen, "Comparison," questions the existence of a polemical motive in Rashi on the Pentateuch, but recognizes it as a key factor elsewhere in his commentaries.
[89] See Cohen, "Comparison," 459; Gevaryahu, "Text of Rashi on Psalms"; Grossman, "Rashi's Commentary on Psalms"; Shereshevsky, "Rashi's and Christian Interpretations."

correct to interpret it about David himself."[90] Esra Shereshevsky has identified a number of other instances in which Rashi's interpretations are opposed to Jerome's, and seem to have been penned specifically to refute them.[91] While in some of the examples that Shereshevsky adduces Rashi's interpretations may not have been motivated by polemical considerations but stemmed, rather, from his own exegetical sensibilities, the possibility that he was aware of Jerome's interpretations cannot be ruled out. Indeed, if Rashi did discuss the Bible with Christian clerics, it is likely that he knew of the special standing the book of Psalms held among Christian interpreters – and this may have motivated him to engage in anti-Christian polemics most vigorously in his Psalms commentary.

In first posing the theory that Rashi's innovative *peshat* program is best understood in the context of the Judeo-Christian conflict, Touitou formulated the following key questions:

> What happened at the end of the 11th century which stimulated the change in the education curriculum of Franco-German Jewry? What were the new needs that were not satisfied by the existing curriculum? ... What is the nature and basic approach of Rashi's commentary, and how does it meet its society's new needs? ... Why did Rashi give his commentary the form which it bears?[92]

The parallels we have noted between Bruno and Rashi suggest a particularly fitting response to these questions. If Rashi became aware of Bruno's Psalms commentary, it would have posed a special danger because the patristic readings cited therein were selected critically and are shown to accord with the language and sequence of Scripture. Given Rashi's stated concern with the perceived threat of Christian learning enticing a potential Jewish audience, this sort of commentary would have called for a particularly sophisticated response. For the purpose of this argument, it is not necessary to presume that Rashi had a detailed knowledge of Bruno's commentary, nor that he intended to refute it psalm

[90] This seems to be Rashi's original formulation, which survives in only one early manuscript, whereas the printed editions follow the other manuscripts, which read, "*Our Rabbis* interpreted this passage in reference to the King Messiah," reflecting a change evidently made for fear of Christian censorship. See Gevaryahu, "Text of Rashi on Psalms," 252–253; Gruber, *Rashi on Psalms*, 177–180. On the expression *teshuvah laminim*, see Cohen, "Comparison," 454 and further references there.

[91] Shereshevsky, "Rashi's and Christian Interpretations." Lasker, "Rashi on Christianity," 3–14, rejects Shereshevsky's conclusions. My feeling is that Shereshevsky's argument is not fully supported by the evidence, but that the scenario he posits is nonetheless plausible. See note 82.

[92] Touitou, "Rashi on Genesis," 160.

by psalm. It would have been sufficient for Rashi to have grasped the gist of Bruno's exegetical project – the aim to demonstrate, through literary analysis, that the Christological readings of the Psalms accurately reflect David's prophetic intentions.[93] This could certainly have caused Rashi to regard the traditional midrashic commentaries on the Psalms as inadequate and impelled him to devise a commentary of his own that draws upon midrashic interpretation selectively in order to demonstrate the cogency of the traditional Jewish readings, and not the Christian ones.

Even if Rashi did have access to the currents of Latin learning in his time and place, including Bruno's teachings on the Bible, the impact that this would have had upon his thinking must be put into proper perspective. Unlike Bruno, Rashi was expert in Biblical Hebrew and also drew heavily upon the expanse of earlier Jewish learning. While Rashi's primary source was rabbinic literature, he had access to important post-rabbinic linguistic-philological sources, such as the works of Menahem ben Saruq and Dunash ben Labrat, as well as the Old French glosses of the Bible. Some scholars assert that Rashi was aware of further exegetical developments in al-Andalus or the philologically oriented Byzantine commentary tradition that emerged in the tenth century, as discussed in the next two chapters. Yet even according to those views (which I consider unlikely), it must be acknowledged that Rashi uses his Jewish sources in a new way and offers innovations of his own within a unique program that integrates a contextual-philological *peshat* program with a critical selection of midrashic interpretation. The "influence" of Bruno raised for consideration in this study relates to the inspiration that would have spurred Rashi to adopt this distinctive program that is not attested in other Jewish exegetical streams. The possibility we are considering is that Rashi became aware of Bruno's endeavor to support a Christological reading of the Psalms through "grammatical" analysis, and that he sought to bolster the Jewish reading of the Bible in a similar way using analogous methods of literary analysis he developed in his talmudic exegesis.

[93] Indeed, Rashi need not have spoken with Bruno himself to have become acquainted with the latter's method of interpretation – exposure to one of Bruno's many students could have been sufficient to familiarize Rashi with the master's methodology. As discussed in the Introduction and earlier in this chapter, Bruno's work reflects a growing trend in the interpretation of the Bible in the cathedral schools in northern France in the latter part of the eleventh century. And so, any substantial contact Rashi might have had with Christian scholars could potentially have exposed him to the mode of thinking exemplified by Bruno's Psalms commentary.

4

Comparison to the Andalusian Exegetical School

Much as the long-accepted view that Rashi was intellectually isolated from his Latin milieu in northern France has been challenged in the last two decades of the twentieth century, recent scholarship calls for reconsideration of the earlier tendency to minimize the cultural ties between the Ashkenazic community and Jews in Muslim lands during the eleventh century. Increasing evidence points to continuous trade among Jewish centers in Christian and Muslim lands, especially between the Rhineland, where Rashi studied, and Byzantium, al-Andalus, North Africa, and Iraq.[1] It probably was along one of these routes that the Babylonian Talmud and the teachings of the Geonim first came to the Rhineland. Based on indications that Rashi had access to Jewish learning in Muslim lands, Avraham Grossman has argued that a key impetus for Rashi's *peshat* revolution was his awareness of the Judeo-Arabic *peshat* tradition that had reached maturity in al-Andalus by the eleventh century.[2] The current chapter aims to evaluate that theory.

TIES TO JUDEO-ARABIC SCHOLARSHIP

Unlike the more conservative attitude of his coreligionists in the Rhineland academies, Rashi was open to intellectual currents emanating from centers of Jewish learning outside Ashkenaz.[3] This is manifested in Rashi's Bible commentaries, for example, in his citations from the teachings of Rabbi Moses ha-Darshan of Narbonne and R. Menahem bar

[1] See Soloveitchik, *Collected Essays II*, 127–144.

[2] See Grossman, "Rejection," 102–105. [3] See Grossman, *France*, 472–473.

Helbo (who seems to have studied in Provence), as discussed in Chapter 1. Rashi also occasionally relies on *Sefer Yosippon* – a medieval paraphrase of Josephus' *Jewish War*, composed in southern Italy in the tenth century.[4] There is evidence that Rashi used manuscripts from Muslim lands to correct the text of the Talmud that circulated in the Rhineland academies, even though the latter bore the authority of the supremely influential Rabbenu Gershom.[5]

It proves more challenging to find indications that Rashi knew of Geonic-Andalusian Bible interpretation – apart from his reliance on Menahem and Dunash, who wrote in Hebrew, unlike virtually all other Jewish authors in Muslim lands, who wrote in Arabic. There are a handful of references to a certain "Rabbi/Rabbenu Saadia" in Rashi's writings. In only one case, however, is it certain that Rashi is referring to Saadia Gaon: in his commentary on Exod 24:12, Rashi mentions Saadia's *Azharot* (i.e., enumeration of the 613 commandments) – composed in versified Hebrew to be used liturgically.[6] On Ps 45:10, Rashi seems to refer to Saadia's otherwise unknown "Treatise on Vocalization"; but this reference is plagued with problems – and even seems to be a textual corruption of Rashi's reference to a masoretic work.[7] Regarding the remaining four citations, it is not clear if Rashi was referring to the works of Saadia, the Gaon of Sura, or to a contemporary Ashkenazic rabbinic scholar named Saadia.[8] In sum, Rashi knew of Saadia Gaon as a rabbinic figure; but there is no evidence that he had access to his Judeo-Arabic Bible commentaries. Although a Hebrew paraphrase of Saadia's philosophical treatise *The Book of Beliefs and Opinions* did circulate in Ashkenaz in the late eleventh century, Rashi never mentions it, and there is no evidence that he knew the work.[9]

Although he did not read Arabic, Rashi seems to have learned of the importance of Hebrew–Arabic comparisons for biblical and talmudic

[4] For Rashi's references to *Sefer Yosippon*, see, e.g., his commentaries on Hag 2:6; Dan 6:29; 7:6; 11:2, 4. See also Dönitz, "Josephus." Some scholars believe that *Sefer Yosippon* was transcribed by Rabbenu Gershom himself in Mainz. See Flusser, *Yosipon*, 2:3–6. But this has been questioned. See Soloveitchik, "Halakhah, Hermeneutics, and Martyrdom," 2:280–282.

[5] See references in Grossman, "Impact," 448.

[6] See Malter, *Saadia*, 150.

[7] See Dotan, "*Niqqud*"; cf. Malter, *Saadia*, 395–396.

[8] See Ta-Shma, *Studies: Germany*, 100–101; Schlossberg, "Saadia on Daniel." Rashi cites the opinions of "Rabbi/Rabbenu Saadia" in his comments on Zech 6:6; Dan 7:25, 8:14; b. *Rosh ha-Shanah* 20b, s.v., עשרים וארבע.

[9] The paraphrase was likely composed toward the end of Rashi's lifetime in 1095, and it therefore may never have even come to his attention. See Keiner, "Paraphrase."

philology.[10] There are approximately twenty cases in which Rashi draws upon a parallel to Arabic in order to illuminate obscure terms in the Bible and Talmud.[11] While Rashi drew some of these parallels from his known written sources, such as Dunash's critical glosses on Menahem's *Maḥberet* or the teachings of R. Moses ha-Darshan, many of them seem to have come to Rashi's attention directly, perhaps through live interaction with Jews from Muslim lands.[12] Rashi explicitly mentions a certain Rabbi Samuel "the pious one," from the city of Barbastro in Aragon.[13] This Rabbi Samuel, and perhaps other learned travelers from Muslim lands, Avraham Grossman conjectures, could have informed Rashi of the highly developed Andalusian Judeo-Arabic exegetical school.

SAMUEL BEN HOFNI'S CONSTRUCTION OF PESHAT

The aforementioned points of contact between Rashi and Judeo-Arabic exegesis amount to sporadic, limited interpretations of a narrow scope, usually the construal of an individual word or phrase. But what could have motivated Rashi to transform the talmudic maxim that "a biblical verse does not leave the realm of its *peshat*" into a cardinal principle of his exegetical system? Grossman, based on the findings of David Weiss Halivni, suggests that Rashi's source for making this pivotal move can be traced to the Judeo-Arabic tradition:

> Halivni engaged in a detailed study of the maxim that "a biblical verse does not leave the realm of its *peshat*." He concluded that the Babylonian Gaon Samuel ben Hofni was the first to utilize this maxim in the sense that would be prevalent in the *peshat* school in northern France, and that he was the source for its use by scholars in Muslim lands. It is possible that the extensive use of this technical term in northern France in the second half of the eleventh century emerged, among other factors, under the influence of these scholars.[14]

In order to evaluate this hypothesis, it is necessary to examine Samuel ben Hofni's actual pronouncements regarding the *peshat* maxim and consider their possible relevance to Rashi.

There are two key passages, both in Judeo-Arabic, that scholars ascribe to Samuel ben Hofni in which he addresses the *peshat* maxim. One is in a manuscript fragment identified by Moshe Zucker as part of Samuel ben Hofni's commentary on Deuteronomy:

[10] See Maman, *Comparative Philology*. [11] Grossman, "Impact," 453–455.
[12] Grossman, "Impact," 453–455. [13] Grossman, "Impact," 449–453.
[14] Grossman, *France*, 563.

The words of God, May He be Exalted ... divide into two: literal language (*ḥaqīqa*) and non-literal language (*majāz*) .... If God or His messengers address us ... it is necessary to take their speech as literal language (*ḥaqīqa*), not as non-literal language (*majāz*), unless there is an indication that proves to us that the intent of that expression is non-literal. As our Sages said, "a biblical verse does not leave the realm of its *peshat*."[15]

In order to understand the terminology and exegetical conceptions in this passage, we must trace its roots within the Judeo-Arabic tradition, as well as the broader intellectual milieu in the Muslim East. Samuel ben Hofni's immediate source is Saadia Gaon, who otherwise is known to have influenced him substantially.

A more extensive investigation of Saadia's methods at this point will be helpful for assessing the originality of Rashi's exegetical program. The following axiom of Bible interpretation is articulated by Saadia in the introduction to his commentary on Genesis:

It is incumbent upon a person of reason to initially grasp the words of Scripture according to the apparent sense (*ẓāhir*) of its words, I mean the well-known meaning (*mashhūr*) understood among speakers of its language .... Unless (1) sense perception, or (2) rational knowledge contradicts the well-known meaning of that phrase, or if (3) the well-known meaning contradicts another verse that is unambiguous or (4) a tradition (i.e., of the Rabbis ...). In those cases we must assume that the verse is not intended according to its apparent sense, but contains a word or words that are *majāz* (i.e., non-literal language). When one discerns the type of *majāz* it is ... then the verse will conform to sensory and rational knowledge, the other verse, and tradition.[16]

For Saadia, like Samuel ben Hofni after him, the baseline assumption of an interpreter must be that any given biblical language expression has its usual, widely known meaning (*mashhūr*), which leads to an interpretation according to what Saadia calls the *ẓāhir*, a term drawn from Qur'an exegesis that connotes *the apparent/obvious or "literal" sense* of a language expression.[17] But when that path creates a contradiction one may posit that the language is used in a sense less commonly known, i.e., it is *majāz*. The term *majāz*, also drawn from Qur'an

15 Zucker, *Saadya on Genesis*, introduction, 42–43 (Arabic and Hebrew translation); French translation in Fenton, *Jardin*, 277. On the question of the attribution of this fragment to Samuel ben Hofni, see Cohen, *Gates*, 50n.

16 Commentary on Genesis, Zucker ed., 17–18 (Ar.), 190–191 (Heb.); see also Brody, *Geonim*, 305. A similar formulation appears in *Beliefs and Opinions* 7:1, Kafih ed., 219. See Ben-Shammai, "Tension," 34–36.

17 See Gleave, *Islam and Literalism*, 49–52.

hermeneutics,[18] is used by Saadia to connote *non-literal language*, including figurative language, as well as a broad range of otherwise unusual usages, such as ellipsis, pleonasm, and inversion.[19] This mode of figurative interpretation was known as *ta'wīl*,[20] a term already well attested in the Qur'an in the general sense of "interpretation" that acquired a more specific technical meaning of "interpretation by way of *majāz*" in Muslim hermeneutics.[21]

Indeed, Saadia's rule can be traced to the widely held rule in Muslim hermeneutics that any given qur'anic verse must, as a rule, be regarded as *ḥaqīqa* and understood according to its *ẓāhir* except when there are compelling reasons to posit that it is *majāz*, in which case *ta'wīl* must be applied to it. In Muslim tradition, the most commonly cited example of this rule is in the passage quoting Joseph's brothers, "Ask the town in which we have been and the caravan in which we returned. We are indeed telling the truth" (Qur'an 12:81–82). Taken literally, the phrase "Ask the town ... " is nonsensical since wood and stone structures do not speak. Therefore the *ẓāhir* must be discounted, and the phrase must be taken as *majāz*, i.e., figuratively, meaning *the people of the town*.[22]

Saadia uses a similar biblical example to illustrate the case of a *ẓāhir* reading to be discounted because it leads to a contradiction with sense perception. Citing Gen 3:20, "Adam called his wife's name Eve, because she was the mother of *all living beings*," Saadia remarks:

> If we leave the expression "all living beings" according to its well-known meaning ... we forsake sense perception, for this implies that the lion, ox, donkey and other animals are Eve's children. Now since there is no trick that will dislodge sense perception, we maintain that there is an elided word (*kalima muḍmara*) in this verse, through which it can be brought into agreement with the unmistakable facts, as I shall explain.[23]

And, indeed, in his commentary on that verse he writes:

[18] See Heinrichs, "Hermeneutics," 257, 265–266.

[19] See the examples discussed below. Although later Arabic (and Judeo-Arabic) authors used the term *majāz* specifically in the sense of *figurative language*, Saadia's usage is more inclusive. See Fenton, *Jardin*, 275–286, 332–339; Cohen, "Poet's Exegesis," 545–546.

[20] See, e.g., the version of Saadia's rule in *Beliefs and Opinions* 7:1, Kafih ed., 220.

[21] See Poonawala, "*Ta'wīl*"; Ben-Shammai, "Tension," 40; Cohen, *Gates*, 36–44. In some schools of Qur'an interpretation, the term was used to connote *allegorical, symbolic*, or *typological interpretation*.

[22] See Gleave, *Islam and Literalism*, 109.

[23] Commentary on Genesis, Zucker ed., 18 (Ar.), 191 (Heb.). See also Fenton, *Jardin*, 280, 296, 339.

In my translation of "the mother of all living beings" I added "human (*nāṭiq*; lit., speaking) beings," in order to make this expression exclude animals such as the horse, donkey and others, which sense perception contradicts.[24]

Invoking the notion of *iḍmār* (ellipsis) common in qur'anic exegesis, Saadia argues that *all living beings* actually means *all human beings*. Samuel ben Hofni, who seems to have sought links between Jewish and Muslim exegetical strategies, regards the rabbinic notion of *derekh qeṣarah* (lit., by way of abbreviation, i.e., abbreviated speech) as a precedent for *iḍmār*.[25]

Saadia goes on in his introduction to Genesis to illustrate the second case that requires *ta'wīl* by citing Deut 4:24, "For the Lord your God, He is a consuming fire." This verse was cited by the Muslim author Abu Uthman Amr b. Baḥr al-Jāḥiẓ (Basra, Baghdad, 781–868) in his criticism of Jewish literal renderings of physical depictions of God.[26] According to al-Jāḥiẓ, the Jews eschewed philosophical speculation and were ignorant of the ways of *ta'wīl*. Richard Steiner thus suggests that Saadia was implicitly replying to al-Jāḥiẓ's critique when he remarked:

If we take this dictum ("He is a consuming fire") according to its apparent sense (*ẓāhir*), reason (*'aql*) will contradict this, for reason indicates necessarily that fire is not self-sufficient (lit., is lacking and needs, i.e., a source of fuel), and that it is subject to change after its termination, and nothing of this is possible [with respect] to the Creator. But with the belief that in this dictum there is something of *majāz*, reason will be in agreement with Scripture.[27]

Saadia's rendering of this verse in Arabic in his *Tafsīr* thus reflects his application of *ta'wīl*: "For the punishment of the Lord your God is fire."[28] This verse is also cited in *Beliefs and Opinions*, where he applies the notion of *iḍmār* and reconstructs this verse in the following way: "for the *punishment* of the Lord your God is *like* fire."[29]

The impact of Saadia's principle on Samuel ben Hofni is evident from another manuscript fragment attributed to him by Zucker, which enumerates guidelines for a biblical interpreter:

[24] Commentary on Genesis, Zucker ed., 78 (Ar.), 296 (Heb.).

[25] See the passage from Samuel ben Hofni's writings in Zucker, *Saadya on Genesis*, 455–456. This passage is cited in full later in this chapter.

[26] See Steiner, *Translation*, 102.

[27] Commentary on Genesis, Zucker ed., 18 (Ar.), 191 (Heb.).

[28] לאן עקאב אללה רבך נאר (Derenbourg ed., 259).

[29] *Beliefs and Opinions* 7:1, Kafih ed., 219: עקאבה כאלנאר תאכל ("His punishment is like fire that consumes").

The seventh matter is that he should leave the texts as they are, and interpret them according to their apparent sense (*ẓāhir*), as the Sages said: "a biblical verse does not leave the realm of its *peshat*." Except for that which (1) clashes with sense perception, or (2) is against reason, or (3) contradicts another text (*naṣṣ*) that is unequivocal (*muḥkam*), or (4) contradicts the tradition (*manqūl*). Under those circumstances, it is necessary to seek for it an interpretation ... to make it consistent with sense perception, reason, the other scriptural verse and the tradition.[30]

Here the *peshat* maxim is cited to support Saadia's rule that a verse must first be interpreted according to its apparent sense (*ẓāhir*), unless doing so leads to one of the four sorts of contradiction enumerated.

Samuel ben Hofni's construal of the *peshat* maxim was influential in al-Andalus. It was invoked, for example, by Samuel ha-Levi ben Joseph (993–1056), known as Samuel ha-Nagid ("the Prince," a reference to his career as a statesman), an intellectual rival of Ibn Janah. Having fled his native Cordoba in 1013, he settled in Granada, serving as vizier to the Berber king, and engaging in military campaigns on his behalf. An accomplished Hebrew poet and Talmud scholar, the Nagid also made substantial contributions in Bible exegesis. A protégé of Hayyuj, he tenaciously attacked Ibn Janah for his critiques of the master.[31] The Nagid penned the twenty-two-section lexicographical work *Kitāb al-Istighnā‘* ("Book of Wealth/Amplitude"), now known only from fragments and citations in later authors.[32] Judging from these later references, it seems that this work exerted substantial influence – rivaling that of Ibn Janah's works.[33] In Talmud scholarship, the Nagid was dependent on the tradition of the Geonim in Iraq (though he departed from their views on specific issues).[34] It is thus not surprising that he adopted Samuel ben Hofni's construal of the *peshat* maxim, as evident from a citation by Isaac Ibn Barun (al-Andalus, early twelfth century):

The Nagid (may God be pleased with him) says that we must not remove a language expression from the category of literal language (*ḥaqīqa*) and deem it non-literal language (*majāz*) unless it is impossible to take it as literal language, because literal language is fundamental (*aṣl*; lit., the root), whereas non-literal language is a deviation (*‘udūl*) from the root, and we do not depart from it unless there is a dire necessity . . . and about this the early Sages, peace be upon them, said: "a biblical verse does not leave the realm of its *peshat*."[35]

30 Zucker, *Saadya on Genesis*, 448 (Ar.); French translation in Fenton, *Jardin*, 276.
31 See Tene, "Hebrew Linguistic Literature," 1356–1357.
32 See Perez, "Quotations."
33 See Maman, "Linguistic School," 267n, 276.
34 On Samuel ha-Nagid's reliance on geonic scholarship in general, see Ta-Shma, *Talmudic Commentary I*, 161.
35 *Kitāb al-Muwāzana*, Kokozoff ed., 24–25; see also Wechter, *Ibn Barun*, 56–57.

Like his geonic predecessors, the Nagid seems to have formulated this rule to justify his applications of *ta'wīl* where necessary. Both the surviving fragments of his own work and citations from later authors indicate that he was quite willing to posit the use of *majāz* in Scripture to resolve exegetical difficulties.[36]

On the basis of Samuel ben Hofni's statements indicating that he took Saadia's exegetical axiom to be the import of the talmudic *peshat* maxim, Halivni comes to the conclusion that "Samuel ben Hofni was the first one ... to interpret the word *peshuto* in the celebrated dictum to mean simple or plain meaning and to make the dictum imply the invincibility of peshat."[37] But this assessment is questionable. True, Samuel ben Hofni deserves credit for making the *peshat* maxim a foundation of the exegetical process, whereas it was marginal in the Talmud. Yet his equation of *peshat* with Arabic *ẓāhir* hardly implies its "invincibility," since (what Halivni calls) the "simple or plain meaning" is actually quite vulnerable. Samuel ben Hofni adopts what we can call a "weak reading" of the *peshat* maxim, since he effectively renders it a rule made to be broken, as the *ẓāhir* is little more than a point of departure, from which further interpretation by way of *majāz* must be considered. And, indeed, both Saadia and Samuel ben Hofni, as well as their Andalusian followers (like Samuel ha-Nagid), regularly applied *ta'wīl* and thereby "removed" many verses from their literal sense – what the latter termed "*peshat.*"[38]

To illustrate this distinction between what the aforementioned Judeo-Arabic exegetes termed *ẓāhir* and what Rashi would term *peshuto shel miqra*, we must explore some examples of how Saadia's rule was applied. In a fragment identified by Zucker as being part of Samuel ben Hofni's Pentateuch commentary, we read:

The sixth type of *majāz* is the elided (or omitted: *muḍmar*), as opposed to the plainly stated expression (*muẓhar*). For the plainly stated is *ḥaqīqa* and the elided is *majāz*. And this phenomenon is what the early sages called "*derekh qeṣarah*" ... and the dean of the academy [Saadia Gaon] al-Fayyumi, God preserve his soul, provided many examples in his writings, such as "For the Lord and for Gideon!" (Judg 7:18), in which the word "a sword ... " is omitted.[39] And "[For I have not dwelt in a house

[36] See, e.g., Ibn Bal'am on Num 22:7, Perez ed., 34 (Ar.), 84 (Heb.). See also Perez, "Quotations," 252–253, 255, 263, 264, 267, 277, 279–280 (on Ps 73:10, 21; 76:6; 77:5; 91:6; 94:17, 20).

[37] Weiss Halivni, *Peshat & Derash*, 90.

[38] See numerous examples in Fenton, *Jardin*, 271–286.

[39] Cf. Judg 7:20, "they shouted 'A sword for the Lord and for Gideon!'"

since the day that I brought up Israel unto this day]; but have gone from tent to tent, and from tabernacle" (1 Chr 17:5), in which "to tabernacle" has been elided.[40]

In the case of an elliptical expression, the *ẓāhir*, i.e., the strictly literal, word-for-word sense of the verse, is untenable, and therefore calls for *ta'wīl*, which entails supplying the missing word.

Another important type of *majāz* is syntactic "inversion" (*maqlūb*), referred to in Arabic treatises on *majāz* in the Qur'an as *muqaddam wa-mu'akhkhar* (lit., the early and the late).[41] Ibn Janah offers a systematic exposition of this phenomenon and its treatment by earlier exegetes.[42] For example, with respect to the biblical depiction of the manna that was left overnight by some Israelites, in defiance of God's command, he remarks:

[Some of them left of it until the morning], and it bred worms and stank (Exod 16:20). Its proper order (*niẓām*) is "and it stank and bred worms," as the stench that results from spoilage, which is the cause of the creation of the worms, precedes the creation of the worms, because the cause must precede the effect.[43]

Indeed, Saadia had applied this analysis in his translation of this verse into Arabic, as he did elsewhere in similar cases.[44]

The notion that a biblical verse might deviate from its natural order is already attested in rabbinic sources, referred to as *miqra mesoras*.[45] For example, the halakhic midrash *Mekhilta* remarks on the verse cited by Ibn Janah:

And it bred worms and stank (Exod 16:20). This is an inverted verse (*miqra mesoras*). Does a thing stink after it breeds worms? No, first it stinks and then it breeds worms, just as it says: "and it did not stink and no worms were in it" (Exod 16:24).[46]

Rashi adopts this very interpretation:

And it stank – this is an inverted verse (*miqra hafukh*), because first it must have stunk and then afterwards have become wormy, just as it is said, "and it did not

40 See Zucker, *Saadya on Genesis*, 455–456; French translation in Fenton, *Jardin*, 279–280.

41 See Versteegh, *Arabic Grammar*, 106, 122–123.

42 This type of syntactic "inversion" is a classic example of *ta'wīl*. See Fenton, *Jardin*, 280–281, 295–297.

43 See Ibn Janah, *Kitāb al-Luma'*, Derenbourg ed., 342; *Sefer ha-Riqmah*, Wilensky ed., 359. (*Sefer ha-Riqmah* is the twelfth-century Hebrew translation of *Kitāb al-Luma'*).

44 See Zucker, *Translation*, 258–260.

45 See Melammed, *Bible Commentators*, 64–67.

46 *Mekhilta de-Rabbi Ishmael, Be-shallaḥ, Vayassa'*, §4, Horovitz and Rabin ed., 167. Translation from Steiner, "*Hysteron Proteron.*"

stink and no worms were in it." And this is the typical manner of all things (*ken derekh kol* ...) that become wormy.[47]

Although Rashi's source is the *Mekhilta*, which is a midrash, this interpretation actually manifests his *peshat* instincts. As noted by Mizrahi in his supercommentary here, Rashi avoided citing another midrashic interpretation that does not "invert" the verse and posits that the spoilage of the manna involved a miracle, a common midrashic assumption.[48] Rashi's remark that "this is the way of all things that become wormy" indicates his general desire to adhere to the laws of the natural world – a tendency Rashbam would develop and refer to as *derekh ereṣ* ("the way of the world") and *nohag she-ba-'olam* ("the manner of the world").[49] Additionally, we have already seen in Chapter 1 how Rashi applies the concept of *miqra mesoras* as part of his *peshat* program on Gen 14:15, by contrast with the word-for-word midrashic reading.

At times, Rashi applies the notion of *miqra qaṣar* in his *peshat* commentaries to offer a stylistic explanation for what would otherwise seem to be an anomalous usage – and that would prompt a midrashic interpretation. On Gen 48:1–2, for example, Rashi remarks:

He said to Joseph – one of the messengers, and this is an elliptical verse (*miqra qaṣar*). But some say that Ephraim was regularly with Jacob for study and when Jacob became ill in the land of Goshen Ephraim went to his father in Egypt and in order to tell him and he told him.

And he – i.e., the messenger – *told Jacob*. It does not state plainly who did the telling. There are many such elliptical verses (*miqra'ot qiṣrei lashon*).[50]

The second opinion that Rashi cites on verse 1 ("But some say") is from *Midrash Tanḥuma*, which sought to identify the unknown speaker – an interpretation adopted by Tobiah ben Eliezer in *Leqaḥ Ṭov*.[51] But Rashi

47 Rashi on Exod 16:20, Berliner ed., 138. Rashi uses the term *miqra hafukh* in the same sense as *miqra mesoras*. See Chapter 1, note 90.

48 *Mizrahi*, Phillip ed., II:234–235.

49 This will be discussed in Chapter 8. Although Rashbam is most often credited with the application of this method, its roots can be traced to Rashi's *peshat* method. See, e.g., the *peshat* commentaries he offers on Gen 14:15 (cited in Chapter 1), Gen 14:18, and 15:10 (also cited in Chapter 1), both in contrast to midrashic interpretations. *Leqaḥ Ṭov* on Exod 16:20 is also based on the *Mekhilta* (i.e., that the manna spoiled before breeding worms), but lacks the observation that "this is the way of all things that become wormy," which is an essential feature of Rashi's *peshat* approach here.

50 Berliner ed., 93. Berliner placed the words "there are many such elliptical verses" in brackets because they do not appear in the Reggio de Calabria edition. However, they do appear in MS Leipzig 1.

51 *Leqaḥ Ṭov*, Buber ed., I: 228.

offers a simpler stylistic explanation based on his observation that many biblical verses are elliptical.[52] The difference between the *peshat* and midrashic approaches is more pronounced in the following double commentary given by Rashi:

Thus he made the candelabrum – The one who made it. And a midrashic *aggadah* explains: by God himself; i.e., it was made on its own.[53]

The midrash deduces from the unspecified subject of the verb "he made" that the candelabrum was fashioned miraculously by God, as though it was made by itself. Rashi's *peshat* interpretation, on the other hand, is predicated on the tendency of the Bible to speak elliptically.

The preceding examples reveal similarities between Rashi's *peshat* exegesis and certain applications of *ta'wīl* in the Judeo-Arabic tradition. This parallel may indicate a transfer of exegetical traditions from Muslim lands to Rashi. To be sure, Rashi in these cases was drawing upon what were originally rabbinic terms and concepts – *miqra mesoras* and *miqra qaṣar*. But, like his Geonic and Andalusian counterparts, he used them as part of a systematic endeavor to identify the Bible's stylistic conventions. Indeed, Rashi occasionally cites the "Baraita of Rabbi Eliezer the son of Rabbi Jose the Galilean on the thirty-two hermeneutical principles (*middot*) by which the Torah is interpreted," which include inversion and ellipsis.[54] Although Rashi accepted the attribution of this work to the tanaitic author of Late Antiquity, modern scholars tend to regard it as the product of the Geonic era – and some believe it is based on a list of hermeneutical rules penned by Samuel ben Hofni to codify the Bible's stylistic conventions.[55]

Yet the parallels we have noted highlight an important difference. Samuel ben Hofni defined "the *peshat* of Scripture" as the *ẓāhir*, i.e., the immediately apparent, strictly literal sense.[56] For him, the talmudic *peshat*

[52] See Rashi on Gen 41:49; Exod 22:22, 32:32; Num 14:24, 24:12.

[53] Rashi on Num 8:4, Berliner ed., 294. The source of this midrashic comment is *Tanḥuma be-Ha'alotekha* §3. Tobiah ben Eliezer makes no remark on this feature of the verse.

[54] See, e.g., Rashi on Gen 2:8 (cited in Chapter 6); 1 Sam 5:11; 2 Sam 24:9; Jer 46:22. Others refer to this work as the Mishnah of Rabbi Eliezer. See Enelow, "Thirty-Two Rules," 359–361.

[55] See Zucker, "Thirty-Two *Middot*." For an alternative view, see Enelow, "Thirty-Two Rules"; Steiner, "*Hysteron Proteron*," 39–40.

[56] In his introduction to the Talmud, Samuel ben Hofni actually glosses the talmudic expression *peshateh di-qera* using the Arabic expression *ẓāhir al-naṣṣ*. See *Prooemium Talmudis*, Abramson ed., 159 (Ar.), 184 (Heb.). (I am grateful to Haggai Ben-Shammai for this reference.)

maxim teaches that the *ẓāhir* must be the exegete's starting point, a baseline assumption. But where the *ẓāhir* is unreasonable, it must be set aside, and *ta'wīl* applied to arrive at the correct interpretation. Where *ta'wīl* is indicated, it overrides "the *peshat* of Scripture," and the rule of *peshat* – being a weak rule – is broken. Rashi, on the other hand, had no exposure to Muslim hermeneutics and did not define "the *peshat* of Scripture" as the *ẓāhir*. For him, "the *peshat* of Scripture" is the most reasonable interpretation that emerges from a philological-contextual analysis that takes into account scriptural stylistic conventions. Rashi works with a dichotomy between *peshat* and midrash, not between *peshat* and *ta'wīl*. In his construction, the rule of *peshat* teaches that the philological-contextual sense remains inviolate, notwithstanding the midrash.

Could Rashi have been informed of Samuel ben Hofni's use of the talmudic *peshat* maxim as a key exegetical principle? This possibility cannot be ruled out. It circulated in al-Andalus in the oral traditions of Samuel ha-Nagid and authors who cited his words (such as Ibn Barun) well into the twelfth century. The trouble is that the conception of *peshat*, and the understanding of the *peshat* maxim, articulated by Samuel ben Hofni Gaon and repeated by Samuel ha-Nagid, do not resemble those of Rashi – and actually are part of a Muslim hermeneutical framework. Within qur'anic hermeneutics, followed by important Judeo-Arabic Bible exegetes, a question commonly raised was whether a given verse is to be taken literally (i.e., as *ḥaqīqa*, and interpreted according to its *ẓāhir*) or figuratively (i.e., as *majāz*, and interpreted via *ta'wīl*).[57] Within this framework Samuel ben Hofni and Samuel ha-Nagid invoked the *peshat* maxim to make the *ẓāhir* a default position, with *ta'wīl* applied where a literal interpretation is unreasonable. But for Rashi, *peshat* is not merely the "apparent" or most literal sense; nor is it merely a default position. Rather, for Rashi, "the *peshat* of Scripture" must be ascertained by taking into account the language and context of a given biblical verse – an interpretation which is indeed inviolate in his view, notwithstanding the validity of the midrashic interpretation. Hence, Rashi often applies what Judeo-Arabic exegetes might term *ta'wīl* to arrive at his *peshat* interpretation, which is not equivalent to the *ẓāhir*.

IBN JANAH'S CONSTRUCTION OF PESHAT

A construal of the talmudic *peshat* maxim that resembles Rashi's more closely was identified in the writings of Ibn Janah by the current author

[57] See Gleave, *Islam and Literalism*.

some years ago – and it has since been marshaled by Grossman to support his theory.[58] Indeed, this "smoking gun" is probably the strongest single piece of potential evidence for the claim that Rashi's conception of *peshat* can be traced to a source in the Andalusian exegetical school. Although Samuel ben Hofni's model of *peshat* was current in al-Andalus, a different one was adopted by Ibn Janah in his highly influential linguistic works, which dealt not only with grammar and lexicography, but also biblical syntax and poetics.

The notion that *ta'wīl* is an exception evidently began to seem unreasonable to Ibn Janah. After all, much of Qur'an exegesis, followed by Judeo-Arabic Bible exegesis, was dedicated to classifying different types of *majāz* and the *ta'wīl* required for their interpretation.[59] This is especially evident in the chapters of Ibn Janah's grammar, *Kitāb al-Luma'*, devoted to what has been termed "lexical substitution," i.e., the use of one word in the sense of another.[60] For example, the expression "the one that shall come out of your intestines (*me'ekha*)" (Gen 15:4) actually means *your progeny*, more properly referred to as emerging from one's "loins" (see, e.g., Gen 35:11).[61] Or, for example, the word "heart" in Ps 16:9 ("my heart rejoices") actually means *soul* or *spirit*, reflecting a usage "by way of metaphor" (*isti'āra*).[62] This premise of linguistic flexibility became prevalent in the Andalusian exegetical school – often in distinction to midrash, which tends to be hyper-literal. Saadia had already established that Scripture often speaks by way of *majāz*. But Ibn Janah introduced a more sophisticated understanding of biblical poetic techniques such as metaphor, metonymy, synecdoche, simile, allegory, and hyperbole, which he drew from Arabic poetics. The elaborate system of such "embellishments" (*maḥāsin al-shi'r*), as classified by Arab experts on poetry, would be applied by Moses Ibn Ezra (c. 1055–1138, Granada),[63] whose poetics *Kitāb al-Muḥāḍara wa-l-Mudhākara* (Book of Discussion and Conversation) outlines the aesthetic features of Hebrew Scripture.[64]

[58] See Cohen, "Spanish Source"; Grossman, "Grammar and Lexicon," 434; Grossman, "Rejection," 104–105.

[59] See Fenton, *Jardin*. [60] See Cohen, *Three Approaches*, 80–81.

[61] *Kitāb al-Luma'*, Derenbourg ed., 295; *Sefer ha-Riqmah*, Wilensky ed., 308.

[62] *Kitāb al-Luma'*, Derenbourg ed., 299; *Sefer ha-Riqmah*, Wilensky ed., 313.

[63] There is no evidence that Moses Ibn Ezra was related to Abraham Ibn Ezra. Since Moses Ibn Ezra is cited in this study only sporadically, he will be referred to by his full name. On the other hand, Abraham Ibn Ezra will be cited simply as "Ibn Ezra," unless there is room for confusion, in which case his full name will be used as well.

[64] See Cohen, "Aesthetic Exegesis"; Cohen, "Poet's Exegesis."

Heralding the maturation of the philological Andalusian exegetical method, the advent of Ibn Janah's works brought to light its sharp divergence from midrash – a chasm Ibn Janah himself sought to address by invoking the authority of the Rabbis. He thus begins his grammar by addressing the critique leveled against his departure from rabbinic exegesis by anonymous talmudists. Such zealots, he argues, act out of

> ignorance of the dictum of our early sages of blessed memory: "Scripture does not leave the realm of its *peshat*" ... and that "the *peshat* of Scripture is one thing [lit., alone], and the halakhah is another [lit., alone]." For it is not impossible that one language expression can bear two correct meanings and more than that, as our Rabbis of blessed memory said: "One verse can have [lit., go out to] a number of meanings, but one meaning cannot come out from two verses" (b.*Sanhedrin* 34a).[65]

Ibn Janah defends his method based on the Talmud, to which he points to assert that Scripture can be interpreted in two alternative, but equally valid, ways: (1) philologically and contextually, yielding "the *peshat* of Scripture" – the realm of his own analysis; (2) according to the midrashic methods of the Rabbis, which determine the halakhah. Notwithstanding the importance of the latter, he asserts that the former is inviolate based on the talmudic *peshat* maxim, which he takes to mean that Scripture cannot be deprived of its philological-contextual sense, i.e., *peshat*.

It is important to note how Ibn Janah's construal of the *peshat* maxim differs from that of Samuel ben Hofni. For the latter, *peshat* is the equivalent of *ẓāhir*, which is merely a default position. Following Saadia's lead, Samuel ben Hofni took rabbinic halakhic interpretation into consideration when weighing the viability of the *ẓāhir*. He distinguished explicitly among different classes of rabbinic exegesis, submitting to halakhic traditions, while feeling free to disregard non-halakhic (aggadic) ones. This dichotomy is reflected in the following programmatic statement, taken from his guidelines for the interpreter:

> The eighth matter: that whatever belongs to the eight categories of the commandments – valid, invalid, forbidden, permitted, unclean, clean, guilty or innocent – he should explain with precision and clarity, without deviation, according to Scripture (*al-naṣṣ*) and the tradition (*al-naql*) alone.
>
> The ninth matter: that whatever is established by an explicit verse or clarified by Scripture or established by rational demonstration, he should state unreservedly and decisively; but of those interpretations which the Sages call *midrashot* or

[65] *Kitāb al-Luma'*, Derenbourg ed., 8; *Sefer ha-Riqmah*, Wilensky ed., 19.

aggadot ... in matters other than the commandments, with which he embellishes his discourse, he should say "It may be," or "It is suitable."[66]

Samuel ben Hofni was willing to deviate from the *ẓāhir* and apply *taw'īl* in light of rabbinic halakhic traditions; but non-halakhic midrash did not command the same authority.

This rule is exemplified in the fourth exception to Saadia's axiom, i.e., a case in which the *ẓāhir* is contradicted by an authoritative "tradition":

An example of the fourth type is the dictum of God in the prohibition: "You shall not cook a kid in its mother's milk" (Exod 23:19). The tradition has come and prohibited eating all meat in all milk. Since the tradition was transmitted by those who witnessed it with their own eyes, we must seek an interpretation ... in order for it to be in agreement with the tradition of the prophets.[67]

Saadia explains why tradition can be regarded as (what he terms elsewhere) *'ilm ḍarūri*, i.e., compelling knowledge: since Scripture was transmitted by people who saw with their own eyes how biblical law was implemented, their words are authoritative in determining its meaning.[68] The tradition therefore has the same status as sense perception, reason, and Scripture itself with respect to *ẓāhir al-naṣṣ*. Accordingly, Saadia adjusts his translation of this verse in the *Tafsīr*: "Do not eat meat with milk."[69] And, indeed, throughout the *Tafsīr* Saadia often abandons the literal sense of Scripture and renders the text according to talmudic halakhah.[70]

To be sure, Saadia was selective in adjusting *ẓāhir al-naṣṣ* to conform to rabbinic halakhic exegesis. His *Tafsīr* at times reflects a literal-contextual reading that diverges from rabbinic halakhic interpretation, as noted above in connection with Deut 25:6.[71] Saadia does not provide a specific theoretical justification for this divergence – at least, not in his extant writings. He probably assumed that the halakhic exegesis was not meant as genuine interpretation, but was employed as an artificial projection onto the text, referred to in the Talmud as *asmakhta*.[72] This,

66 Zucker, *Saadya on Genesis*, 448 (Ar.); English trans. from Brody, *Geonim*, 313.

67 Saadia on Genesis, Zucker ed., 18 (Ar.), 192 (Heb.).

68 See Ben-Shammai, *Leader's Project*, 339. Abraham Ibn Ezra makes a remark in this spirit in his short commentary on Exod 13:9. See Cohen, *Gates*, 149–151.

69 ולא תאכל לחמא בלבן. Derenbourg ed., 115; cf. Zucker, *Translation*, 358.

70 See Zucker, *Translation*, 319–441.

71 See Chapter 2, note 26. On this rather frequent occurrence in the *Tafsīr*, see Zucker, *Translation*, 442–479.

72 See Harris, *Fragmentation*, 76–78. While Saadia does not invoke the concept of *asmakhta* explicitly, this type of reasoning can be inferred from his argument that the midrashic thirteen *middot* were not actually used by the Rabbis to extrapolate halakhah from the

in any case, was the explanation given by others following in Saadia's tradition.[73]

Ibn Janah seems to have been dissatisfied with the inconsistency of the Geonic interpretive system. He did not accept the notion of applying *ta'wīl* to disqualify an otherwise philologically sound interpretation in the face of a contradictory halakhic tradition. It is for such cases that he recruited the *peshat* maxim to assert that the Rabbis acknowledged the validity of the former, notwithstanding the authority of the latter. Unlike his geonic predecessors, who aimed to determine the single correct sense of Scripture through judicious application of *ta'wīl*, Ibn Janah allows the philological-contextual interpretation – which he termed *peshat* – to stand on its own, by positing that Scripture conveys two different meanings simultaneously: the philological *peshat* and the rabbinic halakhic midrash.

Accordingly, two different construals of the *peshat* maxim can be discerned in the Geonic-Andalusian school:

(1) *Weak* reading (Samuel ben Hofni): Scripture must be interpreted according to its obvious, literal sense (*peshat/ẓāhir*) – unless there is a reason to interpret it non-literally.
(2) *Strong* reading (Ibn Janah): Scripture can never be deprived of its philological-contextual sense (=*peshat*), notwithstanding the midrashic reading, which is authoritative for halakhic purposes.

As a Rabbanite, Ibn Janah does not claim that *peshat* is the single correct sense, but rather that it exists alongside the authoritative halakhic reading. He uses the *peshat* maxim to create a niche for the new philological-contextual method and dispense with the need to harmonize it with the talmudic halakhic system, as Saadia and his followers had done.

Notwithstanding this theoretical departure from the Geonic model, Ibn Janah derived much of his exegetical practice from Saadia and Samuel ben Hofni. Ibn Janah privileged the *ẓāhir* as a baseline assumption, but applied *ta'wīl* – liberally – as necessitated by interpretive exigencies (though not to harmonize it with the halakhah). The theoretical difference is that Ibn Janah termed the final product of his analysis "the *peshat* of Scripture," whereas Samuel ben Hofni used that appellation for the *ẓāhir*, which often

biblical text, but rather were used to link laws known from the oral tradition to the text of Scripture. See Cohen, *Gates*, 246–247. On Saadia's complex attitude toward midrashic exegesis in general, see Ben-Shammai, *Leader's Project*, 336–373.

[73] E.g., Judah ha-Levi and Abraham Ibn Ezra. See Cohen, *Gates*, 254–255.

turned out to be a rejected default position. Ibn Janah acknowledged his dependence on the Geonim, as he goes on (in the aforementioned passage) to say that the talmudist zealots who recoil from his interpretive approach do so "because of their scant study of the *peshat* commentaries of Rav Saadia and Samuel ben Hofni, may God be pleased with the two of them."[74] Though Saadia did not characterize his method as *peshat*, and Samuel ben Hofni did not deem *peshat* inviolate, Ibn Janah nonetheless counts them as founders of the *peshat* method of interpretation in a sort of back-projection of his own conception of this hermeneutical category.

For our purposes, it is critical to note that Ibn Janah arrives at his hermeneutical construction by linking two disparate talmudic statements: (a) the *peshat* maxim, and (b) the dictum that "one verse can have a number of meanings." As Kamin noted, this connection is not made in the Talmud and entails a reinterpretation of both statements, whereby, taken together, they express the notion that Scripture conveys dual signification: both *peshat* and midrash.[75] This very connection is made by Rashi in his programmatic introduction to the Song of Songs, as discussed in Chapter 2. Since the connection is distinctive, it points to the possibility that Rashi borrowed it from Ibn Janah, even though the Andalusian linguist is never mentioned by Rashi or even by his students. Grossman argues that Ibn Janah's statement about *peshuto shel miqra* and the achievements of the subsequent Andalusian exegetical school came to Rashi's attention, perhaps in oral reports by travelers from al-Andalus.[76] Even if this scenario is historically plausible, we must consider its hermeneutical implications. What impact could Ibn Janah's *peshat* model have had on Rashi and to what extent does it match his exegetical thought and practice? To answer this question, it is important to place Ibn Janah within the trajectory of the Geonic-Andalusian school and consider whether his conceptions resonate in Rashi's exegetical project.

As discussed in Chapter 1, the Rabbis of Late Antiquity, like the Church Fathers, assumed that Scripture is a cryptic document that must be mined for hints to its truer, deeper meaning that lay beneath its surface. For the Church Fathers, the inner, "spiritual" meaning of Scripture is

74 *Kitāb al-Luma'*, Derenbourg ed., 8; *Sefer ha-Riqmah*, Wilensky ed., 19.

75 See Kamin, *Jews and Christians*, xxxii–xxxiii. The talmudic rule of scriptural multivalence is not limited to two senses, but "many." Both Ibn Janah and Rashi seem to struggle with this. Ibn Janah speaks of Scripture bearing "two correct meanings and more than that." Rashi mitigates this problem by beginning his preface with the verse, "One thing God has spoken; two things have I heard" (Ps 62:12).

76 Grossman, "Grammar and Lexicon," 434–436.

a foreshadowing of the life, death, and resurrection of Jesus Christ. The Rabbis, for their part, applied the midrashic *middot* to derive (or support) the laws and tenets of rabbinic Judaism, which often differed from what is stated plainly in Scripture – a disparity noted, e.g., by Rashbam.[77] With the advent of Islam and the crystallization of the text of the Qur'an, a competing conception of sacred Scripture emerged. As emphasized in recent scholarship, Muslim Scripture is uniquely "self-referential." Not only does it announce itself as sacred Scripture, i.e., the word of God (something often unstated in the Bible), there are verses in the Qur'an that seem to offer guidance for the proper method of its interpretation.[78] In contrast to the assumptions of ancient Jewish and Christian interpreters regarding the supposedly cryptic nature of the Bible, a plethora of qur'anic statements attest that it is written in clear, plain (*mubīn*) language, e.g., "These are the *ayāt* (verses) of the Book, and a clear (*mubīn*) Qur'an" (Qur'an 15:1). While allegorical interpretation of the Qur'an would emerge in Islam,[79] it is not a defining feature of Muslim scriptural interpretation. Christianity and Rabbinic Judaism both inherited their sacred text – the Hebrew Bible – from an earlier context. The Christian community could not embrace this Scripture without positing that its true meaning is something "other" than that what it seems to say, calling for its Christological reinterpretation.[80] Within rabbinic Judaism, likewise, the Bible could no longer serve as a self-standing theological and religious guide. It was therefore mediated through a midrashic rewriting that brought the ancient text in line with contemporary norms of Judaism.[81] But the formation of the Qur'an was roughly coterminous with the birth of Islam, and was directly relevant to the message of the new religion constructed around it.[82] Islam, at the outset, thus did not have the same

77 See, e.g., Rashbam on Gen 37:2.

78 See Madigan, *Self Image*; Wild, *Self-Referentiality*.

79 See Bar-Asher, *Scripture and Exegesis*; Goldziher, *Schools*, 116–166.

80 Some Christians – most notably the followers of Marcion in the second century – took the Hebrew Bible literally, and therefore rejected it as incompatible with Christianity. It was in opposition to this sort of understanding that Marcion's opponents (in what became "Orthodox" Christianity) maintained that the Jews, together with Marcion, did not discern the Hebrew Bible's true "spiritual" meaning. See Ehrman, *Lost Christianities*, 203–212.

81 See Kugel, *Bible as it Was*.

82 Modern scholarship does challenge the traditional narrative of the Qur'an's revelation and dating. Yet the Qur'an is still regarded as a product of the religious culture during the period, broadly speaking, in which Islam emerged. See Neuwirth et al., eds., *Qur'ān in Context*, 2–24.

need to "resituate" its Scripture through midrashic or "spiritual" reinterpretation.[83]

Of special importance in this regard is Qur'an 3:7, taken by Muslim interpreters as a hermeneutical directive said by the angel Gabriel to Muhammad regarding the Qur'an ("the Book") itself:

> It is He who has sent down to you the Book. In it are verses that are clear (*muḥkamāt*; sing. *muḥkam*) – they are the essence (lit., "mother") of the Book. And others are ambiguous (*mutashābihāt*; sing. *mutashābih*). As for those in whose hearts is dissention, they follow that of it which is ambiguous (*mutashābih*), seeking discord and seeking interpretation (*ta'wīl*) for them. And no one knows its interpretation (*ta'wīl*) except Allah and those firm in knowledge. They say, "We believe in it. All is from our Lord."[84]

Accordingly, the clear verses (*muḥkamāt*) of the Qur'an were privileged: they are regarded as its "essence," since they express God's will directly. This led to the default presumption among interpreters that a given qur'anic verse is *muḥkam* rather than *mutashābih*, and must be understood in its "apparent" sense (*ẓāhir*). The *mutashābihāt*, on the other hand, typically employ *majāz*, and therefore require *ta'wīl*, i.e., interpretation in light of contextual, literary, and rational considerations.

This Muslim outlook underlies Saadia's axiom of interpretation. In his introduction to Genesis, after enumerating the three sources of human knowledge – reason, Scripture, and tradition – he writes:

> Since all speech consists of both clear expressions (*muḥkamāt*) and ambiguous expressions (*mutashābihāt*) ... one who interprets the Scriptures must classify as clear expressions (*muḥkamāt*) those expressions that agree with the things that are known from reason ... and the things that are known from tradition ... And he must classify as ambiguous (*mutashābih*) those that contradict one of those two things.[85]

Reflecting the Muslim tendency to privilege the *ẓāhir*, under the assumption that the *muḥkamāt* are the "essence" of God's speech, Saadia diverges from

[83] To be sure, the Qur'an "resituates" biblical motifs within an Islamic framework. It incorporates recollections of the patriarchs and prophets into a new conception of "prophetology" that culminates in Muhammad and advances a new paradigm for the reading of scriptural narratives in an Arabic milieu. See Griffith, *Bible in Arabic*, 54–96.

[84] The translation of this verse is from Wild, "Sura 3:7," 423, with some revision. There is another way of parsing the last two sentences of this verse, which ultimately became dominant in Islam: "And no one knows its interpretation (*ta'wīl*) except Allah. But those firm in knowledge say, 'We believe in it. All is from our Lord.'" According to the first reading above (favored among the Mu'tazilites), there are people "firm in knowledge" capable of interpreting the ambiguous verses, whereas according to this reading God alone knows their interpretation. See Wild, "Sura 3:7," 424–425.

[85] Commentary on Genesis, Zucker ed., 17–18 (Ar.), 190–191 (Heb.).

the midrashic assumption that the Bible is an essentially cryptic document. Accordingly, Saadia generally adhered to the *ẓāhir* in his Pentateuch translation, the *Tafsīr*. Although this Arabic translation is not literal at all points, it effectively marginalizes most of the midrashic readings of Scripture and stood as an example for subsequent Rabbanite interpreters in Muslim lands.[86]

Admittedly, Saadia – followed by Samuel ben Hofni – in practice, often deferred to rabbinic interpretations or applied *ta'wīl* for other reasons. Yet their exegetical axiom brought new prestige to the literal sense of Scripture, which had traditionally been marginalized. This also inspired their successors – especially in al-Andalus – to investigate Biblical Hebrew as a language system. The lexicographic work of Menahem and Dunash (a student of Saadia's) was followed by the breakthroughs in Hebrew linguistics by Hayyuj and Ibn Janah, both of whom drew heavily upon Arabic linguistic scholarship of their day.[87] This, in turn, served as the foundation for subsequent Judeo-Arabic Bible exegesis, as manifested in the influential commentaries of Ibn Chiquitilla and Ibn Bal'am.[88]

As noted above, Halivni oversimplifies matters when he writes that "Samuel ben Hofni was the first one ... to interpret the word *peshuto* in the celebrated dictum to mean simple or plain meaning and to make the dictum imply the invincibility of peshat." Samuel ben Hofni did not make *peshat* "invincible." But Ibn Janah did. Heralding the maturation of the philological Andalusian exegetical method, the great linguist recruited the term *peshat* to connote the philologically correct sense of Scripture – and preserve its integrity notwithstanding its sharp divergence from traditional midrashic exegesis.

FURTHER DEVELOPMENT OF THE PESHAT MAXIM IN THE ANDALUSIAN TRADITION

Ibn Janah's usage of the *peshat* maxim was a turning point that would ultimately gain currency in the Andalusian school. Yet, in the eleventh and early twelfth centuries its impact still seems to have been quite limited. In fact, Ibn Janah rarely even used the Hebrew term *peshat*. He typically relied on Arabic hermeneutical terminology, as his geonic predecessors had done. Neither Ibn Chiquitilla nor Ibn Bal'am (in their extant writings) invoke the maxim that "Scripture does not leave the realm of its *peshat*,"

[86] See Zucker, *Translation*; Steiner, *Translation*. [87] See Becker, *Arabic Sources*.
[88] See Maman, "Linguistic School."

nor does Moses Ibn Ezra – and all of them had ample opportunity to do so, e.g., when classifying rabbinic readings as *derash*.[89]

Somewhat ironically, it was Abraham Ibn Ezra – writing in Hebrew in Christian lands, where he wandered after leaving Spain in 1140 – who played a decisive role in forming the identity of what would come to be known as the "*peshat* movement" that had emerged from the school of Saadia's followers in Muslim lands. Ibn Ezra drew heavily upon Saadia, Ibn Janah, Ibn Chiquitilla, and Ibn Bal'am. However, unlike his predecessors, who wrote in Arabic and rarely used the term *peshat*, Ibn Ezra regularly used it to label his rational, philological-contextual exegetical method, conceivably a response to the culture clash that confronted him in Christian lands, where Rashi had already achieved great popularity.[90]

Whereas Ibn Janah made *peshat* inviolate but acknowledged midrash as a viable alternative, Ibn Ezra argues that *peshat* is the single true sense of Scripture. Echoing the critical attitude of earlier geonic and Andalusian authorities,[91] Ibn Ezra argues that midrash is not necessarily meant to be taken literally, nor was it typically formulated as genuine exegesis: "The *midrashim* of our righteous early Sages ... are of many types. Some are riddles, mysteries and allegories ... others homilies intended to revive exhausted hearts ... to bring faith to those who falter, and to educate the ignorant."[92] Hence, "the *midrashim* are like clothing ... whereas the *peshat* is the body ... as the Sages said, 'Scripture is according to its *peshat*' (*ha-miqra ki-peshuto*)."[93] In this telling paraphrase-modification of the talmudic *peshat* maxim, Ibn Ezra reveals that he took it to mean that the biblical text itself has but a single genuine sense: *peshuto shel miqra*. Indeed, the univocality of Scripture is a tenet expressed clearly by Ibn Ezra:

> The words of any author, whether a prophet or a sage, have but one meaning (*ṭa'am*), although those with great wisdom (i.e., the Rabbis) augment [this] and infer one thing from another thing ... at times by way of *derash* or by way of *asmakhta*. About this the early Sages, of blessed memory, said: "A biblical verse does not leave the realm of its *peshat*."[94]

Not surprisingly, Ibn Ezra elsewhere refers to *peshat* simply as "the truth" (*emet*) and "the essence" (*'iqqar*) of Scripture.[95]

[89] See, e.g., Cohen, "Aesthetic Exegesis," 284–289.
[90] See Mondschein, "One in a Thousand." [91] See Elbaum, *Perspectives*, 47–74.
[92] Ibn Ezra, Introduction to Lamentations This seems to have been his first Bible commentary, composed in Italy in 1140. See Sela and Freudenthal, "Chronological Listing," 23.
[93] Ibn Ezra, Introduction to Lamentations. [94] *Yesod Diqduq*, Allony ed., 86.
[95] See *Safah Berurah*, Wilensky ed., 288, cited in the Introduction, on p. 7.

While Ibn Ezra respects the creative ingenuity of midrash, he does not consider it genuine interpretation, relegating it instead to the status of *derash* and *asmakhta*, terms used in the Talmud to denote fanciful projections onto the biblical text. As Ibn Ezra avers:

> It is not appropriate for an educated person to be ignorant (lit., empty) of biblical wisdom [i.e., knowledge of Scripture], for [otherwise] when he finds written in the Talmud "As it says . . . [i.e., in a biblical citation]," he will not know from which biblical book it is, or if it is by way of *peshat* or *derash* or merely an *asmakhta*, for in their great wisdom and sharp analysis they deduce one thing from another. But they knew the *peshat* more than any of the subsequent generations.[96]

In arguing that the Rabbis themselves "knew the *peshat*," Ibn Ezra seeks to remain loyal to Rabbanite tradition.

For Ibn Ezra, then, "Scripture does not leave the realm of its *peshat*" means that *peshat* exegesis alone determines the correct meaning of the biblical text.[97] His is yet a third construal of the *peshat* maxim, to be placed alongside the two delineated above:

(3) *Very strong* reading – *peshat* is the only genuine interpretation of Scripture, no matter what other "readings" might be projected onto it by way of *derash*.

For Ibn Ezra, the *peshat* maxim announces the supremacy of *peshat* over midrash as the single correct sense of Scripture.

As a staunch Rabbanite, Ibn Ezra never dared challenge talmudic authority. What did he do, then, when the *peshat* contradicted the halakhic exegesis of the Rabbis – based on midrashic interpretation? The solution for Ibn Janah was simple: "the *peshat* of Scripture is one thing [lit., alone], and the halakhah is another [lit., alone]." In other words, Scripture bears both meanings. But Ibn Ezra's singular hermeneutic closed this path, leaving him with two options:

(1) *Deflection.* In many cases Ibn Ezra could deflect the rabbinic "reading" by asserting that a law purportedly "derived" by the Rabbis from a biblical source-text using one of the midrashic *middot* was actually known through an oral tradition given at Sinai. In that case, its midrashic "derivation" is merely an *asmakhta* or *derash*, neither of which impinge on the *peshat*.

(2) *Harmonization.* But in other cases Ibn Ezra was compelled to harmonize the rabbinic reading with his exegetical sensibilities. In

[96] *Yesod Mora* 1:4, Cohen and Simon ed., 77–78. [97] See Cohen, *Gates*, 74–82.

> such cases, he abandoned his own philological-contextual interpretation and deferred to the rabbinic halakhic reading – which he was then forced to acknowledge as the singular *peshat* interpretation.

Ibn Ezra's analysis of Lev 21:2–4, a passage discussed in Chapter 2, illustrates these two different options. The Talmud – followed by Rashi – records that a priest is permitted to defile himself to bury his deceased wife based on the assumption that "his *she'er* is his wife" in verses 1–3, "The Lord said to Moses: Speak to the priests, the sons of Aaron, and say to them: None shall defile himself for any [dead] person among his kin, except for the *she'er* that are closest to him: his mother, his father, his son, his daughter, his brother; also for a virgin sister ... " Ibn Ezra notes that "by way of *peshat*, the wife is never called *she'er*."[98] Instead, Ibn Ezra argues that the term *she'er* means *close kin* in general. This is followed by the detailed list of six permitted relatives: father, mother, son, daughter, brother, sister. In offering this philological interpretation, Ibn Ezra is following both Saadia in his *Tafsīr* and Ibn Janah in his dictionary.[99] Now Ibn Janah had stipulated that his own interpretations by way of *peshat* never impinge on the validity of halakhic midrash, as mentioned above. The dual hermeneutic allows these two layers of interpretation to coexist even when they are at odds with each other. That option, however, was not open to Ibn Ezra because he maintained a singular hermeneutic, i.e., that "the *peshat*" is the single correct sense of the biblical text. Hence, by stating that "by way of *peshat*, the wife is never called *she'er*" Ibn Ezra implicitly deflects the talmudic interpretation of the word. Accordingly, he posits that the Talmud's reading was not actually intended as an interpretation at all; rather, it is an *asmakhta*, i.e., an artificial "support" for the tradition transmitted orally that the wife is the seventh close relative for whom a priest may defile himself.[100]

The strategy of harmonization was required with respect to verse 4, "A husband among his people may not defile himself," about which Ibn Ezra writes:

> It would have seemed to us that ... the meaning of "*A husband* (*ba'al*) *among his people* ... " is that a husband may not defile himself for his wife. However, when we saw that our Rabbis transmitted the law that he may defile himself for his wife ... we must conclude that this interpretation is invalid.[101]

[98] Ibn Ezra on Lev 21:2, Weiser ed., III:72. [99] See Zucker, *Translation*, 387.

[100] Alternate introduction to the Pentateuch, "Fourth Way," Weiser ed., I:141.

[101] Ibn Ezra on Lev 21:4, Weiser ed., III:72.

Ibn Ezra here lets us into the laboratory of his mind, revealing how he would have interpreted these laws on his own: verses 2–3 permit the priest to become ritually defiled for six blood relatives, and verse 4 clarifies that he may not do so for his wife. Ibn Ezra then explains why this path was closed. Though he was willing to classify the rabbinic interpretation of *she'er* in verse 2 as an *asmakhta*, he would not admit a reading of a biblical passage, verse 4, that contradicts the halakhah attached to it.

Modern scholars have noted Ibn Ezra's tendency elsewhere to compromise his philological sensibilities and harmonize his *peshat* reading with the halakhah, something that Ibn Janah – and Rashbam (as discussed in Chapter 9) – do not do.[102] Yet this very strategy of harmonization can be traced to none other than Saadia, who established that a halakhic interpretive tradition may override the apparent sense of the text, i.e., the *ẓāhir*. It is important to note that Samuel ben Hofni equated the *ẓāhir* with the talmudic notion of *peshat*, making it a default option, to be adjusted as necessary. Ibn Ezra, on the other hand, defines *peshat* as the single correct meaning of the biblical text – after taking into account all relevant exegetical considerations, including the halakhic traditions of the Rabbis. For Samuel ben Hofni, *peshat* is the first step in the exegetical process; for Ibn Ezra it is the final conclusion.

Since he was not a talmudist, Ibn Ezra dared not draw halakhic conclusions from his *peshat* exegesis. That bold step would be taken by Moses Maimonides (1138–1204), an Andalusian émigré (born to an important rabbinic family in Cordoba) who fled first to Fez and Palestine but ultimately settled in Fustat. Maimonides is best known for his influential talmudic-halakhic (i.e., legal) works, especially his comprehensive Code of Jewish law, *Mishneh Torah*, and his groundbreaking philosophical opus, *The Guide of the Perplexed*, which recasts traditional Jewish thought through a largely Arabic-Aristotelian lens. Though he did not write running biblical commentaries, Maimonides' works manifest deep familiarity with the Andalusian exegetical tradition, and there is some evidence that he was influenced by the writings of Abraham Ibn Ezra. In any case, as a talmudist, Maimonides was in a position to take the singular hermeneutic formulated by Ibn Ezra to its logical conclusion in the realm of halakhah.

Although the Talmud, in practice, was the source of Rabbanite halakhah, Maimonides sought to identify the scriptural legal basis of the halakhah in his *Book of the Commandments*. That work is a systematic

[102] See Japhet, "Tension"; Simon, *Ear Discerns*, 100–133; Cohen, *Gates*, 365–375.

enumeration of the "613 commandments (*miṣwot*)" – a total number referred to often in rabbinic literature, but without a precise listing. Maimonides establishes as Principle 1 that this enumeration includes only commandments of biblical (*de-orayta*) force, not those commandments instituted by the Rabbis, which are of lesser rabbinic authority (*de-rabbanan*).[103] He thus excludes from this inventory rabbinically instituted commandments such as kindling the Hanukkah lights and reading the scroll of Esther on Purim, stating that the sole source of the 613 commandments is *nuṣūṣ Torah* ("the texts of the Torah"), i.e., the written record of the revelation at Mount Sinai.[104] Although the distinction between biblical and rabbinic law is talmudic, this emphasis on the biblical text is revolutionary, and leads to his formulation of Principle 2, that laws derived using the midrashic *middot* must be excluded from enumeration, as they derive from rabbinic authority only.[105]

Maimonides emphasizes that the commandments derived midrashically are binding. Yet, in his view, they must be excluded from the enumeration of the commandments. To justify this assertion, Maimonides draws upon a distinction in Muslim jurisprudence: the midrashically derived laws are like "branches" (*furūʿ*) extracted from the "roots" (*uṣūl*) – the original core of the 613 biblical commandments. Whereas the "roots" draw authority from the *naṣṣ* (the plain text of Scripture), the "branches" are based upon the sort of inference known in Muslim jurisprudence as *qiyās* (legal analogy or reasoning), the term by which Maimonides characterizes the midrashic hermeneutical rules.[106] To support the unique status of the "roots," Maimonides invokes the talmudic *peshat* maxim:

> The Sages of blessed memory taught us . . . : "a biblical verse does not leave the realm of its *peshat*" and the Talmud in many places inquires: "of what does the verse itself speak?" when they found a verse from which many matters are learned by way of midrashic commentary and inference.[107]

This rule would guide Maimonides in *Mishneh Torah*, his comprehensive code of Jewish law, in which he endeavors systematically to cite verses from the Pentateuch – rather than midrashic derivations – to establish the basis of the halakhah.[108] In this respect, he departs from Ibn Janah – who

[103] *Book of the Commandments*, Kafih ed., 9.
[104] *Book of the Commandments*, Kafih ed., 12.
[105] *Book of the Commandments*, Kafih ed., 12.
[106] *Book of the Commandments*, Kafih ed., 15.
[107] *Book of the Commandments*, Kafih ed., 14.
[108] See Cohen, *Gates*, 439–445; Twersky, *Code*, 57–58.

distinguished between *peshat* and halakhah, the latter being, in his view, based essentially on the midrashic reading of Scripture. Just how revolutionary Maimonides was in this respect can be gauged by the trenchant critique of the great Catalan talmudist Nahmanides (1194–1270):

> Principle 2 ... is shockingly beyond my comprehension, and I cannot bear it, for ... if so ... the truth is the *peshat* of Scripture alone, not the matters derived midrashically, as he mentions from their saying "A biblical verse does not leave the realm of its *peshat*." He thereby uproots the thirteen *middot* by which the Torah is interpreted and most of the Talmud that is established upon them.[109]

Nahmanides zeroes in on the sharp edge of Maimonides' reading of the *peshat* maxim: "the truth is the *peshat* of Scripture (*peshateh di-qera*) alone, not the matters derived midrashically." By "the truth," Nahmanides means to say that (for Maimonides) *peshuto shel miqra* is the single authoritative sense of Scripture. This actually echoes Ibn Ezra's singular model of *peshat*, except that Ibn Ezra refrained from drawing halakhic conclusions based on his *peshat* exegesis and accordingly accepted the notion that some biblical laws were transmitted orally, as mentioned earlier in this chapter.[110] Maimonides argues that *peshat* is the exclusive source of biblical law, whereas laws derived midrashically are of rabbinic authority only. Drawing the implications of the talmudic *peshat* maxim further than any of his predecessors had done, Maimonides transforms the theoretical underpinnings of halakhic jurisprudence.

To be sure, Maimonides' application of this principle of *peshat* primacy was quite complicated in practice, as he most often was forced to accommodate the details of talmudic law.[111] But his theoretical delineation of the halakhah based on the *peshat–derash* dichotomy was a radical step indeed, as were his bold adjustments of the halakhah accordingly in the few cases he did so.[112] It was criticized not only by Nahmanides, but also by other talmudists, such as Rabad of Posquières (c. 1120–1197/8) and Daniel ben Saadia ha-Bavli (Baghdad, twelfth century).[113]

What could have motivated Maimonides to take such a radical step? Three potential motives come to mind: (a) his exposure to Muslim jurisprudence; (b) the Karaite challenge; (c) the increasing prestige of *peshat* within the Rabbanite interpretive tradition.

109 *Hassagot*, Chavel ed., 44. 110 See also Cohen, *Gates*, 369–372.
111 See Cohen, *Gates*, 287–346, 384–401. 112 See Cohen, *Gates*, 401–426.
113 See Cohen, *Gates*, 304, 414–417.

(a) Maimonides embraced the distinction made in Muslim jurisprudence between a clear text (*naṣṣ*), which indicates God's will (*murād Allah*) with absolute certainty, and further inference by analogy (*qiyās*), which yields laws that are known to be correct with only a lesser degree of certainty. Aligning this epistemological–hermeneutical distinction with the *peshat–derash* dichotomy he knew from the Jewish exegetical tradition, Maimonides established a system for differentiating the numerous laws in the Talmud said to be "derived" from Scripture in undifferentiated ways. Muslim jurisprudence provided a set of theoretical categories that enabled Maimonides to separate out the original commandments "stated clearly" in Scripture (*naṣṣ/peshat*) and thus known with certainty to express God's will, i.e., the 613 commandments, as opposed to further midrashic legal inferences and derivations (*qiyās/middot*), which have rabbinic force only.

(b) Maimonides was aware of the Karaite critique of the Rabbis for disregarding what is stated explicitly in the Bible, and it is conceivable that his "rule of *peshat*" was devised to counter it.[114] Despite his professed disdain for Karaism, Maimonides cedes key points to its critique of the traditional Rabbanite account of halakhah.[115] Tacitly accepting a Karaite view, he acknowledges that the Rabbis used the *middot* to extrapolate laws from Scripture, rather than arguing (as some earlier Rabbanite authorities – including Saadia and Ibn Ezra – had done) that those laws were already known through an oral tradition and merely confirmed using the *middot*.[116] Nor could Maimonides return to a naïve reading of rabbinic literature and view the *middot* as genuine methods of interpretation, as talmudists unfamiliar with the *peshat* revolution might have been able to do. The possibility that remained for him was to create a stratified system to distinguish between the text of the Torah (*peshateh di-qera*) and laws derived midrashically.

(c) Notwithstanding the weightiness of the previous two factors, it seems to me that Maimonides probably could not have formulated his rule of *peshat* primacy if not for the increasing prestige ascribed to *peshuto shel miqra* within the Andalusian tradition he inherited.

114 See Twersky, *Code*, 84–86; Lasker, "Karaism," 146–150.

115 Indeed, Maimonides' openly negative attitude did not preclude his adoption of certain Karaite views that he deemed reasonable. See Lasker, "Karaism," 150–161.

116 See Halbertal, *People of the Book*, 55–63.

Ibn Janah turned to the talmudic *peshat* maxim to argue that "the *peshat* of Scripture" is inviolate, notwithstanding the authority he ascribed to midrash. Abraham Ibn Ezra took the next step by rendering *peshat* the single correct construal of Scripture and relegating midrash to a secondary status. As a master jurist, Maimonides built upon that foundation to argue that the halakhic authority of the Pentateuch (Torah, *orayta*) derives from *peshuto shel miqra* alone, to the exclusion of midrash.

Maimonides thus advances a fourth construal of the *peshat* maxim:

(4) *Super-strong* reading: *peshat* alone expresses Scripture's intent, and is the exclusive source of halakhah derived from the Bible (having biblical authority), whereas laws derived midrashically are of rabbinic authority only.

Taking the rule of *peshat* further than any of his predecessors had done, Maimonides transforms the theoretical underpinnings of halakhic jurisprudence.

ANDALUSIAN CONCEPTIONS OF PESHAT VS. CHRISTIAN SENSUS LITTERALIS

It was important to chart the trajectory of the Geonic and Andalusian conceptions of *peshat* in order to better evaluate the theory raised by Grossman that they could have influenced Rashi, in particular that his model can be traced to Ibn Janah's strong construal of the rule of *peshat* As we have seen, Ibn Janah was working with a geonic tradition that privileged the *ẓāhir*, a decisive step away from midrashic assumptions about Scripture that led to further development of biblical linguistics as an independent discipline. Whereas Saadia and Samuel ben Hofni were accomplished halakhic scholars, the great Andalusian linguists Menahem, Dunash, Hayyuj, and Ibn Janah specialized in grammar and philology. The latter therefore recruited the talmudic *peshat* maxim to justify his exclusively linguistic analysis of the biblical text that does not take halakhic interpretation into account. As a Rabbanite, Ibn Janah accepted the authority of rabbinic halakhic interpretation but effectively marginalized it as a special legal interpretive mode, allowing him to make "the *peshat* of Scripture" his exclusive goal. Abraham Ibn Ezra would take the next logical step by asserting that *peshat* is the single genuine sense of Scripture and that midrashic "exegesis" is simply "an added idea," or an *asmakhta*. Maimonides follows this way of thinking about *peshat* to its logical conclusion, arguing that only "the *peshat* of Scripture" yields laws of biblical authority, whereas laws derived through the midrashic *middot* are merely of rabbinic authority.

For Rashi, "the *peshat* of Scripture" is not a final goal, as it was for Ibn Janah – and as it would be for Ibn Ezra. Notwithstanding his strongly articulated interest in "the *peshat* of Scripture," Rashi evidently still regarded midrashic interpretation – conducted within the proper parameters – as the essential conduit for a true understanding the biblical text. In other words, Rashi never really questioned the ancient rabbinic perception of the biblical text as a cipher meant to be decoded through midrashic exegesis. Rashi's thinking about the relationship between "the *peshat* of Scripture" and midrash is illuminated by some of the theoretical remarks made by his grandson Rashbam. Even though the latter focused his attention on "the *peshat* of Scripture," he acknowledged that "the essence (*'iqqar*) of the Torah comes to teach and inform us the *haggadot* (traditions, lore), *halakhot* (laws), and *dinim* (regulations) through the hints of (*remizat*) the *peshat* by way of redundant language, and through the thirty-two hermeneutical rules (*middot*) of R. Eliezer ... and the thirteen hermeneutical rules (*middot*) of R. Ishmael."[117] Both Rashi and Rashbam were steeped in talmudic tradition. Their foray into "the *peshat* of Scripture" entailed the exploration and development of what was effectively an ancillary mode of interpretation intended to supplement, but not to replace, midrashic interpretation.

This conception of *peshat* in Rashi's school can be illuminated by comparison with the Christian characterization of the literal sense as the "foundation" (*fundamentum*) for the spiritual sense. This metaphor is famously articulated by Hugh of St. Victor:

> The student of sacred Scripture ought to look among history, allegory, and tropology ... [as] we see happen in the construction of buildings, where first the foundation is laid, then the structure is raised upon it, and finally, when the work is all finished, the house is decorated by the laying on of color ... You will [not] be able to become perfectly sensitive to allegory unless you have first been grounded in history.[118]
>
> We call by the name "history" not only the recounting of actual deeds, but also the first meaning of any narrative which uses words according to their proper

[117] Rashbam on Gen 37:2, cited in the Introduction, on p. 9.

[118] Hugh, *Didascalicon*, Book Six, Chapters 2–3, Taylor trans., 135–136. See also Minnis and Scott, *Literary Theory*, 74. For a discussion of the implications of this metaphor, see Coolman, "*Pulchrum Esse*," 189–194.

nature [i.e., literally]. And in this sense of the word ... all the books of either Testament ... belong to this study in their literal meaning.[119]

Although Hugh was much younger than Rashi, these words are drawn from a much older source – Gregory the Great's *Moralia in Job*, which Hugh cites:

Just as you see that every building lacking a foundation cannot stand firm, so also is it in learning. The foundation ... is history, from which ... the truth of allegory is extracted ... As [Gregory advised:] "lay first the foundation of history; next, by pursuing the 'typical' meaning, build up a structure in your mind to be a fortress of faith. Last of all, however, through the loveliness of morality paint the structure over as with the most beautiful colors."[120]

Gregory's work was highly influential, and his characterization of the historical sense as the "foundation" for the spiritual senses was commonly repeated in the early Middle Ages by, for example, Bede (673–735), Rabanus Maurus (780–856), and Rupert of Deutz (1075–1129).[121] The recurrence of this hermeneutical conception in the Latin tradition before and during Rashi's time makes it more likely that it would have been known to him if he discussed Bible interpretation with learned Christians.

Even if, historically speaking, Rashi knew of Ibn Janah's construal of the *peshat* maxim, it is evident that he recast it to fit a different hermeneutical hierarchy, in which the philological-contextual interpretation of Scripture (*peshuto shel miqra*) was only a baseline upon which to construct a commentary consisting primarily of a critical selection of rabbinic midrashic interpretations. Here is where the resemblance to the Christian hermeneutical model that emerged in the school of Rheims proves significant, since it provides a closer parallel than Ibn Janah to the way that Rashi negotiated the newly developed philological methods and the midrashic tradition. Like his Christian neighbors in the cathedral schools of northern France who followed Bruno's grammatical hermeneutic, which drew upon patristic interpretations selectively, Rashi did not regard philological-contextual analysis of the Bible as an end unto itself, but rather as a stepping stone for engaging in a systematic, selective commentary drawn from midrashic sources.

119 Hugh, *Didascalicon*, Book Six, Chapter 3, Taylor trans., 138. See also Minnis and Scott, *Literary Theory*, 76.

120 Hugh, *Didascalicon*, Book Six, Chapter 3, Taylor trans., 138. See also Minnis and Scott, *Literary Theory*, 76–77. The citation is from section 3 of the dedicatory epistle to Leander in Gregory's *Moralia in Job*, Adriaen ed., 4, Kerns trans., 51.

121 See de Lubac, *Exégèse médiéval*, I/2:434–439, who traces this image to Origen and Jerome.

Although the hypothesis that Rashi actually knew of Bruno's exegetical work remains conjectural, the comparison between these two eleventh-century northern French Bible interpreters unquestionably helps us better understand their cultural world and sheds light on how Rashi would have conceived his *peshat* project. This, in turn, suggests an answer to the key question that has been asked about Rashi: Given that he knew how to determine *peshuto shel miqra*, why did Rashi not make it the exclusive focus of his commentary? As mentioned in Chapter 2, this question was raised by Moshe Ahrend in criticizing Kamin's understanding that *peshat* was not Rashi's primary interpretive goal. If we were to view Rashi as a puzzle piece, this would be like trying to fit him into the wrong puzzle. The assumption underlying Ahrend's question betrays the modern bias in favor of *peshuto shel miqra* – in the sense used in contemporary discourse, i.e., the "true" meaning of the ancient biblical text, determined through scientific philological study.[122] A medieval precedent for this modern perspective developed in the Andalusian school, influenced by Saadia, who had constructed his hermeneutical system in the spirit of Qur'an 3:7, which privileges the *muḥkamāt.* The idea that these "clear verses" are the "essence" of Scripture powered the marginalization of midrash in the Andalusian school.[123] But both Rashi and his Christian neighbors, much as they disagreed about the "true" meaning of the Hebrew Bible, shared the traditional view that its essence is not to be found at the surface, but rather in its deeper sense. Understandably, then, Rashi's goal was not to devise a *peshat* commentary but rather to compose one that selectively incorporates midrash to "settle the words of Scripture."

There is, as we have mentioned, no direct evidence that Rashi was aware of Bruno's exegetical work, nor of any specifically grammatical- or literal-sense Christian interpretations of Scripture, for that matter. If so, one may ask why this conjecture is any better than the theories that Rashi's *peshat* method was inspired by the Andalusian exegetical tradition. Two answers can be given to this question. To begin with, we would have expected Rashi to quote earlier Jewish authorities – such as Samuel ben Hofni or Ibn Janah – regarding the importance of *peshuto shel miqra* if he knew of any, and the absence of any reference to them in his writings therefore suggests that Rashi was unaware of any Jewish precedents on this matter. Indeed, Rashbam cites Rashi's interest in *peshuto shel miqra*

[122] See Cohen, "Emergence," 204–205.

[123] It is not surprising that Ibn Ezra was especially critical of Christian allegorical readings of the Bible. See Cohen, "Maimonides' Attitude," 459–466, 474–475.

as completely innovative in the Jewish interpretive tradition, which further weakens the theory that either of them was aware of other streams of *peshat* exegesis.[124] On the other hand, if Rashi was, in fact, exposed to Bruno's exegetical methods, it is understandable that he would not have cited a Christian source, even if it prompted him to engage in his novel exegetical program.

More significantly, the methodological parallels between the commentarial modes of Rashi and Bruno are actually closer than those of Rashi to Ibn Janah. The latter treated contextual-philological (*peshat*) interpretation as an end unto itself, implying that it represents the full and proper exegesis of the biblical text. Rashi clearly had a different hermeneutical hierarchy in mind: his interest in *peshuto shel miqra* was part of a larger program to compose a commentary critically drawn from midrashic sources that adhere to systematic criteria, namely correspondence to the sense and sequence of Scripture – in Rashi's words that "settle/are settled upon (*mityashevim 'al*) the words of Scripture," much as Bruno sought to compose a Christological Psalms commentary featuring a critical selection of patristic interpretations that fulfill the criteria of the discipline of *grammatica* that was used to interpret the pagan poets.

[124] See Rashbam on Gen 37:2, Rosin ed., 49, cited in the Introduction, on p. 9.

5

Comparison to the Byzantine Exegetical School

Until almost the very end of the twentieth century, it was assumed that Rashi was the first Rabbanite Jewish interpreter in Christian lands to have composed Bible commentaries that depart from midrashic interpretation and apply a philological-contextual mode of exegesis to arrive at what Rashi termed *peshuto shel miqra*. This assumption was proven wrong with the publication by Nicholas de Lange in 1996 of a commentary by a certain Reuel on Ezekiel and the Minor Prophets found in the Cairo Genizah that is believed to have been completed by the year 1000 in Asia Minor, perhaps in Byzantium itself.[1] Written in Hebrew with occasional Greek glosses, the commentary manifests a remarkably developed contextual-philological mode of interpretation independent of midrashic exegesis. We had long been aware of a Karaite exegetical school in Byzantium, which has its roots in the tenth-century project of Tobiah ben Moses to translate into Hebrew important Karaite exegetical works of the Jerusalem school earlier in the tenth century, which were penned in Arabic.[2] But linguistic and stylistic analysis of Reuel's writing indicates that he was a Rabbanite and not a Karaite.[3] On the other hand, the Byzantine commentary on 1 Kings published by de Lange has been demonstrated by Richard Steiner to be Karaite, perhaps penned by Tobiah ben

[1] De Lange, *Greek Jewish Texts*, 165–294.

[2] Tobiah ben Moses studied in the Jerusalem Karaite school and composed translations of the great Karaite exegetical works of the "Golden Age." See Ankori, *Karaites in Byzantium*, 415–451.

[3] See Steiner, "Byzantine Biblical Commentaries," 260*–262*.

Moses; and Steiner also considers it likely that the highly fragmentary glosses on Genesis and Joshua published by de Lange are also the remnant of a Karaite commentary.[4]

In the same publication de Lange also presents another commentary, actually a collection of glosses, on Genesis and Exodus, termed "Scholia on the Pentateuch" by de Lange, which shares important features with Reuel's commentary and is thought to be from approximately the same time and place.[5] Although the Pentateuch Scholia draws heavily on midrashic sources, it exhibits a keen interest in philological-grammatical issues, and resembles the other Byzantine commentaries, both Rabbanite and Karaite, in its format and style. The Scholia thus suggests that Reuel's commentary was not a unicum, but rather represents the fragmentary remnants of a school of exegesis among Rabbanite Jews in Byzantine lands, one that can even be traced to Hebrew–Greek Bible glossaries dating as early as 900 that indicate lexicographic study of the Bible.[6] Further evidence for the continued vibrancy of this school can be brought from the work of Tobiah ben Eliezer, who wrote his *Leqaḥ Ṭov* commentary in the late eleventh century. Although he is a contemporary (perhaps a younger contemporary) of Rashi, the linguistic and exegetical affinities between his commentaries and the earlier ones indicate the continuity of a Rabbanite Byzantine exegetical school – perhaps in writings that have been lost.[7]

Reuel's commentary and the Scholia have in common what Richard Steiner has termed "a critical lack of linguistic terminology."[8] Although both manifest an interest in grammatical and philological issues, they are severely limited by the meager terminology provided by ancient rabbinic sources. By contrast, by the tenth century a highly developed system of linguistic terminology had been constructed by authors in the Muslim East – both Karaite and Rabbanite – in the Judeo-Arabic school, which drew heavily upon the formidable achievements of Arabic linguistics in the ninth century. As Steiner notes, the Karaite Byzantine commentary on 1 Kings, though written in Hebrew, draws upon that rich linguistic terminology – translated into Hebrew.[9] Even Rashi had access to the

[4] Steiner, "Byzantine Biblical Commentaries," 246*–260*.

[5] See de Lange, *Greek Jewish Texts*, 85–116.

[6] See de Lange, *Greek Jewish Texts*, 71–84; de Lange, "Early Glossary"; Tchernetska, Olszowy-Schlanger, and de Lange, "Hebrew–Greek Glossary."

[7] See Brin, *Reuel*, 449–462. [8] Steiner, "'Lemma Complement,'" 368–369.

[9] Steiner, "'Lemma Complement,'" 369.

linguistic works of Menahem and Dunash, of which there is no trace in Reuel's commentary or the Pentateuch Scholia. Steiner goes on to remark:

> Reuel's commentary and the commentary on Genesis and Exodus show us what medieval biblical exegesis might have looked like had the Jews remained oblivious to the work of the Arab grammarians. They help us to appreciate the magnitude of the revolution brought about by the decision of Saadia Gaon and his Andalusian successors to embrace the systematic study of language.[10]

Notwithstanding that limitation, the sustained interest in linguistic matters manifested in the Rabbanite Byzantine commentaries led them to important achievements in this realm. As Steiner notes, their discovery thus proves to be critically important "for reconstructing the history of Jewish biblical exegesis in the Middle Ages."[11]

The discovery of the tenth- and early eleventh-century Rabbanite Byzantine commentaries led rather rapidly to speculation about their possible impact on later streams of Jewish exegesis, especially on Rashi. Unlike the Judeo-Arabic exegetical works, the Byzantine commentaries, penned in Hebrew, would have been an open book for Rashi – if he indeed had access to them. Israel M. Ta-Shma boldly posited that Rashi must have been aware of this tradition and that it was the chief catalyst for him to focus on "the *peshat* of Scripture."[12] The aim of the current chapter is to evaluate that theory and its implications.

REUEL AND THE SCHOLIA ON THE PENTATEUCH

The lexicographic works of Menahem and Dunash provided Rashi with access to the early linguistic achievements of the Judeo-Arabic school that originated in the Muslim East and was transplanted to al-Andalus in the tenth century. But Menahem's dictionary and Dunash's critical glosses are not Bible commentaries. If Rashi knew of Reuel's commentaries and the Scholia on the Pentateuch, they would have provided him with a model of a running commentary on the Bible guided by linguistic concerns – by contrast to the exclusively midrashic models prevalent in his Ashkenazic milieu. As Ta-Shma notes, Reuel's commentaries, and even the more midrashic Scholia on the Pentateuch, manifest many of the distinctive features that characterize Rashi's *peshat* commentaries. These Byzantine works are consecutive running commentaries on the biblical text that:

10 Steiner, "'Lemma Complement,'" 370.
11 Steiner, "'Lemma Complement,'" 368.
12 Ta-Shma, *Studies: Italy & Byzantium*, 247–248.

- focus on the language of Scripture, rather than primarily seeking its hidden messages beneath the surface, as midrashic interpretation tends to do;
- use vernacular glosses (in Greek) to clarify words and expressions; and
- adhere to principles of philology and grammar, as well as the literary context.[13]

Furthermore, Steiner has also noted a number of distinctive stylistic and methodological parallels between the Byzantine commentaries and Rashi (not typical of midrashic literature), which stem from their shared aim to make the biblical text intelligible on the most basic linguistic level.[14] Very often this simply entails clarifying the referent of a pronoun that is otherwise vague. For example, on Gen 18:10, "Then one said, 'I will return to you next year, and your wife Sarah shall have a son.' Sarah was listening at the entrance of the tent, and it was behind him," Rashi comments:

And it was behind him – the opening was behind the angel.[15]

In the Scholia on this verse we find, similarly:

And it was behind him – ["it" refers to] the opening.[16]

At times the analysis of a vague pronoun is followed by the analysis of a further philological difficulty in the verse. For example, on Exod 17:15, "And Moses built an altar, and he called its name 'The Lord is my miracle'," Rashi comments:

He called its name – [i.e.,] the name of the altar – "*The Lord is my miracle,*" [meaning] The Holy One Blessed be He performed a miracle for us here.[17]

Similarly, in the Scholia, we find:

He called its name – [i.e.,] the name of the altar – saying "*The Lord is my miracle.*"[18]

Both Rashi and the Scholia manifest the identical objective: to clarify the object of the pronoun "its."

[13] Ta-Shma, *Studies: Italy & Byzantium*, 241–247.
[14] The discussion and examples below are taken largely from Steiner, "Rabbanite Biblical Commentaries."
[15] Rashi on Gen 18:10, Berliner ed., 34.
[16] Scholia on Gen 18:10, de Lange, *Greek Jewish Texts*, 88–89.
[17] Rashi on Exod 17:15, Berliner ed., 141.
[18] Scholia on Exod 17:15, de Lange, *Greek Jewish Texts*, 106–107.

This is a case of a style identified by Steiner, which he terms "the lemma complement," i.e., "a quotation from the verse that continues – following the comment – from the point where the lemma left off, a quotation with no subsequent comment."[19] In such cases, the commentator adds a word or a few words into the verse to guide the reader toward its proper understanding, for example, by clarifying the referent of a pronoun that is otherwise vague. As Rashi on Exod 14:20, "And it lit up the night," comments:

And it lit up – i.e., the fire [lit up] – *the night.*[20]

Exactly the same comment is found in the Scholia.[21]

Some of the same sorts of parallel exegetical concerns and shared stylistic features emerge from a comparison between Rashi and Reuel. For example, on Ezek 21:28, "And it shall be unto them as a false divination in their sight," Rashi comments:

And it shall be unto them – what Nebuchadnezzar did shall be for Israel – *as a false divination*, and they will not believe that he will succeed.

Similarly, in Reuel's commentary:

And it shall be unto them – for Israel, the *divination* that Nebuchadnezzar did – *as a false divination in their sight*, for Israel said "the divination of Nebuchadnezzar is false."[22]

At times is it evident that Reuel and Rashi share the same sort of linguistic concerns, even if they comment on different words in the same verse. For example, we can compare the commentaries of Rashi and Reuel on Ezek 7:19–20, "They shall cast their silver in the streets, and their gold shall be removed . . . As for the beauty of his ornament, he set it in majesty: but they made the images of their abominations and of their detestable things therein: therefore have I set it far from them." Rashi comments on the first part of verse 20:

The beauty of his ornament – of God – *which He set in majesty* (Heb. *gaon*) – that is the Holy Temple, which is called "majesty . . . " as it says "Thus saith the Lord God; Behold, I will profane my sanctuary, the majesty (*gaon*) of your strength" (Ezek 24:21). They, *through their abominations and of their detestable things therein* which they did . . .

Reuel comments on verse 20:

[19] Steiner, "'Lemma Complement,'" 370. [20] Rashi on Exod 14:20, Berliner ed., 131.
[21] Scholia on Exod 14:20, de Lange, *Greek Jewish Texts*, 104–105.
[22] Reuel on Ezek 21:28, de Lange, *Greek Jewish Texts*, 212–213.

He put on for pride – fine clothing which he used to put on for pride. *Therefore*: because they used to make out of that gold and silver *images and idols, I have given it* – the gold and the silver – *to them* – to Israel – as *niddah* – ... that the enemy will take and convey to Babylon.[23]

Like Reuel before him, Rashi seeks to explain the connection among the constituent elements in the verse on a simple linguistic level.

Reuel's commentary manifests a distinctively philological style, as he regularly explains difficult biblical locutions based on the immediate context and based on similar expressions within the Bible – a methodology employed, for example, by his Andalusian contemporaries Menahem and Dunash, followed by Rashi. For example, in his commentary on Ezek 9:9 ("The iniquity of the Houses of Israel and Judah is very very great, and the land is full of blood, and the city full of *muṭṭeh* [lit. slanted?]"), Reuel argues that the difficult word *muṭṭeh* in this context must mean *murder victims*, "because [the parallel phrase] 'and the land is full of bloodshed' will not allow you to interpret it in a different sense."[24] Intuitively, Reuel here is following the principle established by Menahem ben Saruq that

The first half of the verse informs us about the second half. It would be enough with that first half, but there is a repetition and the same meaning appears twice in the same verse.[25]

Accordingly, it is possible to discern the sense of a unique biblical term by comparison with the corresponding one used in a parallel verset.[26] This principle, which would be applied by Rashi and, even more so, by Rashbam, was already applied by Reuel – in an ad hoc manner on Ezek 9:9.[27]

Seeking stylistic and linguistic patterns in Biblical Hebrew, Reuel regularly uses the term "you find" (*timṣa'*) or "you often find" (*harbeh timṣa'*) when pointing out that seemingly anomalous grammatical forms can be explained as regular biblical conventions – a departure from the midrashic tendency to seize upon such anomalies to extrapolate new information. For example, he argues that the redundant particle *et* (usually the direct

[23] Reuel on Ezek 21:28, de Lange, *Greek Jewish Texts*, 172–173.

[24] Reuel on Ezek 9:9, de Lange, *Greek Jewish Texts*, 176–177.

[25] *Maḥberet*, s.v., אוב, Sáenz-Badillos ed., 17*. See also *Maḥberet*, s.v., הי, Sáenz-Badillos ed., 137*–139*; Kugel, *Idea*, 176–177. In formulating this rule, Menahem manifests a rudimentary grasp of what later Bible interpreters and scholars would define as biblical "parallelism." See Kugel, *Idea*, 1–15; Watson, *Classical Hebrew Poetry*, 114–159.

[26] See, e.g., *Maḥberet*, s.v., שער, Sáenz-Badillos ed., 385*. Cf. Ibn Ezra, commentary on Gen 49:6.

[27] See Harris, *Discerning Parallelism*, 35–47, 55–73.

object indicator) in Ezek 21:17 and 39:14 is not truly anomalous: "Do not be troubled by the *et* because you can find many similar occurrences, for example, 'And *et* Moses was brought back to Pharaoh' (Exod 10:8)."[28] He similarly notes twice in his Ezekiel commentary that words written defectively are normal in Biblical Hebrew and therefore must be interpreted as if they were written *plene* (i.e., spelled full), an observation at odds with midrashic exegetical practice as noted by Abraham Ibn Ezra.[29] In two cases Reuel notes that a word is attested in the Bible in both masculine and feminine forms, even though the norm for Hebrew words is to be consistently one or the other.[30]

Even though he is hampered by the lack of terminology or systematic grammatical thought, Reuel marks a departure from midrashic interpretation toward philological exegesis – the earliest attested among Jewish authors in Christian lands. As Steiner remarks regarding Reuel's work:

> In this new era of exegesis, the task of the exegete is to find parallels for such forms instead of viewing them in isolation and providing a midrashic explanation. The search for parallels, the quest to eliminate anomalies, the emphasis on *derekh ha-miqra'ot* ("the typical manner of the verses," i.e., biblical style [MC]), is such an integral part of medieval and modern *peshaṭ* exegesis that we often take it for granted, forgetting how subversive it was to the old order. Linguistic anomalies are the life-blood of midrash, and eliminating them reduces the number of pegs on which to hang didactic lessons.[31]

These are indeed features of Rashi's *peshat* exegesis – and that of his students in northern France. It is noteworthy, for example, that Rashi uses a similar formula to assure his readers that seemingly anomalous grammatical phenomena in the text are actually regular features of Biblical Hebrew and need not trigger a midrashic interpretation. For example, in his commentary on Exod 15:2, "The Lord is my strength and might, and He is become [*wa-yehi*] my deliverance," Rashi remarks:

> Do not be puzzled about the expression *wa-yehi*, [i.e.,] that it does not say *hayah* [the normally expected grammatical form], for there are verses worded this way,

[28] Reuel on Ezek 21:17, de Lange, *Greek Jewish Texts*, 210–211.

[29] See, e.g., Reuel on Ezek 39:26 ("You often find [*harbeh timṣa'*] words spelled defectively that are to be interpreted as though they were written *plene*") and a similar note on Ezek 13:18. See de Lange, *Greek Jewish Texts*, 234–235, 188–189. Cf. Ibn Ezra on Exod 20:1 (long commentary). See also Cohen, *Three Approaches*, 245.

[30] Ezek 10:14 ("You find the word *ḥayyah* both in masculine and feminine"). See de Lange, *Greek Jewish Texts*, 178–179. See also the similar comment on Hos 5:9. This grammatical observation is also made in the Scholia on Gen 32:8.

[31] Steiner, "Rabbanite Biblical Commentaries."

and this is an example: "[against] the walls of the house around [both] the temple and the sanctuary, he made (*wa-ya'as*) chambers around [it]" (1 Kgs 6:5). It should have said "He made (*'asah*) chambers around [it]" [instead of *wa-ya'as*].[32]

Rashi expresses himself similarly elsewhere in his commentaries.[33]

Modern scholars have noted a particularly striking exegetical feature shared by Reuel and the Pentateuch Scholia: the concern they manifest, admittedly in only a handful of cases, with the work of a biblical narrator-editor, who arranged the words of the biblical prophets in their current form in Scripture.[34] Although this feature does not have a direct echo in Rashi's exegesis, it does find strong parallels in that of the circle of his students (as discussed in Chapter 9). Reuel uses the term *sadran*, "the one who arranges," to refer to such a narrator-editor, and he attributes three anomalies in the Book of Ezekiel to him. In treating two of them, Reuel presents the *sadran* as editing a single source; in dealing with the third, he portrays him as dealing with multiple, divergent sources.

A key task of the *sadran*, in Reuel's conception, was to decide on the order of presentation in order to regulate the flow of information to the reader. A *sadran* working with a preexisting text might attempt to clarify it by inserting information that would be helpful to the reader at a given point. Reuel assumes that this information was already present in the text, and that the *sadran* merely repeated it at an earlier point for the reader's convenience, in anticipation of a question. For example, the Book of Ezekiel cites the words of the prophet describing how "a spirit lifted me up between the earth and the heaven, and brought me in visions of God to Jerusalem, to the entrance of the inner gate that faces north; that was the site of the infuriating image that provokes fury" (Ezek 8:3). At a later point, Ezekiel's words are cited again: "And he said to me, 'O mortal, turn your eyes northward.' I turned my eyes northward, and behold, north of the gate of the altar, was that infuriating image on the approach" (Ezek 8:5). On this verse Reuel remarks:

that infuriating image on the approach – From here the *sadran* learned of it and mentioned it above.[35]

Reuel argues that the *sadran*, i.e., one who eventually committed Ezekiel's prophecies to writing, added the relative clause "that was the site of the

[32] Rashi on Exod 15:2, Berliner ed., 132–133.

[33] See, e.g., Rashi on Gen 20:13, 24:21, 26:26; Exod 3:2, 15:9; Josh 3:1; Ps 10:3, 118:14.

[34] See Steiner, "Redaction," 124–148.

[35] Reuel on Ezek 8:5, de Lange *Greek Jewish Texts*, 174–175.

infuriating image that provokes fury" in Ezek 8:3, which was not originally included in Ezekiel's words there. His reasoning seems to be that the prophet only first learned of "that infuriating image on the approach" when he subsequently lifted his eyes to the north at the gate of the altar, as recounted in Ezek 8:5. (The expression "and behold ... " [Heb. *we-hinneh*] implies surprise at seeing something for the first time.) It is from that verse that the *sadran* learned of the "infuriating image" and added it in verse 3 to give this information to the reader already at that point.[36]

A similar approach is adopted by Reuel with respect to the detailed description of the cherubs in Ezek 1:8–21. The prophet Ezekiel seems to record his initial vision of cherubs in Ezek 10:8–17, where he provides his own detailed description. On this Reuel remarks:

> From here [the *sadran*] learned well what [the cherubs] were like, and mentioned them above.[37]

Although the *sadran* is not actually mentioned here explicitly, the language of this comment is so similar to the first that there can be little doubt about the subject of this sentence. Here again, Reuel feels that the detailed description of the cherubs in 1:8–21 was not written by Ezekiel but was added by the *sadran*, apparently for the benefit of the curious reader, based on the information given in 10:8–17. Reuel's view, then, is that the author of Ezekiel left temporary lacunae in the reader's knowledge and that the *sadran* filled them with information found later in the book.

The aforementioned two references to the work of the *sadran* by Reuel would seem to have a close affinity to the concept of the *mudawwin* used in tenth-century Karaite exegesis, especially by Yefet ben Eli (late tenth century). The active participle of the verb *d-w-n* in form II, meaning *to put down in writing* (e.g., a collection of poems known as a *diwān*), this term seems to connote the biblical narrator-editor as well. Some scholars posit, or at least entertain the possibility, that Yefet and other Karaite authors used this term to connote a later editor reworking earlier sources.[38] However, as Haggai Ben-Shammai and Eran Viezel argue, convincingly to my mind, the *mudawwin* can usually be identified with the original author of the biblical book, i.e., the prophet arranging or providing a narrative frame for his own prophecies, e.g., Moses (in the Pentateuch)

[36] See Steiner, "Redaction," 125.

[37] Commentary on Ezek 10:8, de Lange, *Greek Jewish Texts*, 178–179.

[38] See Polliack, "Karaite Conception"; Zawanowska, *Abraham Narratives*, 41–57.

or Hosea (in the book bearing his name).[39] Reuel's *sadran*, on the other hand, is clearly a figure other than Ezekiel who arranged and compiled the prophet's writings. Despite this difference, the concepts are closely related. It is thus conceivable that the conception of the *mudawwin* circulated in late tenth-century Byzantium, where the Karaite Jerusalem school exerted substantial influence, and that it came to the attention of Reuel, who adapted it in his conception of the *sadran*.

The second role that Reuel assigns to the *sadran* involves a much bolder claim about the final editing of the prophetic books, at times from multiple and contradictory sources. In his commentary on Ezek 35:6, Reuel remarks:

> The *sadran* found two manuscripts. In one was written: "Therefore, as I live, I shall give you over to blood and blood shall pursue you"; and in the other manuscript was written: "Therefore, as I live, says the Lord God, surely blood you hate and blood shall pursue you."[40]

Evidently disturbed by the redundant language of this verse, Reuel argues that the editor of Ezekiel worked from two manuscripts that had different versions of the same sentence and that he decided to preserve both of them.[41]

There is a precedent for this bold presumption regarding the formation of the biblical text in the late rabbinic works *Numbers Rabbah* and *Avot de-Rabbi Natan*, which speak of "ten dotted expressions in the Torah," i.e., words over which dots appear in the text. According to *Avot de-Rabbi Natan* and one opinion cited in *Numbers Rabbah*, Ezra the Scribe (fifth century BCE) dotted these words because he was unsure about the correctness of the text.[42] The Pentateuch Scholia seems to be referring to this very tradition – and elaborates on it – in the gloss on one of the examples given in both rabbinic sources, "Esau ran to greet him [i.e., Jacob]. He embraced him, and, falling on his neck, and he kissed him; and they wept" (Gen 33:4):

> Why is "and he kissed him" dotted? Some say that Ezra found a manuscript in which the word was written and another in which it was not written, and so he dotted it, and if you remove the word, the verse is not diverted (*ne'ekav*) from its *peshat*. And so it is with all of the dotted words in Scripture.[43]

39 See Ben-Shammai, "*Mudawwin*"; Viezel, "Medieval Commentators on Composition of the Bible," 132–147.

40 Commentary on Ezek 35:6, de Lange, *Greek Jewish Texts*, 226–227.

41 See Steiner, "Redaction," 135.

42 See *Avot de-Rabbi Natan*, version B, chapter 37, Schechter ed., 97–98; *Numbers Rabbah* 3:13. See also Weiss Halivni, *Peshat & Derash*, 139–140; Steiner, "Redaction," 138–139.

43 Scholia on Gen 33:4, de Lange, *Greek Jewish Texts*, 94–95.

We shall return below to the fact that the Scholia here seems to be invoking the talmudic *peshat* maxim. For now we note that, according to the opinion cited here, the doubt that led Ezra to put dots over letters arose from a conflict between two manuscripts – the very same assumption that Reuel adopts in his commentary on Ezek 35:6 cited above.[44]

The text-critical interpretation of the dotted words stands in opposition to the midrashic approach more typically applied in rabbinic sources. In line with the perception of Scripture as a perfect literary composition without errors or internal contradictions, the Rabbis generally did not assume that the dotting indicates doubt about the correctness of the text, but rather about the standing of its literal sense or about the sincerity of the action it describes.[45] Rashi, who does not adopt Reuel's conception of the *sadran*, either in his commentary on Ezekiel or elsewhere, remains faithful to the midrashic approach. As Rashi remarks:

> *And he kissed him* – There are dots over the word. There is controversy concerning this matter in a *baraita* of *Sifrei*. Some interpret the dots to mean that he did not kiss him wholeheartedly. Rabbi Simeon ben Yohai said: It is a well known tradition that Esau hated Jacob, but his compassion was moved at that time, and he kissed him wholeheartedly.[46]

Rashi avoids the text-critical approach and assumes that the dots teach something new about the action described by the expression "and he kissed him." According to the first opinion Rashi cites, the dots indicate that the kiss was not given sincerely, whereas Rabbi Simeon ben Yohai suggests that the dots point to the fact that this kiss, given sincerely, was exceptional for Esau, who otherwise hated Jacob absolutely.

As mentioned above, the early Byzantine exegetes do not seem to have had access to developments in the Andalusian linguistic school reflected in the works of Menahem and Dunash, which were avidly used by Rashi. The result of this disparity can be seen, for example, by comparing the commentary of Rashi with the Pentateuch Scholia on Gen 29:27, in the account of Laban speaking with Jacob about marrying Rachel immediately after having been tricked into marrying Leah. Laban utters a sentence that might, at first glance, be rendered in English: "Let this week (*shevu'a zot*) be completed." However, the author of the Scholia

[44] Cf. Butin, Ten Nequdoth, 113–117.

[45] See Shinan, "Ten Dotted Passages." On the midrashic assumption regarding the "perfection" of Scripture, see Kugel, *Bible as it Was*, 20–21.

[46] Rashi on Gen 33:4, Berliner ed., 68.

points to the fact that the pronoun *zot* ("this") is feminine, whereas the Hebrew term for week (*shavu'a*) is masculine:

Let the week [of] this (τούτης), i.e., of Leah [be completed]. For *shavu'a* (week) is a masculine term.[47]

As Steiner notes, the Scholia fails to make the more important grammatical distinction here, namely that the Hebrew term for week (*shavu'a*) here is in the construct state, as indicated by its pointing (i.e., vocalization): *shevu'a*, meaning "the week of ... " By contrast, Rashi here has a more sophisticated analysis:

Let the week be filled – the word for "week" is in the construct state (lit., attached: *davuq*), as indicated by the pointing of the *shin* with a *shewa*. And it means: *the seven-day period of this one*, i.e., the seven days of the wedding feast ... And it is not possible to say that it means an actual calendar week, because then the *shin* should have been pointed with a *pataḥ* (the term Rashi uses for what we call a *qameṣ*). Additionally, *shavu'a* in the sense of *a week* is masculine... Thus we must conclude that the term *shavu'a* here means *a period of seven days*, *septaine* in the vernacular (*la'az*; i.e., Old French).[48]

Rashi's concern is similar to that of the Scholia. But Rashi had more sophisticated terminology at his disposal that allows him to describe the construct state – using the term *davuq*, which, as Steiner notes, he evidently drew from Dunash.[49] (As Rashbam, following in Rashi's footsteps, would remark: "*davuq* means: a word adjacent to another and the implied word *shel* ("of") is omitted between them."[50]) Rashi also supports his assertion that the term *shevu'a* in this verse is in the construct state by taking note of the pointing of the text, which indicates its proper vocalization, a matter that was of prime importance to Rashi, and for which he avidly consulted the masoretic notes and works available to him.[51] Indeed, Rashi elsewhere in his commentaries regularly explains the relationship between the

47 Scholia on Gen 29:27, de Lange, *Greek Jewish Texts*, 90–91.

48 Rashi on Gen 29:27, Berliner ed., 60. The last part of this comment, from the words "And it is not possible to say ... " are absent in the Reggio di Calabria edition (as indicated by Berliner) and in MS Leipzig 1 and thus may be an addition to Rashi's original commentary. The observation that *shevu'a* in this context means a period of seven days, rendered in Old French *septaine*, is attested in Rashi on Exod 10:22. And so, the comment itself is consistent with Rashi's view.

49 Steiner, "Rabbanite Biblical Commentaries." See also del Valle Rodríguez, *Terminologie*, 50–52.

50 *Dayyaqut*, Merdler ed., 26. See also Merdler, "Rashbam and Hebrew Grammar," 226–227.

51 See Himmelfarb, "Rashi's Use of the Masorah."

pointing and the construct state.[52] By contrast, Steiner argues, the author of the Scholia does not seem to have had a term for the construct state.[53]

A POSSIBLE SOURCE FOR RASHI?

Having noted a range of parallels between Rashi and the early Rabbanite Byzantine commentaries, we must now assess the question of the possible relationship between them, particularly if the latter may have inspired Rashi's *peshat* program. This entails two sorts of investigation. First, a historical one: Could Rashi actually have had access to the Byzantine commentaries? Second, a hermeneutical question: How meaningful are the exegetical parallels between Rashi's *peshat* program and the precedents for it in the Byzantine commentaries? In other words, even if Rashi did know of the Byzantine commentaries, can they be regarded as the impetus for his novel exegetical outlook?

Given the trade links between the Rhineland and Byzantium,[54] it is conceivable that the Byzantine commentaries were available to Rashi already in his youth at the Mainz and Worms academies, though admittedly there is no evidence for this. A stronger possibility is that the Byzantine exegetical tradition was conveyed to Rashi through the conduit of his close student and amanuensis Shemaiah. There is evidence that Shemaiah was from – or at least spent time in – Italy, perhaps in southern Italy, where Byzantine cultural influence was still present in the eleventh century. Shemaiah knew some Greek, and was familiar with Byzantine coins and the customs of Byzantine Jewry.[55] Steiner has identified one instance in which Rashi adopted an idiosyncratic (and otherwise unattested) interpretation by the second-century CE Greek translator Aquila; and this interpretation would have likely have been brought to his attention by Shemaiah.[56] Rashi's use of the Byzantine work *Sefer Yosippon* may also suggest his connection with Byzantine learning.[57]

The historical plausibility of these scenarios, however, has been challenged, particularly by Avraham Grossman.[58] Though Rashi utilized

[52] As noted by Steiner, "Rabbanite Biblical Commentaries." See, e.g., Rashi on Gen 24:2, 37:32; Exod 5:16, 28:11; Lev 22:10; Num 6:5, Deut 4:41, 25:2, 32:13, 32:14.

[53] Steiner, "Rabbanite Biblical Commentaries."

[54] See Soloveitchik, *Collected Essays II*, 127–144; Ta-Shma, *Studies: Italy & Byzantium*, 177–187.

[55] See Steiner, "'Lemma Complement,'" 377–379; Steiner, "Redaction," 145–146.

[56] See Steiner, *Stockmen*, 24.

[57] See Chapter 4, note 4.

[58] See Grossman, "Impact," 458–464. See also Brin, *Reuel*, 12n.

Yosippon, that much older work was composed in southern Italy and, as Grossman notes, does not indicate Rashi's awareness of the exegetical school that emerged in the Balkans in the tenth century. Indeed, the case of *Sefer Yosippon*, which Rashi actually cites by name ("the book of Joseph ben Gurion"), can be brought as evidence that Rashi did not know of Reuel's commentary or the Scholia, as he does not cite them. In other words, Rashi's tendency was evidently to explicitly cite the authorities he drew upon, and if he does not cite the Byzantine commentaries explicitly, then we can conclude that they were unknown to him.

Notwithstanding Grossman's objections, the possibility that the Byzantine exegetical tradition came to Rashi's attention cannot be ruled out categorically. Perhaps Byzantine interpretations were conveyed to him anonymously by Shemaiah, which would explain why Rashi makes no specific reference to their authorship. But it is also important to consider what sort of impact that tradition might have had on his exegetical thinking. Could his potential exposure to the Byzantine tradition, by itself, have inspired Rashi to engage in his otherwise novel exegetical program? In other words, do the Byzantine commentaries truly serve as a precedent for Rashi's commentary?

As discussed in Chapters 1 and 2, philological-contextual exegesis was only one component of Rashi's novel interpretive program. Equally important for the sage of Troyes was the proper critical selection of midrashic material that "settles" the language of Scripture, a goal that actually informs the bulk of his Pentatuech commentary. Perhaps most significant, Rashi manifests a remarkable level of methodological awareness. Guided by the principle that "a biblical verse does not leave the realm of its *peshat*," he regularly distinguishes between *peshat* and midrash, especially in his double commentaries.

One additional example of Rashi's double commentary can be noted here because it helps to demonstrate the contrast to the philological tendency found in the Byzantine exegetical tradition. The Scholia interprets Exod 15:1, "Then Moses sang (*yashir*, lit., will sing)," in the following way:

> *Then Moses sang* – [similarly] "Then Solomon built (*yivneh*, lit., will build; 1 Kgs 11:7)"; in some cases [the prefixed form *yashir*, *yivneh*] can connote the past tense, though in other cases it connotes future tense.[59]

This grammatical point indeed manifests the philological methodology of the *peshat* school: to address the seemingly anomalous use of what is

[59] Scholia on Exod 15:1, de Lange, *Greek Jewish Texts*, 104–105.

normally the form for the future tense where the storyline makes it clear that the verb actually describes an event in the past. But it is illuminating to contrast this with Rashi's note regarding the same grammatical anomaly:

Then Moses sang (*yashir*: lit., will/would sing) – "Then," i.e., when he saw the miracle (of the sea parting), the idea came to him that *he would sing* a song of praise. And thus "Then Joshua spoke (*yedabber*; lit., will/would speak)" (Josh 10:12), and thus "And a house he made (*yivneh*; lit., will/would make) for Pharaoh's daughter" (1 Kgs 7:8), i.e., he thought in his heart that he *would make it* for her. So, too, here, his heart told him to sing, and thus he did, "And they said thus: I shall sing to the Lord" (Exod 15:1). And thus with Joshua, when he saw the miracle, his heart told him to speak, and thus he did "And he said in front of all Israel" (Josh 10:12). And thus the song of the well, which begins "Then Israel sang (*yashir*; lit., will/would sing)" (Num 21:17), it goes on to specify: "Spring up O well, sing to it" (ibid.). "Then Solomon built (*yivneh*; lit., will/would build) a shrine (lit., high place)" (1 Kgs 11:7) our Rabbis explained: He intended to build it but he did not built it (b.*Shabbat* 56b). This teaches us that the *yod* (i.e., the prefix that normally connotes the future tense) indicates an intention to do something in the near future. This [interpretation] is meant to settle its *peshat*.

However our Rabbis of blessed memory (b.*Sanhedrin* 91b) offered a midrashic interpretation: this is a scriptural hint (*remez*) to the resurrection of the dead at the end of days – at which point Moses will once again sing. And thus they interpreted all the similar examples, except "And a house he made (*yivneh*; lit., will/would make) for Pharaoh's daughter," which they explained: He intended to build it but he did not build it.

Now we cannot explain and settle (*leyashev*) this language as [we do] other words written in future tense and they refer to something occurring then [in the narrative], such as "this is what Job always would do (*ya'aseh*; lit., will do)" (Job 1:5), "At the Lord's command they would encamp (*yaḥanu*; lit., will encamp)" (Num 9:18), "And at times the cloud would be (*yihyeh*; lit., will be) upon the tabernacle" (Num 19:20)," as these were all actions that occurred continually, and therefore either past or future tense can be applied to them. But I cannot settle (*leyashev*) this interpretation upon the language in this case (i.e., "Then Moses sang"), which was a one-time occurrence.[60]

Despite the difference in detail between the two commentaries, Rashi and the Scholia share a grammatical perspective toward this verse, which leads them to address the identical anomaly of the future tense form being used where the context indicates that the verb is actually in the past tense. Both commentators also adopt the similar strategy of allowing the context to dictate the sense of the verb, rendering it "Then Moses sang"; and, in order to justify this analysis, they identify a morphological sub-pattern

[60] Rashi on Exod 15:1, Berliner ed., 132.

attested elsewhere in Biblical Hebrew to explain how the future tense form can be utilized to connote a past action. Yet this example also reveals how Rashi differs from the Byzantine commentary, as he labels the grammatical analysis as "the *peshat*" and notes how it diverges from the midrashic interpretation of the Rabbis, who, in typical fashion, seek to derive a theological tenet – faith in the resurrection of the dead at the "end of days" – from this anomalous grammatical form.

The preceding example, typical of Rashi's commentary, highlights the distinctive features of his exegetical program. Rashi displays a heightened methodological sense and regularly distinguishes between *peshat* and midrash. Furthermore, his is not simply a philological commentary. Rashi uses "the *peshat* of Scripture" to tether his midrashic commentary to the biblical text. Rashi draws upon midrashic commentary selectively, with a methodological eye to adherence to the sense and sequence of the text, i.e., that "settles" the language of the text. These are features that find parallels in Bruno the Carthusian, as noted in Chapter 3. But they are absent in the Byzantine commentaries. In fact, even where the Scholia on the Pentateuch juxtaposes (what we can identify as) midrashic and philological interpretations as alternatives, they do not bear the labels *peshat* or midrash.[61] And so, even if Rashi did have access to the early Byzantine commentaries – as might be suggested by the parallels in substance and style noted above – they would have supplied him only with one layer of his exegetical program. The remainder of his program, particularly his methodological awareness and the concomitant use of critical terminology, cannot be attributed to Byzantine influence. His self-aware *peshat* analysis and critical selection of midrashic readings that are "settled upon" the language and sequence of the biblical text reflect an interpretive spirit unique to his intellectual milieu in northern France in the second half of the eleventh century.

In this connection, it is important to note that Reuel never invokes the maxim that "a biblical verse does not leave the realm of its *peshat*," nor does the term *peshat* itself ever appear in his extant commentaries.[62] The talmudic *peshat* maxim is referred to just one time in the Scholia on Gen 33:4, cited earlier in this chapter, in connection with the dots above the expression "and he kissed him." After explaining the dots as a technique used by Ezra the Scribe, in his role as redactor of the Bible, to indicate that in one version of the Pentateuch before him the expression appears and in the other it was missing (an explanation found in rabbinic sources, as

[61] See Brin, *Reuel*, 334n. [62] See Brin, *Reuel*, 335.

mentioned above), the Scholia adds the remark: "And if you remove the word, the verse is not diverted (*ne'ekav*) from its *peshat*. And so it is with all of the dotted words in Scripture."[63] This refracted use of the talmudic *peshat* maxim applies to a rather limited phenomenon – the ten expressions dotted in the Masoretic Text.[64] The term *peshat* is not used here to specifically connote the *literal sense* or the *philological-contextual* sense; the author of this comment evidently means to say simply that the meaning/sense (*peshat*) of the verse is not affected if the dotted word is removed. Thus, the *peshat* maxim is not invoked to privilege (or even preserve the integrity of) the philological-contextual sense of Scripture in relation to midrashic interpretation, as it is in Rashi's commentaries.

"THE PESHAT OF SCRIPTURE" IN LEQAḤ ṬOV

After Reuel's commentary and the Scholia on the Pentateuch, the next extant link in the chain of the Rabbanite commentary tradition from the Byzantine orbit is the *Leqaḥ Ṭov* commentary on the Pentateuch and Five Scrolls by Tobiah ben Eliezer around the turn of the twelfth century. Apparently a native of Kastoria in Bulgaria, Tobiah was an important late eleventh-century rabbinic figure, active in a number of Jewish communities in Greece and Byzantium.[65] Tobiah states that he composed *Leqaḥ Ṭov* to mark the one-year commemoration of the Jewish martyrs of the Mainz community massacred in 1096, though there is evidence that he continued working on the commentary at least until 1108.[66] This dedication suggests that there were lines of communication between the Byzantine community and the Rhineland.[67] Rashi's name is never mentioned by Tobiah, and it would seem that he was unaware of the exegetical work of the Troyes master.[68] Rather, *Leqaḥ Ṭov* reflects Tobiah's

63 Scholia on Gen 33:4, de Lange, *Greek Jewish Texts*, 94–95.
64 On this phenomenon, see, e.g., Kelley, Mynatt, and Crawford, *Masorah*, 32–34.
65 See Molho and Mevorah, *Histoire*, 11–12. Ta-Shma, *Studies: Italy & Byzantium*, 260–261.
66 See Buber, *Leqaḥ Ṭov*, 18–23.
67 See Ta-Shma, *Studies: Italy & Byzantium*, 177–187.
68 See Ta-Shma, *Studies: Italy & Byzantium*, 266. It is similarly likely that Rashi did not know of *Leqaḥ Ṭov*. While there are traces of the latter in Rashi's commentary Touitou argues that these are later interpolations, as they are absent in early Rashi manuscripts and the Reggio di Calabria edition. See Touitou, "Traces." Ta-Shma, on the other hand, questions Touitou's sweeping dismissal of these traces and suggests that the later additions into Rashi's commentary may have been made by the master himself late in his life. See Ta-Shma, *Studies: Italy & Byzantium*, 266 n. 25. But even according to this scenario, *Leqaḥ Ṭov* was not a formative influence on Rashi. In any case, the issue has been

Byzantine cultural setting. He occasionally uses Greek words, and there are marked affinities between his commentaries and the earlier Byzantine ones, though he does not mention them by name.[69] Tobiah seems to have been acquainted with the thriving eleventh-century Byzantine Karaite community and the scholarly works it produced, which included Hebrew translations of the influential Bible commentaries composed in Arabic in the "golden age" of Karaism in the tenth century in Jerusalem.[70] Tobiah regularly polemicizes with the Karaites, criticizing them for engaging in an independent philological analysis of Scripture without considering the rabbinic interpretive tradition.[71]

The vast majority of *Leqaḥ Ṭov* is drawn from rabbinic sources, and it might even be considered a sort of reworked midrashic commentary.[72] In fact, Ibn Ezra singles out *Leqaḥ Ṭov* – together with *Or 'Einayim* by Tobiah's student Meir of Kastoria (a work no longer extant that seems to have been a similar to *Leqaḥ Ṭov*) – as being typical of "the manner of the sages in the lands of Greeks and Romans, who do not heed the rules of grammar (lit. the weights of the scale) and rely instead upon the way of *derash*."[73] After he left Spain, Italy was Ibn Ezra's home for about a decade, and it would seem that the Byzantine works of Tobiah and his student Meir circulated there.

Tobiah invokes the talmudic *peshat* maxim in about a dozen places in his writings. Yet, his purpose in doing so is consistent with the overall midrashic nature of his commentary, and thus is quite different from Rashi's use of the maxim. Generally speaking, Tobiah cites the maxim to acknowledge "the *peshat* of Scripture," by which he evidently means its literal or plain sense, but then goes on to engage in – and even emphasize

revisited by Grossman, who rejects Ta-Shma's argument and sides with Touitou based on a new analysis of the evidence in the earliest Rashi manuscripts now available. See Grossman, "Impact," 464–467.

69 See *Leqaḥ Ṭov* on Exod 3:20, Buber ed., II:20–21. See also Brin, *Reuel*, 419–462. Tobiah refers to the *sadran* twice in his Pentateuch commentary (on Gen 42:34, Num 13:20) to connote the biblical narrator-editor, which seems to be a derivative of Reuel's use of the term *sadran*. See Steiner, "Redaction," 126–127. Some scholars cite this connection to argue that Tobiah conceived of a post-Mosaic editor reworking the ancient sources that made up the Pentateuch. See Brin, *Reuel*, 35–38; Elbaum, "*Sekhel Ṭov*," 82–95. Yet it seems more likely that Reuel identified Moses himself as the *sadran* of the Pentateuch, who arranged its narratives and laws. See Viezel, "Medieval Commentators on Composition of the Bible," 116–117; Mondschein, "Additional Comments."

70 See Frank, "Karaite Exegetical Literature," 530–535.

71 Ta-Shma, *Studies: Italy & Byzantium*, 265–281.

72 Ta-Shma, *Studies: Italy & Byzantium*, 282–292.

73 Ibn Ezra, Standard Introduction to the Pentateuch, "The Fourth Way," Weiser ed., I:7.

the importance of – midrashic exegesis.[74] For example, on Gen 29:2, "There before his eyes was a well in the field; three flocks of sheep were lying there beside it, for the flocks were watered from that well" part of a narrative describing Jacob's arrival in Haran, Tobiah writes:

Our Rabbis of blessed memory said: "a biblical verse does not leave the realm of its *peshat*." Nonetheless, the midrashic interpreters [i.e., the Rabbis] wished to expand [the significance of] the text, and to expound upon it regarding what would occur in history, and to teach that the Holy One, blessed be He, reveals the future from the beginning, and to inform us that the narratives of the patriarchs contain many aspects of the commandments. And thus Rabbi Hama bar Hanina interpreted this verse in six ways in *Genesis Rabbah*.[75]

In citing the *peshat* maxim, Tobiah acknowledges the self-evident *peshat* of this verse (by which he means its obvious literal sense), but goes on to privilege the midrash as its ultimate meaning. According to his characterization, midrash in general aims to extract meanings that are not self-evident from Scripture, and that have relevance for later generations.[76]

Tobiah goes on to enumerate the six typological readings from *Genesis Rabbah*. For example,

The first way:

- *before his eyes there was a well in the field* – this represents the well that would appear for Israel in the desert (Num 21:17);
- *three flocks of sheep were lying there beside it* – Moses, Aaron, and Miriam;
- *for the flocks were watered from that well* – that all of Israel, following the order of their encampments, would draw water from it to their tents.[77]

Tobiah pays homage to "the *peshat*"; but his interests lie in the midrash.

A similar outlook is evident in another comment of Tobiah's on a verse describing Pharaoh's dream, in which the Egyptian king is said to have seen seven cows grazing "in the marsh-reeds (Heb. *aḥu*)":

[74] Touitou, "Exegetical Methodology," 8–21.

[75] *Leqaḥ Ṭov* on Gen 29:2, Buber ed., I:144. Buber's text, "in three (שלשה) ways," is clearly an error. The correct reading must be ששה (six), as Tobiah goes on to enumerate six interpretations. Furthermore, Tobiah's source in *Genesis Rabbah* 70:8, Theodor–Albeck ed., 805–808, also mentions the six ways that Rabbi Hama bar Hanina interpreted this verse.

[76] See Kugel, *Bible as it Was*, 18, 21.

[77] *Leqaḥ Ṭov* on Gen 29:2, Buber ed., I:144–145. The midrashic construal of the word *aḥu* is from *Genesis Rabbah* 89:4, Theodor–Albeck ed., 1090–1091.

Aḥu signifies *friendship, brotherhood* (Heb. *aḥwah*). Even though a biblical verse does not leave the realm of its *peshat*, i.e., that the cows were grazing in the marsh-reeds, as in "Can marsh-reeds (*aḥu*) grow without water?" (Job 8:11), nonetheless, there is a midrash for everything [in Scripture]. And what is the [relevance here of the] language of *friendship, brotherhood*? It teaches that as long as there is plenty in the world, people become friends and brothers to one another and extend brotherhood to one another, as they invite one another to eat, drink and make merry.[78]

Tobiah mentions the philologically determined *peshat* sense of the term *aḥu*, evident from the parallel in Job 8:11, which fits the context of Pharaoh's dream of the grazing cows. Yet Tobiah privileges the midrashic construal of the term in *Genesis Rabbah*, which relates to the deeper symbolic significance of Pharaoh's dream, i.e., the "years of plenty" that the fat cows represent. It is illuminating to compare this with Rashi's commentary:

In the aḥu – in the marsh; *maresc* (i.e., marsh, morass) in the vernacular (*la'az*; i.e., Old French), as in "Can marsh-reeds (*aḥu*) grow without water?" (Job 8:11).[79]

Rashi here offers only the philological construal with the prooftext and a vernacular (*la'az*) rendering.[80] Although he does not specify that this is "the *peshat* of Scripture," it is clear that he avoided the midrashic interpretation in *Genesis Rabbah*, a source that he used often.

It is likewise instructive to compare the interpretations of the two commentators on Exod 2:5, "The daughter of Pharaoh came down to bathe in the Nile." Rashi here addresses a simple linguistic issue regarding the sequence of the verse:

[The daughter of Pharaoh] came down to bathe in the Nile – invert (*sares*) the verse in order to explain it: *The daughter of Pharaoh came down to the Nile to bathe* in it.[81]

As part of his *peshat* program, it is common for Rashi to make such grammatical observations about the syntax of Biblical Hebrew, as he does here by invoking the notion of *miqra mesoras* ("an inverted verse").[82] Tobiah, on the other hand, privileges the rabbinic interpretation that Rashi set aside:

You must understand that even though "a biblical verse does not leave the realm of its *peshat*," the profound midrash is a fine way for learning deeply (lit.,

[78] *Leqaḥ Ṭov* on Gen 41:2, Buber ed., I: 204–205.
[79] Rashi on Gen 41:2, Berliner ed., 81.
[80] On Rashi's tendency to cite Old French renderings in his commentaries, see Chapter 1.
[81] Rashi on Exod 2:5, Berliner ed., 104. [82] See Chapter 1.

understanding one thing from another), to fit the words within the matter [spoken in Scripture]. And thus it is explained in tractate *Soṭah* (12b): "R. Johanan said in the name of R. Simon bar Yoḥai: [this means that] she went down to cleanse herself of the idolatry of her father's household."[83]

Tobiah seems to acknowledge that, according to "the *peshat* of the verse," this narrative simply depicts Pharaoh's daughter engaging in the mundane activity of bathing in the Nile. Yet he asserts that there must be something more to the narrative, a deeper meaning expounded in the Talmud, which casts Pharaoh's daughter as a spiritual heroine abandoning the idolatry of her father's house. Tobiah goes on to elicit evidence for this interpretation from another biblical text, based on a further midrashic interpretation:

And we find an explicit verse in Chronicles that Mered took Bithiah (lit., "daughter of Yah" [a name of God]) the daughter of Pharaoh ... as it is written: "And his Jewish wife bore Jered the father of Gedor, and Heber the father of Socho, and Jekuthiel the father of Zanoah. And these are the sons of Bithiah the daughter of Pharaoh, whom Mered took" (1 Chr 4:18) ... and earlier it says "And the sons of Caleb son of Jephuneh" (1 Chr 4:15) and then it says "And his Jewish wife ... " From this we learn that Caleb's wife was this Jewish one. And it changed his wife's name and his name. As Scripture originally calls him Caleb son of Jephuneh, but later calls him Mered (lit. rebellion); and his wife was originally called "the Jewish one," but later she was called "Bithiah the daughter of Pharaoh." Thus our Rabbis of blessed memory said: "Chronicles was given only for the purpose of engaging in midrashic interpretation of the Torah."[84] Why was he called Mered? Because he rebelled against the evil counsel of the spies. "The Jewish one" – because she converted to Judaism, as anyone who rejects idolatry is called "Jewish" ... and this shows that the midrashic interpretations of the early ones, which the Sages expounded is Torah absolutely. And thus Rabbi Johanan said: [this means that] she went down to cleanse herself of the idolatry of her father's household.[85]

For Tobiah, the verse in Chronicles – a book "given only for the purpose of engaging in midrashic interpretation of the Torah" – confirms the midrashic interpretation of Exod 2:5.

The way the *peshat* maxim is cited by Tobiah indicates a level of methodological awareness, i.e., that his midrashic interpretations diverge from "the *peshat* of Scripture." His need to do so suggests a certain level of self-consciousness about engaging in midrashic interpretation, as though Tobiah must justify his interpretive strategy by acknowledging the literal sense of Scripture, but then going beyond it. What could have made him feel

[83] *Leqaḥ Ṭov*, Buber ed., II:9.

[84] This statement is found in *Leviticus Rabbah* 1:3, Margulies ed., 8 and in *Ruth Rabbah* 2:1, Lerner ed., II:42.

[85] *Leqaḥ Ṭov*, Buber ed., II:9.

self-conscious about engaging in midrashic interpretation, which, after all, had long been the traditional norm of Jewish Bible interpretation?

One might consider the possibility that Tobiah was contending with the strong Karaite tradition of Bible interpretation that had developed in Byzantium during the eleventh century. Perhaps this animus could have prompted him to give a lower profile to "the *peshat* of Scripture" and venerate midrash as the essential meaning of the Bible. Indeed, Tobiah devotes much of *Leqaḥ Ṭov* to midrashic expansions of the biblical text, including extensive digressions on halakhic matters. These halakhic discussions are often attached to anti-Karaite polemics, and are intended to bolster adherence to the tenets of Rabbanite Judaism.[86] The theoretical exegetical foundation for this orientation is made clear by Tobiah on Exod 34:27, "In accordance with these words I make a covenant with you and with Israel":

> This refers to the prescriptions of the Talmud, and it teaches that the essential covenant was made on the basis of the interpretation of the Torah ... for anyone who interprets a verse literally (*ke-ṣurato*; lit. according to its form; see b. *Qiddushin* 49a) without midrashic interpretation and without the thirteen midrashic hermeneutical principles, about him Scripture says: "The fools walks in darkness" (Qoh 2:14).[87]

But this very passage – which is almost certainly directed against the Karaites – suggests that Tobiah's references to the talmudic *peshat* maxim are directed toward a different opposing exegetical viewpoint. After all, the Karaites did not base themselves on the talmudic *peshat* maxim, as they rejected talmudic authority.[88] They engaged in what Tobiah, using a talmudic expression, characterized as "literal" interpretation that ignores the midrashic tradition, what the Karaites often termed the "apparent sense of the text" (*ẓāhir al-naṣṣ*), but not "the *peshat* of Scripture."[89]

In invoking the talmudic *peshat* maxim, it would seem that Tobiah is polemicizing with – but at the same time making a concession to – a Rabbanite audience or a potential interlocutor who sought to interpret Scripture in accordance with that maxim. Perhaps the first address that comes to mind is Rashi's commentary, which indeed emphasizes (at least theoretically) the importance of adherence to "the *peshat* of Scripture." If

86 See Ta-Shma, *Studies: Italy & Byzantium*, 265–279.

87 *Leqaḥ Ṭov*, Buber ed., II:208–209.

88 See Cohen, *Rule of Peshat*, chapter 1; see also Cohen, *Gates*, 45–46, esp. n. 53.

89 See the previous note.

this decisive exegetical move by the sage of Troyes was known to Tobiah, it could have spurred him to hedge his own nearly exclusive focus on midrashic interpretation by citing the talmudic *peshat* maxim to acknowledge the legitimacy of "the *peshat* of Scripture," but at the same time justify his choice to elaborate on Scripture's midrashic dimensions. However, as mentioned above, there is no direct evidence that Tobiah was, in fact, aware of Rashi or his commentaries.

A final possibility that should be considered is that Tobiah was responding to a Byzantine exegetical tradition that privileged "the *peshat* of Scripture." There is evidence, as already mentioned, that Tobiah knew of the earlier Byzantine commentaries of Reuel and the Scholia on the Pentateuch. In fact, at times he seems to engage with them polemically. A comparison of the latter with Tobiah's commentary on Exod 15:1 is thus illuminating:

> *Then Moses sang* (lit., will sing) – It does not say "Then Moses sang (*shar*)," but rather "Then Moses will sing (*yashir*)" – to teach us the doctrine of the resurrection of the dead.
>
> Another interpretation: *Then Moses sang* (lit., will sing: *yashir*) – the *yod* connotes a past action, as in "Then Joshua spoke (lit., will speak; *yedabber*)" (Josh 10:12) ... "Then Solomon built (lit., will build; *yivneh*)" (1 Kgs 11:7).[90]

Tobiah was aware of the simple grammatical explanation of Exod 15:1 in the Scholia (cited above), and offers it as "another interpretation." But Tobiah himself seems to privilege the midrashic interpretation that the *yod* prefix retains its usual grammatical function and connotes the future tense, thus providing support for the rabbinic doctrine of the resurrection of the dead. Although in this case Tobiah does not state the principle that "a biblical verse does not leave the realm of its *peshat*," he seems to apply the same way of thinking: even though there is a *peshat* interpretation, as given in the Scholia, the midrashic interpretation is necessary to extract the "full" meaning of Scripture.[91]

Although neither the Pentateuch Scholia nor Reuel characterized their exegesis as "the *peshat* of Scripture," it is conceivable that Tobiah did – when seeking to circumvent their grammatical focus, which may have set a precedent within the Rabbanite Byzantine community that he could not ignore. To be sure, there are links missing in the Byzantine exegetical

90 *Leqaḥ Ṭov*, Buber ed., II:91.

91 Compare also *Leqaḥ Ṭov*'s midrashic interpretation of Gen 32:9, Buber ed., I:165, which appears to be directed specifically against the simple grammatical analaysis of the Scholia *ad loc.*, de Lange, *Greek Jewish Texts*, 92–93. See also Brin, *Reuel*, 260–262.

tradition in the three generations intervening between Reuel and the Pentatuech Scholia around the turn of the eleventh century and Tobiah around the turn of the twelfth. But it is conceivable that additional commentaries were written during that interval, or that oral interpretive traditions were developed and transmitted in the Byzantine Rabbanite community following the model of Reuel's commentary and the Pentateuch Scholia. As part of this tradition it is possible that the justification for engaging in a linguistic-grammatical analysis of Scripture, rather than midrashic interpretation, was developed on the basis of the talmudic *peshat* maxim. If so, it would then make sense that Tobiah was reacting to this development within his own Byzantine Rabbanite community when seeking to sidestep "the *peshat* of Scripture" and return to a more heavily midrashic exegetical mode.

Armed with this perspective, it is possible to compare how Rashi and Tobiah ben Eliezer recruited the *peshat* maxim to advance their respective interpretive agendas. Tobiah ben Eliezer invoked the *peshat* maxim as part of an effort to highlight the importance of midrash, perhaps as a counterbalance to Byzantine exegetical streams – whether Karaite or Rabbanite – that focused on the philological sense of Scripture alone and ignored midrashic interpretation. Rashi represents a movement in the opposite direction: Coming from a milieu in which midrashic exegesis alone was the norm, Rashi pioneered a *peshat* methodology, training his students to expand it further, and using it as a yardstick by which to evaluate midrashic interpretations critically and select those that "settle the words of Scripture."

PESHAT IN TOBIAH BEN ELIEZER'S SONG OF SONGS COMMENTARY

A glimpse of the Byzantine exegetical tradition that Tobiah inherited comes into view in *Leqaḥ Ṭov* on the Song of Songs, in which Tobiah occasionally cites interpretations in the name of his father, who was probably a generation older than Rashi. Tobiah's father has been identified with a certain "Rabbi Eliezer, son of Rabbi Judah, son of Rabbi Eliezer the Great" mentioned in a letter found in the Cairo Genizah about messianic fervor in the Byzantine Jewish community during the First Crusade. According to this letter, Elijah the prophet appeared to Rabbi Eliezer, son of Rabbi Judah, son of Rabbi Eliezer the Great in Salonika, and this was reported by R. Tobiah – presumably the author of *Leqaḥ Ṭov* – in a missive to the Jewish community of Constantinople.[92] Little else is known about this R. Eliezer, but he may be taken as a fair representative of Byzantine exegetical trends in the mid-eleventh century – approximately midway chronologically between Reuel and the Pentateuch Scholia and Tobiah ben Eliezer.

Leqaḥ Ṭov on the Song of Songs is, on the whole, midrashic, and interprets this biblical book allegorically as a dialogue between God and Israel in the spirit of classical rabbinic tradition. Yet in about a dozen places Tobiah specifically analyzes or refers to the literal sense of the text, in some cases in the name of his father, R. Eliezer. The most dramatic example of this tendency is an interpretation cited by Tobiah in the name of his father that relates to Song 8:11–14. This passage begins with an account of Solomon's vineyard, which had been placed in the care of "guards" (v. 11); but the narrative then shifts to what seems to be a dialogue between Solomon and another interlocutor – perhaps the maiden who speaks elsewhere in the Song – referring to her vineyard (v. 12). The narrative then shifts again to a lover addressing the maiden in the name of "friends" (v. 13), eliciting her response to him as her "beloved" (v. 14):

(11) Solomon had a vineyard in Baal-hamon. He had to post guards in the vineyard: a man would give for its fruit a thousand pieces of silver . . . (12) My vineyard, which is mine, is before me. You may have the thousand, Solomon . . . (13) O you who linger in the garden, friends are listening for your voice; let me hear it. (14) Hurry, my beloved, swift as a gazelle or a young stag, to the hills of spices.

Among the questions that this passage poses is the connections between Solomon's vineyard, its guards, the maiden, and her lover. On this extended passage Tobiah relates:

My father, my teacher, of blessed memory, interpreted "Solomon had a vineyard . . . " literally ("by way of *mashal*") and allegorically ("by way of *meliṣah*").[93]

This methodological distinction is of critical importance because it indicates a clear demarcation between the two levels of interpretation of the Song of Songs – a matter to which we will return below, after exploring how Eliezer, as conveyed by his son Tobiah, interprets the passage literally and allegorically.

In his literal rendering of this passage, Eliezer explains how the two episodes – one about Solomon's vineyards (vv. 11–12), the other a dialogue with the maiden (vv. 13–14) – are logically connected.

[92] See Sharf, "Unknown Messiah," 59–60; Ta-Shma, *Studies: Italy & Byzantium*, 260–261.
[93] *Leqaḥ Ṭov* on Song 8:11, Greenup ed., 104.

Solomon had a vineyard . . . and he gave it to guards to watch over it, and they gave him a thousand pieces of silver to eat its fruits. Now in the vineyard there was a maiden. When the vineyard owner came to retrieve the maiden, the guards said: "All that is in the vineyard is ours!" As it says: "My vineyard, which is mine, is before me," for this is what we stipulated. "You may have the thousand, Solomon," as compensation . . . but the maiden is ours.

O you who linger in the gardens – The vineyard owner says: "Let us ask her."

If she wishes to remain with you, then let her remain with you. But if she does not wish to remain with you, then I will take her for myself. "Friends listen for your voice" – to know your wish – "Let me hear it."

And she answers: "Hurry, my beloved" – There is nothing I can do, as you have handed me over to the guards and I cannot escape from here. So become like a person who steals away and disappear quickly, "swift as a gazelle or a young stag," and return to rescue me from here to bring me "to the hills of spices" – to my land and birthplace.[94]

On the literal level, Tobiah's father, Eliezer, construed out of these verses an episode in which a maiden is caught up in negotiations between the vineyard owner and the vineyard watchers who have seized her.

Eliezer then interprets these verses allegorically in the spirit of the midrashic tradition, casting them as a dialogue between God (the lover/ the vineyard owner) and Israel (the beloved) – a relationship that is threatened by the Gentile nations, Rome and her heirs in particular (the guards who imprison the maiden):

And allegorically it is said of Israel, who are called "the vineyard of Solomon, meaning the one to whom Peace (*shalom*) belongs [i.e., God]," and He [i.e., God] rendered Israel in the hands of the other nations [who are likened to the guards].

In Baal Hamon – [allegorically this means] among the nations. He handed His nation over to them. "Each one pays a thousand pieces of silver for its fruit." "Each man" [means] Se'ir, also called Esau (a symbol for Rome), who seeks to eat the fruit of Israel . . .

My Vineyard is before me – [meaning that] Esau said in his heart, "Israel is in my dominion; they will accept our faith."

God says to them: I did not hand them over to you to do with them as you wish, nor to expel them from under the wings of the divine presence. Let us ask them if they wish to abandon Me to pursue vanity or not.

The one who lingers in the Gardens – this refers to Israel who dwells amongst the nations.

The friends – the nations of the world who invent foreign gods, thus making for me associates ("friends").

Listen for your voice – to know your decision.

Please "Let me hear" your desire.

[94] *Leqaḥ Ṭov* on Song 8:11, Greenup ed., 104.

The congregation of Israel answers: You have already put me into a deep pit, handed me over to the nations, and forced me, with an oath, not to rebel against them.

Make haste, my love – to bring an end to the exile and commence the redemption, and then "resemble a gazelle or a young hart" and quickly lend your support and redeem me, and bring me "to mountains of spices" – those are Mount Zion and the mountain of the holy temple, Mount Moriah, "the mountain upon which God will appear" (Gen 22:14), where there is the pleasant smell of the incense, the place of the "pleasant odor" of the sacrifices.[95]

This reading of Song 8:11–14, reflecting Israel's plight as an oppressed minority among Christian nations who encourage her to abandon Judaism, is entirely in line with the midrashic understanding of the Song of Songs.

What is remarkable about Eliezer's interpretation of these verses is his clear demarcation of two modes of analysis that must be applied to the text of the Song of Songs: the literal, based on the plain sense of the text, which tells of a human love tale, and the allegorical-midrashic reading that pertains to the relationship between God and Israel. To demarcate these two interpretive modes, Eliezer uses the pair of biblical terms *mashal* and *meliṣah* (Prov 1:6), which connote the literal and allegorical senses respectively. In the Bible itself, the meaning of these two terms is not entirely clear; they were recruited by Eliezer (or Tobiah characterizing his father's interpretation) for his purposes as technical exegetical terms. This usage of the terms *mashal* and *meliṣah* is attested earlier in the Byzantine exegetical tradition, in Reuel's commentaries on Ezek 13:5 and 13:10.[96] But neither of those cases relates to midrashic allegorical interpretation; rather, Reuel uses this terminology to interpret what is clearly figurative language employed by the prophet Ezekiel.[97] Eliezer (or Tobiah characterizing his exegesis) may thus be the first to have applied this terminology in the Song of Songs to isolate the literal sense from the midrashic allegorical sense.

It should be noted that this remarkable methodological differentiation attributed to Eliezer in interpreting the Song of Songs is a unicum, attested nowhere else in *Leqaḥ Ṭov*. Furthermore, the distinction is not tied to the differentiation between *peshat* and midrash – as it would be in Rashi. The

95 *Leqaḥ Ṭov* on Song 8:11, Greenup ed., 104–105.

96 Commentary on Ezek 13:5, 10, de Lange, *Greek Jewish Texts*, 185–187, 187–189. Cf. Steiner, "Linguistic Aspects," 43–47.

97 On the distinction between the interpretation of biblical figurative language (on the basis of internal textual and contextual indications) and midrashic allegorical interpretation, see Cohen, *Three Approaches*, 36–48.

peshat maxim is invoked one time in *Leqaḥ Ṭov* on the Song of Songs, in connection with the words of the lover to the beloved, "If you do not know, O fairest of women, go follow the tracks of the sheep, and graze your kids by the tents of the shepherds" (Song 1:8). In the spirit of the midrashic tradition, Tobiah first interprets this verse as God's exhortation to Israel in exile to follow "the way of the fathers" and bring them to "the shepherds' tents," which he interprets accordingly: "synagogues and study halls."[98] He then cites an interpretation of his father's that he considers tenuous, leading him to comment:

> And that is an interpretation by way of *derash*. But the biblical verse does not leave the realm of its *peshat*, [namely,] actual tents (lit., "dwelling places"), a place where the shepherds dwell, i.e., synagogues and study halls.[99]

In this case Tobiah invokes the *peshat* maxim to indicate his preference for one midrashic interpretation over another, but not to distinguish between the different layers of meaning of the biblical text. Nonetheless, it is noteworthy that Tobiah seeks to identify the most fitting midrashic interpretation based on a philological analysis of the language – what Rashi would call "the *peshat* of Scripture."[100]

There are some instances in which Tobiah engages in philological analysis as a precursor to his midrashic allegorical interpretation. For example, on Song 1:2, "May he kiss me (*yishaqeni*) with the kisses of his mouth," he writes:

> The expression *yishaqeni* means actual kissing. And in God's great love for Israel he mentions in connection with this kiss "his mouth," because the custom of eastern kings and southern kings is to kiss the hand. But here it says "of the kisses of his mouth." And its interpretation (*peirusho*): this refers to the Torah, that He taught me wisdom.[101]

He then goes on to offer an interpretation by his father:

> My father interpreted *yishaqeni* to mean "may he purify me," similar to the expression *mashaq gevim* (Isa 33:4),[102] and as the Rabbis in the Talmud say "on the Sabbath one may not bring water into contact (*mashiqin*) with stone vessels to purify them" (t.*Shabbat* 18:7). And its interpretation (*peirusho*) also refers to the Torah, which purifies those who study it.[103]

[98] *Leqaḥ Ṭov* on Song 1:8, Greenup ed., 26.
[99] *Leqaḥ Ṭov* on Song 1:8, Greenup ed., 26.
[100] See Jacobs, "Song of Songs," 228.
[101] *Leqaḥ Ṭov* on Song 1:2, Greenup ed., 12.
[102] It is unclear precisely how Tobiah or Eliezer understood this verse.
[103] *Leqaḥ Ṭov* on Song 1:2, Greenup ed., 12.

Both Tobiah and his father show concern for the literal construal of the words as a proper foundation for the allegorical interpretation, which Tobiah prefaces – in this and a handful of other instances – using the hermeneutical marker "and its interpretation (*peirusho*) is . . . "[104]

Based on the above-cited tendencies, Jonathan Jacobs has argued that the interpretive efforts of Tobiah's father Eliezer may be seen as a Byzantine precedent for Rashi's *peshat* program in the Song of Songs.[105] Although Jacobs is slightly more reticent about suggesting that Eliezer's interpretation of the Song of Songs came to Rashi's attention, he does note that this precedent may strengthen Ta-Shma's view (mentioned above) that the Byzantine exegetical tradition inspired Rashi's *peshat* program. The argument might be developed along the following lines: although *Leqaḥ Ṭov* itself could not have exerted a formative influence on Rashi (and it is uncertain that the work ever came to Rashi's attention[106]), it is conceivable, historically speaking, that the Byzantine exegetical school represented by Tobiah's father, Eliezer, was known to Rashi. If Tobiah's citations of his father's interpretations are to be taken as genuine reflections of the latter's formulations and terminology (and not Tobiah's own reformulations), then Eliezer's interest in the literal sense of the Song of Songs as distinct from its allegorical sense could have been a source of inspiration for Rashi to develop his *peshat* program.

Even if that historical scenario is plausible, it is important to note that Rashi's robust *peshat* program differs substantially from the inchoate one attributed to Eliezer by Tobiah in his Song of Songs commentary. References to "the *peshat* of Scripture" in Tobiah's Song of Songs commentary relate only to individual words. In only one case does Eliezer aim to account for the literal sense of an extended narrative, Song 8:11–14, but he does not use the term *peshat* in this connection, nor do we have evidence that he did so consistently in the Song of Songs. By contrast, Rashi's *peshat* program, as discussed in Chapter 2, entails not only a philological analysis of individual words and verses, but also a comprehensive understanding of the love story that emerges from a literal reading of the Song of Songs. Rashi interprets the Song of Songs as a literary work, a love story – a perspective that would open the door for Rashbam to liken the Song to the *chansons d'amour* of the *trouvères* of medieval France, as discussed in the following chapter.

[104] See Jacobs, "Song of Songs," 229–230.
[105] See Jacobs, "Song of Songs," 240–241.
[106] See note 68.

In sum, the tenth-century Byzantine school, represented by Reuel's commentary and the Pentateuch Scholia, theoretically could have provided Rashi with the model of a non-midrashic running Bible commentary dedicated to linguistic issues and adopting a philological methodology. There is some indirect evidence suggesting subsequent development of a Byzantine exegetical program that included a new focus on "the *peshat* of Scripture," to which Tobiah was responding polemically in his midrashically oriented *Leqaḥ Ṭov* commentary. And some of the interpretations of the Song of Songs that Tobiah cites in the name of his father manifest an interest in the literal sense of that book. If Rashi knew of R. Eliezer's exegesis of the Song of Songs (perhaps in oral form, as we have no evidence that R. Eliezer actually wrote a Bible commentary), it would have provided for him a precedent of using the talmudic *peshat* maxim in connection with the philological interpretation of Scripture, distinct from its midrashic interpretation. But this underscores the innovative literary nature of Rashi's *peshat* program, in which grammar and philology are only a part – albeit an important one. Equally important, for Rashi, is the "arrangement" and "sequence" of the biblical text, values that stem from his keen literary sense and that can be compared productively with trends in contemporaneous Christian interpretation, a subject that will be a focus of the next chapter.

6

Rashi's Literary Sensibilities and Latin *Grammatica*

Precedents for various aspects of Rashi's exegetical program, as discussed in the previous three chapters, can be identified within two Jewish schools of learning, the Andalusian and Byzantine, as well as in the application of the discipline of *grammatica* to the Bible as attested at the cathedral school of Rheims. Rashi does not mention any Andalusian authors beside Menahem and Dunash, who, uncharacteristically, wrote in Hebrew rather than Arabic, nor does he ever refer to the Byzantine exegetical school. As discussed in the preceding two chapters, this suggests that Rashi was, in fact, unfamiliar with their exegetical accomplishments. Rashi, of course, does not mention Bruno or any other Remois interpreters either. But that silence does not necessarily indicate that he was unaware of the Christian interpretive school. If Rashi knew of the Arabic-writing Jewish Andalusian or Jewish Byzantine philologically oriented Bible commentators, he almost certainly would have cited them as authoritative sources – as he does Menahem and Dunash. On the other hand, Rashi understandably would not have cited Bruno, Remigius, or other Christian interpreters as authorities on the Bible. Furthermore, the hypothesis of "influence" raised in Chapter 3 is not that Rashi consciously adopted Christian interpretive methods, but rather that the grammatical Christological mode of reading advanced by Bruno and his circle at Rheims could have come to Rashi's attention and posed a challenge that spurred him to develop an opposing Jewish interpretation "settled upon" the language and sequence of Scripture.

Yet another question still might be raised. If, when all is said and done, all three possibilities of influence are conjectural, why emphasize Rashi's connection to the school of Rheims? After all, the Christian interpretive model would have been inimical to Rashi's worldview, whereas the Andalusian or Byzantine models (if he had access to them) would have been congenial to his thinking. The answer I would propose is that, ironically, the Latin interpretive model – adjusted for differences between Judaism and Christianity – seems to best fit Rashi's distinctive hermeneutical stance. In other words, Bruno and Rashi share much in terms of their interpretive suppositions – despite the bitter enmity between Christianity and Judaism. Rashi and Bruno, as demonstrated in the preceding chapters, share a conviction that the true meaning of Scripture lies beneath the surface, as expounded by the Rabbis and the Church Fathers respectively. Bruno drew upon the discipline of *grammatica* to produce a Psalms commentary made up of critically selected patristic readings that can be construed as capturing the intentions of King David, an insight that does much to elucidate Rashi's exegetical goals in using *peshat* as a yardstick for his critical selection of midrashic readings that "settle" the language and order of Scripture.

This observation leads to a more fundamental point. The historical scenario for Bruno's possible impact on Rashi's exegetical project laid out in Chapter 3 is necessarily conjectural. Yet the interpretive parallels between the sage of Troyes and the Rheims master have independent hermeneutical significance, as they offer a new vantage point from which to assess Rashi's exegetical innovations. The most important source of Rashi's interpretations and terminology is rabbinic literature. Yet just as he drew upon his midrashic sources selectively to create a new sort of commentary, Rashi coined new usages for traditional rabbinic terms in ways that reflected new interpretive agendas.[1]

The preceding three chapters evaluated three alternative theories to answer the key question raised in modern Rashi scholarship: What could have been the source of inspiration for Rashi's novel interpretive program and the role of "the *peshat* of Scripture" within it? Building upon the theory raised by Touitou and Kamin, I have presented the argument that contemporaneous Christian Bible interpretation in northern France, specifically as manifested in the Psalms commentary of St. Bruno, is the most likely source of inspiration for Rashi's new valuation of *peshat* and his

[1] This has been demonstrated, e.g., by Sarah Kamin with respect to Rashi's use of the term *dugma* in the sense of the Latin term *exemplum*. See Chapter 2, note 71. More broadly speaking, of course, we can point to Rashi's use of the term *peshuto shel miqra*. Although this term is talmudic, it was applied by Rashi in a new sense and with far greater methodological awareness.

critical selection of midrashic interpretations accordingly. The current chapter and the next go beyond that narrowly focused question to explore how broader trends in Latin Bible interpretation – of which he may have been aware – shed light on Rashi's innovative exegetical methods and conceptions. As we shall demonstrate, an investigation of the parallels in Bruno and other Latin authors will help to pinpoint some of Rashi's important exegetical innovations and discern the hermeneutical conceptions underlying them, thereby providing a fresh perspective on the *peshat* revolution in northern France in the eleventh century.

CRITICAL SELECTION OF TRADITIONAL (MIDRASHIC, PATRISTIC) COMMENTARIES

Most fundamentally, the methodological parallels to Bruno shed important light on the religious and cultural assumptions about the Bible in Rashi's milieu in eleventh-century northern France. An understanding of this intellectual framework offers a crucial step toward formulating a response to the critique of Kamin's account of Rashi's exegetical program raised by Ahrend, as mentioned earlier in this study. Based on the evidence in Rashi's commentary, Kamin concluded that his goal was not to compose a pure *peshat* commentary or even to privilege *peshat* over *derash*. Rather, according to Kamin, Rashi engaged in *peshat* exegesis as part of an endeavor to compose a running commentary made up largely from midrashic sources that properly "settles" the biblical text, i.e., it corresponds to its language and accounts for its sequence and literary arrangement.[2] Ahrend, however, raised the following question: If Rashi indeed pioneered a method that enabled him to discern "the *peshat* of Scripture," why did he not apply that method consistently rather than relying so heavily on the older rabbinic midrashic mode of reading? By Kamin's account, according to Ahrend, "Rashi ... resembles a craftsman who perfected a new and original technique, but set it aside to display to his audience a haphazard collection of works by his predecessors."[3]

An answer to this question, as discussed in Chapter 4, emerges from a consideration of Rashi's cultural milieu. Even if, historically speaking, Rashi knew of the development of philological-contextual ("*peshat*") interpretation in the Andalusian or Byzantine schools, it is evident that he recast it to fit a different hermeneutical hierarchy. Here is where the resemblance to the Christian hermeneutical model that emerged in the

[2] See Chapter 2. [3] See Chapter 2, p. 77.

school of Rheims proves significant, since it provides a closer parallel to the way that Rashi negotiated the newly developed philological methods and the midrashic interpretive tradition. Like his Christian neighbors in the cathedral schools of northern France who followed Bruno's grammatical hermeneutic, which drew upon patristic interpretations selectively, Rashi did not regard philological-contextual analysis of the Bible as an end unto itself, but rather as a stepping stone for engaging in a systematic, selective commentary drawn from midrashic sources. Both Rashi and his Christian neighbors, as much as they disagreed about the "true" meaning of the Hebrew Bible, shared the traditional view that its essence is not to be found at the surface, but rather in its deeper sense, which was thought to convey messages directly relevant to their respective religious experiences. Within this framework, it makes sense that Rashi did not actually aim to compose a *peshat* commentary per se, but rather to use *peshuto shel miqra* as a foundation for a commentary that incorporates midrashic interpretations that "settle the words of Scripture."

Bruno's interpretive methodology, drawing upon a late Carolingian tradition represented by Remigius of Auxerre, involved "grammatical" analysis, i.e., an endeavor to elucidate the biblical text utilizing the methods applied by grammarians to classical pagan poetry. Applying the skills of *enarratio poetarum* to the Psalms, Remigius, Bruno, and others associated with the school of Rheims sought to interpret each psalm as a cohesive literary unit in order to discern the prophetic intentions of King David (assumed to be the author of the Psalms) – much as the fifth-century grammarian Servius, for example, did in his commentaries on Virgil.[4] Although Rashi did not have access to the tradition of classical poetry and its commentary tradition, there are intriguing points of contact between some of the more innovative aspects of his exegetical work and the methods applied in the Latin school of Rheims. The remainder of this chapter and the next are devoted to investigating three such points of contact, which together suggest that Rashi, likewise, perceived at least certain parts of the Bible as prophetic poetry, a perception that called for a new exegetical methodology that departed from traditional midrashic interpretation.

PROLOGUE FORMAT AND "THE HOLY SPIRIT"

In addition to simply parsing the text of the Psalms, which was akin to the most basic task of *enarratio poetarum*, Bruno recruited the skills of

[4] See Chapter 3.

grammatical analysis as part of his strategy for establishing the cogency of the Christological mystical sense of the Psalms. Bruno was a pioneer in adapting to biblical commentary the so-called type-C prologue form, as classified by R. W. Hunt, which had traditionally been associated with pagan philosophical texts.[5] This prologue form seems to have developed from what Hunt termed the "type-B" form found in late antique glosses, including Servius' prologue to the works of Virgil, and which was used elaborately in Remigius' secular commentaries.[6] These prologues – known as *accessus ad auctores* – typically addressed a variety of general questions about the work being glossed. The "type-C" prologue included, among other things, the *materia libri* (subject matter) and the *ordo libri* (structure). In his general prologue to the Psalms, Bruno takes two other elements from the type-C form, the *intentio auctoris* (authorial intention) and the question *cui parti philosophiae supponitur* (to which part of philosophy does it pertain), and applies them to the Psalms. According to Bruno:

> The intention of this work is shown to be various through the diversity of its individual titles [i.e., the superscriptions]. For he [i.e., David] sometimes intends to prophesy of the Incarnation, the Nativity, the Passion, the Resurrection, and the other acts of Christ, and at other times of the salvation of the good and the damnation of the wicked.[7]

Bruno also discusses in detail the *pars philosophie* (part of philosophy) to which the Psalms can be associated:

> Just as, among secular books, some pertain to physics, some to ethics, and some to logic, so too may we speak of divine books. Some pertain to physics, although in this case the natural phenomena serve as figures – as in Genesis, where the origin of the world is described . . . Others, in place of logic, pertain to ethics, e.g., Job, *Blessed are the undefiled* (see Ps 119:1), and certain other psalms. Others, in place of logic and ethics, pertain to speculation or contemplation – those, that is, which contain the sublime mysteries of God, far removed from comprehension. These include the Song of Songs, in which God is shown speaking with wondrous mystery to the Church, as a Bridegroom to his Bride. This book [i.e., the Psalter], although in part pertaining to ethics, principally pertains to contemplation, since he [i.e., the psalmist] intends

[5] See Dahan, *Lire la Bible*, 64–66 and 395, who suggests that Bruno's Psalms commentary is the first documented application of the type-C form to Bible exegesis. On the type-C and type-B forms, see Hunt, "Introductions," 94–97. On their application to Bible interpretation, see Minnis, *Authorship*, 18–25, 40–72.

[6] See Hunt, "Introductions," 94; Lutz, "Formula"; Minnis, *Authorship*, 15–19, 26–27.

[7] *PL* 152:638A, Aniorté trans., 59. The English translation here is from Kraebel, "Poetry and Commentary," 242.

mysteriously to speak in particular about the Incarnation, Nativity, and the rest of the acts of Christ.[8]

Bruno here draws upon the categories typically used to discuss non-biblical literature to enumerate the three parts of philosophy to which a biblical book may pertain. He adapts the traditional Hellenistic division of philosophy into physics, ethics, and logic to the classification of biblical books by replacing logic with contemplation. Indeed, for Bruno, most psalms pertain to contemplation, since David, as a prophet, contemplates and then writes about future events "far removed from the ordinary comprehension" of his contemporaries.[9]

Bruno at times provides an individual preface to a psalm in which he sets forth its authorial intention, and then goes on, in his verse-by-verse commentary, to demonstrate how that intention is borne out by the psalm's language and structure.[10] On Psalm 18 (MT 19), for example, Bruno writes:

Foreseeing the preachers who will be sent by God for the instruction of the Church, and foreseeing too that, by their wondrous office, the Law will be expounded through the Holy Spirit for the instruction of their successors, making it immaculate and holy, the Prophet, in his joy, intends, through the activity of the Holy Spirit, to prophesy all of these future events as though they were happening in the present.[11]

Accordingly, in his commentary on verse 2, Bruno writes:

The heavens show forth (enarrant) the glory of God, i.e., the Apostles, who, according to the loftiness of their virtues, ought to be called *heavens*. They will tell out (*extra narrabunt*), i.e., in the open, the glorious essence of the Son of God.[12]

The Christological interpretation of "the heavens" as the Apostles is drawn from Augustine, followed by Cassiodorus.[13] But Bruno, both in his introduction to the psalm and in the commentary, makes a distinctive effort to demonstrate how this reading can be construed as David's

[8] *PL* 152:638B–639A, Aniorté trans., 59. English translation from Kraebel, "Poetry and Commentary," 242.

[9] Kraebel, "Poetry and Commentary," 242. See also Levy, "Bruno the Carthusian," 17–18.

[10] Kraebel, "Poetry and Commentary," 243; "*Grammatica*," 89.

[11] *PL* 152:708B–C, Aniorté trans., 160. Translation from Kraebel, "Poetry and Commentary," 243.

[12] *PL* 152:708C, Aniorté trans., 160. Translation from Kraebel, "Poetry and Commentary," 243.

[13] See *Enarrationes*, Coxe trans., 121; Cassiodorus, *Expositio in Psalterium*, Walsh trans., I:196.

intention in the psalm. He thus emphasizes that David foresaw prophetically the preaching activity of the Apostles. Hence, although the psalm is written in the present tense ("the heavens show forth") it can be construed to describe future events ("they will tell out") – echoing a point Bruno had already made in his general prologue to the Psalms.[14]

Rashi normally does not provide full-fledged prologues to his commentaries.[15] An important exception is his introduction to the Song of Songs, which notably bears resemblance to the *accessus* or prologue format employed by Bruno.[16] As discussed in Chapter 2, the first part of Rashi's Song of Songs introduction establishes the importance of "the plain sense" (*mashma'/peshat*) of Scripture, as well as his exegetical criteria for selecting interpretations drawn from midrashic tradition. Rashi goes on to explicate, in a strikingly methodical way, the subject matter and literary structure of the Song of Songs, as well as the intention of its author, King Solomon:

Now I say that Solomon saw with the Holy Spirit that Israel will be exiled, exile after exile, destruction after destruction, and will mourn in this exile over their original glory, and will remember the first love [of God toward them], which made them His chosen among all nations . . . and they will recall His kindness and their transgression, and the good things that He promised to bestow upon them at the end of days.

And he [Solomon] composed (*yissad*) this book with the Holy Spirit in the language of a woman stuck in living widowhood, longing for her husband, pining over her lover, recalling to him the love of their youth, and admitting her sin. Likewise, her lover suffers over her pain, and recalls the goodness of her youth and her beauty, and the excellence of her deeds, through which he was tied to her in powerful love, to say to them that . . . she is still his wife and he is her husband, who will ultimately return to her.[17]

The notion that King Solomon wrote the Song of Songs guided by "the Holy Spirit" is, of course, an ancient rabbinic one.[18] But Rashi uses this concept in a new way in his introduction to the Song of Songs to spell out Solomon's intention in the biblical text that is articulated through

[14] See *PL* 152:639B–C and Kraebel, "Poetry and Commentary," 243; see also Levy, "Bruno the Carthusian," 18.

[15] On the possibility of viewing Rashi's initial comment on Isaiah as a prologue, see Signer, "Restoring the Narrative," 73–74.

[16] See Lawee, "Introducing Scripture," 159. In that study, Lawee explores various reflections of the *accessus ad auctores* style in the medieval Jewish exegetical tradition at large.

[17] Rashi on the Song, Kamin and Saltman ed., 81. For analysis of this text, see Kamin, *Categorization*, 247–249.

[18] See, e.g., Kadari, "'Friends,'" 188.

a particular literary style – a complex love story that he outlines in this introduction, followed by further detail in the commentary itself. For Rashi, the human love story about an older woman and man recalling their youthful love relationship comprises the *peshat* of this biblical text, which, in turn, represents the relationship between Israel and God throughout the ages that King Solomon foresaw with the Holy Spirit.

The themes laid out in Rashi's introduction to the Song of Songs can be compared productively to Bruno's preface to the Psalms. In this introduction, Rashi presents his view of the *materia libri* (subject matter), *ordo libri* (structure), and the *intentio auctoris* (authorial intention) manifested in the Song of Songs. Furthermore, much as Bruno invoked the notion of the Holy Spirit granting David prophetic knowledge of the future that guided him in composing the Psalms, Rashi ascribes such prophetic knowledge to Solomon in the Song of Songs. Rashi, like Bruno, implicitly draws an analogy between biblical and secular literature. In what is believed to be a commentary penned by Rashbam, which is modeled in many respects after that of Rashi, we find an explicit comparison of the literary format of this biblical text with a poetic genre known from contemporaneous secular French popular literature:

> And still nowadays the convention of the *meshorerim* (singers, poets, *trouvères*) is to sing a song that recounts (*mesapper*) the narrative of the love of a couple, with love songs (*shirei ahava* = *chansons d'amour*) as is the practice of all people (*minhag ha-'olam*).[19]

Rashbam here manifests awareness of the *chansons d'amour* sung by the *trouvères* in his time, in the spirit of which, just a generation later, Chrétien de Troyes (1130–1191) would compose Old French romances about courtly love (*fin' amour*) that became widely popular.[20] It is conceivable that Rashi, as well, had this model of secular poetry in mind when describing King Solomon's literary design and intention in the Song of Songs.

Although Rashi did not write full prologues elsewhere in his Bible commentary, he occasionally made brief introductory notes to individual

[19] Rashbam on Song 3:5, Japhet ed., 250. The attribution of this commentary to Rashbam will be discussed in Chapter 8.

[20] See Liss, "Song of Songs," 23–24. On the literary traditions relating to courtly love in Provence and northern France in the eleventh and twelfth centuries, see Dronke, *Medieval Lyric*, 109–131; O'Donoghue, *Courtly Love*, 96–100, 162–166; O'Neill, *Love Songs*, 1–12; Frappier, *Chrétien de Troyes*, 7; Harf-Lancner, "Chrétien's Literary Background," 29–30.

psalms in a quasi-prologue format that deal with questions of authorship and authorial intention. The way in which Bruno supports his interpretation of King David's prophetic Christological intentions illuminates the strategy Rashi employed to interpret the Psalms as prophecies regarding the later history of the Jewish people. On the superscription of Psalm 42, for example, Rashi remarks:

> *A Maskil by the sons of Korah* – Assir and Elkanah and Aviasaph (Exod 6:24). They were originally part of their father's conspiracy, but at the time of his revolt they disassociated themselves. When all those who were around them were swallowed up when the earth opened its mouth, their place remained in the Earth's mouth in accord with what is stated in the Bible, "the sons of Korah did not die" (Num. 26:11). It was there that they sang a hymn of thanksgiving and they ascended and it was there that they composed these psalms [attributed to them: Psalms 42–43, 44–49, 84, 85, 87, 88]. The Holy Spirit rested upon them, and they prophesied concerning the exiles and concerning the destruction of the Temple and concerning the kingship of the Davidic dynasty.[21]

As mentioned in Chapter 2, Rashi interprets Psalm 42 (which continues into Psalm 43) as a national lament of the Jewish people in the Diaspora extending to his own time. This mode of reading the Psalms, of course, is well attested in midrashic interpretation; but Rashi seems intent on providing a rational foundation for it. After all, it might seem more reasonable, from a historical-critical perspective, to suppose that the psalm was composed by an ancient Israelite sadly reflecting upon his own inability to go on a pilgrimage to the Temple in Jerusalem as he had done previously. As noted in Chapter 2, the latter interpretation was indeed given by Rashi's older Andalusian contemporary Moses Ibn Chiquitilla; his interpretation was cited by Abraham Ibn Ezra, who also criticized Rashi for adopting a midrashic approach inconsistent with the psalm's language. In his introductory note on Psalm 42, however, Rashi provides a foundation for his national reading by positing that the psalm was composed through "the Holy Spirit," which gave its author insight into the future and the ability to speak in the voice of the Jewish people in later historical epochs.[22] Rashi thus offers the following interpretation of the anguished lament later in this psalm:

21 Rashi on Ps 42, Gruber ed., 825 (Heb.), 335 (Eng.).

22 To be sure, Abraham Ibn Ezra was prepared to invoke the notion that David and other authors in the Psalms spoke with the aid of the "Holy Spirit," which enabled them to speak of events far in the future. However, Ibn Ezra applies this conception only where it is necessitated by compelling evidence in the biblical text, for example, in Psalms 126 and 137. He does so in response to the view of Ibn Chiquitilla, that these psalms were

O when will I come to appear before God? – i.e., to make a pilgrimage [to Jerusalem] for the festival. [The psalmist] prophesied here concerning the destruction of the Temple, and the utterance three times "Why are you so downcast [my soul]?" (42:6, 12; 43:5) corresponds to the three kingdoms that will in the future put an end to the Temple service. [In each instance] Israel cries out [to God], and they are redeemed: from the kingdom of Babylon, of Greece, and of Edom (i.e., Rome) [respectively].[23]

With this framework in place, Rashi proceeds to interpret the despair expressed in this psalm as the national anguish of Israel in the Diaspora longing for God's salvation and a return to Zion in messianic times.[24]

King David (rather than the Sons of Korah) is the usual vehicle of the Holy Spirit in the Psalms, as Rashi notes regularly, typically to explain how David could refer to events in the far future. For example, in his mini-introduction to Psalm 14, Rashi writes:

There are two [virtually identical] psalms that David said in this book about one matter: the first was said about Nebuchadnezzar (Psalm 14), and the second (Psalm 53) about Titus the wicked. He prophesied that Nebuchadnezzar would barge into the Temple and destroy it, [and it is in reference to him that David says:] "The fool has said in his heart: there is no God" (14:1).[25]

Rashi again invokes the notion of David's prophecy in the course of interpreting Psalm 149, which he takes to be a thanksgiving to God that

composed much later than David's time, e.g., during the Babylonian exile or the subsequent return to Zion, and are prayers uttered in the historical circumstances that they described. See Simon, *Four Approaches*, 126–137, 187–216. By contrast, Rashi, reflecting a distinctively midrashic outlook, applies the concept of the "Holy Spirit" much more broadly – even without compelling textual evidence – to read the Psalms as prayers relevant to the circumstances of the Jewish people in postbiblical times.

23 Rashi on Ps 42:2, Gruber ed., 825 (Heb.), 335–336 (Eng.).

24 See, e.g., his commentaries on Ps 42:3, 5, 9; 42:3. For other instances in which Rashi introduces the concept of "the Holy Spirit" or prophecy in order to interpret a psalm as being relevant for a later point in Jewish history, see, e.g., his commentaries on 74:9, 97:1, and the examples cited further in this chapter.

25 Rashi on Ps 14:1, *Miqra'ot Gedolot ha-Keter*, 38. The first part of this comment is omitted by Gruber, because it does not appear in MS Vienna 220, the base text of his edition of Rashi's commentary (see Gruber, *Rashi on Psalms*, 163). It is also absent in MS Bodleiana 186 (Oppenheim 34). However, the entire commentary is attested in MS Bodleiana 2440. Maarsen, *Parshandatha*, III:13 notes that the full commentary appears in some medieval manuscripts but not others. It is conceivable that the missing words were penned by Rashi, but later removed – either by Christian censors or by Jewish scribes fearful of Christian censorship, since they refer disparagingly to a Roman emperor, and Rome was a typological symbol for Christianity in early medieval Jewish thought. See Grossman, "Rashi on Isaiah," 48–49, 57, 60–61; Walton, "Censorship," esp. 396–397. See also the following note.

that will be uttered by the Jews in the messianic era. Seeking to identify "the judgment that is written" (v. 9) that will be meted out to those who had oppressed Israel, Rashi refers to a verse in Ezekiel, "I shall wreak My vengeance on Edom" (Ezek 25:14). According to the classic rabbinic typology that equates Edom with Rome, Rashi would have taken this to be a reference to the Christian oppressors of Israel.[26] Yet this identification requires the following historical deliberation by Rashi:

> Now should you object: But Ezekiel was not yet born when David composed this Psalm! I would respond: David here prophesied concerning the eschatological redemption. Therefore, when the eschaton will have arrived, this "judgment" will already have been "written" for a long time.[27]

The association of "the judgment that is written" with another prophetic verse can be found in midrashic sources.[28] Rashi's innovation is to explain rationally how King David could refer to such a verse, as he lived well before the era of the literary prophet Ezekiel.

The idea that King David and other authors of the Psalms were inspired by "the Holy Spirit" grants Rashi wide latitude to read into the Psalms depictions of events and sentiments relevant to the long course of Jewish history far beyond the biblical period, a strategy of reading characteristic of midrash.[29] However, Rashi expresses a concern for methodological rigor in applying this notion in order to be certain that he has accurately interpreted David's authorial intention. On Ps 16:7, for example, he accepts a particular midrashic approach that he can attribute to King David – as a recipient of prophecy – while rejecting another midrashic reading that, in his view, does not conform to the language of the text:

> Until this point, David prophesied about the Congregation of Israel [in the far future], who will utter this [psalm of thanksgiving to God]. And now he says [about himself]: "As for me, I too shall praise God . . . " But our Rabbis interpreted it about our father Abraham . . . However, we [do not follow their interpretation, as we] must settle (*leyashev*) the verses according to their sequence (*seder*).[30]

Although Rashi was prepared to apply a midrashic mode of reading to the first part of this psalm, he does not accept the midrashic reading of its second part, which, in his view, does not "settle the verses according

[26] See Cohen, "Esau as Symbol"; Grossman, "Rashi on Isaiah," 52–62.

[27] Rashi on Ps 14:1, Gruber ed., 860 (Heb.), 762 (Eng.).

[28] See *Midrash Tehillim* on Ps 149:9, Buber ed., 541, citing Mal 3:19 and Isa 66:24.

[29] See Kugel, *Bible as it Was*, 18.

[30] Rashi on Ps 16:7, Gruber ed., 816 (Heb.), 227 (Eng.). Rashi is evidently referring to the midrashic interpretation attested in *Midrash Tehillim* on this verse, Buber ed., 122.

to their sequence." He therefore assumes that David refers to his own circumstances, as a straightforward reading of this psalm would suggest, rather than accepting the rabbinic interpretation uncritically. The implications of this reservation are spelled out in Rashi's comment on Ps 51:7, where he remarks: "There are midrashim on this verse, but they do not conform to (lit., are not settled [*mityashevim*] upon; *mityashevim le-fi*) the matter of which this psalm speaks."[31] Rashi's goal is to ascertain the matter of which Scripture "speaks," which can be likened to his endeavor to "settle the text" according to "the manner of Scripture."[32] This seems to be Rashi's way of fathoming the prophetic intention of the biblical author by marshaling empirical evidence from the language and sequence of the biblical text.[33] Interpretations that do not meet these criteria cannot be what David – or other biblical authors – intended to express, either literally or allegorically. In such cases, as already noted, Rashi will specify that the midrashic interpretations lack exegetical cogency – a point he makes often in his commentaries, as we have seen in his introduction to the Song of Songs, and his commentaries on Song 2:7, Exod 6:2–9, and Isa 26:11.[34] This is comparable to the striking challenge that Bruno raises with respect to certain far-fetched allegorical readings in his commentary on Ps 98:3 and on the headings of Psalms 51 and 142.[35] Both eleventh-century northern French exegetes, one Jewish, the other Christian, applied what they regarded as rigorous exegetical standards to accurately ascertain the authorial intention of the prophetic poets who composed the words of Scripture guided by the Holy Spirit.

The parallels between Bruno and Rashi in applying the concept of the "Holy Spirit" in their commentarial prologues, in order to rationally establish the intentions of the prophetic biblical authors, again raise the question: Could it be that Rashi became aware of – and sought to replicate in a Jewish format in his commentaries on the Psalms and the Song of Songs – the critical grammatical methodology Bruno used to establish patristic Christological readings of the Psalms? The need to respond to Christian interpretation was undoubtedly on Rashi's mind in his commentaries on both of these biblical books. Rashi's endeavor to refute Christian interpretations is explicit in his Psalms commentary.[36] In his

31 Rashi on Ps 51:7, Gruber ed., 829 (Heb.), 385 (Eng.). 32 See Chapter 3, note 64.

33 We are speaking here about how Rashi perceived his exegetical project. Naturally, this sort of "conformity" would not satisfy modern historical-critical scholars; nor did it impress Abraham Ibn Ezra, who was a scion of the Andalusian *peshat* school.

34 These examples were discussed in Chapter 1 and Chapter 2.

35 These examples were discussed in Chapter 3. 36 See Chapter 3, p. 99.

Song of Songs commentary this program, while not stated explicitly, lies just beneath the surface. As Sarah Kamin has noted, Rashi's allegorical interpretation of the Song of Songs reworks older midrashic material into a decidedly new reading of this biblical text that was relevant for the Jewish people in "this exile," i.e., in medieval Christian Europe. Rashi read the Song of Songs as an affirmation that God has not abandoned Israel, using this text to rebut the Christian argument that Israel's prolonged exile is evidence that she has been rejected by God. According to Kamin, this is precisely why Rashi interpreted the love story in the Song as a recollection of youthful love told retrospectively by an older woman who, though separated from her husband, continues to express her devotion to him, as he does for her – a representation of Israel and God, who may seem to be separated in the dark exile of medieval Christian Europe, but in actuality remain connected spiritually.[37]

Kamin adduces evidence that Rashi's Song of Songs commentary responds to a traditional Christian reading attested most clearly in Origen's commentary, according to which the book speaks allegorically of the marriage between Christ and the Church.[38] Rashi could have become aware of this reading by being informed of the interpretation of one of the subsequent Latin commentators who adopted his approach, such as Gregory the Great or Haimo of Auxerre (d. 855), as their commentaries on the Song of Songs circulated widely in the tenth and eleventh centuries.[39] The same avenue of intellectual exchange by which Rashi might have come to know of Origen's interpretations could have also exposed him to Bruno's Psalms commentary. It is thus conceivable that Rashi became aware of Bruno's distinctive type-C Psalms prologue format, which was also well known among subsequent Christian scholars, as attested by other late eleventh-century Remois Psalms commentaries.[40] This may have spurred him to engage in a comparable theoretical mode of discussion (otherwise unprecedented in Ashkenazic Jewish scholarship) in his own introduction to the Song of Songs and his quasi-prologues to some of the Psalms.

[37] See Kamin, *Jews and Christians*, 22–35.

[38] Kamin, *Jews and Christians*, 35–57, 69–88. On Origen's Song of Songs commentary, see King, *Origen on Song of Songs*; Layton, "Hearing Love's Language."

[39] See Matter, *Voice of my Beloved*, 34–41; King, *Origen on Song of Songs*, 13–14. Origen's commentary itself, translated into Latin by Rufinus, does not seem to have circulated widely until the twelfth century, when there was a revival of interest in his work. See Leclercq, "Origèn au XIIe siècle."

[40] See Kraebel, "John of Rheims."

LITERARY STRUCTURE: ORDO ARTIFICIALIS VS. ORDO NATURALIS

In addition to discerning the deep intentions of the "Holy Spirit" expressed in the Song of Songs, Rashi manifests acute sensitivity to the literary design of this biblical book as part of his exegetical program to "settle" the allegorical reading upon the language and order of the text, as established within the framework of his *peshat* explication. The Rabbis of Antiquity, of course, were well aware of the literal sense of the individual words and verses that make up the Song of Songs.[41] The truly innovative aspect of Rashi's treatment is the close attention he pays to the human love story that, in his view, runs throughout the Song and makes up the *peshat* narrative, which, in turn, serves as the foundation for his allegorical reading.[42] Rashi does not simply explicate the literal sense of individual words or verses; he seeks to affix ("set") his midrashically inspired allegorical reading upon a comprehensive reading of the human drama that he sees as unfolding in the Song on its *peshat* level.

As discussed in the previous section of this chapter, Rashi's conception of this relation between the allegorical/midrashic and human *peshat* layers of the Song of Songs is made clear in his introduction to that book. There he posits that King Solomon, inspired by the Holy Spirit, foresaw the future of Israel in exile – in Christian Europe, for example – and that there they would long for God and express their faithfulness to Him. Adapting earlier midrashic material, Rashi casts the "beloved" in the Song of Songs as Israel "in this exile," longing to return to her lover, i.e., God. To support this reading, Rashi delineated the human love story that makes up *peshuto shel miqra*, by which he means a contextual-philological analysis of the text – the literary format of which he attributes to King Solomon, inspired by the Holy Spirit.

For Rashi, the underlying human love story in the Song of Songs, which emanates from *peshuto shel miqra*, is that of a long-married woman separated from her husband and seeking to unite with him by reminiscing together with him over the memories of their youthful love. Fulfilling his commitment "to grasp the plain sense (*mashma'*) of the verses, in order to settle their interpretation according to their sequence (*seder*)," and then, accordingly, to set "the rabbinic *midrashim* … one by one, each in its place,"[43] Rashi's commentary on the Song of Songs traces the steps of that

[41] See Kadari, "Models," 74–77. [42] See Chapter 2.

[43] This is Rashi's formulation in his introduction to the Song of Songs. See Chapter 2, p. 73.

complex human love relationship (*peshuto shel miqra*) and how they correspond to the love between God and Israel (the *dugma*). Like that woman stuck in "living widowhood," the people of Israel, suffering in exile from their land and seemingly separated from God, seek to reunite with Him by calling to mind the glory-filled early days of the faith – the exodus from Egypt, the revelation at Sinai, entry into the land of Israel and the building of the Holy Temple. Whereas the midrashic commentaries available to him interpreted the verses of the Song largely in isolation from one another, Rashi created a structural and thematic unity in his commentary, both on the literal and allegorical levels.[44]

This structural-thematic unity depends on Rashi's particularly sophisticated conception of the narrative composition of the Song. Rather than viewing it as a linear account that traces the relationship from beginning to end, Rashi posits that the love story begins *in media res* ("in the middle of things") – with the woman separated from her lover, Israel in exile separated from God – and only later reminisces about the beginnings of the love relationship.[45] The linchpin of this complex account of the narrative is Rashi's commentary on Song 2:7–8, which begins with a critique of the midrashic commentaries he knew and an outline of the more cohesive, systematic allegorical reading he proposes as an alternative:

> There are many midrashic commentaries; but they are not settled on the sequence of the words (*seder ha-devarim*). For I maintain that Solomon prophesied and spoke about the exodus from Egypt, the giving of the Torah, the tabernacle, the entry into the Land [of Israel], the holy Temple, the Babylonian exile, the re-entry [into the Land of Israel to build] the second Temple, and its destruction.[46]

Rashi then addresses the pericope beginning with 2:8, which he identifies as a turning point in the narrative:

> The poet returned to the beginning of the story [lit., "repeats the first things"] (*ḥazar ha-meshorer 'al ha-rishonot*),[47] like a person who initially speaks briefly, and then comes back and says: I did not tell you the beginning of the story. He began by [citing the words of the beloved] saying: "the King drew me into his chambers" (Song 1:4), and he did not recount how he called upon (lit., visited)

[44] See Kamin, *Jews and Christians*, 24. [45] See Alster, "'Forlorn Lady.'"

[46] Rashi on the Song, Kamin and Saltman, ed., 85. This echoes Rashi's more elaborate phraseology in his introduction to the Song of Songs, discussed in Chapter 2, p. 73.

[47] Rashi ascribes a similar structural strategy to "the poet" in his commentary on Psalm 68, as discussed in Chapter 7. For other cases in which Rashi uses the root *ḥ-z-r* ("returning") to make a structural literary observation, e.g., "Scripture returned/returns [to an earlier point in the narrative]," but without the term "the poet," see Viezel, *Commentary on Chronicles*, 212–213.

them in Egypt with loving language. And now he goes back and explains: this "drawing me near" that I told you about – that my lover drew me close and I ran after him – this is what happened: I had lost hope of being redeemed [from enslavement in Egypt] until the completion of the 400 years [of exile] decreed at the covenant between the parts, [when] "Hark! My lover has come!" – before the designated completion [of the exile].[48]

Although Rashi entangles the literal and allegorical narratives here,[49] the literary argument he makes is clear enough, namely that in the early stanzas of the Song the lovers refer only cryptically to their complex past, which is portrayed more fully in the reminiscences that begin at 2:8.

Kamin, as already mentioned, believes that Rashi made his structural observation on Song 2:8 for polemical reasons: by depicting the speaker as an older woman estranged from her husband recalling her earlier love relationship, Rashi can assign the allegorical reading to the present situation of Israel in exile – recalling their close relationship with God in ancient biblical times. It would seem, however, that Rashi was also prompted by his perception of the *peshat* level of the Song of Songs, i.e., the human love story. As Baruch Alster notes, the assumption that the plot begins *in media res* enabled Rashi to chart out a literary design within an otherwise discontinuous narrative.[50] Rashi seems to have felt that the language of Song 1:1–2:7 reflects an already established relationship between the lovers, whereas the language of 2:8ff. makes most sense to be read as a recollection of their initial courtship. As Alster points out, this analysis of the *peshat* level of the Song of Songs was deemed compelling by later medieval Jewish and even Christian commentators, who accepted it even though they did not follow Rashi's allegorical line of interpretation.[51]

The very concept that Scripture does not necessarily follow chronological order can be found already in rabbinic literature, especially in the principle that "there is no earlier or later in the Torah."[52] As Isaac Gottlieb notes, Rashi applies this principle eleven times in his Pentateuch commentary – in every case based on rabbinic sources.[53] In his commentaries on the Prophets and Writings Rashi applies the principle seven times, but in a more independent manner: either without any precedent in rabbinic sources, or (where the Rabbis already noted the diversion from chronological order

[48] Rashi on the Song, Kamin and Saltman ed., 85.

[49] This is not uncommon in Rashi's Song of Songs commentary. See Japhet, "Rashi's Commentary," 212–213.

[50] See Alster, "Human Love," 65–69.

[51] See Alster, "Human Love," 67–68.

[52] See, e.g., b.*Pesaḥim* 6b. See also Gottlieb, *Order*, 21–36.

[53] See Gottlieb, *Order*, 101–102, 153–159.

itself) with a further explanation of why the principle offers the most cogent explanation of the biblical text.[54] As Gottlieb demonstrates, Rashi seems to have been motivated by his objective to "settle the words of Scripture" and recruited the rule that "there is no earlier or later in the Torah" as a tool to account for what would seem to be an illogical arrangement of the biblical text. For example, on Ps 72:20, a sort of postscript that reads: "The prayers of David son of Jesse are ended (*kallu*)," Rashi remarks:

> Our Rabbis interpreted *kallu* to mean "all of these are (*kol ellu*) the prayers of David," so as to subsume under the name of David the entire book, even that portion which Korah and [the rest of the] ten elders composed.[55] The reason that [the entire book is attributed to king David] is that he is called "the sweet singer of Israel" (2 Sam 23:1).
>
> But [properly speaking] one should interpret *kallu* to mean *they have been brought to an end* ... Now if this be so, why was the psalm not written in its place [at the end of the book of Psalms]? [One must say that] "there is no earlier or later in the book." Moreover, it makes sense to suppose that [King David] composed [Psalm 72] in his old age when he made Solomon his son king [in his stead] (see 1 Kgs 1:28–39).[56]

Rashi here addresses the problem that the postscript of Psalm 72 seems to mark the conclusion of the Psalms of David – and yet there are many more psalms ascribed to him later in the Book of Psalms. Rashi begins citing the rabbinic view which construes the Hebrew word *kallu* as if it meant *all of these are* (Hebrew *kol ellu*). While this type of word-play is typical of rabbinic midrashic interpretation, Rashi obviously found it problematic from a philological point of view. He therefore offered an alternative based on the assumption that the word *kallu* retains its normal sense. In order to do so, he argues that the Book of Psalms is not arranged in chronological order, and that Psalm 72 was written toward the end of David's lifetime – a claim he supports by pointing to the dedication to Solomon in the superscription of the psalm.

[54] See Gottlieb, *Order*, 102–104, 159–165.

[55] Other authors, such as "the sons of Korah," are mentioned in the superscriptions of the Psalms. The Rabbis relate that "David wrote the book of Psalms at the hands of ten elders," including Adam, Melchizedek, Abraham, Moses, Heman, Yedutun, Asaph, and three of the sons of Korah. See b.*Bava Batra* 14b. Rashi in his gloss *ad loc.* explains: "he wrote in it things that were said by these elders who preceded him, and there are some among them who lived in his time, such as Asaph, Heman, and Yedutun." Accordingly, in his commentary on Ps 1:1 Rashi enumerates the "ten authors" of the Psalms. For further details of Rashi's opinion regarding the composition of the Book of Psalms, see Viezel, "Formation of Biblical Books, According to Rashi," 19–26.

[56] Rashi on Ps 72:20, Gruber ed., 837 (Heb.), 476 (Eng.). The rabbinic interpretation Rashi cites is from b.*Pesaḥim* 117a.

Rashi's remark on Song 2:8 regarding the non-chronological ordering of the narrative in the Song of Songs can be said to share some methodological features with the structural observations in his commentary noted by Gottlieb. Yet the former manifests distinctive features that are particularly noteworthy. In the Song of Songs Rashi does not simply note that the book is out of order; he argues that it is arranged with a specific literary design in mind – a design he ascribes to "the poet." This poet chose to begin the narrative in the middle of the story and then return to the beginning, to explain to the reader how the love relationship originally developed. This sophisticated conception of a "retrospective" narrative is a far cry from the rabbinic maxim that "there is no earlier or later in the Torah." But it does find illuminating parallels in Latin learning, to which we now turn.

In a remark that reverberated throughout the Latin grammatical tradition, the great poet Horace (65–8 BCE) observed in his *Ars Poetica* that the poet "often … plunges the reader into the midst of things (*in media res*)," rather than simply recounting events as they occurred historically.[57] More broadly, as later authorities in the classical grammatical tradition would argue, there are two ways of arranging a narrative: *ordo naturalis*, which conforms to the chronological events as they occurred; and *ordo artificialis*, which rearranges events according to the narrator's design. The former is characteristic of historical writing, as seen, for example, in the typical definition of *historia* as *ordinata narratio* (ordered narrative) given by Engelbert von Admont (1250–1331), echoing the assurance made by the historian William of Malmesbury (1080–1143) that he "disturbed nothing of the order of events (*rerum ordine*)," nor "corrupted the truth of what occurred."[58] The poet, on the other hand, rearranges events in the narrative "by choice and ingeniously" (*voluntate et ingenio*), as Remigius of Auxerre remarked in his commentary on Marianus Capella's *Marriage of Philology and Mercury*, for artful purposes, yielding an *ordo artificialis*.[59] This preference had already been made especially clear in the so-called *Scholia vindobonensia*, an anonymous Carolingian commentary (thought to have been composed by Alcuin [735–804] or by someone in his circle) on the *Ars Poetica* of Horace, whose advice to "say at the moment what at the moment should be said, reserving and omitting much for the present"[60] is glossed as follows:

[57] Horace, *Ars Poetica*, lines 148–149, Fairclough ed., 462. See also Singerman, *Poesy*, 2–3; Green, *Medieval Romance*, 97.

[58] Green, *Medieval Romance*, 96.

[59] Remigius, *Commentum*, II:97, cited in Green, *Medieval Romance*, 97.

[60] Horace, *Ars Poetica*, lines 42–45; English translation in Singerman, *Poesy*, 288.

Whoever undertakes to write a good poem which will have a lucid order, let him love the artificial order and avoid the natural. Every order is either natural or artificial. The natural order is when one narrates the matter in the order in which it was performed; the artificial is when one does not start from the beginning of the action, but in the middle, as Virgil in the *Aeneid* anticipates something which ought to be said in the present. For where first he should have told of the fall of Troy and then of how Aeneas came to the island of Antandros and through other places until he reached Carthage, and all this following the natural order, instead he changed this order and first told of how Aeneas came to Carthage, which should have been said later; indeed he saved the destruction of the homeland for a better time, when, of course, Aeneas might allure the minds of the feasters with great pleasure.[61]

The author of the scholia was actually drawing upon a much older tradition of commentary on Virgil, as Servius writes regarding the arrangement of the *Aeneid*:

The order is also clear, although some superfluously say that the first book is the second, the second third, and the third first, because first Troy fell, afterward Aeneas wondered, then he came to the realm of Dido. These people do not know this to be the poetic art (*artem poeticam*), so that the beginning from the middle we might recount the first things by narration and always anticipate the future, as if through vaticination, which even Horace prescribed thus in the *Art of Poetry*.[62]

These remarks by Servius reverberated throughout the medieval period, in which the *Aeneid* was often used as the paradigmatic example of the artificial order.[63] The late eleventh-century cleric Bernard of Utrecht, in his commentary on the so-called *Ecloga Theoduli*, a pastoral debate-poem probably composed in the tenth or eleventh century, likens the order of the *Ecloga* to the order of the *Aeneid* which diverges from the "natural order" and adopts an "artificial" order.[64] The German Benedictine monk Conrad of Hirsau (c. 1070–c. 1150) would likewise exemplify the artificial order by noting that "Virgil in the Aeneid . . . puts the narration of events which he did not want to place in the first book into the second book."[65] The *ordo artificialis* would be celebrated by Geoffrey of Vinsauf in his *Poetria Nova* (penned c. 1202), who emphasized the advisability of poetic "transposition" of events for the sake of artistic elegance.[66]

[61] *Scholia vindobonensia*, Zechmeister ed., 5; English translation in Singerman, *Poesy*, 288.
[62] Servius Grammaticus, *In Vergilii carmina commentarii*, I:4–5; English translation in Singerman, *Poesy*, 287.
[63] See Baswell, *Virgil in Medieval England*, 74, 114, 176.
[64] Chance, *Medieval Mythography*, 347–348, 388. [65] See Singerman, *Poesy*, 7, 289.
[66] See Copeland and Sluiter, *Medieval Grammar and Rhetoric*, 598; Singerman, *Poesy*, 6–7, 289. Cf. Horace, *Ars Poetica*, lines 42–45, 148–150; Quintillian, *Institutio Oratoria* 7.10.11–12.

The theoretical preferences of the experts on classical poetry were translated into practice – and the *ordo artificialis* would be employed in medieval vernacular literature, for example, in the romances of Chrétien de Troyes.[67] The distinction between the two *ordines* was also applied on the most basic level to the rudimentary teaching of Latin reading. This is exemplified in the so-called *St. Gall Tractate*, a tenth-century pedagodic treatise believed to have been penned by the Benedictine monk and schoolmaster Notker Labeo (c. 950–1022).[68] Drawing upon classical grammatical and rhetorical works, a distinction is made in this treatise between the "natural" ordering of the grammatical units of a sentence, which is easiest to understand, and the "artificial" order that is the result of poetic meter or rhetorical figures.[69] This distinction underlies the tendency of grammatical commentators on classical works to reconstruct a difficult sentence by rearranging its elements according to the natural order, as exemplified by the *ordo-est* glosses of Servius on Virgil's *Aeneid*.[70]

Rashi's keen interest in the grammatical arrangement of the biblical text on the sentence level was discussed in earlier chapters in connection with his use of the expressions *miqra mesoras* and *miqra hafukh*, which he deploys when "reconstructing" or "reordering" complex biblical locutions to render them in more logically arranged language. To be sure, these expressions themselves are rabbinic. However, the Rabbis of the Talmud typically used them to introduce a midrashic reading using formulas like "Do not read (*al tiqre'*) X, but rather Y," a sort of interpretation that James Kugel paraphrases, "The text may say X, but what it really means is Y."[71] Rashi uses these terms in a new way: to provide a more grammatically transparent formulation that is easier to understand than the original biblical locution – precisely what Latin grammarians did when converting a difficult line of poetry from the *ordo artificialis* to the *ordo naturalis*, and what Remigius and Bruno did when appropriating this grammatical interpretive strategy in their Bible commentaries. Could it be that Rashi knew of this grammatically oriented trend among Christian Bible scholars in the orbit of the cathedral school of Rheims? While there is no direct evidence to support such a conclusion, the possibility should

[67] See Green, *Medieval Romance*, 98–102. [68] See Grotans, *Reading*, 2–13.
[69] See Grotans, *Reading*, 158–166. [70] See Grotans, *Reading*, 167–171.
[71] See Kugel, *Bible as it Was*, 18; cf. Weiss Halivni, *Peshat & Derash*, 3–22. For such examples of rabbinic interpretation using the terms *miqra mesoras* and *miqra hafukh*, see b.*Bava Batra*, 119b, b.*Shabbat* 55b. See also Melammed, *Bible Commentators*, 64–67.

not be discounted – and it would help explain what might have inspired Rashi to use traditional rabbinic terminology in a new way. In any case, the parallel is instructive, as it illustrates Rashi's analogous "grammatical" interests in his Bible commentaries.

Rashi applies grammatical concepts of a different order in his commentary on Song 2:8, where he ascribes a literary design to "the poet." Here he does not merely transpose a difficult line of biblical verse; rather, he describes the artifice of King Solomon in constructing the narrative of the Song of Songs, which begins *in media res*, until "the poet returned to the beginning of the story" in Song 2:8. This concern of Rashi's for literary arrangement in the Bible can be associated with the importance he places on *seder ha-miqra'ot/devarim* (the sequence of the verses/words). This is evident elsewhere in his Bible commentaries, where he makes similar observations about biblical literary structure within the framework of a *peshat* interpretation, which he contrasts to a midrashic one.

For example, as we have already seen in Chapter 1, a *peshat* interpretation – contrasted with a midrashic one – appearing in Rashi's commentary entails an innovative structural analysis of Exodus 6. The linchpin of that interpretation is the argument that Exod 6:29–30 repeats what was already stated in Exod 6:12–13. The redundancy was necessary to reorient the reader:

> Scripture (*ha-katuv*) repeated it ... because it had interrupted the account (lit., matter). And this is typical [of biblical] style (*shiṭṭah*), as a person might say, "Let's go back and review from the beginning [lit., "repeat the first things"] (*naḥazor 'al ha-rishonot*)."[72]

Of particular importance is the note that this sort of "resumptive repetition"[73] is a normal stylistic convention, the way that any account might be presented. As noted in Chapter 1, this passage is missing in a number of early Rashi manuscripts, which suggests that it may not have been part of Rashi's commentary, but rather was added by a later hand. Yet the language here closely resembles Rashi's language on Song 2:8 ("The poet returned to the beginning of the story [*ḥazar* ... *'al ha-rishonot*; lit., repeats the first things]"). And so, even if it was not authored by Rashi himself, it was added by an interpreter following his lead. Rashbam, likewise, writes regarding Exod 6:29–30:

[72] Rashi on Exod 6:30, Berliner ed., 113. For the textual complexities of this note (which may suggest that it was added to Rashi's commentary by a later hand), see Chapter 1, note 93.

[73] On "resumptive repetition," see Chapter 1, note 94.

This passage is identical to the one above, "The Israelites would not listen to me . . . " But above it presented the matter briefly before explaining, "these are the heads of the clans" (v. 14), which informs us who Moses and Aaron were, as they were the ones to speak to Pharaoh.[74]

This note by Rashbam reflects the acceptance of this interpretation in Rashi's *peshat* school.

Although structural analysis is characteristic of Rashi's *peshat* program, in at least one place Rashi credits (what he perceived as) a traditional rabbinic source for his *peshat* sensitivity to the literary arrangement of the biblical narrative. On Gen 1:27, "And God created man in His own image ... male and female He created them," Rashi writes:

But further on (Gen 2:21) it is said: "and He took one of his ribs . . . "! The aggadic midrash [relates]: He created him at first with two faces (i.e., a male and female side) and afterwards He divided them. But the *peshat* of the verse is: here it informs you that both of them were created on the sixth day and it does not explain to you how their creation took place; this it explains to you in another place.[75]

At stake here is the seeming contradiction between the accounts of the creation of man and woman in Gen 1:27, which seems to report their simultaneous creation, and Gen 2:21–22, according to which man was initially created alone, and woman was later created from one of his ribs. The midrash posits that man and woman were initially created as two sides of the same being, literally "male and female He created them." Rashi's *peshat* interpretation is based on the understanding that the biblical narrator first summarized the creation of man and woman (Gen 1:27), and later provided the details (2:21–22).

In his commentary on Gen 2:8, Rashi reveals the source of his *peshat* solution to the discrepancies between the two accounts:

Now I saw in the Baraita of R. Eliezer the son of R. Jose the Galilean on the thirty-two hermeneutical principles by which the Torah is interpreted, and this is one of them:

A general statement followed by a detailed account. [For example,] "the Lord created man [. . .]" (1:27) is the general statement. It did not say from where and how. It returned to explain: "The Lord God fashioned the man" (2:7) . . . "He placed him in the Garden of Eden" (2:15) . . . "So the Lord God cast a deep sleep upon him" (2:21). One who hears this may think that it is a new story, whereas in truth it is simply a detailed account of the first.[76]

[74] Rashbam on Exod 6:30, Rosin ed., 89.
[75] Rashi on Gen 1:27, Berliner ed., 4.
[76] Rashi on Gen 2:8, Berliner ed., 6.

This is indeed the eleventh among the thirty-two hermeneutical rules in the Baraita of Rabbi Eliezer the son of Rabbi Jose the Galilean.[77] The prevailing view among modern scholars is that this work actually originated in the Geonic period, as it bears affinities to the systematic exegetical work of Samuel ben Hofni Gaon.[78] While Rashi assumed that this Baraita was indeed the work of the second-century sage Rabbi Eliezer the son of Rabbi Jose the Galilean, he discerned that the approach it takes to this contradiction is not typical of midrashic interpretation. Rashi therefore classifies this literary solution as "the *peshat* of the verse." Rashbam likewise adopts this literary *peshat* interpretation in his commentary here.[79]

[77] See *Mishnah of Rabbi Eliezer*, Enelow ed., 24–25. [78] See Chapter 4, note 55.

[79] Rashbam on Gen 1:27, Rosin ed., 8. Rashbam also cites the source of this interpretation in the thirty-two hermeneutical rules of Rabbi Eliezer.

7

Rashi's Notion of "the Poet" (*ha-Meshorer*) in the Latin Context

Rashi's conceptual and terminological innovations are sometimes difficult to discern because he draws his vocabulary almost exclusively from rabbinic sources. However, as we have seen in the earlier chapters of this study, there are cases in which he uses traditional Hebrew and Aramaic terminology in innovative ways to advance his new interpretive agenda. This is especially true of his usage of the Hebrew term *ha-meshorer* in the sense of *the poet*, which is the subject of the current chapter. As we shall see, Rashi innovatively uses this term, as well as the related term *kotev ha-sefer*, to connote the implied author-narrator of the biblical text. This literary construct is invoked by Rashi to explain scriptural literary structure in ways that are illuminated by the poetic conceptions articulated among his Latin neighbors.

In Biblical and Rabbinic Hebrew the term *meshorer* (pl. *meshorerim*) means *a singer*.[1] For example, the Psalms were chanted in the Holy Temple by *meshorerim* (2 Chr 29:28), that is, those who performed the liturgical function described in the Talmud (b.*'Arakhin* 11b). Rashi's application of the term *ha-meshorer* in connection with the Psalms is quite different: he employs the term to connote *the poet*, i.e., the author who composed a given psalm, rather than the individual who *sang* the psalm. This extension is not unnatural, since the underlying root *sh-y-r* (*shir/shirah*) seems to connote *poetry* in some contexts already in the Bible, as, for example, in the Song of Songs (*shir ha-shirim*). Indeed, the term *meshorer* would come to be used widely in Medieval Hebrew also to connote *a poet*.

[1] See Brown, Driver, and Briggs, *Lexicon*, s.v., שיר; Jastrow, *Dictionary*, s.v., שיר.

This occurred, however, within the Muslim orbit, where poetic composition was a highly respected endeavor.[2] This usage was not common in Rashi's Ashkenazic milieu.[3] It could have come to his attention through Menahem's *Maḥberet*, in which the term "the poet" (*ha-meshorer*) is used twice to refer to the voice of the poet speaking in the Psalms.[4] Rashi recruited this usage – which represented a neologism in his Ashkenazic tradition – to address structural literary features of the Psalms and Song of Songs.

Within the Muslim orbit, the Hebrew notion of "poetry" (*shir*, *shirah*) was naturally colored by the well-developed discipline of Arabic poetics. Indeed, key Judeo-Arabic authors drew upon the works of Arab experts on poetry (*shiʿr*) when considering the poetic aspects of the Bible and the Hebrew language. Saadia Gaon drew upon Arabic poetic notions in his major treatise on the Hebrew language, *Kitāb Uṣūl al-Shiʿr al-ʿIbrāni* (*The Book of the Principles of Hebrew Poetry*).[5] As mentioned in Chapter 4, Moses Ibn Ezra's Hebrew poetics *Kitāb al-Muḥāḍara wa-l-Mudhākara* presents an elaborate system of "the embellishments of poetry" (*maḥāsin al-shiʿr*) with definitions and examples from the Bible, alongside those from classical Arabic verse. These poetic-aesthetic conceptions informed the Andalusian exegetical tradition, as manifested, for example, in the writings of Ibn Janah, Abraham Ibn Ezra, and Maimonides.

Arabic poetics, of course, was a discipline unknown to Rashi. His conception is aptly summed up by Rashbam, who defines "poetry" (*shirah*) as "the arrangement of words (*siddur devarim*)."[6] The terms *seder/seder ha-devarim*, connoting the arrangement or sequence of the words of Scripture, are prominent in Rashi's programmatic statements, playing an important role in his exegetical agenda, as discussed in earlier chapters of this study. As we shall see in the current chapter, the notion of *siddur devarim* articulated by Rashbam likewise seems to inform Rashi's

[2] See Berlin, *Biblical Poetry*, 61–94.

[3] My thanks to Elisabeth Hollender for confirming this observation in a personal communication. In Ashkenazic writings, the term *payyeṭan* is used occasionally to connote the composer of liturgical poetry (*piyyut*).

[4] See *Maḥberet*, Sáenz-Badillos ed., 35*, 403*. I am grateful to Aharon Maman and Hananel Mirsky of Jerusalem for these references. (The term *meshorer* also appears in the *Maḥberet* on p. 282*, but there it seems to connote *the singer* who chants the psalm.) Theoretically Rashi may have learned of the importance of poets and poetry in Judeo-Arabic culture from Jewish travelers from Muslim lands – the same channel through which he came to learn some Arabic words. See Grossman, "Grammar and Lexicon," 430–433.

[5] See Brody, *Saʿadyah Gaon*, 79–84.

[6] Rashbam on Deut 31:2; Rosin ed., 225. See also Meir, "*Siddur devarim.*"

use of the term *ha-meshorer* in his endeavor to account for the often complex arrangement of the text in the biblical texts labelled *shir(ah)*, i.e., the Song of Songs and the Psalms.

THE "POET'S" STRUCTURAL INTENTIONS

Rashi's commentary on Exod 6:30, discussed in Chapter 6, attributes the narrative strategy of "resumptive repetition" in a rather vague way to "Scripture" (*ha-katuv*). Rashi on Gen 1:27, also discussed in Chapter 6, attributes the structural design of the narrative even more vaguely, using only a pronoun ("it," implicit in the third-person verbs Rashi uses) referring to "the verse" (" . . . the *peshat* of the verse is: here *it* informs you that both of them were created on the sixth day and *it* does not explain to you how their creation took place; this *it* explains to you in another place"). This is indeed typical in Rashi's commentaries. As Eran Viezel notes in a recent study, when Rashi and others in the northern French *peshat* school pointed out literary features of the biblical text, they typically ascribed them vaguely to "Scripture" (*ha-katuv*), "the verse" (*ha-miqra*), or even just the undefined third-person pronoun "it/he" (*hu'*).[7]

Rashi's comment on Song 2:8, cited and discussed in the preceding chapter, is completely different. There Rashi writes:

> The poet (*ha-meshorer*) returned to the beginning of the story, like a person who initially speaks briefly, and then comes back and says: I did not tell you the beginning of the story.

In this remark, Rashi attributes the complex narrative strategy he identifies in the Song of Songs to "the poet" (*ha-meshorer*), a term that seems to connote an implied authorial voice. The term is employed in this sense one more time in Rashi's Song of Songs commentary and thirteen times in Rashi's Psalms commentary (but nowhere else in his writings), and it is worth considering its implications within his interpretive system.[8]

[7] See Viezel, "Medieval Commentators on Composition of the Bible," 124. See, e.g., Rashi on Song 5:2, 3, as well as on Gen 1:27 (cited in Chapter 6) and Exod 6:13 (cited in Chapter 1). The vague term "Scripture" (*ha-katuv*) is typical of rabbinic literature, as noted by Viezel.

[8] The term is used again in Rashi's commentary on Song 5:12. In three of the eleven cases in the Psalms, the term appears in comments that are absent in one or more of the key medieval Rashi manuscripts, as discussed in the notes further in this chapter, where those passages are cited.

On Song 2:8 Rashi ascribes the literary design of the Song of Songs – the choice to begin *in media res* and employ *ordo artificialis* as it were – to "the poet" (*ha-meshorer*).[9] Historically speaking, Rashi took King Solomon to be the author of the Song of Songs, in accordance with the book's superscription.[10] In using the more abstract term "the poet" in his pivotal note on Song 2:8, Rashi seems to be distinguishing, at least conceptually, between Solomon as the historical author of the Song and his voice as the narrator or implied author. In much the same way, this literary "voice," in Rashi's commentary, is also distinct from the voices of the characters (the beloved, the lover) whose words are cited in this biblical book, but mediated by "the poet," i.e., the narrator/implied author who arranged and shaped them.[11]

The importance of distinguishing between the biblical narrator/implied author and the historical authors of the Bible is emphasized by modern literary critics.[12] In discerning the literary design of the Song of Songs and ascribing it to "the poet," Rashi manifests essential features of a literary reading of the text as described by the modern Bible scholar Meir Sternberg:

> The [implied] author/narrator exists only as a construct, which the reader infers and fills out to make sense of the work as an ordered design of meaning and effect. He is what he does in and through the writing, the embodiment of the sense and the composition and the whole reading experience he has devised for us. This makes him the interpreter's mirror image ... [as] reading entails the postulation of a determinate artificer as a strategy of coherence.[13]

While it is important not to ascribe modern literary conceptions to Rashi uncritically, his use of the term "the poet" instead of referring directly to "Solomon" suggests that Rashi wished to speak of King Solomon's literary agency specifically when describing the artistic arrangement of the Song of Songs.

A similar observation can be applied to Rashi's commentaries on the Psalms. Following the Talmud, Rashi attributed the Psalms to King

[9] See Chapter 6.

[10] This is made clear in his introduction to the Song of Songs, cited in Chapter 6, p. 170.

[11] Rashi once again uses the term *ha-meshorer* on Song 5:12 to refer to the implied author/narrator. Occasionally, though, Rashi does refer to the characters themselves as the speakers in the Song. See, e.g., Rashi on Song 1:2.

[12] See Sternberg, *Biblical Narrative*, 64, 74–75. Some modern literary critics distinguish between the implied author and the narrator; but this distinction, suited for some modern literature, does not seem relevant in the Bible.

[13] Sternberg, *Biblical Narrative*, 75.

David – regarding him as their author, or final editor (i.e., of psalms penned by others).[14] And yet, even when discussing psalms explicitly attributed to David in their superscription, Rashi at times uses the abstract literary term "the poet" (*ha-meshorer*) to refer to their implied author. For example, in his commentary on Psalm 68, Rashi uses the term *ha-meshorer* within a series of remarks in which he maps out the complex structure of the psalm. Modern Bible scholars have noted the psalm's lack of a clear structure or unifying theme.[15] Though obviously distant from the thinking of modern critical scholarship, Rashi's exegetical agenda to "settle the words of Scripture" motivated him to address this literary problem, which was not a concern of midrashic commentary. Toward the end of Psalm 68, on verse 29 (out of 36 verses), Rashi uses language reminiscent of his notes on Song 2:8 ("the poet returned ... ") and Gen 2:8 ("it returned to explain")[16] to connect the final stanza of the psalm with its opening in verse 2:

Display strength, O God – Now the poet (*ha-meshorer*) returns to his prayer (*ḥozer li-tefilato*), in which he prayed, "May God arise, and may his enemies be scattered" (v. 2).[17]

According to Rashi, the closing verses of the psalm conclude a supplication addressed directly to God that began in verse 2, "May God arise, may His enemies scatter ... " Rashi intuits a generic distinction described by modern scholars between supplication and praise (so-called hymns) in the Psalms.[18] And so, when Rashi makes the structural point that the supplication in verse 29 returns to the one in verse 2, he is motivated by the interruption to the initial supplication in verse 5, which is a call to the community to utter a hymn of praise to God: "Sing (*shiru*) unto God, sing praises to His name: extol Him that rides upon the heavens by His name YAH, and rejoice before Him." On that verse Rashi comments:

By His name Yah – ... a name referring to fear ... The poet (*ha-meshorer*) says "praise Him," "fear Him," and "rejoice," similar to what is said elsewhere: "rejoice in trembling" (Ps 2:11).[19]

[14] See Chapter 6, note 55.

[15] Many therefore regard it as a patchwork. See, e.g., Gerstenberger, *Psalms*, 2, 34–46.

[16] Rashi on that verse is cited in full in Chapter 6, on p. 185.

[17] Rashi on Ps 68, Gruber ed., 835 (Heb.), 451 (Eng.).

[18] These genre distinctions are applied both to entire psalms and to segments within a given psalm (the latter matching Rashi's intuitive conception of the distinction). See Westermann, *Psalms*, 5–92; Gerstenberger, *Psalms* 2, 9–19.

[19] Rashi on Ps 68, Gruber ed., 834 (Heb.), 445 (Eng.). Rashi uses the term *ha-meshorer* once more in this psalm, on verse 14: "Dunash ben Labrat explained that *ḥaruṣ* means gold, and therefore the poet (*ha-meshorer*) juxtaposed it with silver": Gruber trans., 447; Heb.

Rashi on the next verse ("The father of orphans, the champion of widows, God, in His holy habitation ... ") offers the following structural observation, by noting that this call to praise God extends throughout the greater part of the psalm:

This is the praise that you must sing to Him – the entire matter (*kol ha-'inyan*) until the end of the Psalm.[20]

And indeed, later in the Psalm, in verse 20, we read: "Blessed be the Lord, day by day He supports us, God, our deliverance." On this Rashi comments:

This is part of the hymn (*shir*) referred to above, "Sing to God."[21]

As Rashi reads it, "the poet" makes a supplication to God for national salvation, while at the same time exhorting the community of Israel to sing God's praises – thanking Him for previous salvations. These two elements are arranged in concentric circles within this psalm: the supplication to God forms the outer circle ("Let God arise ... " [v. 2]; "Display strength, O God" [v. 29]); and the inner circle is the hymn that the poet exhorts the community to sing to God ("Sing unto God" [v. 5]; "Blessed be the Lord ... " [v. 20]). Rashi ascribes this sophisticated literary structure to "the poet."

SHIFTS IN PERSPECTIVE, ADDRESSEE, AND THEME

Most of the remaining instances in which Rashi employs the term *ha-meshorer* in his Psalms commentary relate to his endeavor to answer the following questions: for whom, to whom, and about what does the persona, i.e., the implied author, in the psalm speak? These questions are all essential for his distinctive exegetical program, which requires accounting for "the sequence of the verses" (*seder ha-miqra'ot*), i.e., their literary coherence. In order to properly account for this "sequence,"

cited from *Miqra'ot Gedolot ha-Keter*, 204. This line is omitted in Gruber's edition (based on MS Vienna 220), but it does appear in Maarsen, *Parshandatha*, III:63.

20 Rashi on Ps 68, Gruber ed., 834 (Heb.), 445 (Eng.). Perhaps Rashi does not mean until the very end of the psalm, since on verse 29 he says that the poet returns to the prayer he began in verse 2.

21 Rashi on Ps 68, Gruber ed., 834 (Heb.), 449 (Eng.). As Gruber suggests (in the bracketed words included in his translation), Rashi here refers to verses 20–22. It is theoretically possible that Rashi believes that the hymn extends even further within this psalm. See the previous note.

Rashi must explain the shifts in perspective, addressee, and theme throughout each psalm.[22]

To this end, Rashi makes a notable effort to interpret each psalm superscription in accordance with the theme of the body of the psalm – marking a departure from the midrashic tendency to interpret the superscriptions without this restraint.[23] For example, on Ps 5:1, Rashi challenges the midrashic tradition (reflected also in early Christian sources), that the term *neḥilot* in the superscription is related to the concept of "inheritance," for two reasons: first, the word *neḥilot* cannot be construed in this sense philologically; and second, the body of the psalm has nothing to do with inheritance (notwithstanding the fanciful midrashic and patristic readings in this vein).[24] Rashi offers his own analysis as an alternative:

> It is possible to interpret *neḥiloth* as a synonym of *gayyasoth* (military troops) as is suggested by the expression *neḥil shel devorim* (swarm of bees[25]) . . . [This Psalm is thus] a prayer prompted by enemy armies coming to attack Israel. And the poet (*ha-meshorer*) utters this psalm on behalf of the entire people of Israel.[26]

The body of this psalm appears to be a supplication to God for protection against "murderous deceitful men" (v. 7), and Rashi seeks to explain the difficult word *neḥilot* accordingly. Aside from the midrashic interpretation, the sage of Troyes knew that Menahem had offered another approach to the difficult Hebrew terms appearing in the headings of the Psalms, namely that they are the names of musical instruments or melodies.[27] But Rashi suggests a third interpretation, that *neḥilot* means *military troops*, fitting the theme of this psalm understood as a supplication for the defense of Israel from enemies. Since such a reading requires construing the psalm as a collective prayer rather than David's personal supplication for protection from his own enemies, Rashi explains that "the poet utters" its singular language "on behalf of

[22] Rashi does not, however, seek to explain the arrangements of the Psalter as a whole, as Saadia, e.g., had done, prompting Abraham Ibn Ezra's critique. See Viezel, "Formation of Biblical Books, According to Rashi," 24; Simon, *Four Approaches*, 216–220.

[23] Aside from the example cited here, see Rashi's commentaries on Ps 7:1, 8:1, 9:1. On Ps 45:1, as discussed in Chapter 2, Rashi interprets the superscription midrashically – but only because he was able to interpret the body of the psalm accordingly.

[24] See the discussion of Rashi's note here in Chapter 1.

[25] See m.*Bava Qamma* 10:2. It was not uncharacteristic of Rashi to draw upon Rabbinic Hebrew to elucidate Biblical Hebrew usages. See Netzer, "Comparison." Menahem ben Saruq, on the other hand, sharply distinguished between the two linguistic corpuses. See *Maḥberet*, Sáenz-Badillos ed., 13*–14*, 20*.

[26] Rashi on Ps 5:1, Gruber ed., 812 (Heb.), 188 (Eng.).

[27] See Rashi on Ps 5:1, Gruber ed., 812 (Heb.), 188 (Eng.), cited in Chapter 1, on p. 41.

the entire people of Israel."[28] As the psalm was explicitly attributed to David in the heading, Rashi presumably ascribed its composition to him as its historical author. Yet, when writing of the literary voice that speaks in this psalm, Rashi posits a theoretical persona of "the poet," i.e., the implied author who speaks in the psalm.

Rashi arrives at a complex notion of the voice of "the poet" in his commentary on Psalm 19, as evident in his opening comment:

> *The heavens declare the glory of God* – The poet (*ha-meshorer*) himself made this matter explicit: "There is no utterance; there are no words" (v. 4), [which is to say that] they [the heavens] do not speak with people except in so far as *their circuit has gone forth throughout the earth*, and they [the heavens] give light to people. Therefore people *declare the glory of God*, and they acknowledge and bless [Him] on account of the luminaries.[29]

Following the spirit of his commentary on Gen 1:27,[30] Rashi asserts that what is stated originally in verse 2, "the heavens declare the glory of God," becomes clear through the persona speaking in this psalm in verse 4, which clarifies that "There is no utterance; there are no words" – so there can never be any representation of what the heavens "declare." Rather, it is people who "declare the glory of God" when contemplating the heavens – the sun, moon, and stars – and their daily circuit around the earth. It turns out, then, that mankind at large gives a "voice" to the heavens; and "the poet himself" gives a voice to mankind, articulating thoughts essential to the human experience of "the glory of God" through nature.[31]

[28] The notion that David composed some Psalms on behalf of the community can be found already in rabbinic literature. See, e.g., b.*Pesaḥim* 117a.

[29] Rashi on Ps 19:1, Gruber ed., 818 (Heb.), 246 (Eng.).

[30] Rashi's commentary there is cited in Chapter 6, on p. 185.

[31] The term *ha-meshorer* is likewise used to identify the voice of the poet in the standard *Miqra'ot Gedolot* printed edition of Rashi's commentary on Ps 87:5: " ... Another interpretation: the poet says 'I shall mention to my people and to those who know me the great things of Egypt and Babylonia' (=a paraphrase of v. 4ff.)." This is presented as an alternative to the one given by Rashi earlier (on v. 3) that these words are a quotation of a divine utterance. In this instance, then, the term *ha-meshorer* is used in the alternative reading to identify the persona or "speaker" as a human being (as in Rashi's note on Ps 19:1) rather than God. This alternative interpretation is absent in both the Gruber and Maarsen editions of Rashi on Psalms, and it appears in *Miqra'ot Gedolot ha-Keter*, 56, in square brackets indicating its absence in some medieval manuscripts. All of this may suggest that it is a late interpolation into Rashi's commentary. In his critical apparatus, Maarsen, *Parshandatha* III:86, indicates that it is found in two of the medieval manuscripts he checked: Cambridge, St. John's College MS A3 (Ashkenaz, dated 1238); Karlsruhe, Badische Landesbibliothek, Cod. Reuchlin 10 (fourteenth century), in addition to the Salonika 1515 and Bomberg 1523 printed editions of the *Miqra'ot Gedolot*. I have also found it in MS Bodleiana 2440 (Ashkenaz, late twelfth century). Since this

With respect to Rashi's use of the term "the poet" in Psalm 19, it is instructive to consider a midrashic source he cites later in his commentary to the psalm, which notes that "David first mentioned [forgiveness of] 'errors' (v. 13), next 'willful sins' (v. 14), and then 'acts of rebellion' (v. 14)."[32] This midrashic formulation underscores Rashi's innovative move in identifying the literary voice – the implied author or narrator – in this psalm. It is indeed natural for the midrash to refer to David as the speaker in this psalm, since he is said to be its historical author, as its superscription records "A psalm of David." Yet Rashi uses the term *ha-meshorer* to refer to King David's literary agency, i.e., to designate the implied author, the literary voice speaking in this psalm on behalf of mankind at large, much as he posited that "the poet" speaks on behalf of all of Israel in Psalm 5 – another psalm attributed to David in the superscription.[33]

In his commentary on Ps 45:15–18 Rashi uses the term "the poet" (*ha-meshorer*) in the course of clarifying the poetic addressee, which is otherwise rather unclear. As Rashi understands it, verse 15 speaks of gifts brought by maidens "to You" (in the singular), on which Rashi remarks: "the poet (*ha-meshorer*) says this addressing the Holy One Blessed be He."[34] Verse 17, in turn, speaks in a very different vein to what is clearly a group: "your sons will succeed your ancestors; you will appoint them princes throughout the land," on which Rashi remarks: "He says [this] addressing all of Israel."[35] Verse 18 again switches, returning to the singular: "I commemorate Your fame for all generations, so peoples will praise You for ever and ever," on which Rashi comments: "the poet (*ha-meshorer*) says this addressing God."[36] The question Rashi seeks to answer in each of these comments is "To whom is the poet speaking?" – an issue essential for a proper understanding of the sequence and literary coherence of the verses.

commentary appears in the relatively early Cambridge and Bodleiana manuscripts, it is not inconceivable that this addition emanated from Rashi's circle of students (Lisa Fredman, personal communication). In any case, the scribe or commentator who offered this interpretation adopted Rashi's distinctive usage of the term *ha-meshorer*.

32 Rashi on Ps 19:14, Gruber ed., 818 (Heb.), 247–248 (Eng.). The idea behind this midrashic comment appears in *Midrash Tehillim*, Buber ed., 172. Yet Rashi's formulation most closely resembles the version appearing in *Yalqut Shimoni* on this psalm. Although the latter is a thirteenth-century work, it drew upon earlier midrashic sources that seem to have been available to Rashi.

33 Instead Rashi could have said, e.g., "David made this matter explicit" or "David utters this psalm on behalf of the entire people of Israel."

34 Rashi on Ps 45:15, Gruber ed., 827 (Heb.), 352 (Eng.).

35 Rashi on Ps 45:17, Gruber ed., 827 (Heb.), 352 (Eng.).

36 Rashi on Ps 45:18, Gruber ed., 827 (Heb.), 352 (Eng.).

Psalm 87 is classified by many modern scholars as a "Zion Hymn," because it contains praises of the city of Jerusalem.[37] Rashi adopts a similar perspective in his commentary on the second part of the psalm's superscription:

> *Its composition (yesudato) was in reference to the holy mountains* – As for the composition of this psalm, the poet composed it (*yissedo ha-meshorer*) with reference to Mount Zion and Jerusalem.[38]

Although the Biblical Hebrew root *y-s-d* suggests an understanding of this sentence to mean "its foundation is on the holy mountains," Rashi took the word in the medieval Ashkenazic sense commonly used by him (and others in the Franco-German school) to mean literary composition or writing.[39] For Rashi it was important to use the term "the poet" with reference to the literary voice behind the composition of this Psalm when speaking of its subject matter.[40]

THE "POET" VS. THE BIBLICAL EDITOR

In Psalm 45, Rashi uses the term *ha-meshorer* to identify the voice of the poet and implicitly set him apart from a distinct literary figure – an editor who incorporated the poem into the Psalms, quite likely David himself at a later point in his life. As noted in Chapter 2, many modern scholars classify this psalm as a "royal psalm" because it praises the king, i.e., one of the monarchs of ancient Israel, whereas Rashi construes it as a praise of Torah scholars, following midrashic tradition. This is evident in his commentary on the superscription, " … upon lilies, by the sons of Korah" (v. 1):

> *for lilies* – They composed this psalm in honor of Torah scholars, because they are soft as lilies, beautiful as lilies and, like lilies, they make good deeds blossom.[41]

[37] See Gerstenberger, *Psalms*, 2, 138–141.

[38] Rashi on Ps 87, Gruber ed., 844 (Heb.), 559 (Eng.). [39] See Chapter 2, note 45.

[40] The term *ha-meshorer* is used in a similar way in the standard *Miqra'ot Gedolot* printed edition of Rashi's commentary on Ps 118:16, " … And thus the poet says 'the right hand of God, the exalted one, which you created.'" This note is absent in Gruber's edition, as well as in Maarsen's edition. In *Miqra'ot Gedolot ha-Keter*, 158, it appears in square brackets, indicating that the editors question if it is original in Rashi's commentary. In his critical apparatus, Maarsen, *Parshandatha*, III:107, notes that it appears only in the Salonika 1515 and Bomberg 1523 printed editions of the *Miqra'ot Gedolot*, but not in any of the medieval manuscripts he checked. This, then, would seem to be a late addition to Rashi's commentary.

[41] Rashi on Ps 45, Gruber ed., 826 (Heb.), 349 (Eng.).

But then Rashi notes that the speaker of the next verse is different from that of the previous one:

> *My heart is astir* – Thus the poet (*ha-meshorer*) began his poem: "*My heart* motivated within me *gracious words* in praise of you, Torah scholars."
>
> *I say: "My works for the King"* – i.e., this poem that I composed (*yissadti*) and "made," I address to one who is worthy to be king, as it says, "by virtue of me [i.e., Wisdom] kings shall reign (Prov 8:15)."[42]

In Rashi's view, the poet who composed this psalm begins by reflecting on the moment of inspiration – when his heart was "astir" – thus prompting his praise of Torah scholars.[43]

The midrashic approach Rashi employs in his interpretation of this psalm was discussed in Chapter 2. Here we focus on the fact that Rashi seems to differentiate among disparate literary voices in this psalm. He specifies that "the poet," i.e., the personal voice or persona in this psalm (one of the "sons of Korah"[44]), begins to speak only in verse 2, which implies that verse 1, the superscription of the psalm, represents the external "voice" of the literary editor responsible for the arrangement of the Psalter, an activity that Rashi ascribes to King David.[45] Rashi does not spell this out, nor does he make this sort of observation about any other psalm superscriptions.[46] But elsewhere in his Bible commentary he is more explicit about the work of an implied author or narrator to be distinguished from

[42] Rashi on Ps 45, Gruber ed., 826 (Heb.), 349 (Eng.).

[43] Compare Rashi on Ps 8:4–5 ("When I see Your heavens, the work of Your fingers, the moon and stars that You have set in place. What is man that You have been mindful of him?'"): "As for me, *when I see Your heavens*, I wonder to myself '*What is man that you have been mindful of him?*'" (Gruber ed., 813 [Heb.], 198 [Eng.]). In this paraphrase Rashi explains the logical sequence of the otherwise unconnected verses in this psalm by construing verses 4–5 as a description of the moment that inspired the poet's sentiments recorded in the psalm.

[44] See Rashi on Ps 42:1.

[45] See Chapter 6, note 55. There appears to be another complexity in Rashi's perception of the composition of this psalm. Following b.*Pesaḥim* 117a, Rashi posits that the term *maskil* employed in the superscription of this psalm indicates that it was actually written "through the use of a *meturgeman* (lit. a translator)," which Rashi (in his Talmud commentary *ad loc.*) explains: "he spoke and another explicated." See Gruber, *Rashi on Psalms*, 299, 349. Rashi does not, however, identify the *meturgeman* as the one responsible for the superscription of the psalm.

[46] Such a distinction – between the original author of a psalm and a later literary editor – is made explicitly in a note on the superscription of Psalm 137 in the Psalms commentary fragment that some scholars attribute to Joseph Qara. The distinction is made there between the prophet Jeremiah, who authored the original psalm in Babylonia, and Ezra, who incorporated it into the Book of Psalms. See the full citation in Chapter 9, on p. 252.

the "voice" of the characters cited in the narrative – a matter to which we now turn.

"WRITER OF THE BOOK (KOTEV HA-SEFER)"

On Judg 5:31 Rashi notes that the concluding sentence, "And the land was tranquil for forty years," must be distinguished from the victory song uttered by Deborah: "These are not the words of Deborah; rather, they are the words of the writer of the book (*kotev ha-sefer*)."[47] The term *kotev ha-sefer* ("writer of the book") is telling, as it suggests an emergent investigation of biblical authorship and composition independent of midrashic sources, in which such terminology is not used. Another remark by Rashi on 1 Sam 9:9 addresses a similar issue in the biblical text. In the midst of a discussion between Saul and his lad, who were seeking the prophet Samuel, there is an aside in the text: "Formerly in Israel, when a man went to inquire of God, he would say, 'Come, let us go to the seer,' for the prophet of today was formerly called a seer" (1 Sam 9:9). Though these words immediately follow a direct quotation of the words of Saul's lad, Rashi remarks:

> The writer of the book (*kotev ha-sefer*) said this; these are not the words of Saul's lad.[48]

Rashi seeks to clarify that 1 Sam 9:9 is a sort of explanatory gloss by "the writer of the book." That biblical author, Rashi reasons, felt the need to explain why, in the dialogue that follows, the prophet is referred to as "the seer" (1 Sam 10:11, 18, 19). Rashi's comments on 1 Sam 9:9 may suggest – as some scholars have concluded – that he considered this verse to be a late interpolation into the biblical narrative by a later writer (the author of the Book of Samuel according to the Talmud – the opinion Rashi appears to endorse).[49] This historical question, however, is not addressed here explicitly by Rashi. Rather, Rashi's primary concern is a literary one: to

[47] See Gruber, *Rashi on Psalms*, 129–130n.

[48] כותב הספר אמר זאת, ואין זו מדברי נער שאול This seems to be the most accurate text, as attested in *Miqra'ot Gedolot ha-Keter*. See Viezel, "Formation of Biblical Books, According to Rashi," 30. Rashi's commentary in the printed editions of the *Miqra'ot Gedolot* reads הסופר כתב זה ואין זה מדברי נער שאול, a formulation more characteristic of Eliezer of Beaugency (as evident from the citations of his commentary that will be discussed in Chapter 9).

[49] See b.*Bava Batra* 14b–15a, where the books of Judges and Samuel are attributed to Samuel. On Rashi's adoption of this position, and an analysis of his commentary on 1 Sam 9:9, see Viezel, "Formation of Biblical Books, According to Rashi," 29–31; Viezel, "Medieval Commentators on Composition of the Bible," 123.

demarcate the different voices in the narrative, i.e., to distinguish between the voice of the narrator or implied author and the voice of the characters he cites – the issue Rashi clearly addresses in Judg 5:31.[50]

That Rashi's concerns were primarily literary and not historical can be seen by comparison with the comment of Joseph Qara, who – evidently inspired by Rashi's comment – explicitly addressed the historical question of authorship emerging from 1 Sam 9:9. As he remarks:

> *For the prophet of today was formerly called a seer* – What this generation refers to as "a Prophet," the earlier generations referred to as "a seer." This teaches that by the time this book was written they already were calling the "seer" a "Prophet." This indicates that the book was not written in the days of Samuel. If you search all of Scripture you will nowhere else find a prophet called a "seer" . . . This indicates that the generation of Samuel is referred to [in this gloss] as "beforetime." And a generation later than Samuel's is referred when it states "he that is now called a Prophet." Now our Rabbis of blessed memory said that Samuel wrote his book. "The one who illuminates the world will turn darkness into light and will make crooked things straight" (based on Isa 42:16).[51]

For Joseph Qara, it was clear that this verse is the product of a later interpolation – and so, this "voice" is historically and not merely poetically distinct from the authorial voice elsewhere in the book of Samuel.

RASHI'S LITERARY CONCEPTIONS AND POSSIBLE LATIN PARALLELS

Among Rashi's students there would indeed be further development of the issues of the narrative and authorial voices in Scripture – both from literary and historical perspectives. Some of these developments will be addressed in the following two chapters, which explore the literary sensibilities that emerged in the northern French *peshat* school among Rashi's students, followed by some of their students in the twelfth century. But here it is important to consider the implications of the literary observations Rashi himself makes in association with the term *kotev ha-sefer* in his commentaries on Judges and Samuel and his term *ha-meshorer* in his Psalms and Song of Songs commentaries.

[50] Elsewhere Rashi makes a similar literary observation, using the term "the Holy Spirit" to differentiate between the biblical narrator and the words of the characters he cites. See Rashi on Gen 2:24, 37:22. For the rabbinic source of this usage of the term "the Holy Spirit," see m.*Soṭah* 9:6 and Steiner, "Redaction," 130n.

[51] Joseph Qara on 1 Sam 9:9, Eppenstein ed., 57.

Eran Viezel regards the expression *kotev ha-sefer* as a medieval derivative of the common rabbinic term *ha-katuv*, i.e., "Scripture," or "the verse" that is also used frequently by Rashi.[52] Viezel tends to minimize the theoretical significance of this terminological shift from the passive participle of the root *k-t-v*, i.e., "[that which is] written," to the active participle "[the] writer" and argues that the medieval commentators who used the latter term were essentially reflecting the spirit of rabbinic interpretation.[53] In my opinion, however, this terminological innovation suggests a new appreciation for the role of the human writers who shaped the biblical text, guided, of course, by the Holy Spirit. In other words, Rashi does not look at the biblical text exclusively as a final product given by God, but also considers the literary process by which it was produced – through human agency.

Developments in Latin learning may help illuminate this shift of perception that occurred in the northern French *peshat* school. Alastair Minnis has traced changes in Christian perceptions of the Bible as literature and the role granted to its human authors.[54] Traditionally, authorship of the Bible was ascribed to the "Holy Spirit," with its human "authors" regarded as little more than scribes copying the words dictated to them. Gregory the Great, in his *Moralia in Job*, thus minimizes the importance of that biblical book's human author:

> The search for the author of this book is certainly a vain one, because ... the author is the Holy Spirit. The author of a book is the one who dictated it ... who inspired it ... Suppose we receive a letter from some great person and we read the words but wonder by whose pen they were written; it would certainly be ridiculous ... to search out by what scribe the words in it were written down. No, therefore, we know the book, and we know that its author is the Holy Spirit; so when we ask about the writer, what else are we doing but asking who the scribe is, whose words we are reading?[55]

Since the human writer of the Book of Job was simply writing what was dictated by the Holy Spirit, Gregory reasons, he was simply fulfilling an ancillary instrumental role.[56]

52 See Viezel, "Medieval Commentators on Composition of the Bible," 125.

53 See Viezel, "Medieval Commentators on Composition of the Bible," 146. I agree with Viezel that this terminological shift should not be taken as evidence that Rashi questioned rabbinic historical traditions regarding the authorship of the biblical books – as some scholars have suggested. In other words, when speaking of "the writer of the book" in his commentaries on Judges and Samuel, Rashi may well have been referring to the prophet Samuel, who, according to the Rabbis wrote these biblical books. See Viezel, "Medieval Commentators on Composition of the Bible," 122–124.

54 See Minnis, *Authorship*, 33–117.

55 Gregory the Great, *Moralia in Job*, Adriaen ed., 8–9, Kerns trans., 57–58.

56 Minnis, *Authorship*, 37.

This perspective largely prevailed until the thirteenth century. Generally speaking, in the twelfth century "God was believed to have controlled human authors in a way which defied literary description," and therefore "literary criteria and classifications . . . were afforded a relatively unimportant place in Scriptural exegesis."[57] As a result, Minnis argues, the twelfth-century commentators were preoccupied with allegorical interpretation. For Geoffrey of Auxerre (late twelfth century), for example, it was not important to know who wrote the Song of Songs, for whether or not the human *auctor* knew what he was prophesying, "the inspirer (*inspirator*) most certainly knew."[58] What mattered was the prophecy itself, of the mystical marriage of Christ and holy Church. In the thirteenth century emphasis came to be placed on the literal sense of the Scripture – and the exegetes' interest in their texts became more literary, as the emphasis shifted from the divine *auctor* to the human *auctor* of Scripture.[59] Interpreters thus began to explore the roles played by the human authors of Scripture and the literary forms and devices they used – which were classified as features of the literal sense, i.e., as facets of their personal purposes in writing.[60]

In speaking of "the writer of the book" (*kotev ha-sefer*) in his commentaries on Judges and Samuel, Rashi seems to signal a similar shift of attention to the intentions of the human authors who shaped the biblical text. This and similar terminology would be used more regularly in the twelfth century among the circle of Rashi's students, as discussed in Chapter 9. Admittedly, the term *kotev ha-sefer* is truly a minor note in Rashi – attested only twice in his commentaries. However, the term "the poet" (*ha-meshorer*) appears more prominently in his commentaries on the Psalms and Song of Songs, and it suggests a heightened literary sensibility within Rashi's exegetical consciousness. As noted earlier in this chapter, it is quite possible that Rashi derived this usage from the writings of Menahem ben Saruq. Himself a renowned Hebrew poet, the Andalusian linguist would have had in mind the well-developed discipline defined at length in Arabic treatises on poetry. It thus would have been natural for Judeo-Arabic interpreters to perceive the ancient biblical authors as poets and investigate the aesthetic features of Scripture – from the perspective of Arabic poetics. It is unlikely that Rashi had access to this discipline, being that it was transmitted entirely in Arabic, and by some Jewish authors in Judeo-Arabic. If so, we should ask: What could

[57] Minnis, *Authorship*, 58. [58] Minnis, *Authorship*, 38. [59] Minnis, *Authorship*, 39.
[60] Minnis, *Authorship*, 74.

have been behind Rashi's usage of the term "the poet" (*ha-meshorer*) in his commentaries on the Psalms and the Song of Songs?

Based on the examples discussed above, it would seem that Rashi employed the term "the poet" within his endeavor to discern the logic of the "sequence of the matters/verses" (*seder ha-devarim/miqra'ot*), a central goal of his interpretive methodology. In other words, Rashi aimed to discover the literary design of "the poet" in the structure of the biblical text, in the shifts from one verse to the next between different literary voices (who is speaking?) or addressees (to whom?), or transitions in the subject matter (about what?). As already mentioned, Rashbam defined "poetry" as "the arrangement of words (*siddur devarim*)."[61] This conception seems to inform Rashi's use of the term *ha-meshorer* when seeking to account for the often complex arrangement of the text in the biblical texts labelled *shir(ah)*, i.e., the Song of Songs and the Psalms.

It is worth investigating what appears to be a similar understanding of the poetic nature of Scripture in medieval Latin learning. The notion that the Psalms in particular can be viewed as poetic was well represented in Christian tradition going back to Late Antiquity. Despite their disdain for pagan poetry, the Church Fathers Jerome and Augustine found it necessary to argue that the Bible manifests similar literary merit. In his Letter 22 to Eustochium Jerome protests: "What has Horace to do with the Psalter?"[62] Yet this very question implicitly acknowledges that the two can be equated. In his Bible commentaries Jerome remarks that Psalms were "composed in a lyric fashion"[63] and that "David sang a lyric song."[64] The phrase *lyricum carmen* that Jerome uses to describe the Psalms is applied elsewhere in his writings to the works of Pindar and Horace.[65] Citing the authority of Josephus and Origen, Jerome even argues that the Psalms were written metrically in their original Hebrew, just as Horace was in Latin.[66] Augustine, likewise, invoked the opinion of earlier Jewish and Christian authorities who knew Hebrew that "the verses of David" were written in meter.[67] Working within this tradition,

[61] Rashbam on Deut 31:2; Rosin ed., 225.

[62] See *Sancti Eusebii Hieronymi Epistulae*, I:189, cited in Kraebel, "Poetry and Commentary," 227–228. See also Kugel, *Idea*, 151.

[63] Jerome, *Commentarii in Prophetas Minores*, Adriaen ed., II:618.

[64] *In Hieremiam*, Reiter ed., 110.

[65] Jerome, *Commentarii in Prophetas Minores*, Adriaen ed., I:215.

[66] See Kugel, *Idea*, 152.

[67] See Augustine, *Select Letters*, Baxter trans., 196 (Lat.), 197 (Eng.). See also Kugel, *Idea*, 163.

Cassiodorus in his Psalms commentary sought to demonstrate that King David frequently employed the figures and tropes enumerated within the classical traditions of grammar and rhetoric. At times, after he offers an interpretation of a verse, Cassiodorus will then note that the verse exemplifies a particular literary device or rhetorical mood.[68] The result of such a procedure is to turn the Psalter into a book of models useful for the teaching of literary exposition – as illustrated by Isidore of Seville (560–636) and especially in the dedicated work *De schematibus et tropis* of the Venerable Bede (672–735).[69]

But there was a new turn within this tradition in the medieval period. Working at the cathedral school of Rheims, Remigius in the ninth century and Bruno and his followers in the eleventh harnessed this "poetic" perspective to account for the coherence of each of the Psalms as a distinct literary unit. Remigius articulates the formal perception of the Psalms as poetic in the preface to his Psalms commentary:

> A psalm is a hymn or the praise of God. They are called hymns because they recite the praise of God metrically in their original language. For a hymn is praise composed according to a specific meter.[70]

Bruno likewise classifies the Psalms as metrically composed lyrics – a definition adopted by Roscellinus and Gilbertus Universalis.[71] As Andrew Kraebel notes, the perception of the Psalms as poems inspired these commentators to apply a "coherent, poetic hermeneutic" in which the consecutive verses of individual psalms fit together, by contrast with their patristic sources, such as Augustine and Cassiodorus, who tended to gloss each verse discretely, almost to the point of individual verses being the object of brief commentaries unto themselves.[72]

Remigius and those who followed in his footsteps conveyed a sense of internal coherence through prefaces supplied before the verse-by-verse

[68] Cf., e.g., Cassiodorus, *Expositio in Psalterium*, Walsh trans., I:34, 36, 41, 42, 43, 47, 48, 53, 166. For a further discussion of Cassiodorus' use of figures, and the relationship between his commentary and medieval glosses, see Kraebel, "*Grammatica*," 74–75.

[69] See Kugel, *Idea*, 164–170; Copeland and Sluiter, *Medieval Grammar and Rhetoric*, 256–259, 267–269.

[70] MS Rheims 132, f. 1r: *Psalmus uero est hymnus uel laus Dei. Dicuntur autem hymni, quod laudem Dei metrice in sua lingua canunt. Nam hymnus est laus cuiuscumque metri ratione composita.* Cited and translated in Kraebel, "Poetry and Commentary," 231.

[71] See Remigius, MS Rheims 132, f. 1r and *PL* 152: 638B, Aniorté trans., 59, both cited in Kraebel, "Prophecy and Poetry," 448. See also Roscellinus, MS Troyes 1507, f. 25r; Gilbertus Universalis, MS Laon 17, f. 1vb (both cited in Kraebel, "Prophecy and Poetry," 448 n. 89).

[72] Kraebel, "Prophecy and Poetry," 450.

glosses on each psalm. Remigius often adapted Cassiodorus' views in such prefaces that presented a general interpretation of the content of each psalm. For example, before his commentary on Psalm 15 (MT 16), Remigius seeks to explain its Latin heading *tituli inscriptio ipsi David* ("The inscription of a title to David himself"):

> The Prophet speaks in this psalm concerning the Passion of Christ, and so he has given it this particular title, for he sees by divine inspiration the title (*titulum*) that, in the future, Pilate will affix to the Lord's Cross (i.e., "Jesus of Nazareth, King of the Jews"; cf. John 19:19).[73]

The poetic perspective from which this psalm was uttered is made clear by an earlier remark in Remigius' preface: "It should be known that, throughout this psalm, the humanity of Christ speaks, chiefly concerning his Passion and Resurrection," and, as he begins his gloss on the psalm proper, Remigius notes, "This is the voice of Christ calling on his Father in his Passion."[74] This framework explains to the reader how Remigius understood the poetic perspective in this psalm: adopting the voice of Christ, the prophetic poet begins his prayer: "Preserve me, O Lord, for I have put my trust in thee" (Ps 15:1 [MT 16:1]). Some of these elements are drawn from Cassiodorus, who had already made the connection with John 19:19, and, in general, observed that different psalms are spoken in different lyric voices.[75] However, as Kraebel observes:

> [Remigius'] procedure for interpreting what those voices say is more typical of the grammatical tradition of Servius than it is indebted to the patristic exegete. Unlike Cassiodorus, who often simply explains the Christological content of each verse, largely derived from Augustine's *Enarrationes*, Remigius is intent, in his teacherly manner, on explaining how the text of each psalm forms a coherent literary unit.[76]

The aim of the Remois exegetes to impose literary coherence within each psalm can be illustrated through their use of the technical term "apostrophe." In the classical grammatical and rhetorical traditions, this term was used to describe how the poet or speaker "turns away"

[73] MS Rheims 132, f. 19ra: *Locuturus Propheta in hoc psalmo de Passione Christi praetitulauit eum huiuscemodi inscriptione, praeuidens diuina inspiratione futurum quod a Pilato iam dictus titulus dominicae erat cruci affigendus.* Cited and translated in Kraebel, "Poetry and Commentary," 233–234.

[74] MS Rheims 132, f. 19ra: *sciendum quia humanitas Christi per totum hunc psalmum de Passione et Resurrectione sua maxime loquitur*; and f. 19rb: *Vox Christi est Deum Patrem in Passione inuocantis.* Cited and translated in Kraebel, "Poetry and Commentary," 234.

[75] Cassiodorus, *Expositio in Psalterium*, Walsh trans., I:136–137.

[76] Kraebel, "Poetry and Commentary," 234.

from the principal audience to poetically address another (usually unhearing) audience, such as inanimate objects, animals, absent dead people or abstractions.[77] Remigius accounts for the shift between Ps 17:2 (MT 18:2), "I adore you, O Lord," and Ps 17:3 (MT 18:3), "The Lord is my firmament," by identifying the earlier verse as an apostrophe to God. When Ps 17:35 (MT 18:36) refers to God again in the second person, Remigius identifies another instance of apostrophe.[78] Bruno, likewise, applies the term apostrophe in a similar way over one hundred times in his Psalms commentary.[79] For example, he does so in order to explain the logical connection between Ps 2:2, "Kings of the earth take their stand, and regents intrigue together, against the Lord and against His anointed," and Ps 2:3, "Let us break the cords of their yoke, shake off their ropes from us." According to Bruno, in this psalm David speaks, in the voice of Christ, in verse 2 declaratively and generally, but then in verse 3 specifically addresses "his own," i.e., the Church, in an apostrophe.[80]

To be sure, Remigius and Bruno were indebted to patristic interpreters such as Jerome, Augustine, and Cassiodorus for the Christological content of the Psalms. However, their perception of the Psalms' poetic nature drew them to devote energy to the literary coherence of each psalm – at times a challenging endeavor, given the seeming disjointedness of some of these ancient compositions. Using the insight that the Psalms can be likened to lyric poetry, the Remois exegetes harnessed terms and concepts from the tradition of *grammatica* to overcome this challenge. They therefore sought to identify the poetic voice(s) speaking within each psalm, his addressee, which may shift from verse to verse, and his subject matter, which likewise may vary within the psalm.

Rashi can be said to have faced similar interpretive challenges in his commentaries on the Psalms and the Song of Songs, the two biblical texts in which he applied the term *ha-meshorer* to identify the poetic voice speaking within them. The Rabbis of the midrash ascribed prophetic content about the future history of Israel to the Song of Songs, but paid little attention to the literary design of the book. Though Rashi accepted the rabbinic supposition about the prophetic content of the Song of Songs, he criticized the "aggadic *midrashim* on this book ... that do not fit ('are

[77] See *PEPP*, s.v., "Apostrophe." See also Isidore, *Etymologies*, Lindsay ed., I:xxvi–xxvii.

[78] MS Rheims 132, ff. 22v and 25v. [79] Kraebel, "Prophecy and Poetry," 453, n. 103.

[80] *Apostropham facit ad suos, adhortans ne ab illis metu aut blanditiis incorporentur, ne ob id in futuro, sicut et ipsi, damnentur* (*PL* 152:644D–645A, Aniorté trans., 68). See Kraebel, "Prophecy and Poetry," 452.

not settled upon,' (*mityashevim 'al*) the language of Scripture (*leshon ha-miqra*) and the sequence of the verses (*seder ha-miqra'ot*)."[81] Rashi sought to discern the literary design of the book, which he attributed to "the poet" (*ha-meshorer*), a term he used to refer to King Solomon's literary agency in composing the Song of Songs – guided by the Holy Spirit. In his commentaries on the Psalms, likewise, Rashi accepted the general premise of the Rabbis that King David and other authors of the Psalms spoke prophetically, among other things, about events befalling Israel in the far future, as well as their prayers to God in those times. Yet, Rashi endeavored to meet the exegetical challenge posed by these often disjointed or otherwise seemingly discontinuous texts. Beginning with his efforts to demonstrate basic agreement between the superscriptions of each psalm and the verses that follow, Rashi imposed literary coherence upon these texts, and he criticized midrashic interpretations that failed to do so. Underlying this exegetical agenda is an assumption that the Psalms are "poetic" texts, as Rashi employs the term *ha-meshorer* to account for the literary voices (Who is speaking?), the addressees (To whom is he speaking?), and the subject matters (About what is he speaking?) as they shift within each psalm.

It is difficult to determine the extent to which Rashi was aware of developments in Christian interpretation in northern France in his time, as discussed in Chapter 3. It is conceivable that he knew something of the poetic-grammatical hermeneutic of Remigius and Bruno, which circulated in northern France in the last third of the eleventh century, and that this inspired his novel usage of the term *ha-meshorer* in his commentaries on the Song of Songs and the Psalms. But even if that was not the case, this very parallel, like the others noted throughout this study, is illuminating from a methodological perspective, as the implications that Christian interpreters at the school of Rheims drew from what they perceived as the poetic nature of Scripture suggest a new way of appreciating Rashi's intentions in implicitly classifying the Song of Songs and the Psalms as "poetic."

[81] See Chapter 2, p. 73.

8

Joseph Qara and Rashbam: *Peshat* Legacy in Northern France

The pioneering nature of Rashi's *peshat* program was duly noted by Rashbam, who describes how earlier interpreters focused exclusively on midrash, whereas his grandfather "endeavored to interpret the *peshat* of Scripture." In the same breath, though, he adds: "I, Samuel, son of his son-in-law Meir (of blessed memory), debated with him personally, and he admitted to me that if he had the opportunity, he would have to write new commentaries according to the *peshat* interpretations that newly emerge (*ha-mitḥaddeshim*) every day."[1] Rashi recognized that he had not yet completed the work that needed to be done to perfect the *peshat* method, and acknowledged the remarkable advances in this revolutionary endeavor in his own day. It is likely that new *peshat* interpretations were raised orally within Rashi's circle – and that he was referring to them in the comment cited by Rashbam. Indeed, some such interpretations were incorporated into the text of Rashi's commentaries, as noted in earlier chapters of this study. But the most remarkable manifestation of the progress of the *peshat* method was in the separate commentaries penned by Joseph Qara and Rashbam.

It is true that Rashi's commentaries are primarily midrashic, whereas those of Qara and Rashbam are devoted to *peshat*. Some scholars therefore regard the work of those two exegetes as a new phase of "genuine" *peshat* interpretation, separate from Rashi's inchoate conception. In my opinion, however, Rashi had a fairly clear concept of *peshat*, though he did not make it his primary goal – as Sarah Kamin argued. Furthermore, many of the tools utilized by Qara and Rashbam in their *peshat*

[1] See Rashbam on Gen 37:2, Rosin ed., 49, cited in the Introduction on p. 9.

interpretation have their roots in Rashi's work. Precisely for this reason many of the later additions into Rashi's commentaries – originating in interpretations devised by Qara and Rashbam – fit in so seamlessly and are difficult to distinguish from those of the master himself. And so, it would be more accurate to characterize the trilogy of Rashi, Qara, and Rashbam as a continuum of the development of *peshat* interpretation in northern France. It might, in fact, be said that Qara and Rashbam represent the completion of Rashi's *peshat* project – and an understanding of their work is therefore necessary to properly assess the legacy of the Troyes master.

The relationship between Rashi and his students Qara and Rashbam – with respect to the role of *peshat* exegesis in their interpretive work – can be described in the following way. Rashi often used the tools of *peshat* exegesis as a yardstick to evaluate midrashic interpretations and select those that "settle" the language of Scripture. These tools included, primarily, philological-grammatical analysis ("precision of the language/the language of Scripture": *diqduq ha-lashon/leshon ha-miqra*) and respect for the literary context ("sequence of the words/verses": *seder ha-devarim/ha-miqra'ot*).[2] Qara and Rashbam, on the other hand, saw fit to use these tools – which they learned from Rashi and augmented with further refinements – to create an entirely independent *peshat* reading of Scripture. Qara and Rashbam inspired subsequent northern French *pashtanim*, such as Joseph Bekhor Shor and Eliezer of Beaugency (believed to have been Rashbam's direct student), before the school came to a close in the thirteenth century.[3]

In the modern period, Rashbam has generally been better known than Qara, as his Pentateuch commentary has appeared in the *Miqra'ot Gedolot* since the 1705 Berlin edition, whereas Qara's commentaries on the Prophets have been included in the *Miqra'ot Gedolot* only since the 1897 Lublin edition. Interest in Qara grew with the nineteenth-century Wissenschaft des Judentums ("scientific study of Judaism") movement, which sought out his commentaries in manuscript, inspired by this bold intellect fiercely devoted to *peshat*. The mature northern French *peshat* method, characterized by philological, literary, and historical sensitivity, captured the attention of modern scholars, who lauded it as a precursor to modern historical-critical Bible scholarship.[4]

[2] See Chapter 1.

[3] See Grossman, "Literal Exegesis," 363–371; Berger, "Contextual Exegesis"; Cohen, "Eliezer of Beaugency"; Jacobs, *Bekhor Shoro*. On the continued interest in *peshat* in the Ashkenazic milieu in the thirteenth century, see Kanarfogel, "Tosafists."

[4] See Japhet, *Collected Studies*, 21–29. See also Brin, *Qara*.

The clarity and force of the *peshat* method advanced by Qara and Rashbam made it seem superfluous to consider the complexities of their hermeneutics, something required in Rashi's case because of the disparity between his stated *peshat* agenda and reliance on midrash in practice. Many scholars seem to have felt that Qara and Rashbam discerned the "real meaning" of the Bible, i.e., *peshuto shel miqra*. Rashbam's expression "the true *peshat* of Scripture" (*amitat peshuto shel miqra*; comm. on Lev 10:3) was taken to indicate that *peshat* is the "high road" of Bible interpretation.[5] As a result, the mixed signals that Qara and Rashbam emit in speaking of the status of *peshat* vis-à-vis midrash have not been explored sufficiently. Rather than projecting the privileged modern status of *peshat* onto these medieval authors, I believe it is necessary to consider how their hermeneutics emerged organically within their twelfth-century intellectual context, which itself was linked integrally with conceptions prevalent in the eleventh century.

As noted in the preceding chapters of this study, Rashi's exegetical innovations find parallels in Latin Bible exegesis that help explain his new interpretive agenda and the central role that "the *peshat* of Scripture" plays within it. By the twelfth century, with the emergence of the school of St. Victor, the parallels between the new Jewish and Christian interpretive modes had grown stronger.[6] To be sure, such parallels are not needed to explain Rashi's students' very interest in *peshat*, which can be traced directly to the master himself. In other words: while the question had to be asked what motivated Rashi to engage in *peshat* exegesis in the first place, this is not a mystery with respect to his students, since Rashi's *peshat* program would have been a salient model on their intellectual horizon. Yet, when considering how Qara and Rashbam would have sought to balance this new approach in relation to midrashic interpretation, the analogous developments in Latin learning prove illuminating.

The emerging medieval Christian interest in the literal sense of the Bible can be correlated with an increasing tendency to analyze the sacred text using grammatical methods initially devised for secular literature. An analogous correlation, as discussed in the earlier chapters of this volume, seems to inform Rashi's associated conceptions of *peshuto shel miqra* and *yishuv hamiqra* ("settling of Scripture") in his Bible and Talmud commentaries. The

[5] See Japhet, "Tension," 413, 421–422. I do not subscribe to this opinion, as the discussion in this chapter and the next makes clear.

[6] See Kamin, *Jews and Christians*, xxi–lxxiv; Touitou, *Exegesis*, 11–33; Leyra Curiá, *In Hebreo*.

latter had precedents in the Rhineland academies in which Rashi was trained, but the application of philological-contextual analysis to the Bible was Rashi's innovation. This conceptual link between Bible commentary and the analysis of humanly authored texts is critical for understanding the hermeneutics of Qara and Rashbam, since both *pashtanim* also composed commentary-glosses on other forms of Jewish literature, as discussed below.

It is beyond the scope of the current study to survey the commentaries and exegetical methods of Qara, Rashbam, and their circle of students comprehensively. We aim here, rather, to carry forth the comparative investigation advanced in the preceding chapters to show how a comparison with Latin learning can shed new light on the post-Rashi northern French *peshat* school. The argument put forward in this chapter and the next is twofold. First, that the conception of *peshuto shel miqra* developed in northern France in the twelfth century depended on a view of the Bible as a literary work, subject to the modes of analysis that Qara and Rashbam themselves applied in their commentaries on postbiblical Jewish literature. Second, that the ways in which this association was conceived in contemporaneous Latin learning sheds valuable light on how the northern French *pashtanim* negotiated the often conflicting intellectual and theological demands of their rational analysis of the Bible and the traditional midrashic methods. The possibility that Qara and Rashbam were actually aware of – and responded to – the specific Christian interpretive streams cited in this chapter should not be ruled out, since these northern French *pashtanim* manifest a greater familiarity with Christianity and Latin learning than Rashi did. Yet, as was the case in our investigation of Rashi, the probative value of this comparison is independent of the question of influence. In other words, the parallels themselves offer a valuable way to appreciate how the twelfth-century northern French *pashtanim* balanced their innovative literary interests in Scripture with earlier midrashic traditions, much as their Christian neighbors expressing a nascent interest in the *sensus litteralis* balanced it with their abiding allegiance to the "spiritual" Christological sense of the Bible.

BIOGRAPHIC AND BIBLIOGRAPHIC BACKGROUND

Joseph Qara, born in Germany in the 1050s, studied in the Rhineland academies, probably in Worms, in the 1070s and 1080s.[7] Rashi, with whom he came to study in Troyes in the 1080s, is the clearest source of

[7] On Qara's biography, see Grossman, *France*, 254–261.

Qara's conception of *peshat*. Yet he seems to have first been inspired to follow this path from his earlier studies with his uncle Menahem bar Helbo.[8] Joseph's appellation "Qara" (also given to Menahem bar Helbo) evidently connotes special dedication to Bible study (Heb. *miqra*), rather than halakhah.[9] His commentaries probably spanned all of the Prophets and many of the Writings. Later authors cite interpretations of his on Job and the Five Scrolls, and fragments of a Psalms commentary have been attributed with him.[10] There is no extant Pentateuch commentary by Qara.[11] However, there is great importance in his critiques of Rashi that appear in manuscript margins of the master's Pentateuch commentary, with notations such as: "But I Joseph son of Simon say," or "but according to the *peshat* ... " In one instance, Qara records: "Thus I, Joseph son of Simon interpreted, and Rashi acknowledged that my view is correct."[12] These notes, directed at Rashi's midrashic interpretations, highlight Qara's new *peshat* methods – which Rashi himself acknowledged, as reported by Rashbam.[13]

Qara is believed to have written a commentary on the key midrashic work *Genesis Rabbah* (preserved in a manuscript pseudonymously attributed to Rashi).[14] But Qara was better known for his commentaries on the

8 See his commentary on 2 Sam 23:5. Menahem bar Helbo is cited occasionally by Rashi, as mentioned in Chapter 4.

9 See Ahrend, *Qara on Job*, 26–27n; see also Poznanski, "Introduction," XXIV, who cites a reference to *pitronei ha-qara'im* ("interpretations of the Bible experts") in Qara's commentary on Isa 23:13. The term almost certainly does not refer to the Karaites, since that movement was little known in the Ashkenazic community.

10 See Grossman, *France*, 305–316. Among other things, Grossman demonstrates that the Isaiah commentary printed in the Lublin edition of the *Miqra'ot Gedolot*, based on MS NY JTSA (Jewish Theological Seminary of America) Lutzki 777, is far less accurate than the version attested in MS JTSA Lutzki 778. In any case, the manuscripts containing Qara's commentaries at times reveal evidence of having been augmented by later scribes. See Poznanski, "Introduction," XXV–XXXI; Eppenstein, *Qara*, 10–24. Japhet, "Compilatory Commentaries," argues that the Job commentary attributed to Qara is, in fact, a compilation that includes citations from Rashi, Rashbam, and others.

11 Berliner attributed an anonymous fragmentary commentary on Deuteronomy to Qara. But this attribution has been questioned. Grossman made a stronger case for a Pentateuch commentary by Qara based on anonymous fragments (in what has been termed "the Italian Genizah") that resemble Qara's exegetical style. See Berliner, *Pletath soferim*, 6–11; Grossman, *France*, 290–302.

12 See Poznanski, "Introduction," XXV.

13 See Rashbam on Gen 37:2, Rosin ed., 49, a passage discussed further in this chapter and in Chapter 9.

14 See Grossman, *France*, 339–340. Berliner argued that Qara is the author of this commentary, but Eppenstein argued that it is the work of R. Kalonymus of Rome, augmented by Qara. Grossman, on the other hand, believes that the interpretations by Qara in the work

piyyutim, liturgical poetry recited in Ashkenazi prayer rites.[15] While the earliest *piyyutim* originated in Palestine, there was a continuous tradition of *piyyut* composition that came to the Franco-German community through Italy. The great master Rabbenu Gershom composed *piyyutim*, as did Rashi.[16] The language of the *piyyutim* is often extremely difficult, as it is highly allusive and dependent on midrashic material. In response, *piyyut* commentaries were composed in the Rhineland communities. Pioneers in this endeavor included Meshullam ben Moshe (d. 1095) of Mainz, Menahem bar Helbo, and Rashi.[17] But it was Joseph Qara who fully developed this new genre; and he is often referred to simply as "the commentator" in the subsequent *piyyut* commentary tradition.[18] In his *piyyut* commentaries, Joseph Qara cites his uncle, as well as Kalonymus of Rome, with whom he seems to have studied in Worms.[19] Qara continued writing commentaries on the *piyyutim* in Troyes, where he joined Rashi's close student Shemaiah, who likewise engaged in *piyyut* commentary.

Unlike the ancient, sacred, fixed text of the Bible, the *piyyutim* were perceived as a human literary production, especially as many were composed close to Qara's time.[20] The implications of this distinction are reflected in a gloss thought to be from Qara's pen on a line of *piyyut* by Simon ben Isaac (c. 950–1020), a great Ashkenazic *piyyut* composer:

> At the time of the writer of this *piyyut*, the years from the time of the destruction of the Holy Temple in Jerusalem had not yet come to a thousand. Therefore, he wrote: "Over nine hundred and twenty years have passed since it was destroyed." But now that one thousand and fourteen years have passed, one should say "More than a thousand years."[21]

The original *piyyut* was written just after 988 (as medieval Jews dated the destruction of the Second Temple to 68 CE); but the commentator felt he had the authority to adjust it to his time: 1082. Unlike the divine text of the Bible, which obviously was not subject to such updating, this *piyyut* was

were culled by a later author from a separate complete commentary on *Genesis Rabbah* that Qara, like R. Kalonymus, composed.

15 See Grossman, *France*, 325–339; Hollender, *Piyyut*, 36–40.

16 See Gruber, *Rashi on Psalms*, 29–37.

17 Grossman, *France*, 510–528; Hollender, *Piyyut*, 30–36; Gruber, *Rashi on Psalms*, 75–84.

18 Grossman, *France*, 254–255; cf. Hollender, *Piyyut*, 37.

19 See Grossman, *France*, 257.

20 Compare the observation by Hollender, *Piyyut*, 8, on the non-canonical status of *piyyut*.

21 This citation (from Oxford-Bodleian Library MS Mich. 543 [Neubauer 1212], 82v) is taken from Grossman, *France*, 257. Even if this note is not by Qara himself, it probably was by someone in his intellectual circle, perhaps Shemaiah. As such, the attitude it expresses would be an accurate reflection of Qara's thinking.

perceived as an essentially contemporary human text serving as the voice of the community, and as such could be adjusted according to changing circumstances.

Rashbam, who is believed to have been born in Ramerupt (less than 30 miles from Troyes) was a younger colleague of Qara's.[22] He composed commentaries on most of the Bible, though only a small portion survives. Best known is Rashbam's Pentateuch commentary, which was preserved in only a single manuscript (MS Breslau 103) that is now lost, though additional fragments of the commentary, and commentaries attributed to Rashbam on selected verses of the Pentateuch, appear in other manuscripts, at times on the margins of Rashi's commentaries.[23] Commentaries presumed to be by Rashbam on Job, Song of Songs, Qohelet, and Psalms have been discovered and published over the last generation.[24] As mentioned in Chapter 1, Rashbam penned a grammatical work entitled *Dayyaqut* (i.e., "Grammar"), to which he appended a separate, and evidently unfinished, grammatical commentary, which covers only Gen 1:1–7:5. These works deal with Biblical Hebrew phonology, morphology, and syntax, based largely on the works of Menahem and Dunash. It is unclear if Rashbam ever became aware of Hayyuj's works, which were written in Arabic, though they were translated into Hebrew in southern France by Ibn Chiquitilla.[25]

Rashbam was an important talmudist, though his achievements were overshadowed by those of his grandfather Rashi and his own younger

[22] See, e.g., his commentary on Gen 37:13. For a sketch of Rashbam's biography, see Liss, *Fictional Worlds*, 57–58.

[23] MS Breslau 103 was the source of Rashbam's commentary printed in the 1705 *Miqra'ot Gedolot* in Berlin, and of David Rosin's 1882 critical edition, which itself serves as the basis of the new edition published by Martin Lockshin in 2009. See Kislev, "Contribution of MS Hamburg 52"; Liss, *Fictional Worlds*, 59–69; Sokolow, "Rashbam's Pentateuch Commentary." See also the recent PhD dissertation of Hillel Novetsky, "A Reconstruction of Rashbam's Lost Commentary on Bereshit 1–17." (I am grateful to its author for sharing this work with me. Unfortunately, I received it too late to incorporate substantially into this study.)

[24] See Touitou, *Exegesis*, 208–225; Mondschein, "'Lost Commentary,'" 91–129, and the introductions to the published editions of the commentaries attributed to Rashbam on Job, Song of Songs, and Qohelet. Some scholars question whether these commentaries are actually by Rashbam himself and not someone else in his circle of students or colleagues. But to me it seems that their attribution to Rashbam has been demonstrated adequately. Cf. Haas, "Reconsideration"; Kalman, "Methodological Challenges"; Liss, "Song of Songs," 1–8. Some of Rashbam's lost commentaries are cited by later authors and in so-called compilatory commentaries. See Japhet, "Rashbam's Introduction to Lamentations."

[25] See Merdler, "Rashbam and Hebrew Grammar," 309–315.

brother Jacob, renowned as the leading Tosafist Rabbenu Tam. The Tosafists would revolutionize Talmud study by applying a new and robust dialectical method of analysis to this ancient legal compendium.[26] Rashbam wrote commentaries on most of the Talmud; but they now are known only from citations by later authors, apart from sections on tractates *Bava Batra* and *Pesaḥim*, which have long appeared in the standard printed editions of the Talmud.[27] In contrast to Rashi's succinct gloss-note commentary style, Rashbam is expansive. Representing an early Tosafist manner, he goes beyond Rashi's goal of elucidating the text and engages in legal analysis by comparison with other talmudic sources.[28]

Rashbam highlights different interpretive possibilities to a greater extent than Rashi did, in part because he had access to additional talmudic interpretive traditions. Rashbam was the first Ashkenazic talmudist to utilize the commentary of Rabbenu Hananel – who taught at Qayrawan in North Africa.[29] Rashbam also wrote critical glosses (*tosafot*) on Isaac Alfasi's abridgment of the Talmud, which was influential in al-Andalus.[30] Being aware of traditions of talmudic interpretation from the Muslim orbit completely different from that of the Rhineland academies in which Rashi was educated, Rashbam had a clearer grasp of the openness of the talmudic text, and the creative role of the interpreter in determining its meaning.

Rashbam's Talmud commentaries bear the stamp of his forceful, critical personality. In one typical remark, after offering his own interpretation of a talmudic passage, he adds:

> There are many other interpretations ... and there is no substance to them. And the manner (*shiṭṭah*) of the discussion does not settle well with them at all.[31]

Elsewhere, after delineating his own interpretation in opposition to others he rejects, he remarks:

> And the essence of the matter, when you investigate those [other] interpretations, you will not find sense or substance in them ... But rather it is as we have explained ... And there are other interpretations, but there is no substance to

[26] Ephraim Kanarfogel argues that the Tosafists became aware of the dialectic mode of study in the cathedral schools and that this was a catalyst in the development of the revolutionary Tosafist method. See Chapter 3, note 81.

[27] Ta-Shma, *Talmudic Commentary I*, 58.

[28] Ta-Shma, *Talmudic Commentary I*, 59–61.

[29] Ta-Shma, *Studies: Germany*, 43–61.

[30] See Friedman, "Tosafot."

[31] Rashbam on b.*Bava Batra* 80a, cited in Ta-Shma, *Talmudic Commentary I*, 59.

them . . . and it is nonsense and empty words . . . and all of these [other] explanations are empty and misleading.[32]

To evaluate the interpretations available to him critically, Rashbam developed sensitivity to the conventions of talmudic expression, as reflected in the following typical remarks:

This is the manner (*shiṭṭah*) of the Gemara in many places.
This is not the style (lit., language: *lashon*) of the Gemara in any place.
The Gemara abbreviated the language of Rab.
It is not the way of the Gemara to elaborate so much.
Because there are abbreviated matters in this discussion, the scribes erred and the text was (lit. the books were) corrupted.[33]

Rashbam applies the term *shiṭṭah* as used by Rashi to connote *the typical manner or style* of the Talmud, upon which a proper interpretation must "be settled" in order to accurately discern the intention of the author.[34]

ATTITUDES TOWARD CONTEMPORARY MODES OF BIBLE INTERPRETATION

Given the involvement of Qara and Rashbam in *piyyut* and Talmud commentary, respectively, it is not surprising that both manifest acute awareness that their *peshat* method diverges from traditional midrashic interpretation. Rashbam indeed emphasizes the newness of *peshat* interpretation. As he records, Bible interpretation in Ashkenaz had been primarily midrashic, and *peshat* was ignored until his grandfather Rashi first opened this interpretive vista. Rashbam further records debates he had with Rashi, in which the latter acknowledged "the *peshat* interpretations that newly emerge (*ha-mitḥaddeshim*) every day" superior to his own.[35] For Rashbam, *peshat* was nothing less than a revolutionary way of interpreting Scripture – still evolving in his own time.

It is remarkable that a talmudist like Rashbam, in a conservative intellectual rabbinic framework, would readily admit that his exegetical approach departs from traditional Bible interpretation. His younger contemporary Abraham Ibn Ezra, by contrast, argued that the Rabbis "knew

[32] Rashbam on b.*Bava Batra* 104b.

[33] Rashbam's glosses on b.*Bava Batra* 39a, 43a, 51a, 65b, 69a. Rashbam uses the term *shiṭṭah* in his Bible commentary as well. See Rashbam on Exod 9:17, Deut 11:10.

[34] See Chapter 3, p. 94 and note 64.

[35] Rashbam on Gen 37:2. This passage was cited in the Introduction, on p. 9, and will be discussed further in Chapter 9.

the *peshat*" and that his commentaries aim to restore a genuine rabbinic understanding of the Bible.[36] Whereas Ibn Ezra typically invokes earlier authorities, Rashbam celebrates his discovery of *peshat* readings that eluded his predecessors, as reflected in remarks such as these:

Now I shall explicate the interpretations of the early ones, to inform people why I have not interpreted as they did.[37]

He who desires to grasp the essential *peshat* of these verses should be illuminated by this interpretation of mine, as the early ones who came before me did not understand it at all.[38]

In a similar vein, Qara appends the following remark to one of his *peshat* interpretations:

Know that all masters of *aggadah* and Talmud will disparage this interpretation, because they cannot abandon the way the Rabbis interpreted this verse in tractate *Rosh ha-Shanah* and in other tractates and follow my interpretation. Yet the intellectuals (*maskilim*: lit., wise, enlightened ones) will perceive the manner of the Scriptures to establish the matter correctly.[39]

There evidently was a cadre of scholars eager to absorb the new *peshat* method, whom Qara and Rashbam refer to as "lovers of reason," "knowers of reason," and, more generally, "intellectuals" (*maskilim*).[40]

This spirit of intellectual innovation in Bible interpretation finds a parallel in the groundbreaking new method of Talmud scholarship pioneered by the Tosafists, heralded by Rabbenu Tam and his circle. Tosafist learning in northern France, characterized by critical dialectic analysis that departed from the more conservative Talmud study in the Rhineland academies, prized the notion of *ḥiddush*, i.e., innovative legal or textual analysis.[41] Due to the intellectual appeal of this new type of learning, students from the Rhineland began streaming to northern France to study with the Tosafists, reversing the trend – in the tenth and eleventh centuries – of students from France (such as Rabbenu Gershom and Rashi) studying in the Rhineland.[42]

The implications of this revolution can be gauged by a conservative backlash in the thirteenth-century pietist Ḥasidei Ashkenaz movement, as

[36] See Chapter 4, p. 123. [37] Rashbam on Gen 1:1, Rosin ed., 3.
[38] Rashbam on Exod 3:11, Rosin ed., 83. [39] Qara on 1 Sam 1:20, Eppenstein ed., 48.
[40] See the preceding citation from Qara and the citations from Rashbam on Gen 1:1, 37:2, Exod 21:1. See also Touitou, *Exegesis*, 11–15, 98–99, 101–105.
[41] See Soloveitchik, "Rabad," 14; Soloveitchik, "Themes," 339; Ta-Shma, *Talmudic Commentary I*, 71–92.
[42] See Kanarfogel, *Intellectual History and Rabbinic Culture*, 2–9.

reflected in *Sefer Ḥasidim*. According to Haym Soloveitchik, these pietists aimed to redress an imbalance engendered by Tosafist learning:

> In the previous culture, the path to eminence lay in massive scholarship – comprehensive knowledge which could only be acquired by many years of study. If the emblem of excellence, however, was *ḥiddush*, making several subtle distinctions could bring a man rapidly into prominence ... Many of the adherents of the new school may have looked down on the intellectual patrimony of their fathers and on the scholars who embodied it. In sum, it would be surprising if the Tosafist movement ... did not set loose some little foxes who were spoiling the vineyards of the Ashkenazic community. Or so at least it might appear to a conservative contemporary.[43]

For the pietists, the values of the old style of learning had been eclipsed by the Tosafists and their followers:

> As learning in ... [the old Ashkenazic culture] was assimilative rather than creative, the scholarly style was milder, the profile lower. Many of the traits that we associate with Rashi – reticence, modesty, temperateness of expression – are common to the literature of the eleventh century. The equilibrium of the intellectual, imaginative and moral faculties was being upset by this [Tosafist] preemption of aspiration on the part of *talmud torah*. On a deeper level, much of *Sefer Ḥasidim* is an attempt to redress this imbalance.[44]

With its emphasis on *ḥiddush*, Tosafist learning produced what could be perceived as morally problematic by-products, especially hubris:

> Scholars and would-be scholars were busily writing *ḥiddushim* and *tosafot* – *their ḥiddushim* and *their tosafot* to the Talmud. Authorship had come into being, and is it surprising that pride followed close behind? ... The Pietists inveigh regularly against the growing phenomenon of *torah she-lo lishmah* ("study of the Law, not for its own sake"). Intellectual excellence was fast becoming the arête of the age, and he who possessed it was often only too easily tempted to dispense with the humbler and more inconvenient virtues.[45]

Our interest here is not in *Sefer Ḥasidim* or the pietist movement per se, but rather in what they can tell us about cultural and intellectual developments in the twelfth-century Ashkenazic community. Of particular relevance is the new use of the expression *torah she-lo lishmah* in *Sefer Ḥasidim* as noted by Soloveitchik: "The Pietists used the term *she-lo lishmah* at times as synonymous with *lilmod she-lo 'al menat lekayyem*

[43] Soloveitchik, "Themes," 341–342. Cf. Marcus, "History"; Fishman, *People of the Talmud*, 185–198.

[44] Soloveitchik, "Themes," 345–346. On the portrait of Rashi's personality, see Grossman, *Rashi*, 23–30.

[45] Soloveitchik, "Themes," 344.

('study without the intention of fulfilling the Law') ... the reduction of *talmud torah* to a purely intellectual experience."[46] Soloveitchik considers this to be an indictment of the pitfalls opened by Tosafist learning. Yet this critique might have also applied to *maskilim* in the circle of Qara and Rashbam, intellectuals who prized novel *peshat* interpretations that departed radically from older, more traditional ones. Bold, even proud, statements by these *pashtanim* about discovering new readings that had eluded earlier interpreters or that would irritate traditionalists such as those cited earlier in this chapter hardly seem to comport with the eleventh-century values of "reticence, modesty, [and] temperateness of expression." Moreover, *peshat* analysis might appear to be an intellectual pursuit detached from religious observance, since, as Rashbam acknowledges, it sidesteps the halakhic and moral implications of the Bible, which stem exclusively from midrashic interpretation.[47] By pietist standards, this might seem suspiciously close to improper study (*she-lo lishmah*) of the sacred text.[48]

These tumultuous developments in the culture of Jewish learning in northern France might be compared with analogous ones in Latin learning in the transition from the eleventh to the twelfth centuries. The paucity of writings emanating from the eleventh-century cathedral schools by contrast with the numerous works penned in the "twelfth-century renaissance" has long been noted. Yet Stephen Jaeger, who questions the very appellation of twelfth-century learning as a "renaissance," marshals substantial evidence for the vitality of learning in the eleventh-century northern French and German cathedral schools.[49] According to Jaeger, eleventh-century scholars manifested a "charismatic" rather than "intellectual" outlook, and conveyed their learning orally rather than in writing, with the ultimate aim of inculcating within themselves and in their students the values (Latin *mores*) that defined civilized behavior, such as discipline, obedience, and humility.[50] In the twelfth century, "gains in

[46] Soloveitchik, "Themes," 344.

[47] See Rashbam's introduction to Exodus 21, discussed in Chapter 9.

[48] This last statement is offered only as a possibility, since Ḥasidei Ashkenaz did not oppose study of the religious texts of Judaism that had no direct religious application. They even favored study of the talmudic orders *Qodashim* and *Ṭoharot*, which pertain to the era of the Holy Temple and have no contemporary halakhic import. What would be objectionable about the *peshat* project is that it takes the text of the Bible, which – from the midrashic perspective – is replete with halakhic and religious significance, and strips it of those normative dimensions, making the study of the sacred text an intellectual pursuit only.

[49] See Jaeger, "Pessimism." [50] Jaeger, *Envy of Angels*, 4–17.

knowledge, reasoning, success in disputation and in proof" came at the expense of this culture of virtue.[51] Within the twelfth-century cathedral schools there emerged a new critical intellectual spirit that valued the views of the *moderni* alongside the *antiqui*.

Rashbam's bold rejection of the "early ones who came before me" is hard to find in Christian learning. But Peter Abelard (1079–1142) – a chief example cited by Jaeger for his lack of discipline[52] – did assert the need to evaluate the words of the Church Fathers critically for possible errors.[53] Abelard and Gilbert of Poitiers (c. 1080–1154) also manifest an innovative style of Bible commentary that draws upon the arts in new ways to analyze Scripture.[54] These two thinkers were, in fact, well known for applying logical and grammatical thought to the interpretation of Holy Scripture.[55] Furthermore, Abelard and Gilbert were otherwise regarded as radical thinkers. Both were put on trial for views deemed heretical, and were opposed energetically by the more conservative and mystically oriented Bernard of Clairvaux (c. 1090–1153), a devotee of the old charismatic style of learning and the "culture of virtues" it embodied.[56]

Particularly telling is the account offered by Abelard of his encounter with Anselm of Laon (d. 1117), a renowned interpreter of Scripture who would play a key role in the formation of the *Glossa Ordinaria*:

> I was recommended to one Anselm, the very oracle of his time; but to give you my own opinion, one more venerable for his age and wrinkles than his genius or learning . . . Anselm could win the admiration of an audience, but was useless when put to the question. He had a remarkable command of words but their meaning was worthless and devoid of all sense. The fire he kindled filled his house with smoke but not with light; he was a tree in full leaf which could be seen from afar, but on closer and more careful inspection proved to be barren. I had come to this tree to gather fruit, but I found it was the fig tree which the Lord cursed.[57]

As Jaeger notes: "New [learning] confronts old here in as sharp an opposition as we could hope for. Anselm is teaching by eloquence, charisma ... and inertia. Abelard himself makes sense through plain speech and reasoning . . . Abelard has genius, Anselm has slowly acquired polish."[58] Among the areas in which Abelard challenged Anselm was in the interpretation of Scripture. Abelard describes how he attended the old scholar's lecture on Ezekiel but was sorely disappointed, prompting him

[51] Jaeger, *Envy of Angels*, 217–219. [52] Jaeger, *Envy of Angels*, 236.
[53] See Minnis and Scott, *Literary Theory*, 68. [54] See Minnis, *Authorship*, 58–63.
[55] See Copeland and Sluiter, *Medieval Grammar and Rhetoric*, 22–23.
[56] See Evans, "Trial of Gilbert" and Jaeger, *Envy of Angels*, 244–268.
[57] Abelard, *Letters*, 62. [58] Jaeger, *Envy of Angels*, 230.

the next day to deliver his own lecture on this text (which was regarded as particularly difficult) and its interpretation by the Church Fathers.[59] To Anselm's dismay, that lecture proved popular, prompting the audience to request further lectures from Abelard, who eventually set up his own school in Paris.

Though Abelard was exceptional in the Christian world for his audacity, he did make a name for himself and would have been well known in Rashbam's day in northern France. It is therefore suggestive that in one instance Rashbam expresses himself with surprising sharpness, reminiscent of Abelard's remarks:

> You have surely seen how my grandfather, may his saintly name be blessed, interpreted [the difficult locution] "For man is the tree of the field to enter the besieged city before you" (Deut 20:19) to mean "Lest you think that the tree of the field is [like] a man, to enter the besieged city and fight against you." But don't you see that this is nonsense (*hevel*)? For who would be such a simpleton or fool to think that a tree has the abilities of a man? And why would our Master Moses have needed to say something that is not worthy of hearing? But I have explained this properly according to the verses and reason.[60]

This text is from a fragment of Rashbam's writings and may have been part of a private correspondence with a student.[61] In any case, Rashbam's willingness to dismiss his grandfather's interpretation is striking.

Unlike the contentious relationship between Abelard and Anselm, a spirit of reverence for Rashi himself was expressed by Rashbam even when criticizing his interpretations in the above-cited passage. Moreover, rather than resisting his students' innovative interpretations, Rashi acknowledged their value. Rashbam mentions that he debated matters of interpretation with his grandfather, using language reminiscent of the *disputatio* style that characterized the new intellectual mode of Latin learning in the cathedral schools.[62] Rashbam goes on to report that his grandfather valued such "*peshat* interpretations that newly emerge every day" and was prepared to revise his commentaries accordingly.[63] The veracity of this report regarding Rashi's approval for this further

[59] See Smith, *Glossa Ordinaria*, 6–7.

[60] This text appears in Rashbam's name in MS Bodleiana 186 (Oppenheim 34) 116 (Ashkenaz, early thirteenth century). It is cited here from Sokolow, "Rashbam's Pentateuch Commentary."

[61] See Jacobs, "Rashbam's Major Principles."

[62] See Jaeger, *Envy of Angels*, 218, 230. See also Novikoff, *Medieval Culture of Disputation*, 68–70.

[63] Rashbam on Gen 37:2, a passage cited earlier in this chapter.

development of the *peshat* method is supported by remarks made by Qara indicating Rashi's agreement with his new interpretations, even where they depart from those Rashi wrote originally.[64] As discussed in Chapter 1, this unpretentious attitude of Rashi's led to the complex situation of the very text of his commentaries. There is evidence that Rashi actually did revise at least some of his commentaries according to interpretations suggested by his students, either himself, or with the assistance of his amanuensis Shemaiah.[65]

Since we do not have any autographs of Rashi's commentaries, or even of the versions prepared by Shemaiah, it is at times difficult to distinguish between Rashi's original commentaries and those revised or added by him later in life. Furthermore, later scribes seem to have independently added into Rashi's commentaries interpretations by his students, especially Qara and Rashbam. This situation tends to obscure the origins of some of the exegetical innovations within Rashi's school. Insights discovered by Qara or Rashbam, for example, may be found in Rashi's commentary; but their presence there may be second hand, i.e., they may have been added to Rashi's original commentaries, perhaps by Rashi himself, by Shemaiah (at Rashi's request or independently), or by other scribes wishing to augment Rashi's original work. In some cases, though, there are indications that allow us to ascribe particular innovations to Qara or Rashbam.[66] This enables us to trace the development of the *peshat* method from its incipient steps in Rashi's work to its mature state in the exegetical work of his students and their students throughout the twelfth century.

NEW METHODS OF PESHAT

Qara and Rashbam, working with the teachings of Rashi as well as their own keen interpretive intuitions, developed new methods of *peshat* interpretation. In many cases, these new methods are associated with characteristic terminology, which reflects methodological self-awareness. The methods and terms applied by these key northern French *pashtanim* can usefully be delineated in five categories.

[64] See p. 211. On Rashi's openness to learning from his students, see Grossman, *Rashi*, 56–68.

[65] See p. 32.

[66] For example, Rashi acknowledged Rashbam's "discovery" of staircase parallelism, as discussed in Chapter 1.

Self-Sufficiency of Scripture

Perhaps the most fundamental principle of the *peshat* method developed by Qara and Rashbam is the hermeneutical self-sufficiency of the text of the Bible. The assumption underlying midrashic interpretation, as noted in Chapter 1, is that the biblical text is cryptic and requires deep investigation that goes beneath its surface. Qara vigorously opposed this notion: "It is not the manner of a prophet in any one of the twenty-four books of the Bible to obscure the meaning of his words in such a way that they can be ascertained only through the *aggadah*."[67] To be sure, Rashi had pioneered a new method for expounding "the *peshat* of Scripture." But this was only one aspect of Rashi's interpretive program. His ultimate goal was to present a critical selection of midrashic interpretations that comport with ("settle") the language and sequence of the verses. Rashi still accepted the constant need for supplementary information from midrashic tradition to adequately explicate the biblical text. Qara, on the other hand, argued that the Bible is entirely self-explanatory:

> Prophecy was written ... in a complete manner with all that is necessary for its interpretation ... so that there is no need for corroboration from elsewhere, nor midrash, for the Torah, as given, is perfect (cf. Ps 19:8) ... and lacks nothing. But anyone who ... leans toward the midrash ... is like one swept away by the river current ... and grabs anything that comes to hand to save himself. But if he put his heart to the word of God, He would reveal the meaning of the matter and its *peshat*, fulfilling what it says: "If you seek it as you do silver and search for it as for treasures, then you will ... attain knowledge of God" (Prov 2:4–5).[68]

Whereas Rashi often used his sensitivity to the language and sequence of the biblical text as tools for selecting critically among midrashic interpretations, Qara, followed by Rashbam, harnessed these sensitivities exclusively to develop *peshat* as an entirely new interpretive method, predicated on the assumption that the biblical text is "perfect," and can be elucidated entirely from within.[69]

For example, Rashi drew upon midrashic tradition to interpret the intentions of the builders of the tower of Babel, attributing to them the rebellious plan to battle with God based on Gen 11:4: "Come let us build a city, and a tower with its top in the sky, to make a name for ourselves;

[67] Qara on Judg 5:4, Eppenstein ed., 25. [68] Qara on 1 Sam 1:17, Eppenstein ed., 47.

[69] For a midrashic conception of the "perfection" of Scripture, see Kugel, *Bible as it Was*, 20–21.

else we shall be scattered all over the world." Rashbam, on the other hand, writes:

According to the *peshat*, in what manner did the generation of the dispersion sin? If you argue that it is because they said "with its top in the sky," does it not say: "large cities walled up to the sky" (Deut 1:28, 9:1)? But rather, because God commanded them: "Be fertile and increase and fill the earth!" (Gen 1:28, 9:1), but they chose one place in which to dwell and said "lest we scatter"; therefore God scattered them by His decree.[70]

Rashbam's stylistic awareness, coupled with a sense of scientific realism, prompted him to take the expression "with its top in the sky" as hyperbole, just as Moses did not refer to cities actually "walled up to the sky." Seeking evidence for the builders' sin in the Bible (rather than in midrash), Rashbam cited the divine "command" to Adam and repeated to Noah: "Be fertile and increase and fill the earth!" This "precept" was violated by the men of Shinar in their stated intention not to scatter, a sin that invited God's forceful intervention: "Let us, then, go down and confound their speech there, so that they shall not understand one another's speech" (Gen 11:7), leading to the realization of their very fear: "the Lord scattered them ... over the face of the whole earth" (Gen 11:8).

Rationalism

Some scholars have detected in Rashbam – in comments such as one just discussed – a tendency toward rationalism, i.e., a desire to view the events portrayed in the Bible in natural rather than miraculous terms.[71] Yet any discussion of "rationalism" in the northern French *peshat* school must be distinguished from that manifested in the Geonic-Andalusian school, which sought to harmonize Scripture with Greco-Arabic philosophical and scientific learning – an endeavor central in Abraham Ibn Ezra's "way of *peshat*." For example, the tower of Babel episode was cast by Ibn Ezra in anthropological terms, with God's intervention taken as benevolent guidance rather than as a punishment:

If we look carefully by way of *peshat*, we see that the people of the "generation of the dispersion" [i.e., the tower builders] were not punished, but rather were scattered throughout the earth, as opposed to their intention ... And God ... saw fit in His wisdom that they should dwell in many places, as written "and fill the

70 Rashbam on Gen 11:4, Rosin ed., 12. Cf. Rashi on Gen 11:1.

71 See Touitou, *Exegesis*, 123–124, 183; Japhet, *Rashbam on Job*, 134; Grossman, "Literal Exegesis," 352–353.

earth" (Gen 1:28, 9:1), and these are the words of Moses. But they did not know the thoughts of God.[72]

Accordingly, Ibn Ezra reinterprets God's "confounding" the languages of the tower-builders:

In my view . . . they scattered from there, and after they scattered Nimrod reigned over Babylonia, and other kings arose; and over time, with the death of the first generation, the original language was forgotten.[73]

Ibn Ezra thus renders the miraculous biblical depiction a dramatization of a prosaic reality: the builders had a change of heart and abandoned the tower, leading to their dispersion, which over time led to the differentiation of languages among their descendants. Applying what Saadia would call *ta'wīl*,[74] Ibn Ezra reinterprets Scripture to conform to a rational outlook. In fact, one might say that Ibn Ezra's zealous concern for historical feasibility caused him to misunderstand the myth-like tower of Babel tale, which was meant to be taken at face value, as Rashbam did, unencumbered by Ibn Ezra's rationalist concerns.

Literary Context

Menahem ben Saruq – whose *Maḥberet* was influential in Rashi's *peshat* school – relied heavily on the immediate literary context as an exegetical tool, often using the phrase "its context indicates its meaning (*'inyano yoreh 'alayw*)."[75] This allowed Menahem to engage in his philological analysis of Biblical Hebrew without relying on

[72] Ibn Ezra, alternate commentary on Gen 11:4, Weiser ed., I:187–188. For Ibn Ezra, "Be fertile and increase and fill the earth!" is not an actual command that could have been violated by the tower-builders, but rather God's blessing that mankind thrive. (See his commentary on Gen 1:26, Weiser ed., I:19; for the rabbinic view, see b.*Sanhedrin* 59b and Rashi on Gen 9:7.) Moreover, in adding that "these are the words of Moses," Ibn Ezra suggests that they were never even communicated to Adam and Noah (as a literal reading of Gen 1:28 and 9:1 suggests), but merely represent God's unexpressed sentiment toward mankind, which was later recorded by Moses in Scripture, in his role as an omniscient narrator privy to God's inner thoughts. Ibn Ezra elsewhere speaks of Moses' role as the biblical narrator; see alternate commentary on Gen 2:18, Weiser ed., I:168. He would have known this concept from the tenth-century Karaite Yefet ben Eli, who speaks regularly about the activity of the biblical editor-compiler (*mudawwin*), even though Ibn Ezra (who knew Yefet's commentaries well) does not use a comparable Hebrew term for the *mudawwin*. See Steiner, "Redaction," 154–167.

[73] Ibn Ezra, standard commentary on Gen 11:7, Weiser ed., I:49.

[74] See Chapter 4.

[75] *Maḥberet*, s.v., גלב, Sáenz-Badillos ed., 106*; cf. Sáenz-Badillos, "Hebraists," 103. See also Allony, "Vistas," 28–29.

midrashic interpretation.[76] This outlook, in turn, was taken to new heights by Qara and Rashbam. Rashi had used the notion of *seder ha-miqra'ot/devarim* ("the sequence of the verses/words") as a standard by which to critically evaluate midrashic interpretations. Qara uses similar terminology – "the sequence of Scripture (*seder ha-miqra*) and the flow of the verses (*hillukh ha-ketuvim*; lit., 'running' of the verses)" – when seeking to ascertain the *peshat* interpretation. As Qara remarks on a prophecy about the "servant" of the Lord in Isaiah 42, taken in Christianity as a reference to Jesus (see Matt 12:15–21):

> A person not familiar with the order of Scripture (*seder ha-miqra*) and the flow of the verses (*hillukh ha-ketuvim*) might interpret this passage about the King Messiah, and he could cite proofs for his view from many places. But heaven forbid that we disregard the flow of the passage (*hillukh ha-parashah*) and its order (*seder*) and the matter that settles well (*mityashev*), to stitch and connect extraneous subjects to the matter of this prophecy on the basis of two or three verses in the passage that are not consecutive.[77]

Qara, by contrast, interprets this passage as part of a prophecy about the Persian king Cyrus, which he regards as the subject of Isaiah's adjacent prophecies.

For Rashbam, as well, literary context was a useful tool for discerning the correct interpretation of a verse according to its *peshat*. For example, given the cryptic nature of the prohibition "Do not eat upon blood" (Lev 19:26), Rashi evidently felt he had no choice but to turn to the Talmud for its interpretation:

> This is expounded in many different ways in b.*Sanhedrin* (63a): a prohibition to eat from the flesh of holy sacrifices before the sprinkling of the blood; a prohibition to eat from an ordinary animal before its soul has departed; and many more.[78]

Rashbam, on the other hand, offers the following alternative explanation:

> According to its *peshat*, [it is] a matter understood from its context (*davar ha-lamed me-'inyano*), [as the beginning of the verse says:] "Do not practice divination or soothsaying." This, too, means following the manner of the pagan nations, who eat next to the grave of a murdered person for the purpose of witchcraft, so that the death shall not be avenged, or some other type of witchcraft.[79]

The expression *davar ha-lamed me-'inyano*, "a matter understood from its context," is taken from the Talmud, and is actually one of the thirteen

[76] See Maman, "*Peshat* and *Derash*."

[77] Qara on Isa 42:3, *Keter* ed., 273.

[78] Rashi on Lev 19:26, Berliner ed., 253.

[79] Rashbam on Lev 19:26, Rosin ed., 162.

midrashic hermeneutical principles of R. Ishmael.[80] Accordingly, the principle was applied by the Rabbis midrashically in their halakhic explications of Scripture.[81] But Rashbam used this principle in a new way in service of the *peshat* ideal of interpreting the biblical text contextually without recourse to extrabiblical sources.

Biblical Stylistic Conventions

Beyond the immediate context, both Qara and Rashbam were keenly sensitive to the style and conventions of Biblical Hebrew. This *peshat* tendency can be traced to Rashi, who in this connection uses expressions such as "this is the typical style of Scripture/ the scriptures/ the prophets (*ken derekh ha-miqra/ ha-ketuvim/ ha-nevi'im*)."[82] Similar phraseology is used by Qara and Rashbam,[83] augmented by other expressions such as "the usual manner of the language of Scripture (*hergelo shel leshon ha-miqra*)," knowledge of which enables them to undercut midrashic interpretations that had been offered by Rashi.[84]

Both Qara and Rashbam manifest awareness of (what modern scholars refer to as) the "exposition" style in biblical narrative, i.e., the tendency of the biblical narrator to provide seemingly irrelevant information early in an account, by way of "introduction" (*haqdamah*), i.e., in order to prepare the reader to understand something that will be told later. As Rashbam remarks:

This is the essential *peshat* (*'iqqar peshuto*) according to the typical style of the biblical verses (*derekh ha-miqra'ot*). For Scripture often offers introductory information (lit., introduces: *le-haqdim*) and explains something superfluous for the sake of that which is mentioned later on in another place. Hence, it writes, "Shem, Ham and Japhet," and adds "And Ham was the father of Canaan" (Gen 9:18). [The addition is superfluous here] but is intended to

[80] See, e.g., b.*Sanhedrin* 86a. See also Elon, *Principles of Jewish Law*, 64.

[81] See, e.g., b.*Sanhedrin* 86a; b.*Ḥullin* 140a.

[82] See Rashi on Gen 35:27, Isa 63:1, Jer 50:27. See also Rashi on Isa 53:3, 66:4; Job 12:17.

[83] See Qara on Isa 1:18 (*derekh ha-nevi'im*), Ezek 29:5 (*derekh ha-miqra'ot*); Rashbam on Gen 1:1 and Deut 32:23 (both cited in the discussion that follows), as well as on Exod 30:34 (*derekh miqra'ot*), Job 5:19 (*derekh ha-miqra*). Cf. with the term *shiṭṭah* used by Rashi and Rashbam in their Bible and Talmud commentaries. See note 33 earlier in this chapter and Chapter 3, note 64. See also Rashi on Exod 6:30, discussed in Chapter 1.

[84] See Qara's *peshat* gloss on Rashi's midrashic interpretation of Exod 30:13 cited in Berliner, *Pletath soferim*, 19.

explain what was written later [when Noah sought to punish Ham]: "May Canaan be cursed" (Gen 9:25), for had it not been stated earlier who Canaan is, we would not understand why Noah cursed him.[85]

Qara applied this principle to undercut Rashi's midrashic interpretations.[86] Eleazar Touitou and Hanna Liss have demonstrated that Rashbam used it to explain the arrangement of the large and small literary units within the Pentateuch.[87]

Rashbam's substantial insights into the literary conventions of biblical narrative and poetry have been noted by modern scholars.[88] Rashbam's observations about biblical parallelism (discussed in Chapter 1) are particularly significant because they can be viewed as a medieval precursor for the notion of *parallismus membrorum* or "parallelism of the members" (i.e., parts of the verse) articulated by the eighteenth-century English Hebraist Robert Lowth, who defined it as the fundamental characteristic of biblical poetry.[89] As Lowth writes:

The poetical conformation of the sentences, which has been so often alluded to as characteristic of the Hebrew poetry, consists chiefly in a certain equality, resemblance, or parallelism between the members of each period; so that in two lines (or members of the same period) things for the most part shall answer to things, and words to words, as if fitted to each other by a kind of rule or measure.[90]

This "principle of parallelism," as he called it, was capable of "much variety and many gradations; it is sometimes more accurate and manifest, sometimes more vague and obscure endless forms and variations."[91] Lowth would go on to define three main types of parallelism, the most obvious of which he called "synonymous parallelism," which occurred

[85] Rashbam on Gen 1:1, Rosin ed., 3–4.

[86] See, e.g., Qara on 1 Sam 1:3 and his *peshat* gloss on Rashi's commentary on Gen 22:13, cited in Berliner, *Pletath soferim*, 14. See also Jacobs, "Joseph Kara."

[87] Touitou, *Exegesis*, 112–121, 145–164. Liss, *Fictional Worlds*, 78–83, 113, 144. Rashbam's *haqdamah* principle is discussed further in Chapter 9.

[88] On Rashbam's literary awareness, see Lockshin, "Literary Exegete"; Japhet, *Rashbam on Job*, 65–69, 170–187.

[89] See Harris, *Discerning Parallelism*, 1–13, 55–73. Lowth is generally credited with the discovery of biblical parallelism, being the first to regard it as the essential principle of biblical prosody and to describe its workings systematically. James Kugel argues that Lowth's account was not truly original, since it drew upon earlier European Bible scholarship. See Kugel, *Idea*, 266–273. Kugel also challenges Lowth's analysis of biblical parallelism, devising an alternative account of its workings from a literary perspective. See Kugel, *Idea*, 12–58. See also Alter, *Biblical Poetry*, 3–26.

[90] Lowth, *Lectures*, II:34. [91] Lowth, *Lectures*, II:34.

when the same sentiment is repeated in different, but equivalent terms. This is the most frequent of all, and is often conducted with the utmost accuracy and neatness: examples are very numerous, nor will there be any great difficulty in the choice of them: on this account I shall select such as are most remarkable in other respects.[92]

Rashbam notes this phenomenon using the term *kefel* ("double"), and related terminology, throughout his commentaries.[93]

A fine example relates to Deut 32:23, "I will consume (*aspeh*) evils upon them. I will use up (*akhaleh*) My arrows on them." One of the explanations Rashi on this verse offers for the difficult work *aspeh* is "I will consume," for which he cites a proof-text from Gen 19:15, "Lest you be consumed (*tissafeh*)." Rashi's construal of the word *aspeh* in the first verset of Deut 32:23 renders it a synonym of the term *akhaleh* in the second verset. To explain this phenomenon, Rashbam remarks:

I will consume (*aspeh*) *evils upon them* ... *I will use up* (*akhaleh*) ... – [this is a conventional biblical formulation] because it is the typical style of the biblical verses (*derekh ha-miqra'ot*) to double (*likhpol*) their language. So this verse means: I will use every one of the evils that I possess to injure them.[94]

In other words, according to Rashbam, the second verset indeed repeats the very same idea as the first, which is typical of the Bible's stylistic conventions.

Not only did Rashbam note the phenomenon of parallelism in general, he also seems to have discerned the workings of some of its varied manifestations. Lowth's second major category is what he calls "antithetic parallelism," i.e., "when a thing is illustrated by its contrary being opposed to it."[95] As he explains:

This is not confined to any particular form: for sentiments are opposed to sentiments, words to words, singulars to singulars, plurals to plurals, &c. of which the following are examples:

The blows of a friend are faithful / But the kisses of an enemy are treacherous.
The cloyed will trample upon an honey-comb / But to the hungry every bitter thing is sweet. *(Prov 27:6–7)*

There is who maketh himself rich, and wanteth all things / Who maketh himself poor, yet hath much wealth.(Prov 13:7)

[92] Lowth, *Lectures*, II:35.
[93] See Harris, *Discerning Parallelism*, 72–73, and further references cited there.
[94] Rashbam on Deut 32:23, Rosin ed., 228, with the textual emendation (based on MS) in n. 18.
[95] Lowth, *Lectures*, II:45.

The rich man is wise in his own eyes / But the poor man that hath discernment to trace him out will despise him.[96](Prov 28:11)

A careful reading of Rashbam reveals that he perceived the workings of antithetical parallelism. For example, his analysis of Qoh 4:13, "Better is a youth who is poor and wise (*misken we-ḥakham*) than an old and foolish king":

Misken – I cannot interpret this as *wise* to make it synonymous with (lit., a double word [*kefel millah*]) *ḥakham* (wise) as . . . [indicated by a comparison with the use of this root in Isa 40:20 and Job 22:2] . . . [because in this verse] "youth" relates to "old"; "poor" (*misken*) relates to "a king"; "and wise" (*ḥakham*) relates to "and foolish."[97]

There are proof-texts that would have allowed the construal of *misken* to mean *wise*, which would be a synonym of the adjacent work *ḥakham*. But Rashbam gives greater weight to the antithetical structure of this verse that requires an antonym of *a king* here. Accordingly, he construes *misken* to mean *a poor man*.

The third major category classified by Lowth is "synthetic parallelism." In this structure, he explains,

the sentences answer to each other, not by the iteration of the same image or sentiment, or the opposition of their contraries, but merely by the form of construction. To this, which may be called the Synthetic or Constructive Parallelism, may be referred all such as do not come within the two former classes: I shall however produce a few of the most remarkable instances:

> The law of The Lord is perfect, restoring the soul;
> The testimony of The Lord is sure, making wise the simple;
> The precepts of The Lord are right, rejoicing the heart;
> The commandment of The Lord is clear, enlightening the eyes.
> *(Ps 19:8–9)*[98]

What modern scholars term "staircase parallelism" is a subtype of Lowth's "Synthetic or Constructive Parallelism." This structure was defined by Rashbam with remarkable clarity in the following terms: "the first half does not finish the statement until the second half comes and repeats [a phrase] and [then] completes the statement. But the first half mentions about whom it speaks last."[99] As discussed in Chapter 1, Rashbam collates a number of examples to illustrate this biblical poetic convention in his commentary on Exod 15:6, "Your right hand, O Lord,

[96] Lowth, *Lectures*, II:45–46.
[97] Rashbam on Qoh 4:13, Japhet and Salters ed., 128–129.
[98] Lowth, *Lectures*, II:48–49. [99] Rashbam on Exod 15:6, Rosin ed., 102.

glorious in power, Your right hand, O Lord, shatters the foe," a verse that manifests this structure.

Evidently possessing a keen literary intuition, Rashbam was able to discern key elements of biblical poetics using only his deep familiarity with the biblical text itself. Yet the results of his analysis appear rudimentary when compared with the systematic endeavor to outline the Bible's literary techniques by Moses Ibn Ezra in his poetics *Kitāb al-Muḥāḍara wa-l-Mudhākara.*[100] The great Andalusian poet did not have to be as original as Rashbam. He simply drew upon the well-developed discipline of Arabic poetics to define biblical manifestations of twenty "embellishments of poetry" (*maḥāsin al-shi'r*), as they were referred to in Arabic poetics, such as metaphor, simile, and hyperbole, as well as a number of structural techniques. Among the latter are various sub-types of the verse structures defined by Arab experts on poetry that come close to what Lowth would describe as *parallelismus membrorum*, including *muṭābaqa* ("antithesis"), akin to antithetic parallelism; *tardīd* ("reiteration"), akin to "staircase parallelism"; and four verse structures that resemble synonymous parallelism: *taṣdīr* (inclusio), *taqsīm* ("specification"), *tashīm* ("distribution"), and *muqābala* (correspondence).[101] The rich discipline of Arabic poetics equipped Moses Ibn Ezra with a high level of conceptualization, a range of definitions, and an array of terminology unavailable to Rashbam. As Sara Japhet acknowledges, "Rashbam does not present a systematic and structured explanation of the phenomenon of parallelism."[102] For example, he did not even coin a term for the phenomenon of "staircase parallelism," which was referred to only by citing other examples, or with Rashi's designation "Samuel's verses."[103]

Derekh Ereṣ ("Way of the World")

Something similar should be said about the sort of "rationalism" that Qara and Rashbam manifest. Neither was exposed to a systematic study of science or philosophy as their coreligionists in Muslim lands were. Authors like Saadia, Abraham Ibn Ezra, and Maimonides drew upon the works of Plato and Aristotle, supplemented by a rich Arabic commentary tradition. Rather than referring to such a tradition of scientific learning, Rashbam invokes a common-sense type of observation, termed

100 See Chapter 4.
101 See Cohen, "Rashbam vs. Moses Ibn Ezra," 204*–208*; Schippers, "Symmetry," 161–170.
102 Japhet, *Rashbam on Job*, 177.
103 See Chapter 1, p. 51.

"the way of the world" (*derekh ereṣ*), which became a defining feature of his *peshat* interpretation. Rashbam thus states his intention to focus on "the *peshat* of the Scriptures ... to explain the regulations and laws according to 'the way of the world' (*derekh ereṣ*)," in contrast to midrashic interpretation.[104]

The workings of Rashbam's concept of "the way of the world" are evident, for example, in his commentary on Gen 1:2, which describes how "the *ruaḥ* (lit. wind, breath) of God moved over the water." Rashi, following the midrash, took this as a reference to "the throne of divine glory" miraculously "standing in space, hovering over the water by the breath of the mouth of the Holy One, blessed be He, and by His command."[105] Rashbam, however, took *ruaḥ* here to mean *wind*, and explains this step of the creation scientifically:

> *A wind blew over the water* – The wind was needed for what is written below, "And God said: Let the water below the sky be gathered into one area ... " (Gen 1:9), for the water was gathered by means of the wind, just like the splitting of the Red Sea, when the dry land became visible by means of the wind: "and the Lord drove back the sea with a strong east wind all that night and turned the sea into dry ground" (Exod 14:21).[106]

And, indeed, in his commentary on Exod 14:21, Rashbam writes:

> The Holy One acted in accordance with the normal manner of the world (*ke-derekh ereṣ*), for the wind dries and freezes the rivers.[107]

A similar scientific explanation of "the wind" in Gen 1:2 was already offered by Saadia, followed by Ibn Ezra.[108] But those commentators did so as part of a program of harmonizing Scripture with Greco-Arabic scientific learning. By contrast, there is no evidence that Rashbam was working with anything more than an intuitive understanding of "nature"

[104] See Touitou, *Exegesis*, 134–150; Grossman, "Literal Exegesis," 363; Cohen, "Perpetual Motion," 395–396; Japhet, "Rashbam on Job." See also Rashbam's introduction to Exodus 21, discussed in Chapter 9. The term *derekh ereṣ* is originally found in rabbinic literature, but Rashbam recasts it (like the term *peshat*) for his own purposes. The expression "in the custom of the world" (*be-nohag she-ba-'olam*) is used in Rashbam's commentary on Job in the same way. See Japhet, *Rashbam on Job*, 148–149; see also Rashbam's introduction to Lamentations, which is cited in Chapter 9, on p. 258. On the roots of these concepts in Rashi's commentaries, see Chapter 4, note 49.

[105] Rashi on Gen 1:2, Berliner ed., 1.

[106] Rashbam on Gen 1:2, Rosin ed., 4–5.

[107] Rashbam on Exod 14:21, Rosin ed., 100.

[108] Saadia on Gen 1:2, Zucker ed., 29 (Ar.), 214 (Heb.); Ibn Ezra, standard commentary *ad loc.*, Weiser ed., I:14.

and "science" – and a desire to avoid the supernaturalism typically posited in midrashic tradition.

Yet there is an instructive parallel between Rashbam's naturalistic tendency and a dramatic development in contemporary Latin learning. The cathedral school of Chartres (about 100 miles from Rashbam's native Ramerupt and about 40 miles from Paris, where Rashbam is known to have traveled) achieved renown in the late eleventh and early twelfth centuries as a center of learning, especially in mathematics and "natural philosophy," i.e., science, as it was known from the works of the ancient Greek philosophers. Bernard of Chartres (d. before 1130) was considered an authority on Plato, and appealed to the works of his such as the *Timaeus* (a dialogue on the nature of the physical world) to explicate Christian Scripture and doctrine.[109] This process was further developed by William of Conches (c. 1090–1154).[110] Adelard of Bath (1080–1152), another member of the Chartres school, traveled widely – from Spain to Antioch – in his search for Arabic and Greek philosophical and scientific works, which he translated.[111] The tendency of such scholars to rely on human reason was criticized by more conservative Christian figures such as Bernard of Clairvaux and William of St. Thierry, who regarded the Church Fathers as the essential authority for explicating the Bible and theology.[112]

Notwithstanding this controversy, the availability and prestige of this new learning had an influence on Thierry of Chartres (d. slightly after 1156),[113] in the preface to his *Hexameron* (commentary on the six days of creation):

> I am going to expound the first part of Genesis, and the seven days and the division between the six works in relation to physics and the literal sense (*secundum phisicam et ad litteram*) . . . I shall proceed to the exposition of the historical literal sense, so I shall completely leave beside the allegorical and moral readings, which holy expositors have lucidly accomplished.[114]

[109] See Dutton, ed., *Glosae*. Recent scholarship challenges the long-held view of the "School of Chartres" as "the nurse of humanist values and intellectual freedom in the early twelfth century." See Wetherbee, "Philosophy," 21. See also Jeauneau, *School of Chartres*; Southern, "Paris and Chartres." Yet by most accounts the "Chartres School" reflects intellectual trends (regardless of how revolutionary or radical) in Latin learning, and thus provides a broader context for Rashbam's work.

[110] See Elford, "William."

[111] See Burnett, *Adelard: English Scientist*; Burnett and Ronca, *Adelard: Conversations*.

[112] See Jeauneau, *School of Chartres*, 20–21, 52–54.

[113] On Thierry of Chartres, see Dronke, "Thierry."

[114] Thierry, *De sex dierum operibus*, Haring ed., 553. English translation from White, *Nature*, 77. See also Dronke, "Thierry," 375–382.

The parallel to Rashbam is striking: both authors pay homage to the earlier traditional interpreters, while focusing their own attention on a newer scientific approach. In fact, Thierry's conceptual combination *secundum physicam et ad litteram* resembles Rashbam's association of *peshat* and *derekh ereṣ*. Occasionally Rashbam reveals the particular coloration he gives to this term by adding other expressions to it: "*derekh ereṣ* and a matter of wisdom (*devar ḥokhmah*)"/ "*derekh ereṣ*, according to the human wisdom (*ḥokhmat benei adam*)."[115]

Rashbam's phraseology suggests that his rationalism was based on common sense and rudimentary scientific observation, rather than a body of scientific or philosophical literature. There is no evidence that Rashbam had access to the glosses on Plato's *Timaeus* by his Christian contemporaries, or any other Latin philosophical or scientific works for that matter. It is possible, however, that he knew of such works from conversations with his Christian neighbors – which may have included some "intellectuals" like himself. His negative reference, for example, in his Qohelet commentary to the type of "wisdom" that deals with the secrets of creation (which he refers to with the Rabbinic Hebrew term *ma'aseh bereshit*) may indicate that he was aware of this branch of Latin learning.[116]

It would seem that *derekh ereṣ*, being a universal (rather than specifically Jewish) type of wisdom, provided a common ground on which Rashbam could converse with Christian neighbors. This explains the association of that term with Rashbam's occasional "responses" to Christianity. For example, on Lev 11:34 he offers a rationale for a biblical law for "one who wishes to give a reason (*ṭa'am*) for the commandments[117] according to *derekh ereṣ* and as a response to the Christians (*minim*)."[118] Rashbam likewise points to the empirical benefits of adhering to the prohibition to eat certain ("non-kosher") animals:

> According to the *peshat* of Scripture and as a response to the *minim*: all of the animals, beasts, birds, fish, and types of locusts and swarming things that God prohibited to Israel are referred to as "impure," since they are disgusting. They also harm and heat the body. And the great doctors say so as well, and in the Talmud (b.*Shabbat* 86b) [it is also written]: "Gentiles who eat insects and reptiles harm themselves."[119]

[115] See Touitou, *Exegesis*, 145. [116] See Kamin, *Jews and Christians*, lxi–lxix.

[117] On the endeavor to identify a rationale for the commandments in the northern French *peshat* school, see Grossman, *France*, 302–304; Touitou, *Exegesis*, 182.

[118] Rashbam on Lev 11:34, Rosin ed., 154. On the term *minim* and the expression "response to the *minim*," see Chapter 3, pp. 96 and 99.

[119] Rashbam on Lev 11:3, Rosin ed., 153. A similar hygienic explanation is also given by Maimonides in his *Guide of the Perplexed*, III:48, Pines trans., 598.

From the connection he makes between "the *peshat* of Scripture" and "a response to the *minim*" it would seem that Rashbam discussed Scripture with his Christian neighbors and found the rational *peshat* method congenial for portraying the virtue of its Jewish interpretation.[120] The yardstick of rationalism (*derekh ereṣ*) that Rashbam applied to Scripture enabled him to provide an explanation to Christians for Jewish adherence to the Law.

In this vein, Rashbam identifies a common theme of a group of three biblical laws in commenting on Deut 22:6, which requires that a mother bird be chased away before one collects her eggs or chicks to eat:

According to *derekh ereṣ* and as a response to the *minim*, I have already explained on the verse "You shall not cook a kid in its mother's milk" (Exod 23:19), and also on "No animal shall be slaughtered on the same day with its young" (Lev 22:28), that it is a sort of (lit., resembles) cruelty and gluttony to take, slaughter, cook or eat a mother and its young together.[121]

The term *derekh ereṣ* here connotes a sense of morality, which Rashbam evidently regarded as an aspect of human reason. Elsewhere Rashbam uses a slightly different term, saying that in these laws "Scriptures aims to teach you civilized/ refined behavior (*derekh tarbut*)."[122] Rashbam's term *derekh tarbut* would seem to be another aspect of *derekh ereṣ*; in other words, human wisdom includes proper, refined behavior.[123]

Rashbam's use of the expression *derekh tarbut* can, of course, be traced to the use of the term *tarbut* in Rabbinic Hebrew to connote *domestication*, "domesticated animals" (*benei tarbut*), in opposition to wild animals.[124] A related, probably derivative, usage is the Rabbinic Hebrew expression *tarbut ra'ah*, i.e., (human) *bad behavior*.[125] Rashbam's use of the expression *derekh tarbut* to connote *civilized, refined behavior* was a neologism that seems to have developed in Rashi's school.[126] It is not unreasonable to suppose that it was coined to express in Hebrew a concept from the surrounding culture. Given the context of polemical dialogue with Christians that he mentions explicitly, it is not unlikely that Rashbam here had in mind the medieval Latin ideals of *civiles mores* (civil behavior) and, more broadly, *civilitas* (civility), as well as *venustas morum* (beauty of manners/ conduct) celebrated in

[120] See Touitou, *Exegesis*, 143–144. [121] Rashbam on Deut 22:6, Rosin ed., 220.
[122] Rashbam on Exod 23:19, Rosin ed., 121. [123] See Touitou, *Exegesis*, 144.
[124] See m.*Bava Qamma* 1:4. [125] See m.*Niddah* 10:8. Cf. Num 32:14.
[126] See Ben-Yehuda, *Dictionary*, s.v., תרבות.

Western Christian society in the eleventh and twelfth centuries.[127] It would seem that Rashbam intends to say that these very values, which he refers to as *derekh tarbut*, are inculcated by adherence to the Law in its literal sense – as practiced by the Jews.

Rashbam's notion of *derekh ereṣ* reflects not only an interest in "natural philosophy" and ethics, but also historical sensitivity, i.e., an awareness of the *realia* of the Bible's historical setting.[128] This represents a departure from midrashic modes of reading, which tended to downplay the historical, realistic, and mundane aspects of the biblical narrative and regard it in a supernatural way – for a spiritual purpose.[129] The Rabbis' endeavor to seek moral and religious relevance in the biblical text, in fact, typically led them to blur the chronological gap between their own circumstances and the historical world of the Bible. Rashi and his students inherited this hallowed tradition and lived their Jewish lives by it – as their "spiritual sense" of the Bible (to use a Christian term). But the *peshat* method as it began to emerge in Rashi's school entailed an effort to make sense of Scripture independently as a literary reflection of ancient Israelite circumstances, akin to what was regarded as the "historical" sense of the Old Testament in Christian exegesis.[130]

This dimension of *peshuto shel miqra* is already found in Rashi, for example, in his commentary on Abraham's "covenant between the parts" (*berit bein ha-betarim*) with God in Genesis 15, as discussed in Chapter 1. Most often, however, Rashi still relied exclusively on the ahistorical midrashic approach, leaving it to Qara and Rashbam to offer the historically oriented *peshat* approach. For example, to explain why Abraham ordered his servant: "Put your hand under my thigh and I will make you swear by the Lord" (Gen 24:2), Rashi, drawing upon midrashic tradition, interprets this ritual as a reference to Abraham's circumcision, following the assumption that one must hold a sacred object (a Torah scroll in Rabbinic times), when taking an oath.[131] Rashbam, however, adopts a historical-anthropological outlook based on internal biblical evidence:

[127] See Jaeger, *Envy of Angels*, 27–35, 245, 292–296, 325–326; Jaeger, *Origins of Courtliness*, 135–136. See also Scaglione, *Knights and Courts*, 47–51.

[128] One can likewise discern a historical sensibility in the work of the Tosafists in their analysis of the Talmud. See Fishman, *People of the Talmud*, 148.

[129] See Kugel, *Bible as it Was*, 17–24.

[130] See Smalley, *Study of the Bible*, 100–102, 145–149; White, *Nature*, 79.

[131] Rashi on Gen 24:2, drawing upon a midrashic tradition reflected in *Genesis Rabbah* 59:8, Theodor–Albeck ed., 636 and *Tanḥuma ha-Qadum*, *Ḥayyei Sarah* §6, Buber ed., I:120.

Various ways of establishing a covenant are found in the Bible: (1) "the calf which they cut in two [so as to pass between the halves]" (Jer 34:18); "[a flaming torch] which passed between those pieces" (Gen 15:17) – this is [one way of] establishing a covenant; (2) "Is the palm of Zebah and Zalmmuna in your hand?" (Judg 8:6), "[My son, if you have stood surely for your fellow], given your hand to another" (Prov 6:1); this, too, is [a way of] establishing a covenant. (3) And placing a hand on [i.e., beneath] the thigh, we find with a son – Joseph; and Eliezer, a servant, when the father or master made them take an oath. And a son's honor [for his father] was equated with a servant [for his master,] as written: "A son should honor his father and a slave his master" (Mal 1:6). And this was their practice in those days.[132]

Indicating awareness of the historical gap between his own circumstances and those in antiquity, Rashbam seeks biblical evidence to reconstruct the various conventions that governed the establishment of a covenant in biblical times.

Abraham Ibn Ezra offers an explanation similar to Rashbam's about the oath Abraham administered to his servant, except that he adds that "this custom is still practiced in India."[133] This parallel raises the intriguing question of whether Ibn Ezra was actually influenced – here and elsewhere – by Rashbam, although it is also plausible that two *peshat* exegetes, using the same biblical evidence, might arrive at similar conclusions. It is equally important, however, to note the cultural disparity that emerges between the two authors. Having lived in Muslim Spain, Ibn Ezra (whose own son Isaac traveled to Egypt and possibly even Iraq[134]) had extensive knowledge of the East and could therefore cite practices current there to support his conjectures regarding biblical times. Rashbam, on the other hand, had only the internal biblical evidence to utilize for this purpose.

At times the *peshat* interpretation of Qara and Rashbam is based on observable human behavior. This type of anthropological-psychological *peshat* sensibility is evident, for example on Exod 17:11, which describes how Israel prevailed in battling Amalek only as long as Moses' hands were raised. The Rabbis (m.*Rosh ha-Shanah* 3:8) explained this correspondence in religious terms, saying that when Moses raised his hands to

[132] This comment is attributed to Rashbam in a marginal note on Rashi's commentary on Gen 24:2 in MS Vienna 220, where many such comments by Rashbam, Qara, and others appear in the margins. See Touitou, *Exegesis*, 192; Liss, *Fictional Worlds*, 61–69. In Rosin's edition (based on the now lost MS Breslau 103), Rashbam's commentary on Gen 24:2 is much briefer, though it reflects the same basic approach.

[133] Ibn Ezra, standard commentary on Gen 24:2, Weiser ed., I:74.

[134] See Schmelzer, *Poems*, 9–11.

heaven, Israel turned their hearts to God, thereby earning merit to be granted a miraculous victory, an interpretation adopted by Rashi on that verse. Qara offers the following alternative, as recorded in a note on the margin of Rashi's commentary:

According to the *peshat*, it is this way: when someone raises the flag, *fondon* in the vernacular (*la'az*; i.e., Old French), it serves as a good omen for his army, and they battle mightily as long as it is raised. But when he lets it down, they say, "We are defeated," and this is a signal for them to retreat and flee.[135]

Rashbam refines this observation by highlighting the fact that it is based on typical human behavior:

This is the typical manner of those who wage war (*derekh 'orkhei milḥamah*); as long as they see the raising of their battle flag, *confanion* in the vernacular (*la'az*; i.e., Old French), they prevail, but when it is cast down, they typically flee and are vanquished.[136]

Rashbam here employs phraseology characteristic of his anthropological-psychological commentaries, "it is the typical manner of (*derekh* . . .) those who . . ., " a formula also adopted by Eliezer of Beaugency in his *peshat* commentaries.[137]

As discussed in Chapter 1, this tendency and phraseology can be traced to Rashi.[138] Especially noteworthy are the cases in which the Troyes master cites a midrashic interpretation but then juxtaposes it with an alternative *peshat* interpretation, for example, based on "the typical manner (*derekh*) of those who divide up to pursue enemies fleeing in different directions" (Gen 14:15) or "the typical manner (*derekh*) of those who made covenants in biblical times" (Gen 15:10). Having learned it from the master, Rashi's students applied this method more extensively in their own commentaries. In this way, Rashi's innovative *peshat* methodology inspired an entire school of exegesis dedicated to what, as Rashbam records, he regarded as "the *peshat* interpretations that newly emerge (*ha-mitḥaddeshim*) every day."

135 Berliner, *Pletath soferim*, 18.

136 Rashbam on Exod 17:11, Rosin ed. 106. See also Touitou, *Exegesis*, 139.

137 See Cohen, "Eliezer of Beaugency." Similar expressions occur in Rashbam on Exod 32:19 ("the typical manner [*derekh*] of those who throw down heavy items . . . "); and Song 4:1 ("this is the typical manner [*derekh*] of women . . . "). Cf. Rashbam on Gen 19:17.

138 See p. 46.

9

Literary Sensibilities of *Peshat* within a Latin Context

Within a mere two generations – from Rashi to Joseph Qara to Rashbam – the rules of Ashkenazic Bible interpretation were rewritten in northern France, as outlined in the preceding chapter. No longer was the Bible viewed exclusively as a divine cryptic document, to be decoded through the tools of midrashic inquiry. The *peshat* project entailed analyzing the Bible as an open book like others, its meaning to be understood through contextual-philological analysis. Rather than mining the sacred text for moral and halakhic "instruction," the *pashtanim* aimed to understand the ancient Scripture within its human historical context in the Near East of biblical times. It is thus not surprising that this movement has been viewed as a precursor of modern historical-critical Bible scholarship.[1] But the twelfth-century *pashtanim* were not modern Bible scholars. It is necessary to consider how they perceived this new interpretive model within their cultural-intellectual framework and to ask: what was the status of this *peshat* method – in their view – vis-à-vis the traditional midrashic mode of reading Scripture? As we shall demonstrate in this chapter, a new appreciation of the Bible's literary nature – which finds illuminating parallels in Latin learning – was essential for negotiating the narrow straits between the traditional midrashic outlook and the powerful *peshat* methodology that emerged in the circle of Joseph Qara, Rashbam, and their students in twelfth-century northern France.

[1] As discussed in Chapter 8.

HERMENEUTICS: STATUS OF PESHAT IN RELATION TO MIDRASH

Joseph Qara took a spirited stance in declaring what would seem to be the hermeneutical self-sufficiency of *peshat*. In a key passage cited in the previous chapter, Qara uses stark, evocative terms to depict *peshat* as a sure-footed quest for intellectual treasure guided by the "perfection" of God's word, whereas midrashic interpretation is likened to aimless, hopeless flailing by one being swept away by a raging river current.[2] In a similar vein, in his commentary on Isa 5:9 Qara remarks:

> Incline your ear and bend over toward Scripture, for every verse that our Rabbis interpreted midrashically ... when they concluded their midrashic homily, they themselves said in the end: "Scripture does not leave the realm of its *peshat*," for there is no manner of study in Scripture greater than ... *peshuto shel miqra*.[3] And thus Solomon King of Israel said: "Incline your ear [and listen to] the words of the Sages, and put your heart to My knowledge" (Prov 22:17). Its meaning is this: "Even though you are obligated to listen to the words of the Sages," "Put your heart to My [i.e., God's] knowledge (Heb. *de'ah*)" – i.e., the very essence (lit., body; Heb. *guf*) of the matter. It does not say "to their knowledge," but rather "to My knowledge."[4]

Qara creates a clear demarcation: *peshuto shel miqra* is the true meaning of Scripture, the "knowledge" conveyed by God Himself in the sacred text, whereas midrash conveys only the opinions of the Sages.[5] This suggests that

[2] See p. 222.

[3] This is an imprecise citation from the Talmud, at best an adaptation of the maxim, "One who studies Scripture – that is a somewhat meritorious manner of study (lit., a manner, but not a manner: *middah we-einah middah*) ... one who studies Talmud, there is no manner [of study] greater than this" (b.*Bava Meṣi'a* 33a). Elsewhere Qara repeats this point: "There is no manner [of study] in Scripture greater than the *peshat* of the matter, for even where there is a midrash, our Rabbis expounded: 'Scripture does not leave the realm of its *peshat*'" (commentary on Isa 1:18, *Keter* ed., 9). Cf. Rashbam's more precise citation in his commentary on Gen 37:2, cited later in this chapter.

[4] Qara on Isa 5:9, *Keter* ed., 37.

[5] This distinction, of course, was made by the Karaites to reject the authority of the talmudic sages. See Frank, *Search Scripture*, 5–16, 33–39. Yet there is no evidence that Joseph Qara knew much about Karaism. Sara Japhet has argued that Rashbam likewise considered *peshat* to be the single original meaning of the biblical text, what he elsewhere refers to as "the truth of its *peshat*" (comm. on Lev 10:3), whereas the *derash* is the product of subsequent rabbinic exegesis. The latter is the exclusive determinant of halakhah, "fundamental" for Jewish practice, "but it does not represent the meaning of the biblical text as is ... [as] midrashic interpretation is not the 'high road' of the biblical text," a distinction held by *peshat* alone. See Japhet, "Tension," 413, 421–422. Although this would explain Rashbam's emphatic adherence to *peshat*, it is out of character for an Ashkenazic talmudist. See Cohen, *Gates*, 450–453. An alternative account of Rashbam's *peshat* model is thus offered in the discussion that follows.

peshuto shel miqra is the superior form of Bible interpretation. No wonder, then, that Qara elsewhere speaks of *peshat* representing the "truth" – which the "intellectuals" of his day were beginning to appreciate – in opposition to the midrash.[6]

To be sure, Qara had considerable expertise in, and even love for, midrashic interpretation. Apart from (evidently) having written a commentary on *Genesis Rabbah* (as mentioned in Chapter 8), he drew heavily on midrash in his *piyyut* commentaries. This is understandable, since the *piyyutim* are based on midrashic interpretations of the biblical verses. Hence, in order to arrive at a correct understanding of the intention of the authors of the *piyyutim*, one must clarify which midrashic interpretations they had in mind.[7] Yet, Qara's commentaries on Isaiah – surprisingly – include extensive citations from midrashic sources.[8] For example, the very passage cited above from Qara's commentary on Isa 5:9, in which he extols the virtue of *peshat*, occurs in the midst of a reference to the interpretation offered by the Rabbis, and he in fact continues:

> Until here I have interpreted this according to its context and *peshat*. But now I shall return to the words of the Rabbis, may their bones flourish like grass . . .[9]

Midrash was never far from Qara's mind, even where he seems to set it aside, as evident in his characteristic remarks:

> This is the *peshat* of the verse, and its midrashic interpretation is well-known (lit., in everyone's mouth).[10]
>
> . . . and in the annals of the *aggadah* the Rabbis offer different interpretations, but they are not convincing (lit., are not settled [*mityashevim*] upon the heart).[11]

In one revealing instance, Qara cites a midrashic interpretation in full and labels it as such ("this is its midrash"), but then remarks:

> . . . yet I do not know how to settle this matter on its place, and this is not its *peshat* interpretation.[12]

He goes on in this passage to express his frustration at not being able to arrive at an adequate *peshat* interpretation. Given his remarks about the

[6] See p. 216. [7] See Grossman, *France*, 327–339. [8] Grossman, *France*, 317.
[9] Qara on Isa 5:9, *Keter* ed., 37. [10] See the examples cited in Grossman, *France*, 298.
[11] Qara on 2 Sam 12:30, Eppenstein ed., 87–88. Qara's use of the verb "to settle" (Heb. *y-sh-b*) is noteworthy, as it reflects Rashi's usage, as discussed in earlier chapters of this study. On Qara's tendency elsewhere to use this verb in a manner similar to the way it is used by Rashi, see Gelles, *Rashi*, 32. See also the following note.
[12] Qara on Judg 5:4, Eppenstein ed., 24. Here, too, Qara speaks of "settling" the text. See previous note.

relative value of *peshat* and *derash*, it is difficult to imagine that Qara would have been satisfied with the midrashic resolution of the exegetical crux in question.

Yet elsewhere Qara hints that at times there may be no other choice. In his commentary on 1 Sam 17:55, he addresses a perplexing issue regarding the composition of the Book of Samuel. The previous biblical chapter (1 Sam 16:19–23) recounts that David played the harp for King Saul to alleviate his depression, and that the king "loved him very much and he became his armor bearer" (v. 21). Yet after slaying Goliath, David seems to be unknown to Saul, who inquires, "Whose son is that boy?" (1 Sam 17:55). Qara raises this question and then provides an elaborate answer based on midrashic sources. At that point he remarks cryptically:

> This is explained in the midrash, and in tractate *Yevamot*. But to settle the text without its midrashic explanation I cannot do successfully. And "Scripture does not leave the realm of its *peshat*."[13]

Qara seems to acknowledge that there is no satisfactory *peshat* solution to this crux.[14]

In sum, though Qara was a brilliant *pashtan*, there are inconsistencies between his exegetical theory and practice, an indication, perhaps, that the northern French *peshat* school was still not ready for such a radical theoretical break with midrashic tradition.[15] It is conceivable that Rashbam's pronouncements about *peshuto shel miqra* were designed as a corrective, as he offers critical self-reflection on the emergence of the new interpretive agenda in Ashkenazic culture:

> Let lovers of reason (*sekhel*) comprehend and understand that our Rabbis taught us that "a biblical verse does not leave the realm of its *peshat*," even though the essence (*'iqqar*) of Torah comes to teach and inform us of the *haggadot* (traditions,

[13] Qara on 1 Sam 17:55, Eppenstein ed., 67. Modern scholars resolve this difficulty by positing that the two accounts reflect different sources of the biblical narrative that record different traditions as to how David came to be a member of Saul's court.

[14] Compare Rashi on Gen 1:1, Berliner ed., 1: "This verse tells us clearly that it must be interpreted midrashically." The Talmud likewise notes an exception to the rule that "a biblical verse does not leave the realm of its *peshat*" (b. *Yevamot* 24a), in which case the midrashic interpretation supersedes the *peshat*. This may be comparable to Origen's notion that some parts of the Bible have no literal meaning, and can be interpreted only spiritually. See Paget, "Alexandrian Tradition," 513.

[15] Theoretically, one could interpret Qara's comments about his inability to resolve the difficulties he mentions according to *peshuto shel miqra* as a veiled way of questioning the integrity of the Masoretic Text of the Bible. However, it is difficult to assess such a possibility, since it is based on conjecture about thoughts Qara may have had and not articulated.

lore), *halakhot* (laws) and *dinim* (regulations) through the hints of the *peshat*,[16] by way of redundant language, and through the thirty-two hermeneutical rules of R. Eliezer ... and the thirteen rules of R. Ishmael. Now the early generations, because of their piety, tended to delve into the *derashot*, since they are essential (*'iqqar*), and therefore were not accustomed to the deep *peshat* of Scripture. And also because the Sages said "Do not let your children do a great deal of recitation [of Scripture]."[17] And they also said: "One who studies Scripture – that is a somewhat meritorious manner of study (lit., a manner [*middah*], but not a manner) ... one who studies Talmud, there is no manner [of study] greater than this" (b.*Bava Meṣi'a* 33a).[18] Therefore they were not very accustomed to delve into *peshuto shel miqra*, as it recounts in Tractate *Shabbat*: "I was eighteen years old and I had studied the entire Talmud and I did not know that 'Scripture does not leave the realm of its peshat.'" (b. *Shabbat* 63a). Now our master, Rabbi Solomon, the father of my mother, luminary of the Diaspora, who interpreted Torah, Prophets and Writings, aimed (*natan lev*) to interpret the *peshat* of Scripture. And I, Samuel, son of Meir, his son-in-law (of blessed memory), debated with him personally, and he admitted to me that if he had the opportunity, he would have to write new commentaries according to the *peshat* interpretations that newly emerge (*ha-mitḥaddeshim*) every day.[19]

Despite being an ardent *pashtan*, Rashbam describes the sources and principles of midrashic interpretation, which he deems the "essence" of Scripture.

In this detailed programmatic statement Rashbam presents a dual model of Bible interpretation that balances midrashic tradition and the novel *peshat* mode. He takes the maxim that "a biblical verse does not leave the realm of its *peshat*" to mean that the *peshat* is inviolate, notwithstanding the primacy of midrash. This departs from Qara's construal of the *peshat* maxim and returns, at least in theory, to that of Rashi, who still regarded midrashic interpretation – conducted within the proper parameters – as the essential conduit for a true understanding of the biblical text. Indeed, Rashbam corrects Qara's

[16] When speaking of "the hints of the *peshat*" Rashbam uses the term *peshat* in the sense of *the biblical text itself*. See Touitou, *Exegesis*, 99.

[17] This is a paraphrase of b.*Berakhot* 28b ("Keep your children from recitation [*higayon*]"). The meaning of *higayon* (lit., articulation of language) is subject to debate. According to one interpretation in Rashi *ad loc.* (evidently the understanding Rashbam had in mind) it means the study of Scripture. It is well known that Jews in Muslim lands took *higayon* to mean *logic*, which corresponds to Arabic *manṭiq* (logic: lit., speech).

[18] This is a precise citation of the talmudic statement, as opposed to its adaptation by Qara (see note 3).

[19] Rashbam on Gen 37:2, Rosin ed., 49. On this exegetical manifesto, see Touitou, *Exegesis*, 98–104.

imprecise quotation of the talmudic maxim regarding the relative merit of studying Scripture and studying Talmud.[20] As Rashbam understood well, traditional Jewish Bible study was based on the Talmud, and *peshuto shel miqra* is an innovation – albeit an important and exciting one – of his time. The "early generations" focused their attention on midrashic interpretation. By Rashbam's account, it was only with the advent of Rashi that *peshat* become an important objective, one that continued to develop subsequently. But all of this was contingent on an acknowledgement of midrash as "the essence of Torah."

PESHAT VS. HALAKHAH

The implications of Rashbam's dual hermeneutic are especially pertinent in the case of halakhic passages, as evident from his programmatic preface to the first full-length law-code in the Pentateuch:

> I have not come to explain *halakhot*, even though they are essential, as I explained in Genesis, for the *haggadot* and *halakhot* can be inferred from the redundancies of the Scriptures, and some of them can be found in the commentaries of Rabbi Solomon my grandfather (may the memory of the righteous be blessed). I, on the other hand, have come to interpret the *peshat* of the Scriptures, interpreting the *dinim* and *halakhot* according to the way of the world (*derekh ereṣ*). Yet the *halakhot* (i.e., as interpreted by the Rabbis) remain essential (*'iqqar*), as our Rabbis said: "halakhah uproots Scripture" (b.*Soṭah* 16a).[21]

This should be compared with the proviso by Thierry of Chartes in his Bible commentary:

> I shall proceed to the exposition of the historical literal sense, so I shall completely leave beside the allegorical and moral readings, which holy expositors have lucidly accomplished.[22]

Like Thierry, Rashbam acknowledges the interpretive authority of the earlier "expositors," even while proceeding to engage in his own very different mode of interpretation.

He remarks, furthermore, at the conclusion of his Exodus commentary, which also serves as a preface to the book of Leviticus:

[20] See note 18.

[21] Rashbam on Exodus 21, introduction, Rosin ed., 113. See Touitou, *Exegesis*, 105; Lockshin, "Does Halakhah Uproot Peshat?"

[22] See Thierry, *De sex dierum operibus*, Haring ed., 553, English translation from White, *Nature*, 77. This passage was cited in full in Chapter 8, on p. 232.

He who puts his heart to the word of our Creator must not budge from the explanations of my grandfather, our Master Rabbi Solomon, and must not depart from them. For most of the *halakhot* and *derashot* in them are close to the *peshat* of the Scriptures, and all of them can be deduced [from the redundancies and anomalies of] the language. And it is best for you to take this commentary as I have interpreted the Pentateuch, but not forgo (lit., let go of) Rashi's commentaries. The Book of Leviticus contains many *halakhot*. Now wise men: study the commentaries of my grandfather, because I will elaborate only where there is a need to explicate the *peshat* interpretations of the verses.[23]

Rashbam thus stipulates that his *peshat* interpretation cannot stand alone, but must be regarded as a supplement to the traditional midrashic understanding, which conveys the halakhah that is central to Jewish practice.[24]

Whereas the Rabbis of the Talmud applied the midrashic *middot* to ascertain the halakhah, Rashbam would aim for *peshuto shel miqra* guided by his own reasoning and "the way of the world."[25] Manifesting ingenuity and originality in his analysis, which is often at odds with rabbinic halakhic interpretation, Rashbam effectively creates an alternative, non-talmudic "shadow" system of halakhah based his reading of Scripture itself.[26] It was the midrash–*peshat* hierarchy Rashbam posited that freed him to engage in an independent analysis of the legal sections of the Pentateuch, because ultimately the halakhah is not determined by *peshuto shel miqra* as he conceived it. For example, the Rabbis (b. *Menaḥot* 34b–37b) took Exod 13:9, "And this shall serve you as a sign on your hand and as a reminder between your eyes – in order that the teaching of the Lord may be in your mouth – that with a mighty hand the Lord freed you from Egypt," as a source for every Jewish male's obligation to don phylacteries (*tefillin*). Following the Talmud, Rashi writes that the phylacteries are the "sign" placed literally on the arm and head, as a reminder of the exodus.[27] But Rashbam remarks:

[23] Rashbam, conclusion to Exodus, Rosin ed., 144–145. The words in brackets in this passage were missing in (the now lost) MS Breslau 103 (where there was an empty space) and were inserted by Rosin in his edition, based on a comparison with Rashbam's language elsewhere. According to Rosin, the words "The Book of Leviticus" are not part of the body of Rashbam's discourse, but rather serve as a heading for what follows, indicating the beginning of a new section of the commentary. But I accept the opposing view of Kislev, "Rashbam's Methodological Preface," who argues that this passage is to be read continuously.

[24] See Lockshin, "Tradition or Context," 184.

[25] See Chapter 8, note 104.

[26] See Touitou, *Exegesis*, 126–139; Japhet, "Tension"; Liss, *Fictional Worlds*, 195–219.

[27] Rashi on Exod 13:9, Berliner ed., 127.

As a sign on your hand – According to its deep *peshat*: it will always be on your mind, as if it were written on you hand. As in the verse, "Place me as a seal on your heart, [as a seal on your arm]". (Song 8:6)

Between your eyes – like an ornament or a gold chain that is customarily put on the forehead for decoration.[28]

Whereas Rashi took these phrases literally, Rashbam interpreted them figuratively, knowing that Scripture often employs metaphoric locutions. The appearance of similar poetic imagery in Song 8:6 served him as an apt example of this stylistic tendency.[29] He argues that this verse does not refer to anything actually placed on the hand or between the eyes, but is, instead, Moses' exhortation to the Israelites to preserve the memory of the exodus, as if it were imprinted "on ... [the] hand" and an adornment "between ... [the] eyes." Rashbam regarded this meaning as the "deep *peshat*" because it best accords with the context of this verse. The rabbinic interpretation breaks the connection between Exod 13:9 and the surrounding pericope (Exod 13:3–10), which is devoted exclusively to the annual celebration of the unleavened bread festival in commemoration of the exodus. Rashbam's reading preserves the pericope's contextual unity by construing Exod 13:9 as a command to continuously keep the exodus from Egypt in mind.[30]

The audacity of Rashbam's non-halakhic interpretation of Exod 13:9 can be gauged by the harsh criticism it elicited from Abraham Ibn Ezra, who criticizes "those who disagree with our holy forebears and say that 'as a sign ... and reminder' is metaphorical."[31] In his view "it is in its literal sense, to make phylacteries (*tefillin*) of the hand and phylacteries of the head." As Ibn Ezra remarks, "since the Sages, of blessed memory, transmitted thus, the first interpretation is void, for it does not have trustworthy witnesses as the second interpretation has."[32]

28 Rashbam on Exod 13:9, Rosin ed., 98. This would seem to be an adaptation of the interpretation of the tenth-century Andalusian linguist Menahem ben Saruq. See *Maḥberet*, s.v., טף, Sáenz-Badillos ed., 200*.

29 See Rashbam on Song 8:6, Japhet ed., 277.

30 On the expression "its deep *peshat*" (*'omeq peshuto*) and others like it in Rashbam's lexicon – *'iqqar peshuto* (its essential *peshat*), *amitat peshuto* (its true *peshat*) – see Kamin, *Categorization*, 268. On literary context as a critical ingredient in the northern French concept of *peshat*, see Harris, "Literary Hermeneutic," 280–301.

31 Ibn Ezra, long comm. on Exod 13:9, Weiser ed., II:87.

32 Ibn Ezra, short comm. on Exod 13:9, Weiser ed., II:264. The short commentary was written in Italy in the early 1140s, the long commentary in northern France a decade later. On the historical question of when Ibn Ezra could have become aware of Rashbam and

Even more dramatically, Rashbam at times offers interpretations that actually contradict the halakhah.[33] In his commentary on Gen 1:5, "And there was evening and there was morning, a first day," for example, Rashbam comments:

> The evening of the first day arrived and the light faded away, and there was morning, the morn of the night, meaning that the dawn arrived. At that point one of the six "days" that God spoke of in the Ten Commandments ("For in six days God made the heaven and the earth" [Exod 20:8]) was complete.[34]

Rashbam indicates that "a day" in the Bible begins and concludes at dawn, contradicting the talmudic principle that "the night follows the day," i.e., that the time-span of "a day" (e.g., the Sabbath) is from sundown to sundown. This was noted by Abraham Ibn Ezra, who seems to have become aware of Rashbam's commentary in England toward the end of his life, prompting him to pen "The Epistle of the Sabbath" to demonstrate that the sundown-to-sundown observance of the Sabbath is mandated by *peshuto shel miqra*.[35]

Whereas Ibn Ezra could not countenance the possibility that the halakhah would contradict *peshuto shel miqra*, Rashbam's dual hermeneutic implied precisely that. In Rashbam's view, evidently, Scripture was formulated originally with two different levels of meaning: *derash*, to be derived according to the midrashic hermeneutical rules, and *peshat*, a literary, philological-contextual analysis of the text.[36] Touitou regards this as an irrational theory and referred to it as a "mystical" notion by analogy with the kabbalistic model of Nahmanides.[37] But to me it seems that the connection to Nahmanidean mysticism is out of place and that this conception actually would have been quite natural in Rashbam's twelfth-century northern French intellectual milieu, since a similar duality was posited by his Christian neighbors.[38] The notion that Scripture conveys multiple layers of meaning simultaneously was a cornerstone of

his commentaries, see Liss, *Fictional Worlds*, 92–96; Mondschein, "Inter-Relationship"; Simon, *Ear Discerns*, 102–111. In any case, he would have known this figurative interpretation from Menahem ben Saruq; and so, he is reacting to the interpretation per se – and it is not certain that he is reacting specifically to Rashbam.

33 See Japhet, "Tension"; Simon, *Ear Discerns*, 100–133.

34 Rashbam on Gen 1:5, Rosin ed., 5.

35 See Simon, *Ear Discerns*, 68–133.

36 See Simon, *Ear Discerns*, 100–133; Lockshin, "Tradition or Context." Cf. the account of Rashbam's *peshat* model by Japhet cited in note 5.

37 Touitou, *Exegesis*, 54. As Touitou writes: "How is it possible, according to the rules of human logic, that one verse would have two completely different – and at times contradictory – meanings, and that both are correct?"

38 See Kamin, *Jews and Christians*, xxi–xxxv.

Church tradition, and even the twelfth-century exegetes who devoted attention to the literal sense still saw it as a stepping stone to the deeper and more spiritual allegorical and anagogical senses of the biblical text. With this supposition permeating Rashbam's intellectual milieu, it should not be surprising that he believed his devotion to *peshat* could go hand in hand with a genuine commitment to what he regarded as Scripture's "essence" (*'iqqar*), i.e., rabbinic tradition embodied in *derash*.[39]

One can point to an illustrative parallel in twelfth-century Christian Bible interpretation in the monastic school of St. Victor outside of Paris founded in 1108 by William of Champeaux (1070–1121; himself a student of Anselm of Laon and a one-time teacher of Abelard). The Victorines in general were known for their interest in the literal sense. Andrew of St. Victor (c. 1110–1175) was famous (and controversial) for his learned investigation of the Hebrew text of the Old Testament – for which he at times relied on Jewish sources.[40] Andrew's teacher and Rashbam's contemporary, Hugh of St. Victor, is often credited with the emerging twelfth-century Christian interest in the literal sense of Scripture in northern France.[41] And yet, Hugh regarded the literal sense merely as a vehicle for arriving at the more lofty spiritual senses of Scripture.[42] Rashbam of course did not embrace the Christological senses of Scripture; but the underlying conception of the biblical text's multivalence offered a fitting way for him to posit the coexistence of *peshat* alongside traditional rabbinic midrashic exegesis.

Comments of Rashbam's scattered throughout his commentaries indicate that he was aware of Christian opinions regarding the Hebrew Bible. As mentioned above, Rashbam at times specifically registers his "responses" to the Christians.[43] In one telling instance, he records a conversation that he himself had with Christians about a Hebrew

[39] On the way in which Rashbam conceptualized the relationship between these two layers of scriptural signification, see Cohen, "New Look," 98–101, 111–117.

[40] See Smalley, *Study of the Bible*, 112–186; Leyra Curiá, *In Hebreo*; van Liere, "Andrew of St. Victor."

[41] See Smalley, *Study of the Bible*, 83–111.

[42] See, e.g., Evans, *Language and Logic*, 67–71. Cf. the citation from Hugh of St. Victor on p. 130, where the literal sense is characterized as the "foundation." A similar point can be made about other twelfth-century Christian interpreters who manifested an interest in the literal sense, such as Rupert of Deutz and Richard of St. Victor. See Zemler-Cizewski, "Rupert"; van 't Spijker, "Literal and Spiritual."

[43] See Rashbam on Gen 3:22; Lev 11:3; Deut 22:6. The last two examples are discussed in Chapter 8.

word rendered imprecisely in the Vulgate.[44] It is thus not implausible that Rashbam had knowledge of theoretical developments in Christian Bible interpretation in his time, especially since he is known to have traveled to Paris and other centers of Latin learning in northern France.[45] In any case, the argument made here is not for Christian influence on Rashbam as such. Rather, the parallel to the Victorines points to an underlying *Zeitgeist* in twelfth-century northern France and suggests how Rashbam could have navigated the theological complexities of introducing a new mode of Bible interpretation seemingly at odds with the traditional one in his religious community.

CONCEPTIONS OF THE BIBLICAL NARRATOR-EDITOR

The notion that Sacred Scripture is entirely of divine origin was well entrenched in Jewish tradition since Antiquity.[46] To be sure, the Talmud lists the human "authors" of the books that make up the Hebrew Bible. But little attention is paid within rabbinic literature to the personal contributions of these figures, since they are assumed to have written down what they received through divine inspiration.[47] The Jewish attitude toward biblical authorship was not unlike that expressed in the commentary on Job by Gregory the Great, who maintained that "The search for the author of this book is certainly a vain one, because ... the author is the Holy Spirit."[48]

A break with this tendency within Jewish tradition seems to have first emerged within Karaite interpretation, where increasing focus was placed on the role of the so-called *mudawwin* (editor-compiler), a human figure responsible for the literary selection and arrangement of the original words of God appearing in the Bible in its current form.[49] Within the Rabbanite tradition, a parallel conception of a human biblical editor-compiler, referred to in Hebrew as the *sadran*, emerged in the Byzantine school in the eleventh century as discussed in Chapter 5. Intriguingly, the

44 Rashbam on Exod 20:13. The extent of Rashbam's knowledge of Latin is unclear. See Japhet, "Did Rashbam Know the Vulgate."

45 See, e.g., Rashbam on Num 11:35 and Leyra Curiá, *In Hebreo*, 335–338; see also the references cited in Japhet and Salters, *Rashbam on Qohelet*, 13. On the other side of the equation, there is some evidence that interpreters such as Hugh and Andrew of St. Victor consulted Jewish scholars. See note 40 and Smalley, *Study of the Bible*, 104–105, 364.

46 See Kugel, *Bible as it Was*, 21–23.

47 See b.*Bava Batra* 14b–15a; Simon, *Four Approaches*, 182–186.

48 See the full citation in Chapter 7, on p. 200.

49 See Chapter 5, p. 142.

same Hebrew root (*s-d-r*; "to arrange") is used by Rashbam in reference to the editorial process behind the biblical text in its current form.[50] As Rashbam remarks regarding the opening verses of the book of Qohelet:

> These two verses (1:1–2), "the words of Qohelet," "Vanity of vanities" were not said by Qohelet, but by the one who arranged (*sidder*) the words as they stand.[51]

Likewise, Rashbam observes regarding the concluding verses:

> Now the book is completed; those who arranged (*sidderu*) it speak from here on.[52]

Traditionally, Qohelet has been attributed to King Solomon, referring to himself within this book as "Qohelet."[53] Rashbam, however, discerned that these opening and closing verses speak in a different voice than the rest of this biblical book, indicating that these are not the words of Qohelet himself.[54] Here Rashbam identifies the work of an anonymous figure or figures, "the one(s) who arranged the words/it," responsible for the literary organization of the book. To be sure, one might endeavor to reconcile Rashbam's view on this matter with rabbinic tradition by pointing to the talmudic opinion that "Hezekiah and his men (or: group, party) composed Isaiah, Proverbs, Song of Songs and Qohelet" (b.*Bava Batra* 15a). Rashbam probably was thinking of this group when speaking of the "the one(s) who arranged the words/it."[55] And yet, there is an innovative spirit in Rashbam's words that goes beyond his talmudic source, as he employs this rabbinic tradition to differentiate between the words of King Solomon himself and the editorial voice(s) speaking in the opening and closing verses of Qohelet. Equally important, he refers to the activity of "those who arranged the words," i.e., those who conceived the literary design of King Solomon's original words in their current format in the Book of Qohelet. It was their literary intentions that Rashbam sought to understand in his commentary.

[50] The possibility that Rashbam was actually influenced by the Byzantine tradition in this respect is discussed later in this chapter.

[51] Rashbam on Qoh 1:1, Japhet and Salters ed., 92–93.

[52] Rashbam on Qoh 12:8, Japhet and Salters ed., 212–213.

[53] The Rabbis identified "Qohelet son of David" in the superscription of Qohelet as Solomon. See *Song of Songs Rabbah* 1:10, Dunski ed., 3; *Qohelet Rabbah* 1:1, Hirshman ed., 2; Wyrick, *Authorship*, 84–86. Although the Talmud (b.*Bava Batra* 15a) states that these three books were "written" by "Hezekiah and his group," this was taken to mean that they recorded and edited Solomon's words. See Simon, *Four Approaches*, 182–186; Wyrick, *Authorship*, 28–29, 32–57.

[54] See Japhet and Salters, *Rashbam on Qohelet*, 34–35.

[55] See Viezel, "Medieval Commentators on Composition of the Bible," 153–154.

This observation by Rashbam reverberated in the later northern French *peshat* school. Eliezer of Beaugency, believed to have been his student,[56] makes a similar claim about Ezek 1:2–3 (which breaks out of the first-person style of the surrounding pericope, told by the prophet himself), arguing that these verses make up an editorial gloss by the biblical editor (*sofer*). As Eliezer writes:

I saw visions of God (...) and lo, a stormy wind (1:1, 4) – This is all that Ezekiel said originally; he did not even give his name ... But the scribe (*sofer*) who put all of his words together in writing (*she-katav kol devaraw*) went on to make explicit in these two verses (1:2–3) what he left unsaid and abbreviated.[57]

To be sure, Rashi – seeking to account for "the sequence of the verses/ words" – had already noted that verses 2–3, which speak about the prophet in the third person, interrupt the flow of Ezekiel's first-person account in verses 1, 4. But Rashi (followed by Qara) attributed this interruption vaguely to "the Holy Spirit."[58] Eliezer of Beaugency, on the other hand, boldly ascribes the biographical information about Ezekiel provided in verses 2–3 to "the scribe" who edited Ezekiel's prophecies, an important transition from the notion of divine authorship to human literary agency.

What is perhaps the most sweeping remark regarding the work of the editor/redactor in a number of biblical books, evidently inspired by Rashbam's above-cited comments, is found in the following comment on the superscription to the Song of Songs ("The Song of Songs by Solomon"; Song 1:1) in an anonymous northern French *peshat* commentary:

The Song of Songs by Solomon – the scribe (*ha-sofer*) tells us that Solomon composed this poem, and these are not Solomon's words. And the beginning of the book is "May he kiss me of the kisses [of his mouth] (Song 1:2). And thus "The Words of Qohelet" (Qoh 1:1) are the words of a scribe. And thus "The Proverbs of Solomon son of David" (Prov 1:1) are the words of a scribe.[59]

[56] See Cohen, "Eliezer of Beaugency," 674.

[57] Eliezer of Beaugency on Ezek. 1:1, Poznanski ed., 1–2. See Harris, "Literary Hermeneutic," 210; Harris, "Awareness," 294. Translation taken from Steiner, "Redaction," 129.

[58] Rashi on Ezek 1:1, *Keter* ed., 2. Rashi elsewhere uses the term "Holy Spirit" in the sense of the *narrator*, following a convention attested in rabbinic literature. See Steiner, "Redaction," 130. See also Cohen, "Eliezer of Beaugency"; Harris, "Awareness."

[59] Japhet, "Anonymous Commentary," 231. A note in Rashi's comm. on Prov 1:7, Fredman ed., 90, which appears in the printed editions of the *Miqra'ot Gedolot*, likewise attributes the first six verses of that book to an editor rather than King Solomon himself. Lisa Fredman, in her critical apparatus on this verse, observes that this note is absent in all of the early manuscripts she checked, and appears only in the printed editions (and in a sixteenth-century manuscript that itself seems to be based on a printed edition). This,

Sara Japhet identifies this anonymous commentator as a student of Eliezer of Beaugency,[60] and so it is not surprising that he uses the term "the scribe" (*ha-sofer*) – characteristic of Eliezer – to refer to the biblical editor.[61]

Rashbam's use of the root *s-d-r* to connote the biblical narrator-editor and the associated term *ha-sofer* among his successors seems to suggest an incipient historical-critical awareness. In other words, exegetes in the circle of Rashbam and Eliezer of Beagency challenged the traditional conceptions of biblical authorship and recognized that the current text of the Bible is made up of earlier texts that were edited by later hands. Further evidence for this awareness can be brought from a remarkable point made in (what is believed to be) Rashbam's commentary on Psalms, in connection with the fifteen "Songs of Ascents" in Psalms 120–134:

A Song of Ascents – According to its *peshat*, during their pilgrimage, from the time of David and Solomon until the time between the first Temple and the Second Temple they composed "songs" about those "ascents." And from that point onward they recited them at all times in the Temple. And there were those that were composed during the emigration of Ezra and his group from Babylonia. And the language of these psalms demonstrates this.[62]

As Aaron Mondschein notes, the preface of this comment ("According to its *peshat* ... ") is directed against Rashi's reliance on midrash to explain the locution "A Song of Ascents."[63] Rashi adhered to the traditional view of the authorship of the Psalms, and he therefore states that King David composed the "Songs of Ascent," citing the explanation given in the Talmud that they were intended "to raise up the water table ('the depths')."[64] Rashbam, on the other hand, argues that the *peshat* method must be guided by the language of these psalms themselves, some of which indicate that they were composed in Babylonia, and from the exiles returned to the land of Israel once the Babylonian captivity was brought to an end by the Persian king Cyrus.

Nor is this comment by Rashbam a unicum within the northern French *peshat* school. As mentioned in Chapter 7, Joseph Qara notes that 1 Sam

then, would seem to be an addition by a later scribe or commentator. Eran Viezel believes that it can be attributed to Rashbam or one of his students. See Fredman, *Rashi on Proverbs*, 17; Viezel, "Formation of Biblical Books, According to Rashi," 39–40.

60 Japhet, "Anonymous Commentary," 229–230. 61 See Chapter 7, note 48.

62 Mondschein, "Lost Commentary," 130. On the attribution of this commentary to Rashbam, see Chapter 8, note 23.

63 Mondschein, "Lost Commentary," 125.

64 See Rashi on Ps 120:1, Gruber ed., 698–699.

9:9 is an interpolation into the original narrative by a later hand. And in his commentary on 1 Sam 17:55, cited earlier in the current chapter, Qara seems to recognize that the Book of Samuel incorporates different – and contradictory – traditions regarding Saul's first encounter with David. Perhaps most dramatically, in an anonymous fragment of a twelfth-century northern French commentary on Psalms, the following argument is made about Psalm 137, a lament of the Jews "on the rivers of Babylon":

It would appear ... that David did not compose (*katav*) this [psalm], but rather in the time of the Second Temple, when they were exiled to Babylonia, Jeremiah composed (*katav*) it. And when Ezra emigrated from Babylonia and composed (*katav*) all of the books [of the Bible], he composed (*katav*) this book [of Psalms] as well, and he added this one that Jeremiah wrote and juxtaposed it here to [the verse] " ... that He remembered us in our abject condition / [for His mercy endures forever]" (Ps 136:23) – and now as well He remembered (i.e., and eventually redeemed) us in our abject condition, for they had emigrated from Babylonia.[65]

Some scholars maintain that this commentary was penned by Joseph Qara.[66] In any case, the author of this commentary identifies two literary stages with respect to Psalm 137: it was first written by Jeremiah on behalf of the Jews of his time exiled to Babylonia; but later it was incorporated into the Book of Psalms by Ezra, described here as having "composed all the books" of the Bible. Ezra did not change the language of the psalm, but he decided to include it in the biblical canon and chose where best to place it. Additionally, the placement of this psalm, according to this commentator, illustrates that God, in His enduring mercy, did not forsake the Jews in their abject condition in the Babylonian captivity, and redeemed them through the agency of Cyrus, who allowed them to return to Zion. Ezra, the later editor of the Book of Psalms, was granted this perspective, a perspective that Jeremiah, the original author of Psalm 137, could not have known.

The next generation of northern French *pashtanim* – commentators influenced by Qara and Rashbam – continued to speak boldly about the role of the biblical narrator/editor in shaping the biblical text.[67] So-called Pseudo-Rashi on Ezra–Nehemiah (i.e., the commentary attributed to Rashi in the Rabbinic Bible), believed to have been written around 1150 by a student of Rashbam, argues that "the writer of the book" (*kotev ha-*

[65] From MS Hamburg 32, cited in Ta-Shma, "Bible Criticism in Franco-Germany," 457–459. The precise connotations of the root *katav* in this passage will be discussed later in this chapter.

[66] See Ta-Shma, "Open Bible Criticism in an Anonymous Commentary," 418–420.

[67] See Harris, "Awareness," 291–292n.

sefer), i.e., the editor who compiled the list of the exiled Judeans returning from Babylon to Jerusalem with Zerubbabel in Nehemiah 7, took some liberties and reworked the original list recorded in Ezra 2:1ff.[68] Similarly, Pseudo-Rashi on Chronicles (2 Chr 32:25), believed to have been penned around 1155 by a scholar of the same circle, notes that "the writer of the book" (*kotev ha-sefer*) abbreviated his source material from Kings and Isaiah when recording certain aspects of Hezekiah's reign in Chronicles.[69]

Eran Viezel, however, argues that the critical tendencies of Qara, Rashbam, and their circle should not be overstated. In his view, the genuinely "critical" comments by these exegetes are few and far between, and even in cases where they actually make reference to the biblical "narrator-editor," whether using the root *s-d-r*, *ha-sofer*, or *kotev ha-sefer*, the essential point they wish to make is literary and not historical-critical. In other words, these commentators, with only rare exceptions, had no intention of challenging the traditional attributions of biblical authorship by the Rabbis.[70] I believe that Viezel is fundamentally correct in this matter, though I think that greater emphasis can be placed on the implications of the literary innovations behind this new use of terminology.

In support of Viezel's view, it should be noted that the terminology used by the northern French *peshat* exegetes to connote *an editor* reworking earlier sources is the very same term they used to connote *the narrator* within the original biblical text.[71] Joseph Qara uses the expression "the prophet who wrote (*she-katav*) the/this book" to distinguish between remarks by the biblical narrator and the words of the characters cited in the narrative. For example, on Judg 13:18 ("The angel said to him: You must not ask for my name. It is unknowable"), Qara argues that the words "It is unknowable" were not uttered by the angel to Manoah, but rather were added by "the prophet who wrote (*katav*) the book." In other words,

[68] See Viezel, "Ezra–Nehemiah," 145–146, 178–180. As Viezel notes, the anonymous expression "the writer of the book" probably refers to the (unnamed) compiler of the historical list in Nehemiah 7, rather than to Nehemiah himself (whom this commentator took to be the author of the Book of Nehemiah; see his comment on Neh 1:1).

[69] See Viezel, *Commentary on Chronicles*, 233, 319–333. On 2 Chr 32:19 the commentator identifies that verse as a remark by "the one who wrote this book," as opposed to the words Sennacherib's messenger cited in the previous verses – an observation about the biblical narrator that more closely resembles those of Rashi and Qara cited above.

[70] Viezel, "Medieval Commentators on Composition of the Bible," 153–155.

[71] In the commentary on Psalm 137 cited earlier, the verb *katav* ("he wrote") is used both in connection with Jeremiah's role as the *author* of the psalm and Ezra's role as *editor* of the Book of Psalms.

this is the voice of the narrator explaining to the reader why the angel refused to fulfill Manoah's request.[72] On Judg 17:6, "In those days there was no king in Israel; every man did as he pleased," Qara writes:

> The prophet who wrote (*katav*) this book said this so that readers in later generations should not wonder [why the king did not prevent the illicit activity described in this chapter]. He therefore explains that this is the way things were in those days, because "in those days there was no king in Israel" and there was no one to stop their behavior and "every man did as he pleased."[73]

It is true that this comment entails a historical observation about the composition of the biblical text. But it does not necessarily imply any challenge to the rabbinic view that the prophet Samuel composed the Book of Judges. Indeed, it does not even necessarily imply that this verse was added to the "original" Book of Judges by a later hand, since Samuel himself could have inserted such a remark in the monarchal era of Israelite history which began with the reign of King Saul. Qara's objective is simply to identify the voice of the narrator of the account and distinguish it from the voices of the characters within the story.

It is also worth noting how Eliezer of Beaugency, who undoubtedly refers to the work of a later editor of Ezekiel's prophecies in his comment on Ezek 1:1–4, uses the term *ha-sofer* elsewhere in his commentaries. For example, on Jonah 1:10, "The men were greatly terrified, and they asked him, 'What have you done?' And when the men learned that he was fleeing from the service of the Lord – for so he told them," Eliezer writes:

> *Because he had told them* – earlier, in answering their question, "From where did you come?" (v. 8). But the narrator (lit., scribe: *ha-sofer*) held back this detail until they said to him: "What have you done?" And this style is common Scripture (*harbeh shiṭṭot ka-zeh ba-miqra*).[74]

Eliezer of Beaugency manifests keen awareness of the way that the narrator/implied author of the biblical account controls the flow of information to the reader.[75] In a similar way, in his commentary on Isa 7:2, Eliezer remarks:

[72] A similar observation can also be made with respect to Qara's commentary on 1 Kgs 1:15.

[73] Qara on Judg 17:6, Eppenstein ed., 40.

[74] Eliezer of Beaugency on Jonah 1:10, Poznanski ed., 158.

[75] There are instances in which he makes observations about the role of the biblical narrator in shaping the text – but without using the term "the scribe." See, e.g., his commentary on Isa 20:2, *Miqra'ot Gedolot, Keter* ed., 137.

> The typical manner of the [biblical] narrator (*derekh ha-sofer*; lit., "the scribe") is to relate the essential aspect of the matter briefly at the beginning ... and then go on to offer a more elaborate exposition.[76]

Eliezer ascribes a literary stylistic convention to "the scribe," a term he uses here in the sense of the narrator or implied author responsible for structuring the biblical narrative.[77] His expression *derekh ha-sofer* resembles the expression *derekh ha-miqra'ot* used by others in the northern French *peshat* school, though it is significant that he speaks of an authorial convention rather than simply speaking of the typical manner of the verses.

A modern eye will immediately distinguish between the work of a narrator or implied author shaping the words of the characters in a narrative and a redactor editing, reworking or combining preexisting literary sources. However, the medieval commentators, especially in the northern French *peshat* school, do not seem to have differentiated sharply between these literary activities, as suggested by their using similar terminology in reference to both.[78] We thus find the northern French *pashtanim* using terms like *kotev ha-sefer* and *ha-sofer* for both at different places in their commentaries.

Given the pivotal role Rashbam plays within this tradition, it is not surprising that some scholars have turned to his terminology for possible indications of the source of the conceptions of the biblical editor/narrator among the northern French *pashtanim*. Richard Steiner suggests that Rashbam's expression "the one who arranged the words (*oto she-sidder ha-devarim*) in their current sequence" may be "a paraphrase of the term *sadran*" used in the Byzantine *Leqaḥ Ṭov* and *Sekhel Ṭov* Pentateuch commentaries to connote the biblical narrator/editor who controls the flow of information to the reader.[79] By implication, this would also suggest that Rashbam could have been influenced by the earlier usage of the term *sadran* used in the earlier Byzantine commentaries to connote a biblical editor reworking earlier sources. However, this linguistic hypothesis must be put into proper context. To begin with, it appears that *Leqaḥ Ṭov* – cited once by Rashbam – was probably not available to him until late in his career, and the evidence that he knew *Sekhel Ṭov* (written a generation after *Leqaḥ Ṭov*)

[76] Eliezer of Beagency on Isa 7:2, *Miqra'ot Gedolot*, *Keter* ed., 53.
[77] See Harris, "Literary Hermeneutic," 159–164.
[78] See Harris, "Awareness," 289–290; cf. Steiner, "Redaction," 124.
[79] Steiner, "Redaction," 133.

remains inconclusive.[80] More importantly, we would argue that Rashbam's sensitivity to the work of the biblical narrator-editor has its roots in the literary-exegetical concerns that Rashi displays in his distinctive use the term *ha-meshorer*, in addition to his less frequent usage of the term *kotev ha-sefer*. In other words, even if Rashbam's terminology was borrowed from the Byzantine commentaries, the literary conceptions underlying it would have already been familiar to him from his exposure to Rashi, who was his first and most important teacher.[81] In order to assess this possibility of organic development within the northern French *peshat* tradition, we will now turn to investigate how Rashi's literary terms and concepts related to the biblical narrator/editor seem to reverberate in the work of Rashbam.

REFLECTIONS OF RASHI'S NOTION OF "THE POET" (HA-MESHORER) IN RASHBAM

Rashbam does not use the term *ha-meshorer* in his commentaries exactly as Rashi did.[82] Yet he adapted Rashi's coinage in his discussion of the literary perspective represented in (what is believed to be) his commentary on the Song of Songs. As Rashbam remarks in his introduction:

> [Solomon] wrote his ... "Song" ... [speaking] like a maiden longing and lamenting the loss of her lover, who left her ... She recalls him and his eternal love for her, and she sings (*meshoreret*) and says: such strong love my darling manifested toward me when he was still with me. And she recounts (*mesapperet*) to her girlfriends and her maidens: such and such my darling said to me and this is how I responded.[83]

Notwithstanding the similarities between them, Rashbam's usage certainly differs from Rashi's. Whereas Rashi used the masculine participle form as a noun, preceded by the definite article *ha-* ("the"), yielding *ha-*

[80] See Lockshin, "Connection"; Jacobs, "Clarification." There is no evidence that Rashbam had access to the earlier tenth/eleventh-century Byzantine commentaries that use the related term *sadran*.

[81] On Rashi's foundational influence on Rashbam, see Touitou, *Exegesis*, 68–76; Japhet, *Rashbam on Song of Songs*, 63–65.

[82] Rashbam does not use the term *meshorer* in the sense of a narrator or implied author in (what is believed to be) his Psalms commentary. (I thank Aaron Mondschein for providing this information from manuscript of this commentary, which he intends to publish.) The term *ha-meshorer* is used in the sense that Rashi used it in a note regarding Ps 141:4 by Benjamin of Canterbury (a student of Rabbenu Tam) in his gloss on Joseph Kimhi's *Sefer ha-Galui*, Mathews ed., 16. See Bacher, "Commentator," 168.

[83] Rashbam, Introduction to Song of Songs, Japhet ed., 233.

meshorer ("the poet"), Rashbam uses the feminine participle as a present-tense verb: *meshoreret* ("she sings/speaks poetically").[84] Furthermore, whereas Rashi posits an external literary voice that narrates for the beloved, Rashbam identifies the beloved herself, a character in the story, as the narrator who "recounts" (*mesapperet*) her own love tale.[85] Yet the similar point that both *pashtanim* make – with closely related terminology – is that the narrator in the Song of Songs must be distinguished from its historical author, King Solomon.[86]

On the second verse of the Song – the first time the maiden's voice is heard – Rashbam remarks:

> Sometimes the bride sings (*meshoreret*) as though speaking with her lover; and sometimes she recounts to her girlfriends about him, that he is not together with her.[87]

Later in the commentary, Rashbam makes a similar point and clarifies that it applies to the work as a whole:

> This is the manner of this "Song" – that she sings (*meshoreret*) and grieves in all of them about her love for her darling, and after recounting ... her love to her girlfriends ... they scold her, responding: "Forget his love, because he has scorned you and will not return to you ... " And she adjures them that they must not speak of this to her because she shall never forsake his love ... And still nowadays the convention of the *meshorerim* (singers, poets, *trouvères*) is to sing a song that recounts (*mesapper*) the narrative of the love of a couple, with love songs (*shirei ahava = chansons d'amour*) as is the practice of all people (*minhag ha-'olam*).[88]

[84] It was characteristic of Rashbam to adapt and modify his grandfather's terminological innovations. E.g., the distinctive term *dugma* (=*exemplum*) that Rashi used to connote the Song of Songs' allegorical layer of meaning (see Chapter 2, note 71) was adapted by Rashbam, who employs the term *dimyon* (=similitude) to serve this function. See Liss, "Song of Songs," 8–19.

[85] There is, of course, a more fundamental difference between the two exegetes' approaches: Rashi construes the beloved as an elderly woman in "living widowhood" reminiscing about her youthful love, whereas Rashbam casts the beloved and her lover as young lovers experiencing the vicissitudes of their initial relationship. On these differences between the approaches of Rashi and Rashbam, see Japhet, *Rashbam on Song of Songs*, 137–143.

[86] This usage by Rashbam is also reflected in another twelfth-century northern French Song of Songs commentary that appears to have emanated from Rashbam's scholarly circle, who remarks: "Solomon composed (*yissad*) this song and formulated it from the perspective of the beloved, who sings (*meshoreret*) about her lover, for she utters all the words of the Song that are not direct quotations." From MS BML (Florence) Acq. e Doni 121, cited in Alster, "Human Love," 14–16, 70–71.

[87] Rashbam on Song 1:2, Japhet ed., 233.

[88] Rashbam on Song 3:5, Japhet ed., 250. On the Old French love songs of the *trouvères*, see Chapter 6, note 20.

Rashbam here introduces another speaker-group whose words are cited in the Song: the maiden's "girlfriends," who advise her to forsake him – advice that elicits a reconfirmation of her steadfast love. To support his claim about the shifting speakers and addressees of the beloved's words, Rashbam cites "the practice of all people," i.e., the literary conventions of the *meshorerim* in the general culture around him, probably a reference to the *trouvères* of twelfth-century France.[89] It is conceivable that Rashi's introduction of the term *ha-meshorer* into the analysis of the Song of Songs opened the door to Rashbam's analogy between this sacred text and the *chansons d'amour* of the *trouvères*. In any case, Rashbam's use of the terms *meshoreret/meshorerim* resembles the way that Rashi had used the term *ha-meshorer* in his Psalms commentary to identify the voice of the speaker in a given psalm, whose perspective he adopts, and to whom he speaks.[90]

Rashi had coined the usage of the term *ha-meshorer* to designate the narrator or implied author, but applied it only in the Song of Songs and the Psalms, probably because it is only in these biblical books that the term is naturally applicable: the Hebrew title of Song of Songs is *shir ha-shirim*, and the Psalms are said to have been sung by *meshorerim* (see 2 Chr 29:28).[91] Rashbam adapted this usage in his commentary on the Song of Songs, but evidently sought to widen it, as we see in his commentary on Lamentations.[92] Traditionally, Lamentations – a book of national lament over the tragedies of the destruction of the Temple and the exile of Israel – was attributed to the prophet Jeremiah, as recorded in the Talmud, followed by Rashi.[93] Although Rashbam faithfully records that this was the opinion of the Rabbis, he begins his analysis in a different vein:

The "lamentor" (*ha-meqonen*) that composed (*yissad*) the scroll of Lamentations selected his style (*shiṭṭah*) following the practice of all people (*nohag she-ba-'olam bi-benei adam*). As might occur typically in the case of a widow, remaining completely alone, bereft of her children and husband, she calls upon trained "lamenting women" to utter many lamentations for her. Sometimes they express their lamentations speaking in the voice (lit., in place) of the widow herself . . . And

[89] See Japhet, *Rashbam on Song of Songs*, 100–104, 118–120.

[90] On these aspects of Rashi's use of the term *ha-meshorer*, see Chapter 7.

[91] Abraham Ibn Ezra, e.g., regularly uses the expression "the poet (*ha-meshorer*) said" when citing verses from Psalms.

[92] On this commentary, of which only fragments survive, see Japhet, "Rashbam's Introduction to Lamentations," 231–232.

[93] Rashi on Lam 1:1, based on b.*Bava Batra* 15a. See Viezel, "Formation of Biblical Books, According to Rashi," 26–27. This opinion was also adopted by early Christian authorities, as is reflected in the placement of Lamentations immediately following the Book of Jeremiah in Jerome's Vulgate and in subsequent Christian versions of the Bible.

sometimes they speak to the widow in their lamentations and bemoan her misfortune. And sometimes they recount the events that befell the widow to others in their lamentations. In this way this "lamentor" (*meqonen*: i.e., the author of the book of Lamentations) composed (*yissad*) his lamentation for Israel. Sometimes he speaks in the voice of (lit., in place of) the people of Israel, and sometimes he speaks to her. And sometimes he speaks to others about her.[94]

Although he would go on in the following lines to cite the rabbinic view that Jeremiah authored Lamentations without any reservations, Rashbam first identifies the literary voice – the "lamentor" – speaking in the book. The term he recruited for this purpose is the participle *meqonen* (attested in Biblical Hebrew – see below), manifesting the same grammatical form as *meshorer*. Just as Rashbam invokes "the practice of all people" in his Song of Songs commentary to draw an analogy between sacred Scripture and the *chansons d'amour*, here he does so to interpret Lamentations in light of the style of professional women "lamentors" that a recently widowed woman might invite to mourn her tragedy. In this instance, Rashbam does not, as he might have, cite a contemporary medieval practice (like *chansons d'amour*), but rather a feature of ancient Israelite society in biblical times, as attested by the description of "dirge-singers" (*meqonenot*) in Jer 9:16–17. As the biblical depiction of these women suggests, their dirges aimed to bring the listeners to tears. Rashbam's specific purpose in drawing this analogy is to explain the shifts of perspective and addressee in Lamentations: at times the "lamentor" speaks in the voice of Israel wailing over her tragedies, at times he speaks to Israel about her tragedies, and at times he speaks in his own voice to others about Israel's tragedies.[95] These shifts resemble those delineated by Rashbam in his Song of Songs commentary (using the term *meshoreret*) and by Rashi in his Psalms commentary (using the term *ha-meshorer*).

As discussed in Chapter 7, Rashi – in his commentaries on Song 2:8 and Psalm 68 – referred to "the poet" (*ha-meshorer*) as the narrator or implied author responsible for the structure and organization of the biblical text. Rashbam in his Pentateuch commentary boldly ascribes to Moses the role of selecting and organizing the narratives of the Pentateuch – as detailed in recent studies by Hanna Liss, Martin Lockshin, Eleazar Touitou, and Eran Viezel.[96] In other words, it was Moses who conceived the literary design of the Pentateuch, and the arrangement of the laws in it – cited in God's

94 Japhet, "Rashbam's Introduction to Lamentations," 232–233.

95 See Japhet, "Rashbam's Introduction to Lamentations," 237–240.

96 See Liss, *Fictional Worlds*, 75–168; Lockshin, "Moses"; Touitou, *Exegesis*, 120–121; Viezel, "Rashbam on Moses' Role."

words verbatim, as indicated with formulas such as "And God spoke to Moses saying ... "[97] Admittedly, in the case of the Pentateuch Rashbam does not distinguish between the historical author, i.e., Moses, and the more conceptual anonymous reference to the narrator/implied author responsible for the organization of the text, as he and other northern French *pashtanim* (including Rashi) did elsewhere in the Bible.[98] Yet it is evident that a key goal of Rashbam's *peshat* program was to discern the literary design of the biblical text, as intended by Moses.

In sum, it is clear that Rashbam devised a number of ways to refer to the biblical narrator/editor, and the expression "the one who arranged the words (*oto she-sidder ha-devarim*) in their current sequence" is only one of them. It is certainly conceivable that Rashbam devised this locution to connote the biblical narrator under the influence of the usage of the term *sadran* in *Leqaḥ Ṭov and Sekhel Ṭov*. But there is an ample background for this phrase and – more importantly – the literary conceptions it implies in the work of Rashi. To begin with, Rashi himself refers – albeit only one time, in his Talmud commentary – to the activity of Moses in arranging the Torah using the term *sidder*.[99] More prominently, as discussed in Chapter 7, Rashi designated the work of the biblical narrator with the term *ha-meshorer* ("the poet") on Song of Songs and Psalms. It stands to reason that this profoundly influenced Rashbam, who sought to apply similar insights about literary structure even in biblical books in which the term *meshorer* is not applicable, such as Lamentations and the Pentateuch. As a close student of Rashi's, Rashbam would have regarded it a central interpretive objective to discern the logic of "the sequence of the words/verses" (*seder ha-*

97 In one passage in his Talmud commentary Rashi states that "Moses wrote and arranged (*katav we-sidder*) the Torah" (comm. on b.*Ḥullin* 100b, s.v., אמרו לו). See Viezel, "Formation of Biblical Books, According to Rashi," 36. By itself, this comment does not necessarily imply that Moses played an active role in the organization of the Pentateuch, but it may have been suggestive for Rashbam, inspiring him to think along these lines. We should note that later northern French exegetes do speak of Moses' active editorial activity in the Pentateuch using the root *s-d-r*. See Joseph Bekhor Shor on Deut 1:1 (with Harris, "Awareness," 303; Steiner, "Redaction," 132) and Hizkuni on Exod 34:32. Bekhor Shor's view is discussed at length in Jacobs, *Bekhor Shoro*, 242–244.

98 It is beyond the scope of this study to conjecture why Rashbam did not distinguish between the historical author and implied author/narrator in the Pentateuch – as he does in other biblical books. We can remark briefly, though, that Rashbam may have been deterred from making this distinction on theological grounds, because the authorship of the Pentateuch was a particularly sensitive matter. And so, he may have wished not to suggest, even implicitly, that anyone but Moses authored the Pentateuch.

99 See note 97.

devarim/miqra'ot). We must recall Rashbam's remark, "poetry (*shirah*) is the arrangement of words (*siddur devarim*)."[100] For Rashbam, then, the task of the poet is to arrange the words in their proper sequence, the logic of which the *peshat* exegete must discern. Although the term *ha-meshorer* may be relevant only in relation to the Psalms and Song of Songs, the idea of *siddur devarim* can be applied widely to any text of the Bible. Following Rashi, Rashbam would have regarded this usage of the root *s-d-r* as a natural way of describing the literary work of the biblical narrator and thereby fulfill the goal of accounting properly for the "sequence" of the biblical text, as Rashi had done using the term "the poet."

The lineage of Rashbam's use of the root *s-d-r* to connote the biblical editors who arranged the words of Qohelet is not simply a matter of historical detective work. Rather, it suggests something about Rashbam's interpretive motives. Rashbam's interest, like Rashi's in using the term *ha-meshorer*, was to account for the shift in voices that can be discerned in the opening and closing verses of Qohelet. In other words, as Viezel argues, Rashbam's interests are literary rather than historical-critical. But the importance of this literary sensibility must not be underestimated: it implied that human writers had a hand in the literary design of Scripture. It was the goal of *peshat* interpretation to discern the literary intentions of those writers, just as one would do when seeking to interpret other, completely humanly authored literary compositions, as Qara did for *piyyut* (and is believed to have done for *Genesis Rabbah*), and Rashbam did for Talmud.

INNOVATION IN A TRADITIONAL FRAMEWORK: PESHAT AND HUMAN LITERARY AGENCY

The literary investigations opened by Rashi at times served as a springboard for further development among later northern French *pashtanim*. A particularly dramatic case relates to the Song of Songs, a special biblical text that prompted Rashi to express his hermeneutical conceptions elaborately and clearly, as discussed in earlier chapters of this study. A number of later Jewish commentaries on this book from the northern French *peshat* school have survived, some in fragmentary form, and all of them anonymous or mistakenly attributed to Rashi.[101] Among these, one Song of Songs

[100] See Chapter 7, note 6.
[101] See, e.g., Alster, "Human Love," 13–16; Japhet, "Anonymous Commentary."

commentary has been identified as Rashbam's, as mentioned in the previous chapter.[102] The introduction to this work begins by presenting *peshat* as its objective:

The discerning man must incline his heart to understand the language of eloquence (*meliṣah*) of this book. To teach and convey its *peshat*, according to its style and word[ing], in accordance with its structure and language … Solomon wrote (*katav*) his … "Song" … [speaking] like a maiden longing and lamenting the loss of her lover, who left her and went to a faraway land.[103]

The imprint of Rashi's approach is evident here. Yet Rashbam's specific reading of the *peshat* framework is new, as he identifies the beloved as a young maiden, not an older already married woman in "living widowhood."[104]

The allegorical sense of the Song of Songs is not mentioned in Rashbam's introduction; but it features prominently throughout the commentary, as evident in his comment on the first verse:

[The Song …] of Solomon – King Solomon composed it (*yissedo*) through the Holy Spirit, for he saw that Israel would grieve in their exile over God, who has become distant from them, as a groom separated from his beloved. He began to sing his song representing the people of Israel, who are like a bride for Him.[105]

Rashbam attributes the prophetic content of the Song of Songs to the Holy Spirit, as Rashi had done in his introduction. However, whereas Rashi attributed the human love story that comprises the literary format of the Song of Songs to the Holy Spirit as well ("[Solomon] composed (*yissad*) this book with the Holy Spirit in the language of a woman stuck in living widowhood … "[106]), Rashbam speaks only of Solomon's authorship in that connection:

Solomon wrote (*katav*) his … "Song" … [speaking] like a maiden longing and lamenting the loss of her lover, who left her and went to a faraway land (as cited above).

[102] See Chapter 8, note 24.

[103] Rashbam, introduction to Song of Songs, Japhet ed., 233. The remainder of this passage was cited on p. 256.

[104] Presumably he felt that this better captures the spirit of playful, youthful love in the Song of Songs – and did not wish to read these retrospectively, as Rashi had done, as discussed in Chapter 6.

[105] Rashbam on Song 1:1, Japhet ed., 233.

[106] See the full citation of Rashi's introduction in Chapter 6, p. 170.

Solomon, rather than the Holy Spirit, is credited for the imaginative literary framework of this book, i.e., the object of its *peshat* analysis.[107]

For Rashbam, it would seem, the poetic garb of the Song of Songs is a product of human literary ingenuity, as opposed to the book's divine prophetic content. This would explain the analogy Rashbam draws between this holy text and the profane love songs, the *chansons d'amour* popular in France in his time, as discussed in Chapter 6. Indeed, as recent studies by Sara Japhet and Hanna Liss have shown, Rashbam analyzes the Song of Songs as secular love poetry more fully than had ever been done before in the Jewish interpretive tradition.[108]

Rashbam's alignment of *peshuto shel miqra* with the human literary dimension of the biblical text finds an instructive parallel in developments in Latin learning. As Alastair Minnis has shown, the privileging of the literal sense of Scripture in late medieval Western Christian interpretation was integrally linked with the emergence of more sharply defined conceptions of the Bible as literature and its human authorship. Traditionally, the literal sense was of lesser interest in Christianity by comparison with the spiritual sense associated with the "Holy Spirit" that endowed the words of the Bible with deeper meaning. Its human "authors" were seen as little more than scribes copying the words of God, as Gregory the Great, for example, remarked.[109] But by the thirteenth century Christian exegetes began to consider more seriously the role of the human authors of Scripture and their intentions. New interest in "the intention of the speaker" emerged, i.e., the human being through whom the Holy Spirit communicated. Albert the Great (writing shortly after 1270) maintained that "the intention of the speaker as expressed in the letter is the literal sense."[110] This new appreciation for the human authors of Scripture brought with it a new appreciation for pagan authors: "Writers from

[107] In medieval Ashkenazic writing, the verbal root *y-s-d* was used to connote *writing, literary composition*; see Chapter 2, note 45. As such, it is essentially synonymous with the verb *k-t-v*, i.e., *to write*. And yet, Rashbam's choice here to use the term *katav* instead of copying Rashi's term *yissad* may hint at his desire to declare independence from his grandfather with regard to Solomon's authorial activity in the composition of the Song. On the other hand, in connection with the allegorical interpretation, Rashbam faithfully uses Rashi's term *yissad*.

[108] See Japhet, *Rashbam on Song of Songs*, 133–146; Liss, "Song of Songs." By contrast, Abraham Ibn Ezra, in his introduction to the Song of Songs, makes a deliberate effort to distinguish this biblical book from profane Arabic love poetry. See Cohen, *Gates*, 206.

[109] See the full citation in Chapter 7, on p. 200. [110] Minnis, *Authorship*, 73.

both camps, the Scriptural and the secular, were being credited with comparable literary and moral achievements."[111]

Aristotle's notion of multiple forms of causality was recruited to maintain the traditional hierarchy that granted supremacy to the spiritual sense attributed to the Holy Spirit, even while carving out a niche for the literal sense, defined as the intention of the human author. Using Aristotelian terminology, the Holy Spirit was described as the "principal efficient cause" of Scripture, i.e., its ultimate source, whereas the divinely inspired human authors were characterized as the "instrumental efficient cause."[112] As a result:

> The influence of Aristotle's theory of causality as understood by late-medieval schoolmen helped to bring about a new awareness of the integrity of the individual human *auctor*. Henceforth, each and every inspired writer would be given credit for his personal literary contribution ... [For] Nicholas Trevet, the greatest scholar among the English "classicising friars" of the early fourteenth century ... the literal sense ... is the expression of the *prima intentio*; it was provided by the inspired human *auctor*, while the mystical senses were the work of the Holy Spirit ... Trevet's Psalter-commentary manifests the conviction that the Jews were, and are, adept at expounding the words of the human *auctor*, even though they fail to grasp the spiritual significance intended by the divine *auctor*.[113]

The new literary appreciation of Scripture brought with it an increased interest in its literal sense, even though it was not regarded as the ultimate meaning of Scripture.

The trends described by Minnis blossomed only in the thirteenth and fourteenth centuries. But they had roots in the twelfth century: "Peter Abelard (1079–1142) ... anticipates literary attitudes which were widely held in the thirteenth century. [He] was ... interested in the individual literary activity of the human *auctor* of Scripture, especially in the author's intention and the rhetorical force of his writing."[114] The same goes for Gilbert of Poitiers:

> Anselm of Laon ... had little to say about the eloquence of the prophet David. For many of Anselm's successors, the Psalter's *modus tractandi* remained, as it were, the property of the Holy Spirit, not of the human author or authors of the Psalter. But many exegetes did not share Anselm's reticence ... Gilbert of Poitiers (c. 1080–1154) was more interested in the persuasive force of the psalms than his master, Anselm of Laon had been.[115]

111 Minnis, *Authorship*, 75. 112 Minnis, *Authorship*, 78–79.
113 Minnis, *Authorship*, 85–86. 114 Minnis, *Authorship*, 58–60.
115 Minnis, *Authorship*, 49–50.

Thierry of Chartres laid special emphasis on the literal sense.[116] Hugh of St. Victor, likewise, invoked the need to ascertain the author's intention in defending the importance of investigating the literal sense.[117] In Rashbam's time, then, there were bold Christian thinkers who began to focus on the intentions of the human authors of Scripture.

These parallels illuminate Rashbam's attribution of the literary format of the Song of Songs to King Solomon himself (rather than the Holy Spirit), and his use of the analogy from contemporary love poetry to elucidate *peshuto shel miqra*. Like the Christian interpreters discussed by Minnis, Rashbam posits that the Song of Songs was composed with the guidance of the Holy Spirit, and as such contains a divine prophetic message – conveyed by the midrash. Rashbam's innovative move was to argue that it was Solomon, as a human author, adopting human literary conventions, who fashioned its literary form, which therefore must be interpreted as one would interpret any similar human composition – and this is the domain of *peshuto shel miqra*.

The implications of the dichotomy established by Rashbam were drawn out by a subsequent anonymous northern French *peshat* commentator, who remarks in his opening comment on the book:

> *The Song of Songs of Solomon* – Solomon ... wrote many poems (lit., songs), as it is written "his poems numbered a thousand and one" (1 Kings 5:12) ... From among his poetry the Wise Men selected these poems and combined them, in order to impart a lesson about God and the Community of Israel. And this is what the opening verse means: "A poem that was prepared from Solomon's poetry" – that they anthologized his poems and arranged (*sidderu*)[118] this collection as a testimonial regarding God and the Community of Israel, and the remainder they did not use. For this book was composed (*nityassed*)[119] with the Holy Spirit and was included in the Sacred Writings because it is holy of holies, for the Wise Men arranged the words of Solomon, as it is written: "These are the sayings of Solomon that the men of Hezekiah transmitted" (Prov. 25:1).[120]

Using the vocabulary of Rashi and Rashbam, this commentator boldly posits two aspects of the authorship of the Song of Songs. In his view, the book is a selection of love poems by King Solomon – what Rashi defined as the *peshat* layer of the book. However, a later group of editors, Hezekiah's

[116] See the citation from Thierry's *Hexameron* in Chapter 8, on p. 232.

[117] See Minnis and Scott, *Literary Theory*, 66–67; Smalley, *Study of the Bible*, 94–95.

[118] Note the use of the root *s-d-r* to connote the arrangement of Solomon's original words, a usage that certainly can be traced to the influence of Rashbam, for example in his Qohelet commentary, as cited on p. 249.

[119] On the use of this term, see note 107 above.

[120] Eppenstein, "Fragment," 243–244.

"Wise Men," is responsible for the anthology of poems that makes up the biblical work we now have as the Song of Songs – and they endowed it with its allegorical sense, inspired by the Holy Spirit.[121] Going a step beyond Rashbam, he argues that Solomon himself is responsible solely for the literary format of the Song of Songs, and that the Holy Spirit inspired only the later authors, who endowed the text with its allegorical sense regarding the relationship between God and Israel. While this bold view was not advanced by Rashbam, it reflects a possibility for which he opened the door by distinguishing between the human and divine components of the Song of Songs and coordinating them using the *peshat–derash* dichotomy, aligning the *peshat* with the literary intentions of the human author, and the midrashic interpretation with the prophecy conveyed by the Holy Spirit.

"MOSAIC" AUTHORSHIP OF THE PENTATEUCH

Rashbam advanced a novel perspective on Mosaic authorship of the Pentateuch within the framework of *peshuto shel miqra*.[122] Traditionally it was assumed that the Pentateuch reflects the word of God conveyed to Moses, and written down word for word from this divine dictation.[123] Yet in two salient passages Rashbam speaks of the intentions of Moses himself as the author of the Pentateuch. The first of these is in his commentary on Genesis 1:1–5, where Rashbam addresses a question that had been raised by his grandfather. Positing that the primary purpose of the "Torah" (lit., the Law) is to convey the precepts of Judaism (the *miṣwot*), Rashi pondered why it was necessary for it to begin with an account of the creation of the world.[124] Whereas Rashi drew upon midrashic sources to answer this question in a theological vein, Rashbam offers a literary solution, which

121 This account of the formation of the Song of Songs accords with the rabbinic view that this biblical book, along with Isaiah, Qohelet, and Proverbs, was compiled by "Hezekiah and his party." See Viezel, "Medieval Commentators on Composition of the Bible," 153–154.

122 See Touitou, *Exegesis*, 112–121.

123 The Mishnah in *Sanhedrin* 10:1 refers to the doctrine that "the Torah is from Heaven" (i.e., the word of God Himself). The Talmud (b.*Sanhedrin* 99b) clarifies that this required belief is comprehensive, and excludes "someone who says that the entire Torah is from the Almighty except for a particular verse which was written by Moses on his own." There is some ambiguity about this elsewhere in the Talmud, however, since we do find a view that sections of Deuteronomy "Moses said them on his own" (b. *Megillah* 31b).

124 See Rashi on Gen 1:1.

he characterizes as *peshat*.[125] In fact, in this opening comment on the Pentateuch, he invokes the talmudic *peshat* maxim to underscore the importance of maintaining the integrity of *peshuto shel miqra* notwithstanding the primacy of midrashic interpretation:

Let lovers of reason (*sekhel*) understand that all of the words of our Rabbis and their *derashot* are valid and true. And this is what is said in b.*Shabbat* (63a): "I was eighteen years old and I did not yet know that 'Scripture does not leave the realm of its *peshat*.'" And the essence of the *halakhot* and the *derashot* can be extracted from the redundancies of the verses or from their anomalous language, because the *peshat* of Scripture[126] is written in a way that one can deduce from it the essence of the derivation (*derashah*). For example: "Such is the story of the heaven and the earth when they were created" (Gen 2:4), and the Sages derived midrashically, ["By the merit of the future actions of] Abraham,"[127] triggered by the redundancy of the language, since it did not need to say "when they were created."[128] And now I shall explicate the interpretations of the earlier ones on this verse, to inform people why I did not interpret as they did.

After reviewing earlier interpretations that he rejects, Rashbam writes:

But this is the essential *peshat* (*'iqqar peshuto*) according to the typical style of the biblical verses (*derekh ha-miqra'ot*). For Scripture often offers introductory information (lit., introduces: *le-haqdim*) and explains something superfluous for the sake of that which is mentioned later on in another place ...

So, too, our Master Moses composed this account of the "labor" (i.e., creation) of the six days, as well as introductory information to clarify what God would say ... [later, in the Ten Commandments]: "Remember the Sabbath day to sanctify it ... for in six days God created the heaven and the earth ... and He rested on the seventh day" (Exod 20:8). And this is what was written: "And it was evening and it was morning, *the* sixth day," i.e., the sixth ... to which God referred later. Therefore Moses said to Israel, to inform them that God's words are true, as if to say: "Do you think that this world always existed as you see now, filled with all that is good? It was not so. But rather ... it was completely desolate, and had nothing upon it [at which point God labored for six days to create all that is in it now]."[129]

Rashbam goes on to explain the creation account. When he reaches verse 5, "And God called the light 'day,'" he makes a point of recording another aspect of his *peshat* commentary:

[125] See Kamin, *Jews and Christians*, lx.

[126] In this context, the words "the *peshat* of Scripture" connote *the very text of Scripture*. See note 16.

[127] *Genesis Rabbah* 12:8, Theodor–Albeck ed., 107.

[128] Hebrew בהבראם, which can be "rearranged" to spell Abraham (אברהם).

[129] Rashbam on Gen 1:1, Rosin ed., 3–4. The first part of this passage was cited in Chapter 8, on p. 226. For a detailed analysis of Rashbam's commentary in this passage and the next, see Kislev, "Rashbam on Creation"; Liss, *Fictional Worlds*, 78–83.

You must wonder, according to the *peshat*, why did God have to call the light "day" when it was created? But this is what Moses wrote (i.e., it is not a record of God's speech at the time of creation, but rather a feature of Moses' literary composition of the Pentateuch) as if to say that whenever we see in the words of God "day" or "night," for example "And day and night will not cease" (Gen 8:22), it means the light and darkness that were created on the first day – and God refers to them consistently as "day" and "night." And similarly all verses of the form "And God called ... " in this section have the same sense.[130]

In Rashbam's view, it would seem, Moses was the one who decided to include the creation story in the Bible, and it is he who formulated it in order to provide clarification for the laws later appearing in the Pentateuch. Rashbam thus introduces, as part of his *peshat* program, the investigation of Moses' literary intentions in composing the Pentateuch.

Rashbam likewise discusses Moses' intentions in his discussion of the historical presentation of the sons of Jacob in Genesis 37. Here, too, he begins with the methodological-programmatic statement about the relation between *peshuto shel miqra* and midrashic interpretation, a passage cited earlier in this chapter (see p. 241), after which he writes:

The intellectuals (*maskilim*) must recognize as nonsense the interpretation of the earlier scholars that "These are the generations of Jacob" means *these are the occurrences that befell Jacob*. For every occurrence of the expression "These are the generations" in the Pentateuch or in the Writings spell out either the children or grandchildren of the individual named ... And thus, with respect to Jacob, it says earlier "And Jacob's sons were twelve" (Gen 35:22) ... and now its writes "These are the generations of Jacob" – meaning his grandchildren, who numbered seventy and how they were born. How did this occur? "Joseph was seventeen years old" (Gen 37:2) and his brothers were jealous of him, and because of this Judah descended ... and bore children ... and through a chain of events Joseph was taken to Egypt and he bore Manasseh and Ephraim ... until they were seventy. And all of this, Moses had to write because later he rebuked them saying: "Your forefathers descended to Egypt numbering seventy souls ... " (Deut 10:22).[131]

In his final comment in this passage, Rashbam speaks of how Moses organized the historical narratives in Genesis to support his "rebuke" of Israel recorded in the Book of Deuteronomy.

As Eleazar Touitou has noted, these remarks suggest that Rashbam conceives of the Pentateuch as having two distinct aims: (1) to convey the precepts commanded by God; (2) to provide supporting narratives, and Moses' "rebuke" in Deuteronomy. Touitou argues further that Rashbam maintains, according to *peshuto shel miqra*, that the essence of the

[130] Rashbam on Gen 1:5, Rosin ed., 5. [131] Rashbam on Gen 37:2, Rosin ed., 50.

Pentateuch – the words that God Himself communicated – is limited to its main legal sections, whereas the narratives and Deuteronomy were formulated by Moses to provide a framework.[132] Touitou raises, but does not answer, the question of how Rashbam reconciles this position with the talmudic doctrine that every verse of the Pentateuch – without even one exception – was dictated by God Himself to Moses.[133] In other words, it is puzzling that Rashbam would ignore the fundamental doctrine of the absolute divine authorship of the Pentateuch and posit that Moses played an active role in shaping its text.[134]

I would like to suggest that the key to solving this conundrum may be found upon consideration of the fact that the two key passages of Rashbam's Pentateuch commentary that speak of Moses' authorship of Genesis (on Gen 1:1–5 and 37:2) also contain his apologia for interpreting *peshuto shel miqra*, notwithstanding the authority of midrashic interpretation. In both passages, Rashbam explains that midrashic interpretation operates by focusing on the special features of the language of Scripture – its anomalies and redundancies, which "hint" at deeper messages – the *haggadot, derashot* and *halakhot*. This interpretive operation treats the sacred text as a God-given finished product, to be investigated deeply through the midrashic hermeneutical rules. Rashbam's exploration of *peshuto shel miqra* is based on different assumptions. He seeks to

132 Touitou, *Exegesis*, 112–121. Evidence for Mosaic authorship of Deuteronomy can be adduced by the opening verse of the book: "These are the words that Moses spoke to all of Israel ... " (Deut 1:1). It is perhaps this outlook of Rashbam's that underlies a comment by Hizkuni: "'The Torah was given scroll [by scroll]' (see b.*Giṭṭin* 60a). [That is to say:] when Moses received each law from the Holy One Blessed be He, he would write it in its own scroll. And when he was about to depart from this world, he arranged (*sidder*) the [entire] book of the Torah and he established the order of the chapters in their current form according to the appropriate juxtapositions, as our Rabbis expounded" (comm. on Exod 34:32, Chavel ed., 323). Hizkuni was a thirteenth-century northern French Bible commentator about whom little is known; but it is clear that he was heavily influenced by Rashbam. See Japhet, *Collected Studies*, 364–372.

133 See Touitou, *Exegesis*, 121, n. 24. See also note 123 earlier in this chapter.

134 It is true that other medieval Jewish commentators faithful to rabbinic tradition likewise modified the traditional doctrine regarding the authorship of the Pentateuch – by positing that some verses are post-Mosaic additions. See Ta-Shma, "Bible Criticism in Franco-Germany," who cites examples in thirteenth-century Ashkenazic commentaries. See also Simon, *Ear Discerns*, 407–464, who discusses Ibn Ezra's view. Nonetheless, advancing such a position was often perceived as being potentially heretical. For this reason, Ibn Ezra merely alluded to his opinion on this matter rather than stating it openly. Yet it seems that in Ashkenazic circles this was less of a concern, perhaps because critique of the integrity of the biblical text was not common in the surrounding intellectual milieu. See Soloveitchik, "Two Notes."

understand how the Pentateuch was compiled by Moses, who committed God's communications to writing and arranged them with a particular design in mind. To discover Moses' intentions, Rashbam explores the style and structure of the text (rather than delving beneath its surface) within its historical context, and by considering the literary conventions that can explain its seeming anomalies and redundancies.

The theory advanced here is that Rashbam maintained a dualistic approach to interpreting the Pentateuch and that this allowed him the freedom to investigate Moses' intentions in shaping the text of the Pentateuch. On the one hand, he believed that Moses penned the Pentateuch at God's dictation. In that sense, it is entirely a divine document – the deep eternal religious secrets of which are to be fathomed by midrashic interpretation. Yet Rashbam's keen sensitivity to evidence of the process of biblical authorship and editing manifested in his commentaries on Psalms, Qohelet, and Song of Songs would have prompted him to evaluate this notion critically. In light of the verses identifying Moses as the author of the Torah (see, e.g., Deut 31:9, Josh 23:6, 2 Kgs 23:25, Mal 3:22, Neh 8:1), Rashbam evidently concluded that Moses played an active role in shaping the text. The endeavor to understand Moses' intentions in shaping the biblical narrative – through literary analysis of the sort that one would apply to human literature – is what Rashbam terms *peshuto shel miqra*.[135] The legitimacy of this literary investigation derives from the talmudic *peshat* maxim.

FROM RASHI TO RASHBAM: PESHAT AND THE LITERARY DIMENSIONS OF SCRIPTURE

Rashi had initiated a "grammatical" approach to the Bible guided by the notion of authorial intention akin to the one he applied in his Talmud commentary. Yet, still seeking the intentions of the Holy Spirit, he did so in his Bible commentary to select midrashic readings that "are settled upon" the language and order of Scripture. Within two generations, though, academic-style analysis of non-divine Hebrew literature grew more powerful and critical – as evident in Qara's *piyyut* commentaries and Rashbam's Talmud commentaries. Rashi had opened the door to

[135] Through a detailed investigation of Rashbam's Genesis commentary, Hanna Liss argues that his analysis of the narratives of the Pentateuch reflects an understanding of the poetic techniques of twelfth-century courtly literature in northern France, e.g., the romances of Chrétien de Troyes. See Liss, *Fictional Worlds*, 126, 169–194.

applying the tools of literary analysis to the Bible; but the dramatic development of those tools subsequently called for a new *peshat* approach. This need – felt acutely by the "intellectuals" inspired by Rashi – was met by Qara and Rashbam, who directed their *peshat* analysis to discover the intentions of the Bible's human authors. While in this respect Qara was just as profound as Rashbam, the latter more successfully conceptualized this new interpretive mode within a traditional framework. Rashbam recognized the theoretical difficulty of interpreting the Bible simply using the tools of analysis one would apply to contemporary writings, which the commentator might even feel free to adjust.[136] Rashbam's dual hermeneutic, based on the talmudic *peshat* maxim, addresses this difficulty: Scripture is indeed a divine work that must be analyzed midrashically for its hidden meanings; but the Rabbis acknowledged that the Bible also is subject to *peshat* interpretation, as one would interpret a humanly authored document. This interpretation, as conceived by Rashbam, is aligned with the intention of the human author who served as the conduit for recording God's word.

Although it is clear that Rashbam had some interaction with Christians knowledgeable about Bible interpretation, we do not know precisely how familiar he was with contemporary Latin learning. Yet the developments in the notion of biblical authorship in Christian interpretation in northern France in his time help us understand Rashbam's way of thinking. In particular, the emerging Christian theories about the relation between the human biblical authors' intentions and the Holy Spirit ultimately responsible for the deeper meaning of the sacred text go a long way to explain how Rashbam might have conceptualized his novel *peshat* method. Consideration of the Latin intellectual context clarifies how Rashbam could speak of Moses as the author of the Pentateuch and explore his literary intentions in its composition by analyzing its language according to "the way of the world" (*derekh ereṣ*) and its stylistic conventions. All of this was done "according to the *peshat*." But within the hierarchy of Bible interpretation, *peshat* remained subservient to midrashic interpretation, which reflects the deeper meaning of the text (and thus its halakhic authority) with which it was endowed as the word of God Himself.

[136] See the gloss on the *piyyut* cited in Chapter 8, on p. 212.

Bibliography

The Hebrew Bible is cited according to *Tanakh, The Holy Scriptures: The New Jewish Publication Society Translation According to the Traditional Hebrew Text* (Philadelphia: Jewish Publication Society, 1985), with minor adjustments to reflect the medieval commentators' understanding of the text. Bible commentaries are cited from critical editions where available, as listed below, and otherwise from the best available version of the Rabbinic Bible, *Miqra'ot Gedolot ha-Keter* (ed. Menachem Cohen, Ramat Gan: Bar-Ilan University Press, 1990–). Volumes not available in print are accessible online at www.mgketer.org/

MANUSCRIPTS

The manuscripts listed below all contain Rashi's commentaries, some with notes citing other Bible exegetes, such as Joseph Qara and Rashbam.

Berlin 140. Berlin, Staatsbibliothek 140. Ashkenaz, dated 1335.

Berlin 514. Berlin, Staatsbibliothek Or. Qu. 514. Italian script, dated 1289.

Bodleiana 186. Oxford, Bodleian Library 186 (Oppenheim 34). Ashkenaz, early thirteenth century.

Bodleiana 2440. Oxford, Bodleian Library 2440 (Corpus Christi College, MS 165). Ashkenaz, late twelfth century.

De Rossi 175. Parma, Biblioteca Palatina, de Rossi 175. Spain, dated 1305.

De Rossi 181. Parma, Biblioteca Palatina, de Rossi 181. Ashkenaz, thirteenth or fourteenth century.

Karlsruhe 10. Karlsruhe, Badische Landesbibliothek, Cod. Reuchlin 10. Ashkenaz, fourteenth century.

Leipzig 1. Leipzig, Universitätsbibliothek B.H. 1. Ashkenaz, thirteenth century.

London 26917. London, British Library. Add 26917. Ashkenaz, dated 1273.

Munich 5. Munich, Staatsbibliothek 5. Ashkenaz, dated 1273.

St. John's College 3. Cambridge, St. John's College 3 (A3). Ashkenaz, dated 1238.

Vienna 220. Vienna, Nationalbibliothek 23, Hebr. 220. Ashkenaz, thirteenth or fourteenth century.

RABBINIC WORKS CITED

The Jerusalem and Babylonian Talmuds are cited according to the traditional printed editions. Other rabbinic texts are cited either from the standard printed editions or, where available, from critical editions, as enumerated below, each according to its own paragraph system and/or pagination, as applicable.

Avot de-Rabbi Natan, ed. Solomon Schechter. New York: Feldheim, 1967.

Genesis Rabbah, ed. Julius Theodor and Chanoch Albeck. Jerusalem: Wahrmann, 1965.

Leviticus Rabbah, ed. Mordecai Margulies. Jerusalem: Ministry of Education, 1953–1960.

Mekhilta de-Rabbi Ishmael, ed. Saul Horovitz and Israel A. Rabin. Jerusalem: Bamberger et Wahrmann, 1960.

Midrash Tehillim, ed. Salomon Buber. Vilnius: Rom, 1891.

The Mishnah of Rabbi Eliezer or The Midrash of Thirty-Two Hermeneutic Rules, ed. Hyman G. Enelow. New York: Bloch, 1933.

Pesikta de-Rav Kahana, ed. Bernard Mandelbaum. New York: JTS, 1962.

Qohelet Rabbah (*Midrash Kohelet Rabbah 1–6*), ed. Marc Hirshman. Jerusalem: Schechter Institute, 2016.

Ruth Rabbah ("Book of Ruth in Aggadic Literature and Midrash Ruth Rabba"), ed. Myron B. Lerner. PhD dissertation, Hebrew University of Jerusalem, 1971.

Song of Songs Rabbah (Midrash Rabbah Shir ha-Shirim), ed. Samson Dunski. Jerusalem: Devir, 1980.

Tanḥuma ha-Qadum, ed. Salomon Buber. Jerusalem: Ortsel, 1964. (*Midrash Tanḥuma* is cited from the standard printed editions.)

PRIMARY SOURCES

Abelard, Peter. *The Letters of Abelard and Heloise*, trans. Betty Radice. London: Penguin, 2003.

Aquinas, Thomas. *Summa theologiae*, ed. Pietro Caramello, 5 vols. Turin: Marietti, 1952–1956; English trans. in *Basic Writings of Saint Thomas Aquinas*, ed. Anton Pegis, 2 vols. New York: Modern Library, 1945.

Augustine. *Enarrationes in Psalmos*, ed. Eligius Dekkers. Turnhout: Brepols, 1956; English trans. *St. Augustine: Exposition on the Book of Psalms*, trans. A[rthur] Cleveland Coxe, vol. 8 of *A Select Library of the Nicene and Post-Nicene Fathers of the Christian Church*. Edinburgh: T&T Clark, 1886.

Select Letters, trans. James Houston Baxter. London: Heinemann, 1930.

Bekhor Shor, Joseph ben Isaac. Pentateuch Commentary. *Perushe Rabi Yosef Bekhor Shor 'al ha-Torah*, ed. Yehoshafaṭ Nevo. Jerusalem: Mossad Harav Kook, 1994.

Bruno the Carthusian. Psalms Commentary. *Expositio in Psalmos. PL* 152: 637–1420; French trans. *Commentaire des Psaumes attribué à saint Bruno*, trans. A. Aniorté. Le Barroux: Sainte Madeleine, 2017.

Commentary on the Pauline Epistles. *PL* 153: 9–565.

Cassiodorus. *Expositio in Psalterium* in *Magni Aurelii Cassiodori senatoris opera*. Turnhout: Brepols, 1958; English trans. *Cassiodorus: Explanation of the Psalms*, trans. P. G. Walsh. New York: Paulist Press, 1990.

Eliezer of Beaugency. *Kommentar zu Ezechiel und den XII kleinen Propheten von Eliezer au Beaugency*, ed. Samuel A. Poznanski. Warsaw: Mekize Nirdamim, 1913.

Gregory the Great. *Moralia in Job*, ed. Marcus Adriaen. Turnhout: Brepols, 1979; English trans. *Moral Reflections on the Book of Job*, trans. Brian Kerns. Collegeville, MN: Liturgical Press/Cistercian Publications, 2014.

Hezekiah ben Manoah. Pentateuch Commentary. *Hizkuni: Perush ha-Torah*, ed. Hayyim Dov Chavel. Jerusalem: Mossad Harav Kook, 1981.

Horace. *Ars Poetica*. In *Satires, Epistles and Ars Poetica*, ed. and trans. H. Rushton Fairclough, 450–489. Cambridge, MA: Harvard University Press, 2005.

Hugh of St. Victor, *Didascalicon*, ed. Charles Henry Buttimer. Washington, DC: Catholic University of America, 1939; English trans. *The Didascalicon of Hugh of St. Victor: A Medieval Guide to the Arts*, trans. Jerome Taylor. New York: Columbia University Press, 1991.

Ibn Bal‘am, Judah. “Rabbi Judah Ibn Bal‘am’s Commentary on Numbers and Deuteronomy” (Hebrew), ed. and trans. Maaravi Perez. MA thesis, Bar-Ilan University, 1970.

Ibn Barun, Isaac. *Kitāb al-Muwāzana*, ed. Paul Kokozoff. St. Petersburg, 1890; repr. Jerusalem: Kedem, 1971.

Ibn Ezra, Abraham. Pentateuch Commentary. *Perushei ha-Torah le-Rabbenu Avraham Ibn Ezra*, ed. Asher Weiser. Jerusalem: Mossad Harav Kook, 1977.

Safah Berurah, ed. G. H. Lippmann. Fürth, 1839; partial annotated ed., Michael Wilensky, *Devir* 2 (1924): 274–302.

Sefer Moznayim (Spanish), ed. and trans. Lorenzo Jimenez Paton and Angel Sáenz-Badillos. Cordoba: El Almendro, 2002.

Yesod diqduq, ed. Nehemia Allony. Jerusalem: Mossad Harav Kook, 1985.

Yesod mora ve-sod Torah [The foundation of piety and the secret of the Torah], ed. Joseph Cohen and Uriel Simon. 2nd ed. Ramat Gan: Bar-Ilan University Press, 2007.

Ibn Ezra, Moses. *Kitāb al-Muḥāḍara wa-l-Mudhākara/Sefer ha-‘iyyunim we-ha-diyyunim* [*Book of Discussion and Conversation*] (Hebrew), ed. and trans. A. S. Halkin. Jerusalem: Mekize Nirdamim, 1975.

Ibn Janah, Jonah. *Kitāb al-Luma‘* (*Le livre de parterres fleuris: Grammaire hébraïque en arabe d‘Abou’l-Walid Merwan Ibn Djanah de Cordoue*), ed. Joseph Derenbourg. Paris, 1886; Hebrew trans. *Sefer ha-Riqmah*, trans. Judah Ibn Tibbon, ed. Michael Wilensky, 2nd ed. Jerusalem: Academy for the Hebrew Language, 1964.

Isidore of Seville. *Etymologies (Isidori Hispalensis episcopi Etymologiarum sive originum libri XX)*, ed. W. M. Lindsay, 2 vols. Oxford: Clarendon, 1911.

Jerome. *Commentarii in Prophetas Minores*, ed. M. Adriaen, 2 vols. Turnhout: Brepols, 1969–1970.

Hebraicae quaestiones in libro Geneseos, Liber interpretationis hebraicorum nominum, Commentarioli in Psalmos, Commentarius in Ecclesiasten, ed. Paul de Lagarde. Turnhout: Brepols, 1959.

In Hieremiam Libri VI, ed. Siegfried Reiter. Turnhout: Brepols, 1960.

Jerome's Commentary on Daniel, trans. Gleason L. Archer. Grand Rapids: Baker Book House, 1958.

Sancti Eusebii Hieronymi Epistulae, ed. Isidore Hilberg, 3 vols. Vienna: Tempsky, 1910–1918.

Kimhi, Joseph. *Sefer ha-Galui, with the Corrections of a Certain Benjamin*, ed. Henry J. Mathews. Berlin: Iṭtsḳovsḳi, 1887.

Maimonides, Moses. *Book of the Commandments: Sefer ha-Mitzvot*, ed. and trans. Joseph Kafih. Jerusalem: Mossad Harav Kook, 1971.

Guide of the Perplexed, trans. Shlomo Pines. Chicago: University of Chicago Press, 1963.

Menahem ben Saruq. *Maḥberet* (Spanish), ed. and trans. Angel Sáenz-Badillos. Granada: Universidad de Granada, 1986; older ed. Herschell E. Filipowski. London: Ḥoveret Yeshanim, 1854.

Mizrahi, Elijah. Commentary on Rashi. *Perush le-perush Rashi*, ed. Moshe Phillip. Petah-Tikvah: Moshe Phillip, 1992.

Nahmanides, Moses. *Hassagot (Sefer ha-Mitzvot 'im Hassagot ha-Ramban)* [Critique of Maimonides' Book of the Commandments]), ed. Chaim D. Chavel. Jerusalem: Mossad Harav Kook, 1981.

Qara, Joseph. Commentary on Former Prophets. *Perushei Rabbi Yosef Qara li-nevi'im rishonim*, ed. Simon Eppenstein. Jerusalem: Mossad Harav Kook, 1972.

The Commentaries of Rabbi Joseph Qara on the Book of Job (*Perushei Rabbi Yosef Qara le-sefer Iyyov*), ed. Moshe Ahrend. Jerusalem: Mossad Harav Kook, 1988.

Quintillian. *Institutio Oratoria*, trans. H. E. Butler. Cambridge, MA: Harvard University Press, 1995.

Rashbam (Samuel ben Meir). Pentateuch Commentary. (1) *Perush ha-Torah asher katav Rashbam*, ed. David Rosin. Breslau: Shottlender, 1881. (2) *Perush ha-Torah le-Rabenu Shemu'el ben Me'ir 'im shinuye nusḥa'ot, tsiyune meḳorot, he'arot u-mafteḥot*, ed. Martin (Me'ir Yitsḥak) Lockshin. Jerusalem: Horev, 2009.

The Commentary of Rabbi Samuel Ben Meir (Rashbam) on the Book of Job, ed. Sara Japhet. Jerusalem: Magnes, 2000.

The Commentary of R. Samuel ben Meir (Rashbam) on Qoheleth, ed. and trans. Sara Japhet and Robert Salters. Jerusalem and Leiden: Magnes and Brill, 1985.

The Commentary of Rabbi Samuel Ben Meir (Rashbam) on the Song of Songs, ed. Sara Japhet. Jerusalem: Magnes, 2008.

Dayyaqut me-Rabbenu Shemuel [ben Me'ir (RaSHBaM)], ed. Ronela Merdler. Jerusalem: Hebrew University of Jerusalem, 1999.

Rashi (Rabbi Solomon ben Isaac) Pentateuch Commentary. *Raschi: der Kommentar des Salomo B. Isak über den Pentateuch*, ed. Abraham Berliner, 2nd ed. Frankfurt am Main: J. Kauffmann, 1905.

Rashi's Commentaries on the Prophets and Psalms. *Parshandatha: The Commentary of Rashi on the Prophets and Hagiographs, Edited on the Basis of Several Manuscripts and Editions*, ed. Isaac Maarsen, 3 vols. Amsterdam: Hertzberger, 1930–1936.

Rashi's Commentary on the Book of Proverbs, ed. Lisa Fredman. Jerusalem: World Union of Jewish Studies, 2019.

Rashi's Commentary on Psalms, ed. Mayer I. Gruber. Leiden: Brill, 2004.

Rashi's Commentary on the Song of Songs, according to JTSA MS Lutzki 778. In *Secundum Salomonem: A Thirteenth Century Latin Commentary on the Song of Songs*, ed. S. Kamin and A. Saltman, 81–99 (Hebrew section). Ramat Gan: Bar-Ilan University Press, 1989.

Remigius of Auxerre. *Commentum in Martianum Capellam*, ed. Cora Lutz. Leiden: Brill, 1962.

Saadia Gaon. *Beliefs and Opinions* (*Kitāb al-Mukhtār fi-l-Amānāt wa-l-I'tiqādāt; Sefer ha-Nivḥar be-emunot we-de'ot*) (Hebrew), ed. and trans. Joseph Kafih. Jerusalem: Mossad Harav Kook, 1970.

Tafsīr (translation of the Torah). In *Oeuvres complètes de R. Saadia ben Iosef al-Fayyoûmî*, ed. Joseph Derenbourg. Paris: E. Leroux, 1893.

Saadya's Commentary on Genesis (Hebrew), ed. and trans. Moshe Zucker. New York: JTS, 1984.

Samuel ben Hofni Gaon. *Rabbi Shmuel B. Chofni: Liber Prooemium Talmudis* (Hebrew), ed. and trans. Shraga Abramson. Jerusalem: Mekize Nirdamim, 1990.

Scholia vindobonensia ad Horatii Artem poeticam, ed. Joseph Zechmeister. Vienna: C. Gerold, 1877.

Servius Grammaticus. *In Vergilii carmina commentarii*, ed. G. Thilo and H. Hagen, 2 vols. Hildesheim: Olms, 1961.

Thierry of Chartres, *De sex dierum operibus*. In *Commentaries on Boethius by Thierry of Chartres*, ed. Nicholas M. Haring, 553–575. Toronto: Pontifical Institute of Medieval Studies, 1971.

Tobiah ben Eliezer. *Leqaḥ Ṭov Commentary on the Song of Songs*, ed. A. W. Greenup. London: n.p., 1909.

Leqaḥ Ṭov Commentary on the Torah, ed. Salomon Buber. Vilnius: Romm, 1884.

SECONDARY SOURCES

For studies listed below published in Hebrew, translated titles are used where available, followed by the notation (Hebrew). Otherwise, the Hebrew title is transliterated, followed by my own English translation, as necessary for clarification.

Abulafia, Anna Sapir, and G. R. Evans. *The Works of Gilbert Crispin, Abbot of Westminster*. London: Published for the British Academy by the Oxford University Press, 1986.

Ahrend, Moshe. "The Concept Peshuto Shellamiqra' in the Making" (Hebrew). In Japhet, ed., *Bible In Light of its Interpreters*, 237–261.

Qara on Job. See under Qara, Joseph, in Primary Sources.

Allen, Judson Boyce. *The Friar as Critic: Literary Attitudes in the Later Middle Ages*. Nashville: Vanderbilt University Press, 1971.
Allony, Nehemia. "Vistas caraistas en el Mahberet de Menahem" (Hebrew). *Tesoro de los Juios Sefardies* 5 (1962): 21–54.
Alster, Baruch. "The 'Forlorn Lady' in the Interpretation of the Song of Songs" (Hebrew). *JSIJ* 5 (2006): 101–122.
"Human Love and its Relationship to Spiritual Love in Jewish Exegesis on the Song of Songs" (Hebrew). PhD dissertation, Bar-Ilan University. Ramat Gan, 2006.
Alter, Robert. *The Art of Biblical Poetry*. New York: Basic Books, 1985.
Andrée, Alexander. "Laon Revisited: Master Anselm and the Creation of a Theological School in the Twelfth Century." *Journal of Medieval Latin* 22 (2012): 257–281.
Ankori, Zvi. *Karaites in Byzantium: The Formative Years, 970–1100*. New York: Columbia University Press, 1959.
Bacher, Wilhelm. "The Title הקורא Given to Joseph Kimchi by the Commentator of his Sepher Ha-galui." *JQR* 5 (1892): 167–168.
Baer, Isaac. "Rashi and the Historical Reality of his Time" (Hebrew). *Tarbiz* 20 (1949): 320–332.
Banitt, Menahem. "*Les Poterim*," *REJ* 125 (1966): 21–33.
Rashi, Interpreter of the Biblical Letter Tel Aviv: Tel Aviv University Press, 1985.
Bar-Asher, Meir M. *Scripture and Exegesis in Early Imāmī Shiism*. Leiden: Brill, 1999.
Bar-Asher, Moshe, Dalit Rom-Shiloni, Emanuel Tov, and Nilil Wazana, eds. *Shai le-Sara Japhet: Studies in the Bible, its Exegesis and its Language*. Jerusalem: Magnes, 2007.
Basch, Rivka. "*Peshuto shel Miqra* and *Sensus Litteralis*: A Comparative Examination of Jewish and Christian Interpretations in the Twelfth Century" (Hebrew). MA thesis, Baltimore Hebrew University, 2003.
Baswell, Christopher. *Virgil in Medieval England: Figuring the Aeneid from the Twelfth Century to Chaucer*. Cambridge: Cambridge University Press, 1995.
Becker, Dan. *The Arabic Sources of R. Jonah Ibn Janāḥ's Grammar* (Hebrew). Tel Aviv: Tel Aviv University Press, 1998.
Ben-Shammai, Haggai. *A Leader's Project: Studies in the Philosophical and Exegetical Works of Saadya Gaon* (Hebrew). Jerusalem: Bialik Institute, 2015.
"On the *Mudawwin* – Editor of the Biblical Books – in Judeo-Arabic Exegesis" (Hebrew). In *From Sages to Savants: Studies Presented to Avraham Grossman*, ed. Joseph R. Hacker, Yosef Kaplan, and B. Z. Kedar, 73–110. Jerusalem: Zalman Shazar Center, 2010.
"The Tension between Literal Interpretation and Exegetical Freedom." In McAuliffe et al., eds., *Reverence for the Word*, 33–50.
Ben-Yehuda, Eliezer. *Dictionary and Thesaurus of the Hebrew Language*. New York: Thomas Yoseloff, 1960.
Benson, Robert L., and Giles Constable, eds. *Renaissance and Renewal in the Twelfth Century*. Cambridge, MA: Harvard University Press, 1982.
Benton, John F. "The Court of Champagne as a Literary Center." *Speculum* 36 (1961): 551–591.

Berger, David. "From Crusades to Blood Libels to Expulsions: Some New Approaches to Medieval Anti-Semitism." In Berger, *Persecution, Polemic, and Dialogue*, 15–39.

"Mission to the Jews and Jewish–Christian Contacts in the Polemical Literature of the High Middle Ages." In Berger, *Persecution, Polemic, and Dialogue*, 177–198 (originally appeared in *American Historical Review* 91 (1986): 576–591.)

Persecution, Polemic, and Dialogue. Boston: Academic Studies Press, 2010.

"Study of the Early Ashkenazic Rabbinate" (Hebrew; review of Avraham Grossman, *The Early Sages of Ashkenaz*). *Tarbiz* 53 (1984): 479–487.

Berger, Yitzhak. "The Contextual Exegesis of Rabbi Eliezer of Beaugency and the Climax of the Northern French *Peshat* Tradition." *JSQ* 15 (2008): 115–129.

Berlin, Adele. *Biblical Poetry through Medieval Jewish Eyes*. Bloomington: Indiana University Press, 1991.

Poetics and Interpretation of Biblical Narrative. Sheffield: Almond Press, 1983.

Berliner, Abraham. *Pletath soferim: Beiträge zur jüdischen Schriftauslegung im Mittelalter*. Jerusalem: Maqor, 1971 [1872].

Raschi. See under Rashi, in Primary Sources.

Beyer, Hartmut, Gabriela Signori, and Sita Steckel, eds. *Bruno the Carthusian and his Mortuary Roll: Studies, Text, and Translations*. Turnhout: Brepols, 2014.

Brandin, Louis. *Les gloses françaises (Loazim) de Gerschom de Metz*. Paris: A. Durlacher, 1902.

Brin, Gershon. *Reuel and his Friends: Jewish Byzantine Exegetes from around the Tenth Century CE* (Hebrew). Tel Aviv: Tel Aviv University Press, 2012.

Studies in the Biblical Exegesis of R. Joseph Qara (Hebrew). Tel Aviv: Tel Aviv University, Chaim Rosenberg School of Jewish Studies, 1990.

Brody, Robert. *The Geonim of Babylonia and the Shaping of Medieval Jewish Culture*, 2nd ed. New Haven: Yale University Press, 2013.

Sa'adyah Gaon, trans. Betsy Rosenberg. Oxford: Littman Library of Jewish Civilization, 2013.

The Textual History of the She'iltot (Hebrew). New York: American Academy for Jewish Research, 1991.

Brown, Francis, S. R. Driver, and Charles A. Briggs. *A Hebrew and English Lexicon of the Old Testament*. Oxford: Clarendon Press, 1907.

Buber, Salomon. *Leqaḥ Ṭov*. See under Tobiah ben Eliezer, in Primary Sources.

Sekhel Ṭov. See under Menahem ben Solomon, in Primary Sources.

Burnett, Charles. *Adelard of Bath: An English Scientist and Arabist of the Early Twelfth Century*. London: Warburg Institute, 1987.

Burnett, Charles, and Italo Ronca, eds. *Adelard of Bath, Conversations with his Nephew: On the Same and the Different, Questions on Natural Science, and on Birds*. Cambridge: Cambridge University Press, 1998.

Burnett, Stephen G. *Christian Hebraism in the Reformation Era (1500–1660): Authors, Books, and the Transmission of Jewish Learning*. Leiden: Brill, 2012.

"The Strange Career of the Biblia Rabbinica among Christian Hebraists, 1517–1620." In *Shaping the Bible in the Reformation: Books, Scholars and Readers in the Sixteenth Century*, ed. Matthew McLean and Bruce Gordon, 63–83. Leiden: Brill, 2012.

Butin, Romain F. *The Ten Nequdoth of the Torah: Or, The Meaning and Purpose of the Extraordinary Points of the Pentateuch (Massoretic Text). A Contribution to the History of Textual Criticism among the Ancient Jews*. Baltimore: J. H. Furst Co., 2009.

Castaño, Javier, Talya Fishman, and Ephraim Kanarfogel, eds. *Regional Identities and Cultures of Medieval Jews*. London: Littman Library of Jewish Civilization, 2018.

Chance, Jane. *Medieval Mythography: From Roman North Africa to the School of Chartres, AD 433–1177*. Gainesville: University Press of Florida, 1994.

Châtillon, Jean. "Sainte Anselm et l'écriture." In *Les Mutations socio-culturelles au tournant des XIe–XIIe siècles*, ed. Raymonde Foreville, 431–442. Paris: Centre national de la recherche scientifique, 1984.

Chazan, Robert. "Rashi's Commentary on the Book of Daniel: Messianic Speculation and Polemical Argumentation." In *Rashi et la culture juive en France du Nord au moyen âge*, ed. Gilbert Dahan, Gérard Nahon, and Elie Nicolas, 111–121. Paris: E. Peeters, 1997.

Cohen, Gerson D. "Esau as Symbol in Early Medieval Thought." In *Jewish Medieval and Renaissance Studies*, ed. Alexander Altmann, 19–48. Cambridge, MA: Harvard University Press, 1967.

Cohen, Mordechai Z. "The Aesthetic Exegesis of Moses Ibn Ezra." In *HBOT* I/2, 282–301.

"Eliezer of Beaugency." In *Encyclopedia of the Bible and its Reception*, VII:674–677. Berlin: de Gruyter, 2013.

"Emergence of the Rule of Peshat in Jewish Bible Exegesis." In Cohen and Berlin, eds., *Interpreting Scriptures in Judaism, Christianity and Islam*, 204–223.

"Maimonides' Attitude toward Christian Biblical Hermeneutics In Light of Earlier Jewish Sources." In *New Perspectives on Jewish-Christian Relations: In Honor of David Berger*, ed. Elisheva Carlebach and Jacob J. Schacter, 455–476. Leiden: Brill, 2012.

"Malbim: Rabbinic Scholar, Biblical Exegete." In *The YIVO Encyclopedia of Jews in Eastern Europe*, ed. Gershon D. Hundert, 1145–1147. New York: YIVO, 2008.

"A New Look at Medieval Jewish Exegetical Constructions of Peshat in Christian and Muslim Lands: Rashbam and Maimonides." In Castaño et al., eds., *Regional Identities*, 93–121.

Opening the Gates of Interpretation: Maimonides' Biblical Hermeneutics in Light of His Geonic-Andalusian Heritage and Muslim Milieu. Leiden: Brill, 2011.

"A Poet's Biblical Exegesis." *JQR* 93 (2003): 533–556.

"A Possible Spanish Source for Rashi's Concept of *Peshuto Shel Miqra*" (Hebrew). In *Rashi: The Man and his Work* (Hebrew), ed. Avraham Grossman and Sara Japhet, 353–379. Jerusalem: Zalman Shazar Center, 2008.

"Rashbam Scholarship in Perpetual Motion." *JQR* 98 (2008): 389–408.

"Rashbam vs. Moses Ibn Ezra: Two Perspectives on Biblical Poetics." In Bar-Asher et al., eds., *Shai le-Sara Japhet*, 193*–217* (English section).

"Reproduction of the Text: Traditional Biblical Exegesis in Light of the Literary Theory of Ludwig Strauss." *The Torah U-Madda Journal* 17 (2015/16): 1–33.

The Rule of Peshat: Jewish Constructions of the Plain Sense of Scripture in their Christian and Muslim Contexts, c. 900–1270. Philadelphia: University of Pennsylvania Press, 2020.

Three Approaches to Biblical Metaphor: From Abraham Ibn Ezra and Maimonides to David Kimhi. Leiden: Brill, 2003.

Cohen, Mordechai Z., and Adele Berlin, eds. *Interpreting Scriptures in Judaism, Christianity and Islam: Overlapping Inquiries*. Cambridge: Cambridge University Press, 2016.

Cohen, Shaye D. "Does Rashi's Torah Commentary Respond to Christianity? A Comparison of Rashi with Rashbam and Bekhor Shor." In *The Idea of Biblical Interpretation: Essays in Honor of James L. Kugel*, ed. Hindy Najman and Judith H. Newman, 449–472. Leiden: Brill, 2004.

Colish, Marcia L. "*Psalterium Scholastocorum*: Peter Lombard and the Emergence of Scholastic Psalms Exegesis." *Speculum* 67 (1992): 531–548.

Collins, Ann Ryan. *Teacher in Faith: and Virtue Lanfranc of Bec's Commentary on Saint Paul*. Leiden: Brill, 2007.

Coolman, Boyd Taylor. "*Pulchrum Esse*: The Beauty of Scripture, the Beauty of the Soul, and the Art of Exegesis in Hugh of St. Victor." *Traditio* 58 (2003): 175–200.

Copeland, Rita. "Rhetoric and the Politics of the Literal Sense in Medieval Literary Theory: Aquinas, Wyclif, and the Lollards." In *Interpretation: Medieval and Modern. The J. A. W. Bennett Memorial Lectures, Perugia, 1992*, ed. Piero Boitani and Anna Torti, 1–23. Cambridge: D. S. Brewer, 1993; repr. in *Rhetoric and Hermeneutics in our Time*, ed. Michael Hyde and Walter Jost, 335–357. New Haven: Yale University Press, 1997.

Copeland, Rita, and I. Sluiter. *Medieval Grammar and Rhetoric: Language Arts and Literary Theory, AD 300–1475*. Oxford: Oxford University Press, 2009.

Dahan, Gilbert. "Les Commentaires bibliques d'Étienne Langton: exégèse et herméneutique." In *Étienne Langton: prédicateur, bibliste, théologien*, ed. Louis J. Bataillon, 201–239. Turnhout: Brepols, 2010.

"La Connaissance de l'exégèse juive par les chrétiens du XIIe au XIVe siècle." In *Rashi et la culture juive en France du Nord au moyen âge*, ed. Gilbert Dahan, Gérard Nahon, and Elie Nicolas, 343–359. Paris: E. Peeters, 1997.

Les Intellectuels chrétiens et les juifs au Moyen Âge. Paris: Éditions du Cerf, 1990.

Lire la Bible au Moyen Âge: essais d'herméneutique médiévale. Geneva: Droz, 2009.

"Thomas Aquinas: Exegesis and Hermeneutics." In *Reading Sacred Scripture with Thomas Aquinas: Hermeneutical Tools, Theological Questions and New Perspectives*, ed. Piotr Roszak and Jörgen Vijgen, 45–70. Turnhout: Brepols, 2015.

de Lange, Nicholas R. M. "An Early Hebrew–Greek Bible Glossary from the Cairo Genizah and its Significance for the Study of Jewish Bible Translations into Greek." In *Studies in Hebrew Literature and Jewish Culture Presented to Albert van der Heide on the Occasion of his Sixty-Fifth Birthday*, ed. M. F. J Baasten and Reinier Munk, 31–39. Dordrecht: Springer, 2007.

Greek Jewish Texts from the Cairo Genizah. Tübingen: J. C. B. Mohr (Paul Siebeck), 1996.

de Lubac, Henri. *Exégèse médiéval: les quatre sens de l'écriture*. Paris: Aubier, 1961.

de Visscher, Eva. *Reading the Rabbis: Christian Hebraism in the Works of Herbert of Bosham*. Boston: Brill, 2014.

del Valle Rodríguez, Carlos. *Die grammatikalische Terminologie der frühen hebräischen Grammatikern*. Madrid: Consejo Superior de Investigaciones Científicas, Instituto Francisco Suárez, 1982.

Dönitz, Saskia. "Josephus Torn to Pieces: Fragments of 'Sefer Yosippon' in Genizat Germania." In *Books within Books: New Discoveries in Old Book Bindings*, ed. Andreas Lehnardt and Judith Olszowy-Schlanger, 83–95. Leiden: Brill, 2014.

Dotan, Aharon. "*Niqqud Rav Se'adya*: Fact or Fiction?" (Hebrew). *Tarbiz* 66:2 (1997): 247–257.

Sefer Diḳduḳe ha-ṭe'amim: 'al pi kitve yad 'atiḳim. Jerusalem: Academy of the Hebrew Language, 1967.

Dove, Mary. "Literal Senses in the Song of Songs." In *Nicholas of Lyra: The Senses of Scripture*, ed. Philip D. Krey and Lesley Smith, 129–146. Leiden: Brill, 2000.

Dronke, Peter. *The Medieval Lyric*. New York: Cambridge University Press, 1977.

"Thierry of Chartres." In *A History of Twelfth-Century Western Philosophy*, ed. Peter Dronke, 358–385. New York: Cambridge University Press, 1988.

Dutton, Paul Edward, ed. *Glosae super Platonem of Bernard of Chartres*. Toronto: Pontifical Institute of Mediaeval Studies, 1991.

Ehrman, Bart D. *Lost Christianities: The Battles for Scripture and the Faiths we Never Knew*. Oxford: Oxford University Press, 2005.

Eisenstat, Yedida. "Taking Stock of the Text(s) of Rashi's Commentary: Some 21st Century Considerations and the Case for Leipzig 1." In *To Fix Torah in their Hearts: Essays in Biblical Interpretation and Jewish Studies in Honor of Barry Levy*, ed. Jacqueline S. du Toit, Jason Kalman, Hartley Lachter, and Vanessa R. Sasson, 199–232. Cincinnati: Hebrew Union College Press, 2019.

Elbaum, Jacob. "The Anthology *Sekhel Ṭov*: *Derash*, *Peshaṭ* and the Issue of the Redactor (the *Sadran*)" (Hebrew). In *A Word Fitly Spoken: Studies in Mediaeval Exegesis of the Hebrew Bible and the Qur'ān Presented to Haggai Ben-Shammai*, ed. Meir M. Bar-Asher, Simon Hopkins, Sarah Stroumsa, and Bruno Chiesa, 71–96. Jerusalem: Ben-Zvi Institute, 2007.

Medieval Perspectives on Aggadah and Midrash (Hebrew). Jerusalem: Bialik Institute, 2000.

Eldar, Ilan. "The Grammatical Literature of Medieval Ashkenazi Jewry." In *Hebrew in Ashkenaz: A Language in Exile*, ed. Lewis Glinert, 26–45. New York: Oxford University Press, 1993.

Elford, Dorothy. "William of Conches." In *A History of Twelfth-Century Western Philosophy*, ed. Peter Dronke, 308–327. New York: Cambridge University Press, 1988.

Elon, Menachem. *The Principles of Jewish Law*. [Jerusalem]: Encyclopaedia Judaica, 1975.

Enelow, H. G. "The Midrash of Thirty-Two Rules of Interpretation." *JQR* 23 (1933): 357–367.

Eppenstein, Simon. "*Fragment d'un commentaire anonyme du Cantique des Cantiques.*" *REJ* 53 (1907): 242–254.

Eppenstein, *Qara*. See under Qara, Joseph, in Primary Sources.

Evans, Gillian R. "Godescalc of St. Martin and the Trial of Gilbert of Poiters." *Analecta Praemonstratensia* 57 (1981): 196–209.

The Language and Logic of the Bible: The Earlier Middle Ages. Cambridge: Cambridge University Press, 1984.

Fenton, Paul. *Philosophie et exégèse dans le Jardin de la métaphore de Moïse Ibn 'Ezra*. Leiden: Brill, 1997.

Fishbane, Michael A., ed. *The Midrashic Imagination Jewish Exegesis, Thought, and History*. Albany: State University of New York Press, 1993.

Fishman, Talya. *Becoming the People of the Talmud: Oral Torah as Written Tradition in Medieval Jewish Cultures*. Philadelphia: University of Pennsylvania Press, 2011.

Flusser, David. *Sefer Yosipon*. Jerusalem: Bialik Institute, 1980.

Frank, Daniel. "Karaite Exegetical and Halakhic Literature in Byzantium and Turkey." In Polliack, ed., *Karaite Judaism*, 529–558.

Search Scripture Well: Karaite Exegetes and the Origins of the Jewish Bible Commentary in the Islamic East. Leiden: Brill, 2004.

Frappier, Jean. *Chrétien de Troyes, the Man and his Work*, trans. Raymond J. Cormier. Athens, OH: Ohio University Press, 1982.

Fredman, *Rashi on Proverbs*. See under Rashi, in Primary Sources.

Fredrickson, Paula. "Allegory and Reading God's Book: Paul and Augustine on the Destiny of Israel." In *Interpretation and Allegory: Antiquity to the Modern Period*, ed. Jon Whitman, 125–149. Leiden: Brill, 2000.

Friedman, Shamma. "Mi-tosafot Rashbam la-Rif" [From the Tosafot of Rashbam on Alfasi]. *Qoveṣ 'al yad* 8 (1975): 187–226.

Fudeman, Kirsten Anne. *Vernacular Voices: Language and Identity in Medieval French Jewish Communities*. Philadelphia: University of Pennsylvania Press, 2010.

Geiger, Ari. "The Commentary of Nicholas of Lyra on Leviticus, Numbers and Deuteronomy" (Hebrew). PhD dissertation, Bar-Ilan University, Ramat Gan, 2006.

"A Student and an Opponent: Nicholas of Lyra and his Jewish Sources." In *Nicolas de Lyra, franciscain du XIVe siècle, exégète et théologien*, ed. Gilbert Dahan, 167–203. Turnhout: Brepols, 2011.

Gelles, Benjamin. *Peshat and Derash in the Exegesis of Rashi*. Leiden: Brill, 1981.

Gerstenberger, Erhard S. *Psalms, Part 1, With an Introduction to Cultic Poetry*. Grand Rapids: Eerdmans, 1988.

Psalms, Part 2, and Lamentations. Grand Rapids: Eerdmans, 2001.

Gevaryahu, Hayyim. "*Nusḥa'ot Rashi le-Tehillim we-ha-ṣenzurah*" [The text of Rashi on Psalms and censorship]. In *Haim M. I. Gevaryahu Memorial Volume*, ed. Ben-Zion Luria, 248–261(Hebrew section). Jerusalem: World Jewish Bible Center, 1989.

Gibson, Margaret. "The *Artes* in the Eleventh Century." In *Arts libéraux et philosophie au moyen âge*, 121–126 and 148–153. Paris: Vrin, 1969.

"Lanfranc's Commentary on the Pauline Epistles." *Journal of Theological Studies* n.s. 22 (1971): 86–112.

Giraud, Cédric. *Per verba magistri: Anselme de Laon et son école au XIIe siècle*. Turnhout: Brepols, 2010.

Gleave, Robert. *Islam and Literalism: Literal Meaning and Interpretation in Islamic Legal Theory*. Edinburgh: Edinburgh University Press, 2011.

Goldziher, Ignaz. *Schools of Koranic Commentators*, trans. Wolfgang Behn. Wiesbaden: Harrassowitz, 2006.

Goodwin, Deborah. *Take Hold of the Robe of a Jew: Herbert of Bosham's Christian Hebraism*. Leiden: Brill, 2006.

Gottlieb, Isaac. *Order in the Bible* (Hebrew). Jerusalem: Magnes, 2009.

Grabois, Aryeh. "The *Hebraica Veritas* and Jewish–Christian Intellectual Relations in the Twelfth Century." *Speculum* 50:4 (1975): 613–634.

Graves, Michael. *Jerome's Hebrew Philology*. Leiden: Brill, 2007.

Green, D. H. *The Beginnings of Medieval Romance: Fact and Fiction, 1150–1220*. Cambridge: Cambridge University Press, 2002.

Greenberg, Moshe. "The Relationship between Rashi and Rashbam to the Pentateuch" (Hebrew). In *Isaac Leo Seeligmann Volume*, ed. Alexander Rofé and Yair Zakovitch, II:559–567. Jerusalem: E. Rubinstein, 1983.

Griffith, Sidney H. *The Bible in Arabic: The Scriptures of "The People of the Book" in the Language of Islam*. Princeton: Princeton University Press, 2013.

Gross, Avraham. "Spanish Jewry and Rashi's Commentary on the Pentateuch" (Hebrew). In *Rashi Studies*, ed. Z. A. Steinfeld, 27–56. Ramat Gan: Bar-Ilan University Press, 1993.

Grossman, Avraham. "The Commentary of Rashi on Isaiah and the Jewish–Christian Debate." In *Studies in Medieval Jewish Intellectual and Social History: Festschrift in Honor of Robert Chazan*, ed. David Engel, Lawrence H. Schiffman, and Elliot R. Wolfson, 47–62. Leiden: Brill, 2012.

The Early Sages of Ashkenaz: Their Lives, Leadership and Works (900–1096) (Hebrew). Jerusalem: Magnes, 1981.

The Early Sages of France (Hebrew). Jerusalem: Magnes, 1995.

"The Impact of Rabbi Samuel of Spain and Reuel of Byzantium on Rashi's School" (Hebrew). *Tarbiz* 82 (2014): 447–467.

"*Peirush Rashi le-Tehillim we-ha-pulmus ha-Yehudi–Noṣri*" [Rashi's commentary on Psalms and the Jewish–Christian debate]. In *Meḥqarim ba-Miqra u-be-ḥinnukh*, ed. Dov Rappel, 59–74. Jerusalem: Touro College, 1996.

Rashi, trans. Joel A. Linsider. Oxford: Littman Library of Jewish Civilization, 2012.

"Rashi's Rejection of Philosophy." *Jahrbuch des Simon-Dubnow-Instituts* 8 (2009): 95–118.

"The School of Literal Jewish Exegesis in Northern France." In *HBOT* I/2, 321–371.

"The Treatment of Grammar and Lexicon in Rashi's Commentaries: Rashi's Ties with the Islamic Lands" (Hebrew). *Leshonenu* 73 (2011): 425–448.

Grossman, Avraham, and Sara Japhet, eds. *Rashi: The Man and his Work* (Hebrew). Jerusalem: Zalman Shazar Center, 2008.

Grotans, Anna A. *Reading in Medieval St. Gall*. Cambridge: Cambridge University Press, 2006.

Gruber, *Rashi on Psalms*. See under Rashi, in Primary Sources.

Haas, Jair. "Rashbam on the Song of Songs: A Reconsideration" (Hebrew). *JSIJ* 7 (2008): 127–146.

"Rashi's Criticism of Mahberet Menahem" (Hebrew). In *Zer Rimonim: Studies in Biblical Literature and Jewish Exegesis Presented to Professor Rimon Kasher*, ed. Michael Avioz, Elie Assis, and Yael Shemesh, 449–463. Atlanta: Society of Biblical Literature, 2013.

Hailperin, Herman. *Rashi and the Christian Scholars*. Pittsburgh: University of Pittsburgh Press, 1963.

Halbertal, Moshe. *People of the Book: Canon, Meaning and Authority*. Cambridge, MA: Harvard University Press, 1997.

Harf-Lancner, Laurence. "Chrétien's Literary Background." In *A Companion to Chrétien De Troyes*, ed. Norris J. Lacy and Joan T. Grimbert, 26–42. Cambridge: D. S. Brewer, 2005.

Harkins, Franklin T. *Reading and the Work of Restoration: History and Scripture in the Theology of Hugh of St. Victor*. Toronto: Pontifical Institute of Mediaeval Studies, 2009.

Harris, Jay M. *How do we Know This? Midrash and the Fragmentation of Modern Judaism*. Albany: State University of New York Press, 1995.

Harris, Robert A. "Awareness of Biblical Redaction among Rabbinic Exegetes of Northern France" (Hebrew). *Shnaton: An Annual for Biblical and Ancient Near Eastern Studies* 12 (2000): 289–310.

Discerning Parallelism: A Study in Northern French Medieval Jewish Biblical Exegesis. Providence, RI: Brown Judaic Studies, 2004.

"The Literary Hermeneutic of R. Eliezer of Beaugency." PhD dissertation, Jewish Theological Seminary of America, 1997.

Heinrichs, Wolfhart P. "Scriptural Hermeneutics and Literary Theory in Islam." *Zeitschrift für Geschichte der arabische-islamischen Wissenschaften* 7 (1991/2): 253–284.

Heller, Marvin J. *Printing the Talmud: A History of the Earliest Printed Editions of the Talmud*. New York: Im Hasefer, 1992.

Himmelfarb, Lea. "The Link between the Jewish–Christian Polemic and the Masorah Notes in Rashi's Bible Commentary." *JJS* 59:2 (2008): 292–307.

"On Rashi's Use of the Masorah Notes in his Bible Commentary" (Hebrew). *Shnaton: An Annual for Biblical and Ancient Near Eastern Studies* 15 (2005): 167–184.

Hoffmann, Hartmut. *Die Würzburger Paulinenkommentare der Ottonenzeit*. Hanover: Hahnsche, 2009.

Hollender, Elisabeth. *Piyyut Commentary in Medieval Ashkenaz*. Berlin and New York: Walter de Gruyter, 2008.

Holmes, Urban T., and M. Amelia Klenke. *Chrétien, Troyes, and the Grail*. Chapel Hill: University of North Carolina Press, 1959.

Hunt, R. W. "The Introductions to the 'Artes' in the Twelfth Century." In *Studia Mediaevalia in Honorem Admodum Reverendi Patris Raymundi Josephi*

Martin, Ordinis Praedicatorum S. Theologiae Magistri LXXUM Natalem Diem Agentis. Bruges: De Tempel, 1948.

Irvine, Martin. *The Making of Textual Culture: Grammatica and Literary Theory, 350–1100*. Cambridge: Cambridge University Press, 1994.

Jacobs, Jonathan. *Bekhor Shoro Hadar Lo: R. Joseph Bekhor Shor between Continuity and Innovation* (Hebrew). Jerusalem: Magnes, 2017.

"Clarification of the Extent to which Rashbam Knew Midrash Leqaḥ Tov." In *Ta-Shma: Studies in Judaica in Memory of Israel M. Ta-Shma*, ed. Avraham Reiner, 475–499. Alon Shevut: Tevunot, 2012.

"The Leqah Tov Commentary on Song of Songs: Its Place in the History of Biblical Exegesis and its Relationship with the Commentary of Rashi" (Hebrew). *Shnaton: An Annual for Biblical and Ancient Near Eastern Studies* 23 (2014): 225–241.

"Rabbi Joseph Kara as an Exegete of Biblical Narrative: Discovering the Phenomenon of Exposition." *JSQ* 19 (2012): 73–89.

"Rashbam's Major Principles of Interpretation as Deduced from a Manuscript Fragment Found in 1984." *REJ* 170 (2011): 443–463.

Jaeger, C. Stephen. *The Envy of Angels: Cathedral Schools and Social Ideals in Medieval Europe, 950–1200*. Philadelphia: University of Pennsylvania Press, 1994.

The Origins of Courtliness: Civilizing Trends and the Formation of Courtly Ideals, 939–1210. Philadelphia: University of Pennsylvania Press, 2010.

"Pessimism in the Twelfth-Century 'Renaissance.'" *Speculum* 78:4 (2003): 151–183.

Japhet, Sara. "The Anonymous Commentary on the Song of Songs in Ms Prague" (Hebrew). In *To Settle the Plain Meaning of the Verse: Studies in Biblical Exegesis* (Hebrew), ed. Sara Japhet and Eran Viezel, 206–247. Jerusalem: Bialik Institute, 2011.

Collected Studies in Bible Exegesis (Hebrew). Jerusalem: Bialik Institute, 2008.

"Did Rashbam Know the Vulgate Latin Translation of the Song of Songs?" *Textus* 24 (2009): 263–285.

"The Nature and Distribution of Medieval Compilatory Commentaries in the Light of Rabbi Joseph Kara's Commentary on the Book of Job." In Fishbane, ed., *Midrashic Imagination*, 98–130.

Rashbam on Job. See under Rashbam, in Primary Sources.

Rashbam on Song of Songs. See under Rashbam, in Primary Sources.

"Rashbam's Introduction to his Commentary on Lamentations" (Hebrew). *Shnaton: An Annual for Biblical and Ancient Near Eastern Studies* 19 (2009): 231–243

"Rashi's Commentary on the Song of Songs: The Revolution of the *Peshat* and its Aftermath" (Hebrew). In Grossman and Japhet, eds., *Rashi*, 205–226.

"The Tension between Rabbinic Legal Midrash and the 'Plain Meaning' (Peshat) of the Biblical Text – an Unresolved Problem? In the Wake of Rashbam's Commentary on the Pentateuch." In *Sefer Moshe: The Moshe Weinfeld Jubilee Volume*, ed. Chaim Cohen, Avi Hurvitz, and Shalom M. Paul, 403–425. Winona Lake, IN: Eisenbrauns, 2004.

Japhet, Sara, ed. *The Bible in Light of its Interpreters: Sarah Kamin Memorial Volume*. Jerusalem: Magnes, 1994.

Japhet and Salters, *Rashbam on Qohelet*. See under Rashbam, in Primary Sources.

Jastrow, Marcus. *A Dictionary of the Targumim, the Talmud Babli and Yerushalmi and the Midrashic Literature*. New York: Pardes, 1950.

Jeauneau, Édouard. *Rethinking the School of Chartres*, trans. Claude Paul Desmarais. Toronto: University of Toronto Press, 2009.

Jeudy, Colette. "L'œuvre de Remi d'Auxerre." In *L'École carolingienne d'Auxerre: De Murethach à Remi, 830–908*, ed. Dominique Iogna-Prat et al., 373–396. Paris: Beauchesne, 1991.

Kadari, Tamar. "'Friends Hearken to your Voice': Rabbinic Interpretations of the Song of Songs." In *Approaches to Literary Readings of Ancient Jewish Writings*, ed. K. A. D. Smelik and Karolien Vermeulen, 183–209. Leiden: Brill, 2014.

"Rabbinic and Christian Models of Interaction on the Song of Songs." In *Interaction between Judaism and Christianity in History, Religion, Art and Literature*, ed. Marcel Poorthuis, Joshua Schwartz, and Joseph Turner, 65–82. Leiden: Brill, 2009.

Kahana, Menahem. "The Halakhic Midrashim." In *The Literature of the Sages, Second Part: Midrash and Targum, Liturgy, Poetry, Mysticism, Contracts, Inscriptions, Ancient Science and the Languages of Rabbinic Literature*, ed. Shmuel Safrai, 3–106. Assen: Royal Van Gorcum, 2006.

Kalman, Jason. "When What you See is not What you Get: Rashbam's Commentary on Job and the Methodological Challenges of Studying Northern French Jewish Biblical Exegesis." *Religion Compass* 2:5 (2008): 844–861.

Kamin, Sarah. "Affinities between Jewish and Christian Exegesis in 12th Century Northern France." In *Proceedings of the Ninth World Congress of Jewish Studies: Panel Sessions, Bible Studies and Ancient Near East*, ed. Moshe Goshen-Gottstein, 141–155. Jerusalem: Magnes, 1988; repr. in Kamin, *Jews and Christians*, xxi–xxxv (English section).

Jews and Christians Interpret the Bible (Hebrew), ed. Sara Japhet, 2nd ed. Jerusalem: Magnes, 2009.

Rashi's Exegetical Categorization with Respect to the Distinction between Peshat and Derash (Hebrew). Jerusalem: Magnes, 1986.

Kanarfogel, Ephraim. "Ashkenazic Talmudic Interpretation and the Jewish–Christian Encounter." *Medieval Encounters* 22 (2016): 72–94.

The Intellectual History and Rabbinic Culture of Medieval Ashkenaz. Detroit: Wayne State University Press, 2013.

"Tosafists as *Peshat* Exegetes: A Century after S. A. Poznanski's *Introduction to Biblical Exegesis in Northern France*" (Hebrew). *Michlol* 1 (2016): 147–160.

Kearney, Jonathan. *Rashi – Linguist Despite Himself: A Study of the Linguistic Dimension of Rabbi Solomon Yishaqi's Commentary on Deuteronomy*. London: T&T Clark, 2012.

Keiner, Ronald C. "The Hebrew Paraphrase of Saadiah Gaon's *Kitāb al-Amānāt wa'l-I'tiqādāt*." *AJS Review* 11 (1986): 1–25.

Kelley, Page H., Daniel S. Mynatt, and Timothy G. Crawford. *The Masorah of Biblia Hebraica Stuttgartensia: Introduction and Annotated Glossary*. Grand Rapids: Eerdmans, 1998.

Kennedy, Robert George. "Thomas Aquinas and the Literal Sense of Sacred Scripture." PhD dissertation, Notre Dame. 1985.
Kessler, Stephan C. "Gregory the Great: A Figure of Tradition and Transition in Church Exegesis." In *HBOT* I/2, 135–147.
Khan, Geoffrey. *The Early Karaite Tradition of Hebrew Grammatical Thought*. Leiden: Brill, 2000.
King, Christopher. *Origen on the Song of Songs as the Spirit of Scripture: The Bridegroom's Perfect Marriage-Song*. Oxford: Oxford University Press, 2005.
Kislev, Itamar. "The Contribution of MS Hamburg 52 for Improving the Text of Rashbam's Torah Commentary" (Hebrew). *Alei Sefer* 26/27 (2017): 41–70.
"'Exegesis in Perpetual Motion': The Short Commentary of Ibn Ezra as a Source for Rashbam in his Commentary on the Pentateuch" (Hebrew). *Tarbiz* 79 (2010): 413–438.
"Rashbam's Commentary on the Story of the Creation" (Hebrew). *JSIJ* 10 (2012):95–107.
"'Whoever has Heeded the Words of our Creator': Rashbam's Methodological Preface to Leviticus and the Relationship between Rashi's and Rashbam's Commentaries" (Hebrew). *Tarbiz* 73 (2004): 225–237.
Klepper, Deanna. *The Insight of Unbelievers: Nicholas of Lyra and Christian Readings of Jewish Texts in the Later Middle Ages*. Philadelphia: University of Pennsylvania Press, 2007.
Kraebel, A. B. "*Grammatica* and the Authenticity of the Psalms-Commentary Attributed to Bruno the Carthusian." *Mediaeval Studies* 71 (2009): 63–97.
"John of Rheims and the Psalter Commentary Attributed to Ivo II of Chartres." *Revue Bénédictine* 122 (2012): 252–293.
"The Place of Allegory in the Psalter-Commentary of Bruno the Carthusian." *Mediaeval Studies* 73 (2011): 207–216.
"Poetry and Commentary in the Medieval School of Rheims: Reading Virgil, Reading David." In Cohen and Berlin, eds., *Interpreting Scriptures in Judaism, Christianity and Islam*, 227–248.
"Prophecy and Poetry in the Psalms-Commentaries of St. Bruno and the Pre-Scholastics." *Sacris Erudiri* 50 (2011): 413–459.
Kugel, James L. *The Bible as it Was*. Cambridge, MA: Harvard University Press, 1997.
The Idea of Biblical Poetry: Parallelism and its History. New Haven: Yale University Press, 1981.
Lasker, Daniel J. "The Influence of Karaism on Maimonides" (Hebrew). *Sefunot* n.s. 5 (1991): 145–161.
"Rashi and Maimonides on Christianity. In *Between Rashi and Maimonides: Themes in Medieval Jewish Thought, Literature and Exegesis*, ed. Ephraim Kanarfogel and Moshe Sokolow, 3–21. New York: Ktav, 2010.
Lausberg, Heinrich. *Handbook of Literary Rhetoric: A Foundation for Literary Study*, ed. David E. Orton and R. Dean Anderson. Leiden: Brill, 1997.
Lawee, Eric. "Introducing Scripture: The "Accessus ad Auctores" in Hebrew Exegetical Literature from the Thirteenth through the Fifteenth Centuries." In McAuliffe et al., eds., *Reverence for the Word*, 157–179.
"The Reception of Rashi's *Commentary on the Torah* in Spain: The Case of Adam's Mating with the Animals." *JQR* 97 (2007): 33–66.

Layton, Richard. "Hearing Love's Language: The Letter of the Text in Origen's Commentary on the Song of Songs." In *The Reception and Interpretation of the Bible in Late Antiquity: Proceedings of the Montréal Colloquium in Honour of Charles Kannengiesser, 11–13 October 2006*, ed. Lucian Turcescu, Lorenzo DiTommaso, and Charles Kannengiesser, 287–315. Leiden: Brill, 2008.

Leclercq, Jean. "Monastic Commentary on Biblical and Ecclesiastical Literature from Late Antiquity to the Twelfth Century," trans. A. B. Kraebel. *The Medieval Journal* 2:2 (2012): 27–53.

"Origèn au XIIe siècle." *Irenikon* 24 (1951): 425–439.

Leibowitz, Nehama. "Darko shel Rashi be-hava'at midrashim be-ferusho la-Torah" In *Iyyunim ḥadashim be-sefer Shemot*, 497–524. Jerusalem: World Zionist Organization, 1975. English trans. "Rashi's Method in Citing Midrashim in his Torah Commentary." In *Nehama Leibowitz on Teaching Tanakh: Three Essays*, ed. and trans. Moshe Sokolow, 31–70. New York: Torah Education Network, 1986.

Levy, Abraham. *Rashi's Commentary on Ezekiel 40–48: Edited on the Basis of Eleven Manuscripts*. Philadelphia: Dropsie College for Hebrew and Cognate Learning, 1931.

Levy, Ian Christopher. "Bruno the Carthusian: Theology and Reform in his Commentary on the Pauline Epistles." In *Analecta Cartusiana 300*, ed. James Hogg, Alain Girard, and Daniel Le Blévec, 5–61. Salzburg: FB Anglistik und Amerikanistik, Universität Salzburg, 2013.

Leyra Curiá, Montse. *In Hebreo: The Victorine Exegesis of the Bible in the Light of its Northern-French Jewish Sources*. Turnhout: Brepols, 2017.

Liss, Hanna. "The Commentary on the Song of Songs Attributed to R. Samuel ben Meïr (Rashbam)." *Medieval Jewish Studies* 1 (2007): 1–27.

Creating Fictional Worlds: Peshaṭ-Exegesis and Narrativity in Rashbam's Commentary on the Torah. Leiden: Brill, 2011.

Lockshin, Martin. "The Connection between Rabbi Samuel ben Meir's Torah Commentary and Midrash Sekhel Tov." In *Proceedings of the Eleventh World Congress of Jewish Studies*, I:135–142. Jerusalem: World Union of Jewish Studies, 1993.

"Does Halakhah Really Uproot Peshat?" *Diné Israel* 32 (2018): 211*–226*.

"Moses Wrote the Torah: Rashbam's Perspective." *HUCA* (2015): 109–125.

Rabbi Samuel Ben Meir's Commentary on [Torah]: An Annotated Translation, 5 vols. Lewiston, NY, Lampeter (Wales), and Queenston (Ontario): Edwin Mellen Press, 1989–2004.

"Rashbam as Literary Exegete." In McAuliffe et al., eds., *Reverence for the Word*, 83–91.

"Tradition or Context: Two Exegetes Struggle with Peshat." In *From Ancient Israel to Modern Judaism: Intellect in Quest of Understanding. Essays in Honor of Marvin Fox*, ed. Jacob Neusner et al., II:173–186. Atlanta: Scholars Press, 1989.

Lowth, Robert. *Lectures on the Sacred Poetry of the Hebrews*, trans. G. Gregory, 2 vols. London: J. Johnson, 1787.

Lutz, Cora. "One Formula of *Accessus* in Remigius' Works." *Latomus* 19 (1960): 774–780.

Mack, Hannanel. "The Bifurcated Legacy of Rabbi Moses ha-Darshan and the Rise of Peshat Exegesis in Medieval France." In Castaño et al., eds., *Regional Identities*, 73–91.

The Mystery of R. Moses Hadarshan (Hebrew). Jerusalem: Bialik Institute, 2010.

Madigan, Daniel A. *The Qur'ân's Self Image: Writing and Authority in Islam's Scripture*. Princeton: Princeton University Press, 2001.

Malter, Henry. *Saadia Gaon, his Life and Works*. Philadelphia: Jewish Publication Society of America, 1921.

Maman, Aharon. *Comparative Semitic Philology in the Middle Ages*. Leiden: Brill, 2004.

"The Linguistic School." In *HBOT* I/2, 261–281.

"*Peshat* and *Derash* in Medieval Hebrew Lexicons." In *Israel Oriental Studies* XIX, *Compilation and Creation in Adab and Lugha: Studies in Memory of Naphtali Kinberg (1948–1997)*, ed. Albert Arazi, Joseph Sadan, and David J. Wesserstein, 343–357. Winona Lake, IN: Eisenbrauns, 1999.

Marcus, Ivan G. "History, Story and Collective Memory: Narrativity in Early Ashkenazic Culture." In Fishbane, ed., *Midrashic Imagination*, 255–279.

"Rashi's Choice: The Humash Commentary as Rewritten Midrash." In *Studies in Medieval Jewish Intellectual and Social History: Festschrift in Honor of Robert Chazan*, ed. David Engel, Lawrence H. Schiffman, and Elliot R. Wolfson, 29–45. Leiden: Brill, 2012.

Matter, E. Ann. *The Voice of my Beloved: The Song of Songs in Western Medieval Christianity*. Philadelphia: University of Pennsylvania Press, 1990.

McAuliffe, Jane Dammen, Barry D. Walfish, and Joseph W. Goering, eds. *With Reverence for the Word: Medieval Scriptural Exegesis in Judaism, Christianity, and Islam*. Oxford: Oxford University Press, 2003.

Melammed, Ezra Zion. *Bible Commentators* (Hebrew). Jerusalem: Magnes, 1978.

Meir, Amirah. *Siddur devarim qaruy shirah: parshanuto shel Rashbam le-shirat ha-Torah* [Poetry is the arrangement of words: Rashbam's exegesis of biblical poetry]. *Beth Mikra* 42 (1997): 34–44.

Merdler, Ronela. "*Dayyaqut me-Rabbenu Shemuel*: Rashbam's Grammatical Commentary on the Bible and its Exegetical Contribution" (Hebrew). *Shnaton: An Annual for Biblical and Ancient Near Eastern Studies* 14 (2004): 241–255.

"Rabbi Samuel ben Meir (Rashbam) and Hebrew Grammar, his Grammatical View on Topics of Phonology and Morphology, his Place in the History of Hebrew Linguistics, and his Character as a Grammarian" (Hebrew). PhD dissertation, Hebrew University of Jerusalem, 2004.

Mews, Constant. "Bruno of Reims and the Evolution of Scholastic Culture in Northern France, 1050–1100." In Beyer et al., eds., *Bruno and his Mortuary Roll*, 49–81.

"Bruno of Reims and Roscelin of Compiègne on the Psalms." In *Latin Culture in the Eleventh Century*, ed. Michael Herren et al., 129–152. Turnhout: Brepols, 2002.

Minnis, Alastair. "Figuring the Letter: Making Sense of Sensus Litteralis in Late-Medieval Christian Exegesis." In Cohen and Berlin, eds., *Interpreting Scriptures in Judaism, Christianity and Islam*, 159–182.

Medieval Theory of Authorship: Scholastic Literary Attitudes. Philadelphia: University of Pennsylvania Press, 2008.

Minnis, Alastair, and A. B. Scott, with the assistance of David Wallace. *Medieval Literary Theory and Criticism c.1100–c.1375: The Commentary Tradition*. Oxford: Oxford University Press, 1991.

Mirsky, Hananel. "The Linguistic Theory of Menahem ben Saruq." PhD dissertation, Hebrew University of Jerusalem. 2014.

"Shalosh sugyot me-ḥokhmat ha-lashon mi-bet midrasho shel Menaḥem ben Saruq" [Three topics in the discipline of language from the school of Menahem ben Saruq]. *Mehkarim be-Lashon (Language Studies)* 14–15 (2013): 99–131.

Molho, Michael, and Abraham Mevorah. *Histoire des israélites de Castoria*. Thessaloniki: M. Molho, 1938.

Mondschein, Aharon. "Additional Comments on *ha-Sadran* and *ha-Mesadder*" (Hebrew). *Leshonenu* 67 (2005): 331–346.

"On the Attitude of R. Abraham Ibn Ezra to the Exegetical Use of the Hermeneutic Norm *Gematri'a*" (Hebrew). In *Te'uda 8: Studies in the Works of Abraham Ibn Ezra*, ed. Israel Levin, 137–161. Tel Aviv: Tel Aviv University Press, 1992.

"Concerning the Inter-Relationship of the Commentaries of R. Abraham Ibn Ezra and R. Samuel ben Meir to the Pentateuch: A New Appraisal" (Hebrew). In *Te'udah 16–17: Studies in Judaica*, ed. Yair Hoffman, 15–46. Tel Aviv: Tel Aviv University Press, 2001.

"Only One in a Thousand of his Comments may be Called *Peshat*": Toward Ibn Ezra's View of Rashi's Commentary to the Torah" (Hebrew). In *Studies in Bible and Exegesis V: Presented to Uriel Simon*, ed. Moshe Garsiel et al., 221–248. Ramat Gan: Bar-Ilan University Press, 2000.

"On Rashbam's Rediscovered 'Lost Commentary' on Psalms" (Hebrew). *Tarbiz* 79 (2010): 91–141.

Murphy, James Jerome. *Rhetoric in the Middle Ages: A History of Rhetorical Theory from Saint Augustine to the Renaissance*. Berkeley: University of California Press, 1974.

Netzer, Nissan. "Comparison with Mishnaic Hebrew: One of Rashi's Strategies in his Biblical Commentary" (Hebrew). In *Rashi Studies*, ed. Zvi Arie Steinfeld, 107–136. Ramat Gan: Bar-Ilan University Press, 1993.

Neuwirth, Angelika, Nicolai Sinai, and Michael Marx, eds. *The Qur'ān in Context: Historical and Literary Investigations into the Qur'ānic Milieu*. Leiden: Brill, 2010.

Novetsky, Hillel. "A Reconstruction of Rashbam's Lost Commentary on Bereshit 1–17" (Hebrew). PhD dissertation, Hebrew University of Jerusalem, 1971.

Novikoff, Alex J. *The Medieval Culture of Disputation Pedagogy, Practice, and Performance*. Philadelphia: University of Pennsylvania Press, 2013.

Ocker, Christopher. *Biblical Poetics before Humanism and Reformation*. Cambridge: Cambridge University Press, 2002.

O'Donoghue, Bernard. *The Courtly Love Tradition*. Manchester: Manchester University Press, 1982.

Ofer, Yosef. "When Was '*Dayaqot*' – R. Shmuel Ben Meir's Grammatical Treatise – Written?" (Hebrew). *Shnaton: An Annual for Biblical and Ancient Near Eastern Studies* 17 (2007): 233–251.

O'Neill, Mary J. *Courtly Love Songs of Medieval France: Transmission and Style in the Trouvère Repertoire*. Oxford: Oxford University Press, 2006.

Owens, Jonathan. *The Foundations of Grammar: An Introduction to Medieval Arabic Grammatical Theory*. Amsterdam: J. Benjamins, 1988.

Paget, James N. B. Carleton. "Christian Exegesis in the Alexandrian Tradition." In *HBOT* I/1, 478–542.

Penkower, Jordan. "The End of Rashi's Commentary on Job. The Manuscripts and the Printed Editions." *JSQ* 10 (2003): 18–48.

"Rashi's Commentary on Ezekiel: On the Occasion of its New Edition in *Miqra'ot Gedolot Haketer*" (Hebrew). In *Studies in Bible and Exegesis VII: Presented to Menachem Cohen*, ed. Shmuel Vargon, Yosef Ofer, Jordan S. Penkower, and Jacob Klein, 425–474. Ramat Gan: Bar-Ilan University Press, 2005.

"Rashi's Corrections to his Commentary on the Pentateuch" (Hebrew). *JSIJ* 6 (2007): 141–188.

"Rashi's Corrections to his Commentary on the Prophets" (Hebrew). *Shnaton: An Annual for Biblical and Ancient Near Eastern Studies* 15 (2005): 185–212.

"The Textual Transmission of Rashi's Commentary on Ezekiel 27:17" (Hebrew). *Tarbiz* 63 (1994): 219–234.

Pereira-Mendoza, Joseph. *Rashi as Philologist*. Manchester: Manchester University Press, 1940.

Perez, Maaravi. "Quotations from *Kitab al-Istighna* by R. Shmuel ha-Nagid in an Anonymous Commentary on the Book of Psalms" (Hebrew). *Shnaton: An Annual for Biblical and Ancient Near Eastern Studies* 12 (2002): 241–287.

Polliack, Meira. "Karaite Conception of the Biblical Narrator (*Mudawwin*)." In *Encyclopaedia of Midrash: Biblical Interpretation in Formative Judaism*, ed. J. Neusner, A. J. Avery-Peck, and W. S. Green, I:350–374. Leiden: Brill, 2004.

"Major Trends in Karaite Biblical Exegesis." In Polliack, ed., *Karaite Judaism*, 363–413.

Polliack, Meira, ed. *Karaite Judaism: A Guide to its History and Literary Sources*. Leiden: Brill, 2003

Poonawala, Ismail. "*Ta'wīl*." In *Encyclopedia of Islam*, 2nd ed., X:390–392. Leiden: Brill, 2000.

Poznanski, Samuel A. *Fragments de l'exégèse biblique de Menahem bar Helbo*. Warsaw: Schuldberg, 1904.

"Mavo 'al ḥakhmei ṣorfat mefarshei ha-miqra" [Introduction to the Bible commentator sages of France]. In *Kommentar zu Ezechiel und den XII kleinen Propheten von Eliezer au Beaugency*, ed. Samuel A. Poznanski, IX–CLXVI. Warsaw: Mekize Nirdamim, 1913.

Pradié, Pascal. *Bruno de Cologne, Ludolphus de Saxonia, Denys le Chartreux, Le commentaire des Psaumes des montées: une échelle de vie intérieure*. Paris: Beauchesne, 2006.

Prebor, Gila. "The Use of Midrash in Rashi's Commentary on Ecclesiastes" (Hebrew). *Shnaton: An Annual for Biblical and Ancient Near Eastern Studies* 19 (2009): 209–229.

Reiner, Avraham. "Bible and Politics: A Correspondence between Rabbenu Tam and the Authorities of Champagne." In *Entangled Histories: Knowledge, Authority, and Jewish Culture in the Thirteenth Century*, ed. Elisheva Baumgarten, Ruth

Mazzo Karras, and Katelyn Melser, 59–72. Philadelphia: University of Pennsylvania Press, 2017.

"From Rabbeinu Tam to R. Isaac of Vienna: The Hegemony of the French Talmudic School in the Twelfth-Century." In *The Jews of Europe in the Middle Ages (Tenth to Fifteenth Centuries)*, ed. Christoph Cluse, 273–281. Turnhout: Brepols, 2004.

"Rabbenu Tam and his Contemporaries: Relationships, Influences and Methods of Interpretation of the Talmud" (Hebrew). PhD dissertation, Hebrew University of Jerusalem, 2002.

Rosenthal, Judah. "Ha-pulmus ha-anti noṣri be-Rashi 'al ha-Tanakh" [Anti-Christian polemic in Rashi on the Bible]. In Judah Rosenthal, *Studies and Texts in Jewish History, Literature and Religion*, 101–116. Jerusalem: Rubin Mass, 1967.

Sáenz-Badillos, Angel. "Early Hebraists in Spain: Menahem Ben Saruq and Dunash ben Labrat." In *HBOT* I/2, 96–109.

Scaglione, Aldo. *Knights and Courts: Courtliness, Chivalry, & Courtesy from Ottonian Germany to the Italian Renaissance*. Berkeley: University of California Press, 1991.

Schippers, Arie. "Symmetry and Repetition as a Stylistic Ideal in Andalusian Poetry: Moses Ibn Ezra and Figures of Speech in the Arabic Tradition." In *Amsterdam Middle Eastern Studies*, ed. M. Woidich, 160–173. Wiesbaden: Ludwig Reichert, 1990.

Schlossberg, Eliezer. "Le-gilgulo shel perush Rasag 'al Daniel 3:10" [The development of R. Saadia Gaon's commentary on Daniel 10:3]. In *Studies in Hebrew Literature and Yemenite Culture: Jubilee Volume Presented to Yehuda Ratzaby*, ed. Judith Dishon and Ephraim Hazan, 81–87. Ramat Gan: Bar-Ilan University Press, 1991.

Schmelzer, Menahem H. *Isaac Ben Abraham Ibn Ezra: Poems* (Hebrew). New York: Jewish Theological Seminary of America, 1979.

Schmitt, Jean-Claude, and Alex J. Novikoff. *The Conversion of Herman the Jew: Autobiography, History, and Fiction in the Twelfth Century*. Philadelphia: University of Pennsylvania Press, 2003.

Schwartz, Baruch J. "Rashi's Commentary on Exodus 6:1–9: Reconsideration" (Hebrew). In *To Settle the Plain Sense of Scripture*, ed. Sara Japhet and Eran Viezel, 100–112. Jerusalem: Magnes, 2010.

Sela, Shlomo, and Gad Freudenthal. "Abraham Ibn Ezra's Scholarly Writings: A Chronological Listing," *Aleph* 6 (2006): 13–55.

Shapira, Amnon. "Rashi's Twofold Interpretations (Peshuto and Midrasho): A Dualistic Approach?" (Hebrew). In Japhet, ed., *Bible in Light of its Interpreters*, 287–311.

Sharf, Andrew. "An Unknown Messiah of 1096 and the Emperor Alexius." *JJS* 7 (1956): 59–70.

Shereshevsky, Esra. "Inversions in Rashi's Commentary ('*Mikrah Mesoras*')." In *Gratz College Anniversary Volume: On the Occasion of the Seventy-Fifth Anniversary of the Founding of the College, 1895–1970*, ed. Isidore David Passow and Samuel Tobias Lachs, 263–268. Philadelphia: Gratz College, 1971.

"Rashi's and Christian Interpretations." *JQR* 61 (1970): 76–86.

Shinan, Avigdor. "The Midrashic Interpretations of the Ten Dotted Passages in the Pentateuch." In Japhet, ed., *Bible in the Light of its Interpreters*, 198–214.

Signer, Michael. "Restoring the Narrative: Jewish and Christian Exegesis in the Twelfth Century." In McAuliffe et al., eds., *Reverence for the Word*, 70–82.

"Vision and History: Nicholas of Lyra on the Prophet Ezechiel." In *Nicholas of Lyra: The Senses of Scripture*, ed. Philip D. W. Krey and Lesley Smith, 147–171. Leiden: Brill, 2000.

Simon, Uriel. *The Ear Discerns Words: Studies in Ibn Ezra's Exegetical Methodology* (Hebrew). Ramat Gan: Bar-Ilan University Press, 2013.

Four Approaches to the Book of Psalms: From Saadiah Gaon to Abraham Ibn Ezra, trans. Lenn Schramm. Albany: State University of New York Press, 1991.

Singerman, Jerome E. *Under Clouds of Poesy: Poetry and Truth in French and English Reworkings of the Aeneid, 1160–1513*. New York: Garland Publications, 1986.

Smalley, Beryl. "Andrew of St. Victor, Abbot of Wigmore: A Twelfth-Century Hebraist." *Recherches de théologie ancienne et médiévale* 10 (1938): 358–373.

"A Commentary on the *Hebraica* by Herbert of Bosham." *Recherches de théologie ancienne et médiéval* 18 (1951): 29–65.

"Stephen Langton and the Four Senses of Scripture." *Speculum* 6 (1931): 60–76.

The Study of the Bible in the Middle Ages, 3rd ed. Notre Dame: University of Notre Dame, 1983.

Smith, Lesley. *The Glossa Ordinaria: The Making of a Medieval Bible Commentary*. Leiden: Brill, 2009.

Sokolow, Moshe. "Rashbam's Pentateuch Commentary: New Material" (Hebrew). *Alei Sefer* 11 (1984): 73–74.

Soloveitchik, Haym. *Collected Essays I*. Oxford: Littman Library of Jewish Civilization, 2013.

Collected Essays II. Oxford: Littman Library of Jewish Civilization, 2014.

"Halakhah, Hermeneutics, and Martyrdom in Medieval Ashkenaz." *JQR* 94:1 (2004) 77–108; 2: 278–299.

"Rabad of Posquières: A Programmatic Essay." In *Studies in the History of Jewish Society Presented to Professor Jacob Katz on his Seventy-Fifth Birthday*, ed. Immanuel Etkes and Yosef Salmon, 7–40. Jerusalem: Magnes, 1980.

"Three Themes in *Sefer Ḥasidim*," *AJS Review* 1 (1976): 311–357.

"Two Notes on the 'Commentary on the Torah' of R. Yehudah he-Hasid." In *Turim: Studies in Jewish History and Literature: Presented to Dr. Bernard Lander*, ed. Michael A. Shmidman and Bernard Lander, 241–251. New York: Touro College Press, 2007.

Southern, R. W. "The Schools of Paris and the School of Chartres." In Benson and Constable, eds., *Renaissance and Renewal*, 113–137.

Spiegel, Yaakov. *Chapters in the History of the Jewish Book: Writing and Transmission* (Hebrew). Ramat Gan: Bar-Ilan University Press, 2005.

Steckel, Sita. "*Doctor doctorum*: Changing Concepts of 'Teaching' in the Mortuary Roll of Bruno the Carthusian (d. 1101)." In Beyer et al., eds., *Bruno and his Mortuary Roll*, 83–116.

Steiner, Richard C. *A Biblical Translation in the Making: The Evolution and Impact of Saadia Gaon's Tafsir*. Cambridge, MA: Harvard University Press, 2011.

"The Byzantine Biblical Commentaries from the Genizah: Rabbanite vs. Karaite." In Bar-Asher et al., eds., *Shai le-Sara Japhet*, 243–262.

"A Jewish Theory of Biblical Redaction from Byzantium: Its Rabbinic Roots, its Diffusion and its Encounter with the Muslim Doctrine of Falsification." *JSIJ* 2 (2003): 123–167.

"The 'Lemma Complement' in Hebrew Commentaries from Byzantium and its Diffusion to Northern France and Germany." *JSQ* 18 (2011): 367–379.

"Linguistic Aspects of the Commentary on Ezekiel and the Minor Prophets in the Hebrew Scrolls from Byzantium" (Hebrew). *Leshonenu* 59 (1996): 39–56.

"'*Muqdam u-Me'uḥar*' and '*Muqaddam wa-Muaḥḥar*': On the History of Some Hebrew and Arabic Terms for *Hysteron Proteron* and *Anastrophe*." *Journal of Near Eastern Studies* 66 (2007): 33–45.

"The Rabbanite Biblical Commentaries from the Genizah and their Place in the History of Biblical Exegesis." Unpublished MS.

Stockmen from Tekoa, Sycomores from Sheba: A Study of Amos' Occupations. Washington, DC: Catholic Biblical Association of America, 2003.

Stercal, Claudio. *Stephen Harding: A Biographical Sketch and Texts*, trans. Martha F. Krieg. Trappist, KY: Cistercian Publications, 2008.

Stern, David. *The Jewish Bible: A Material History*. Seattle: University of Washington Press, 2017.

Sternberg, Meir. *The Poetics of Biblical Narrative: Ideological Literature and the Drama of Reading*. Bloomington: Indiana University Press, 1985.

Sweeney, Eileen C. *Anselm of Canterbury and the Desire for the Word.* Washington, DC: Catholic University of America Press, 2012.

Taitz, Emily. *The Jews of Medieval France: The Community of Champagne.* Westport, CT: Greenwood Press, 1994.

Ta-Shma, Israel M. "Bible Criticism in Early Medieval Franco-Germany" (Hebrew). In Japhet, ed., *Bible in Light of its Interpreters*, 453–459.

"Hebrew-Byzantine Bible Exegesis ca. 1000, From the Cairo Genizah" (Hebrew). *Tarbiz* 69 (2000): 247–256.

"Open Bible Criticism in an Anonymous Commentary on the Book of Psalms" (Hebrew). *Tarbiz* 66 (1997): 417–423.

Studies in Medieval Rabbinic Literature (Hebrew). Vol. I: *Germany*. Jerusalem: Bialik Institute, 2004; vol. III: *Italy & Byzantium*. Jerusalem: Bialik Institute, 2005.

Talmudic Commentary in Europe and North Africa, Part I: 1000–1200 (Hebrew). Jerusalem: Magnes, 1999.

Tchernetska, Natalie, Judith Olszowy-Schlanger, and Nicholas de Lange. "An Early Hebrew–Greek Biblical Glossary from the Cairo Genizah." *REJ* 166 (2007): 91–128.

Tene, David. "Hebrew Linguistic Literature." In *Encyclopaedia Judaica*, XVI:1352–1390. Jerusalem: Encyclopaedia Judaica, 1972.

"Hebrew Linguistic Tradition." In *Concise History of the Language Sciences, from the Sumerians to the Cognitivists*, ed. E. F. K. Koerner and R. E. Asher, 21–28. Oxford: Pergamon, 1995.

Touitou, Eleazar. "Concerning the Presumed Original Version of Rashi's Commentary on the Pentateuch" (Hebrew). *Tarbiz* 56 (1987): 211–242.

Exegesis in Perpetual Motion: Studies in the Pentateuchal Commentary of Rabbi Samuel ben Meir (Hebrew). Ramat Gan: Bar-Ilan University Press, 2003.

"Rashi's Commentary on Genesis 1–6 in the Context of Judeo-Christian Controversy." *HUCA* 61 (1990): 159–183.

Review of Sarah Kamin, Rashi's Exegetical Categorization in Respect to the Distinction between Peshat and Derash (Hebrew). *Tarbiz* 56 (1987): 439–447.

"Shiṭato ha-parshanit shel Rashbam 'al reqa' ha-meṣi'ut ha-hisṭorit shel zemano" [Rashbam's exegetical system within the context of the historical reality of his time]. In *Studies in Rabbinic Literature, Bible and Jewish History [Dedicated to Professor Ezra Zion Melammed]*, ed. Y. D. Gilat, C. Levine, and Z. M. Rabinowitz, 48–74. Ramat Gan: Bar-Ilan University Press, 1982.

"Traces of *Leqaḥ Ṭov* in the Text of Rashi's Commentary to the Torah" (Hebrew). *'Alei Sefer* 15 (1988/9): 37–44.

Touitou, Inbal. "The Exegetical Methodology of Rabbi Tobias ben Eliezer in his Commentary *Leqaḥ Ṭov* to the Pentateuch" (Hebrew). MA thesis, Bar-Ilan University, 2005.

Twersky, Isadore. *Introduction to the Code of Maimonides*. New Haven: Yale University Press, 1980.

Urbach, Efraim Elimelech. *Arugat ha-bosem*. Jerusalem: Mekitse Nirdamim, 1939.

Vaciago, Paolo. *Glossae Biblicae*. Turnhout: Brepols, 2004.

van Liere, Frans. "Andrew of St. Victor, Jerome, and the Jews: Biblical Scholarship in the Twelfth-Century Renaissance." In *Scripture and Pluralism: Reading the Bible in the Religiously Plural Worlds of the Middle Ages and Renaissance*, ed. Thomas J. Heffernan and Thomas E. Burman, 59–75. Leiden: Brill, 2005.

van 't Spijker, Ineke. "The Literal and the Spiritual: Richard of Saint-Victor and the Multiple Meaning of Scripture." In van 't Spijker, ed., *Multiple Meaning of Scripture*, 225–247.

van 't Spijker, Ineke, ed. *The Multiple Meaning of Scripture: The Role of Exegesis in Early-Christian and Medieval Culture*. Leiden: Brill, 2009.

Versteegh, Kees. *Arabic Grammar and Qur'anic Exegesis in Early Islam*. Leiden: Brill, 1993.

Viezel, Eran. *The Commentary on Chronicles Attributed to Rashi* (Hebrew). Jerusalem: Magnes, 2010.

"The Commentary on Ezra–Nehemiah Attributed to Rashi" (Hebrew). *JSIJ* 9 (2010): 123–180.

"An Examination of Statements in Rashi's Commentaries concerning Targum Onkelos" (Hebrew). *Shnaton: An Annual for Biblical and Ancient Near Eastern Studies* 16 (2006): 181–203.

"The Formation of Some Biblical Books, According to Rashi." *JTS* 61 (2010): 16–42.

"Medieval Bible Commentators on the Question of the Composition of the Bible: Research and Methodological Aspects" (Hebrew). *Tarbiz* 84 (2016): 103–158.

"Rashbam on Moses' Role in Writing the Torah" (Hebrew). *Shnaton: An Annual for Biblical and Ancient Near Eastern Studies* 22 (2013): 167–188.

"The Secret of the Popularity of Rashi's Commentary on the Torah," *Review of Rabbinic Judaism* 17 (2014): 201–217.

"Targum Onkelos in Rashi's Exegetical Consciousness," *Review of Rabbinic Judaism* 15 (2012):1–19.

Walton, Michael T. "In Defense of the Church Militant: The Censorship of the Rashi Commentary in the *Magna biblia rabbinica*." *Sixteenth Century Journal* 21 (1990): 385–400.

Watson, Wilfred G. E. *Classical Hebrew Poetry: A Guide to its Techniques*. Sheffield: JSOT Press, 1986.

Wechter, Pinchas. *Ibn Barun's Arabic Works on Hebrew Grammar and Lexicography*. Philadelphia: Dropsie College, 1964.

Weiss Halivni, David. *Peshat & Derash*. New York: Oxford University Press, 1991.

Westermann, Claus. *The Psalms: Structure, Content and Message*. Minneapolis: Augsburg Publishing House, 1980.

Wetherbee, Winthrop. "Philosophy, Cosmology and the Twelfth-Century Renaissance." In *A History of Twelfth-Century Western Philosophy*, ed. Peter Dronke, 21–53. New York: Cambridge University Press, 1988.

White, Hugh. *Nature, Sex and Goodness in a Medieval Literary Tradition*. New York: Oxford University Press, 2000.

Whitman, Jon. "The Literal Sense of Christian Scripture: Redefinition and Revolution." In Cohen and Berlin, eds., *Interpreting Scriptures in Judaism, Christianity and Islam*, 133–158.

Wild, Stefan, ed. *Self-Referentiality in the Qur'an*. Wiesbaden: Harrassowitz Verlag, 2006.

"The Self-Referentiality of the Qur'an: Sura 3:7 as an Exegetical Challenge." In McAuliffe et al., eds., *Reverence for the Word*, 422–436.

Williams, John R. "The Cathedral School of Rheims in the Eleventh Century." *Speculum*, 29:4 (1954): 661–677.

Wright, David. "Augustine: His Exegesis and Hermeneutics." In *HBOT* I/1, 701–730.

Wyrick, Jed. *The Ascension of Authorship: Attribution and Canon Formation in Jewish, Hellenistic, and Christian Traditions*. Cambridge, MA: Harvard University Press, 2004.

Yadin, Azzan. *Scripture as Logos: Rabbi Ishmael and the Origins of Midrash*. Philadelphia: University of Pennsylvania Press, 2013.

Zawanowska, Marzena. *The Arabic Translation and Commentary of Yefet ben 'Eli the Karaite on the Abraham Narratives (Genesis 11:10–25:18)*. Leiden: Brill, 2011.

Zemler-Cizewski, Wanda. "The Literal Sense of Scripture according to Rupert of Deutz." In van 't Spijker, ed., *Multiple Meaning of Scripture*, 203–224.

Ziomkowski, Robert. *Manegold of Lautenbach: Liber Contra Wolfelmum*. Paris: Peeters, 2002.

Zohory, Menahem. *Grammarians and their Writings in Rashi's Commentaries* (Hebrew). Jerusalem: Carmel, 1994.

Zucker, Moshe. "Le-pitron be'ayat 32 middot u-mishnat Rabi Eliezer" [On the resolution of the problem of the thirty-two *middot* and *Mishnat Rabbi Eliezer*]. *Proceedings of the American Academy of Jewish Research* 23 (1954): 1–39.

Rav Saadya Gaon's Translation of the Torah (Hebrew). New York: Feldheim, 1959.

Saadya on Genesis. See under Saadia, in Primary Sources.

General Index

a biblical verse does not leave the realm of its *peshat* (talmudic maxim), 5, 8, 9, 37, 45, 63, 66, 67, 72, 73, 104, 105, 108, 115, 121, 122, 123, 126, 127, 147, 149, 152, 153, 156, 161, 239, 241, 242, 267
Abelard, Peter, 219, 220, 264
accessus ad auctores, 168, 170
aggadah/haggadah, 9, 38, 39, 40, 41, 46, 55, 56, 69, 70, 73, 75, 92, 112, 115, 116, 130, 185, 205, 216, 222, 240, 241, 243, 269
Ahrend, Moshe, 9, 77, 132, 166
Albert the Great, 263
Alfasi, Isaac, 27, 214
Andrew of St. Victor, 3, 14, 247
Anselm of Canterbury, 17
Anselm of Laon, 17, 18, 20, 219, 264
apostrophe (rhetorical technique), 204, 205
Aquinas, Thomas, 14, 15, 16
Aristotle, 16, 125, 230, 264
asmakhta, 62, 64, 116, 122, 123, 124, 125, 129
Augustine, 15, 19, 23, 84, 85, 87, 88, 89, 169, 202, 203, 205
authorial intention, 16, 23, 87, 168, 169, 171, 172, 174, 175, 270

Baraita of R. Jose the Galilean, 112, 185, 186
Bede, 81, 131, 203
Bekhor Shor, Joseph, 62, 63, 208
Berger, David, 93
Berliner, Abraham, 33
Bernard of Chartres, 232
Bernard of Clairvaux, 219, 232
biblical authorship and redaction. *See also kotev ha-sefer*; *mudawwin*; *oto she-sidder ha-devarim*; *sadran*; *sofer, ha-sofer*; *see also under* Christian interpretation
  Pentateuch, Mosaic authorship, 151, 266, 269
  Psalms, Davidic and post-Davidic authorship, 173, 174, 180, 191, 196, 197, 251, 252
Bruno the Carthusian
  biography, 4, 19, 20
  commentary on Psalms, 18, 19, 21, 167, 169, 203
  commentary on the Pauline Epistles, 81
  concept of Holy Spirit, 169, 171
  concern for sequence of the verses, 82, 86, 89
  critical selection of patristic commentary, 19, 87, 88, 89, 90, 91, 95, 100, 175
  grammatical learning, interpretive method, 18, 20, 79, 81, 87, 94, 167, 183, 205
  influence on later interpreters, 18, 19, 20, 81
  influenced by Remigius, 18, 80, 82, 205
  interpretive methods
    allegorical, mystical, typological, 83, 84, 87
    historical-literal, 83, 84, 85, 86, 89

Bruno the Carthusian (cont.)
and Rashi, 4, 19, 20, 21, 82, 86, 90, 91, 95, 96, 100, 132, 133, 164, 165, 167, 171, 172, 175, 206
use of prologue format, 168, 170, 176

Cairo Genizah, 134, 157
Cassiodorus, 19, 23, 81, 85, 86, 87, 88, 89, 169, 203, 204, 205
chansons d'amour, 162, 171, 257, 258, 259, 263
Chrétien de Troyes, 171, 183, 270
Christian interpretation
allegory, allegorical interpretation, 15, 83, 85, 86, 87, 89, 90, 119, 131, 176, 201, 232
conception of human biblical authorship, 16, 200, 201, 263, 264
literal-historical sense, 3, 13, 14, 15, 16, 19, 24, 83, 130, 201, 232, 263, 264
see also sensus litteralis
theory of multiple senses, 15, 83, 130
typological, 15, 87, 88

de-orayta laws, 126
de-rabbanan laws, 126
derash, derashot, 2, 7, 8, 9, 38, 44, 55, 59, 66, 70, 71, 91, 122, 123, 127, 128, 151, 161, 166, 241, 242, 244, 246, 266, 267
derekh ereṣ. See under Rashbam, method
derekh ha-miqra/miqra'ot/nevi'im ketuvim (typical style of Scripture), 140, 226, 228, 255, 267
diqduq (grammar, linguistic precision), 44, 52, 53, 54, 79, 208
disputatio, 32, 220
dugma, 73, 91, 178
Dunash ben Labrat, 5, 7, 29, 37, 101, 121, 129, 145, 164

Eliezer of Beaugency, 208, 237, 250, 251, 254
enarratio poetarum, 18, 25, 79, 94, 167

Gelles, Benjamin, 8, 69, 70, 94
gematria, 58, 59
gezerah shawah, 63
Gilbert of Poitiers, 219, 264
Gilbertus Universalis, 18, 203
Glossa Ordinaria, 17, 219
grammatica, 18, 23, 25, 79, 81, 90, 94, 133, 164, 165, 205
Greenberg, Moshe, 4, 8
Gregory the Great, 15, 83, 131, 176, 200, 248, 263
Grossman, Avraham, 10, 11, 29, 35, 94, 102, 104, 118, 146

Hananel ben Hushiel, 27, 214
Ḥasidei Ashkenaz (German pietists), 216, 217, 218
Hayyuj, Judah, 7, 11, 108, 121, 129
Henry I, 98
Herbert of Bosham, 3, 98
Herman of Cologne, 99
ḥiddush, 216, 217
hillukh ha-ketuvim, 225
Holy Spirit, 16, 23, 75, 76, 170–175, 200, 248, 250, 262, 263, 264, 265, 266, 271
Horace, 181, 182, 202
Hugh of St. Victor, 3, 14, 15, 16, 130, 131, 247, 265

Ibn Bal'am, Judah, 7, 11, 37, 121, 122
Ibn Chiquitilla, Moses, 7, 11, 37, 59, 121, 122, 172, 213
Ibn Ezra, Abraham
asserted that the "Rabbis knew the *peshat*", 123, 215
attitude toward midrash, 58, 122, 123, 127, 128, 140
critique of *Leqaḥ Ṭov*, 59, 151
critique of Rashbam, 245
critique of Rashi, 6, 7, 8, 59, 60, 70, 172
deferred to Rabbis in exegesis related to halakhah, 123, 124, 125, 245, 246
definition of *peshat*, 122, 123, 125
historical sensibility, 60
influence on Maimonides, 125
philosophy, 223, 230
programmatic statements, 122, 123
and Rashbam, 236
rationalism, 224, 231
rejected *gematria*, 59
and Saadia Gaon, 6
singular hermeneutic, 122, 123, 124, 127, 129
sources of influence, 7, 11, 122, 188
viewed *peshat* as the essence (*'iqqar*), 122
Ibn Ezra, Moses, 114, 122, 188, 230
Ibn Janah, Jonah, 7, 11, 23, 108, 110, 113–133, 188

intentio auctoris, 23, 168, 171
Isaac ben Judah, 26, 27

Jacob ben Yaqar, 26, 30
Jacobs, Jonathan, 162
Jaeger, Stephen, 14, 17, 218, 219
Jerome, 3, 15, 19, 23, 81, 84, 87, 98, 202, 205
John of Rheims, 18
John of Salisbury, 98

Kalonymus of Rome, 212
Kamin, Sarah, 8, 13, 14, 44, 70, 71, 76, 77, 92, 118, 166, 176
Karaism, Karaite interpretation, 6, 11, 53, 127, 128, 134, 135, 142, 143, 151, 155, 157, 248
Kimhi, Joseph, 7
kotev ha-sefer, 187, 198, 199, 200, 201, 252, 253, 255, 256
Kraebel, Andrew, 18, 82, 89, 203, 204
Kugel, James, 37, 38, 183

la'az (vernacular), 29, 39, 58, 145, 153, 237
Lanfranc of Bec, 17, 81
Langton, Stephen, 15
Leibowitz, Nehama, 69
Leipzig 1 Rashi manuscript, 35, 36, 49, 51
Leqaḥ Ṭov, 24, 39, 46, 50, 58, 59, 111, 135, 150–163, 255
leshon ha-miqra, 2, 44, 52, 73, 74, 206
levirate marriage, 61, 62
Liss, Hanna, 227, 259, 263, 270
Lockshin, Martin, 259
Lowth, Robert, 227, 228, 229, 230

Mack, Hananel, 30
Maimonides, Moses, 125, 126, 127, 128, 129, 188, 230
Mainz, 1, 2, 10, 20, 26, 27, 29, 92, 93, 146, 150, 212
majāz, 105, 106, 107, 108, 109, 110, 113, 114, 120
Manegold of Lautenbach, 17
mashal, 158, 160
mashhūr, 105
mashma', 2, 42, 52, 62, 65, 71, 72, 73, 74, 170, 177
maskilim, 216, 218, 268
Masorah, masoretic notes, works, 29, 53, 103, 145
meliṣah, 158, 160, 262
Menahem bar Helbo, 30, 103, 211, 212
Menahem ben Saruq, 5, 29, 40, 41, 53, 56, 91, 101, 121, 139, 188, 193, 201, 224
meshorer, 24, 68, 178, 187, 189, 190, 191, 192, 193, 194, 195, 196, 197, 199, 201, 202, 205, 206, 256, 257, 258, 259, 260, 261
Mews, Constant, 18, 19
middot, 9, 38, 55, 63, 112, 119, 123, 126, 127, 128, 130, 244
minhag ha-'olam, 171, 257, 258
minim, teshuvah la-minim, 96, 99, 233, 234
Minnis, Alastair, 16, 200, 201, 263, 264
miqra hafukh, 110, 183
miqra mesoras, sares ha-miqra, 46, 82, 86, 110, 111, 112, 153, 183
miqra qaṣar / derekh qeṣarah, 107, 109, 111, 112
Mizrahi, Elijah, 65, 69, 71, 111
Mondschein, Aaron, 59, 251
Moses ha-Darshan, 30, 102
muḥkam, 108, 120
mutashābih, 120

Nahmanides, Moses, 127, 246
naṣṣ, 108, 115, 116, 126, 128, 155
Nathan ben Jehiel, 92
Nicholas of Lyra, 3, 16, 45

Old French, 5, 29, 30, 39, 40, 58, 97, 101, 145, 153, 171, 237
omnisignificance, 38
ordo artificialis, 181, 182, 183, 190
ordo naturalis, 181, 183
ordo verborum, 23, 80, 82
Origen, 15, 176, 202
oto she-sidder ha-devarim, 249, 255, 260, 265, 269

parallelism, 50, 51, 227, 228, 229, 230
Pentateuch Scholia (Byzantine commentary), 135–150, 156–158, 163

peshat. *See also* "a biblical verse does not leave the realm of its *peshat*" and under Ibn Ezra, Abraham; Qara, Joseph; Rashbam; Rashi
  as conceived by Jonah Ibn Janah, 113–121
  as conceived by Maimonides, 126–129
  as conceived by Samuel ben Hofni Gaon, 104–111, 118, 125
  as conceived by Tobiah ben Eliezer, 150–162
peshat interpretations that newly emerge (*ha-mitḥaddeshim*) every day, 4, 9, 31, 32, 35, 36, 207, 215, 220, 237, 242
piyyut, 33, 212, 240
Plato, 230, 232
prologue format, type-C prologue, 168, 170, 176
Pseudo-Rashi on Chronicles, 31, 253
Pseudo-Rashi on Ezra–Nehemiah, 31, 67, 252

Qara, Joseph
  attitude toward midrash, 209, 215, 216, 222, 239, 240, 241
  on biblical authorship, 199, 251, 253
  on biblical editor-narrator, 253
  biography, 210
  conception of *peshat*, 208, 209, 210, 216, 218, 221, 222, 239, 241
  glosses on Rashi, 32, 34, 51, 52, 221
  and Latin learning, 99, 209, 210
  method
    biblical stylistic conventions (*hergelo shel leshon ha-miqra*), 226
    context (*seder ha-miqra, hillukh ha-ketuvim, hillukh ha-parashah*), 225
    derekh ha-miqra'ot, 226
    historical sensitivity, 199, 235, 252
    self-sufficiency of *peshat*, 222, 239
  midrash commentary, 240
  piyyut commentary, 99, 240
  programmatic statements, 222, 239
  and Rashi, 2, 31, 208, 221
  rationalism, 230, 236
  sources of influence, 31, 207, 271
  works
    Bible commentaries, 211
    midrash commentary, 211
    piyyut commentary, 211

Rabanus Maurus, 79, 131
Rabbenu Gershom, 1, 2, 26, 27, 28, 30, 92, 212, 216
Rabbinic Bible, 3, 31, 33
Rashbam
  amitat peshuto shel miqra, 209
  anti-Christian polemics, 97, 233, 247
  attitude toward midrash, 130, 209, 215, 243
  on biblical narrator, 257, 258, 259, 260
  on biblical style, 184, 226, 227, 230, 267
  biography, 213
  concept of *peshat*, 9, 208, 209, 210, 215, 218, 221
  Dayyaqut, 54, 213
  dual hermeneutic, 242, 243, 244, 246
  glosses on Alfasi, 214
  glosses on Rashi, 32, 34, 51, 52, 221
  invoked *derekh* ... ("the typical manner of those who do X"), 237
  Latin knowledge, 97, 233
  and Latin learning, 209, 210, 219, 232, 233, 246, 247, 248, 263, 265
  method
    be-nohag she-ba-'olam, 111
    contextual interpretation, 225
    davar ha-lamed me-'inyano, 225, 226
    derekh ereṣ, 47, 111, 230, 231, 233, 234, 235, 243, 271
    derekh ha-miqra'ot, 226, 228, 267
    derekh tarbut, 234
    haqdamah, 226, 267
    historical sensitivity, 46, 235, 236
    self-sufficiency of *peshat*, 222, 223
  non-talmudic *peshat* interpretation of legal passages, 62, 65, 243, 244, 245, 246
  on parallelism, 50, 51, 227, 228, 229
  programmatic statements, 9, 31, 241, 243, 267
  and Rashi, 2, 4, 10, 31, 51, 65, 208, 220
  rationale for the commandments, 233, 234
  rationalism, 223, 230, 233, 236
  siddur devarim, 188, 202, 261
  Song of Songs interpretation, 171, 256, 257, 262, 263, 265
  sources of influence, 31, 46, 207, 271
  Talmud commentary, 213, 214

view of Mosaic authorship of the Pentateuch, 266, 268, 270
view of the role of human authors, editors in shaping the Bible, 249, 251, 255
viewed midrash as "the essence (*'iqqar*) of Torah", 9, 130, 241, 243
works, 213, 214
Rashi
aimed to "settle the verses", 52, 70, 71, 72, 178, 180
anti-Christian polemics, 99
attitude toward midrash, used selectively, 40, 41, 42, 66, 71, 74, 75, 77, 91, 95, 101, 130, 166
biography, 1, 19, 20, 26, 27
Christian interpretation and, 13, 91, 96, 98, 100, 130, 132, 175, 176, 183, 209
cited by Christian interpreters, 3
commentaries, list of, 30
concept of Holy Spirit, 23, 75, 76, 170, 172, 173, 174, 177, 200, 206, 250, 262
concept of the *meshorer*, 187–196, 202, 205, 206, 256, 258–261
derekh ha-miqra /miqra'ot / ketuvim (typical style of Scripture), 226
differentiated between *peshat* and midrash, 31, 36, 39, 43, 44, 46, 56, 57, 70, 147, 149, 185
dual hermeneutic, 44, 73, 74, 148
encouraged students' independence, 32, 36, 51, 207, 215, 220
exegetical terminology, 44, 52, 53
grammatical sensibilities, 47, 94, 95, 145, 148, 167, 183, 184
historical sensibilities, 45, 174
and Ibn Janah, 24, 118, 129, 131, 133
interpretations
halakhic, 61, 63
midrashic, 5, 56, 58, 67, 68, 144
peshat (explicitly labeled as such), 39, 40, 45, 46, 47, 49
typological, 45, 59, 60, 172, 173, 174
invoked *derekh* ... ("the typical manner of those who do X"), 45, 46, 111, 237
lemma complement format, 138
personality traits, 217
philological sensibilities, 29, 40, 41, 42, 52, 57, 140, 153, 193
programmatic statements, 69, 72, 73, 75
quasi-prologue format, 171, 173, 176
revised his commentaries, 32, 35, 36, 51, 221
sensitive to "sequence" of the biblical text, 43, 52, 71, 202
Song of Songs interpretation, 72, 73, 74, 75, 76, 162, 170, 171, 176, 177, 178
sources of influence for his *peshat* method
Menahem ben Saruq, 5, 10, 29, 40, 91, 104, 136
poterim, 5, 29
Targums, 5, 29
supercommentaries on, 69
Talmud commentary, 1–3, 10, 28, 94
textual complexity of commentary
additions to the commentary, 33, 34, 50, 221
glosses on the commentary, 32, 34, 213
view of the role of the editors who shaped the Bible, 196, 198, 251, 260
Reggio di Calabria edition (of Rashi), 33, 48, 51, 150
Remigius of Auxerre, 18, 19, 23, 80, 82, 84, 85, 88, 91, 164, 167, 168, 181, 183, 203, 204, 205, 206
resumptive repetition, 48, 49, 184, 189
Reuel (early Byzantine commentator), 11–12, 37, 134–151, 156–160
Rhineland talmudic academies, 1, 2, 10, 20, 26, 27, 29, 92–95, 102, 210, 214, 216
Roscellinus of Compiègne, 18
Rupert of Deutz, 99, 131

Saadia Gaon, 6, 23, 57, 103, 105–110, 114, 116, 117, 118, 120, 121, 122, 124, 125, 128, 129, 132, 136, 188, 224, 230, 231
sadran, 141, 142, 143, 144, 151, 248, 255, 260
Samuel ben Hofni Gaon, 7, 23, 104, 105, 107, 108, 109, 112, 113, 114, 115, 116, 117, 118, 121, 125, 129, 132, 186
seder, seder ha-miqra'ot, 2, 8, 23, 44, 52, 71, 73, 74, 75, 86, 174, 177, 178, 184, 188, 192, 202, 206, 208, 225, 260

Sefer ha-'Arukh, 92
semikhah, 43, 91
sensus litteralis, 3, 14, 210
sequentia, sequential reading of Scripture, 23, 86, 90
Servius, 80, 82, 87, 167, 168, 182, 183, 204
Shemaiah, 12, 32, 33, 35, 36, 51, 146, 147, 212, 221
shiṭṭah, *shiṭṭot*, 48, 94, 184, 214, 215, 254, 258
Smalley, Beryl, 3, 14, 15, 16, 38, 55
sofer, *ha-sofer*, 250, 251, 253, 254, 255
Soloveitchik, Haym, 92, 93, 217, 218
Steiner, Richard, 107, 134, 135, 136, 137, 138, 140, 145, 146, 255
Sternberg, Meir, 190

ta'wīl, 106, 107, 109, 110, 112, 113, 114, 117, 120, 121, 224
Tam, Rabbenu Jacob, 28, 62, 97–98, 214, 216
Targum, 29, 39, 40, 93
Ta-Shma, Israel M., 12, 136, 162
tefillin, 244, 245
there is no earlier or later in the Torah (rabbinic maxim), 179, 180, 181
Thierry of Chartres, 232, 265
Tobiah ben Eliezer, 12, 24, 39, 45, 46, 57, 58, 59, 111, 135, 150, 151, 152, 153, 154, 155, 156, 157, 158, 160, 161, 162, 163
Tobiah ben Moses, 134
Tosafists, 28, 98, 214, 216, 217, 218
Touitou, Eleazar, 11, 13, 14, 34–35, 44, 100, 165, 227, 246, 259, 268–269
tower of Babel, 222–224
Trevet, Nicholas, 264
trouvères, 162, 171, 257, 258
Troyes, 1, 20, 22, 27, 28, 96, 210
twelfth-century renaissance, 4, 13, 14, 218

Viezel, Eran, 142, 189, 200, 253, 259, 261
Virgil, 23, 80, 87, 167, 168, 182

Weiss Halivni, David, 104, 109, 121
William of Champeaux, 247
William of Conches, 232
Worms, 1, 20, 26, 27, 28, 29, 146, 210, 212

Yefet ben Eli, 142, 224
yishuv, *yishuv ha-miqra*, "settling the words of Scripture," 2, 23, 43, 70, 72, 73, 75, 133, 148, 174, 175, 206, 209, 225, 240
y-s-d in the sense of writing, 67, 68, 76, 170, 196, 197, 258, 259, 262, 263

ẓāhir, 105–110, 112, 113, 115–117, 120, 121, 125, 129, 155

Index of Scriptural References

Genesis
1:2, 231
1:5, 246
1:27, 185, 189, 194
2:8, 185, 191
2:21–22, 185
3:8, 69, 76, 92
3:20, 106
3:24, 39
5:24, 97
11:4, 222
11:7, 223
11:8, 223
11:28, 56–57
14:14, 57
14:15, 46, 111, 237
15:2, 58
15:4, 114
15:10, 45, 237
15:17, 45, 236
15:18, 45
18:10, 137
19:15, 228
24:2, 235
29:2, 152
29:27, 144
33:4, 143, 149
33:19, 40
35:11, 114
35:16, 40, 41
37:2, 268
39:1, 49
48:1–2, 111
48:6, 63
49:22, 51
Exodus
2:5, 53, 153, 154
6:2–9, 42, 72, 88, 175
6:13, 48, 49, 184
6:29–30, 184
6:30, 189
10:8, 140
13:9, 244, 245
14:20, 138
14:21, 231
15:1, 147, 148
15:2, 140
15:6, 49, 229
16:20, 110
17:11, 236
17:15, 137
20:13, 97
23:2, 72
23:19, 116, 234
24:12, 103
34:27, 155
Leviticus
11:34, 233
14:34, 97
19:19, 97
19:26, 225
21:1–4, 64
21:4, 71

Numbers
8:4, 112
21:17, 148
Deuteronomy
4:24, 107
22:6, 234
25:5–6, 61
31:9, 270
32:23, 228
Joshua
23:6, 270
Judges
5:31, 198, 199
13:18, 253
17:16, 254
1 Samuel
9:9, 198, 199, 252
10:11, 198
10:18, 198
10:19, 198
17:55, 241, 252
2 Samuel
22:42, 47, 80
23:1, 180
2 Kings
5:19, 40
Isaiah
5:9, 239
7:2, 255
26:11, 44, 72, 175
64:3, 35
Jeremiah
9:16–17, 259
34:19, 45
Ezekiel
1:2–3, 250
1:8–21, 142
2:1, 98
7:19–20, 138
8:3, 141, 142
8:5, 141, 142
9:9, 139
10:8–17, 142
13:5, 160
13:10, 160
21:17, 140
21:28, 138
24:21, 138
25:14, 174
35:6, 143, 144
39:14, 140
Amos
9:9, 41
Jonah
1:10, 254
Psalms
2:1, 99
2:2, 205
2:3, 205
5:1, 41
5:7, 193
14:1, 173
16:1, 204
16:7, 174
16:9, 114
18:2, 205
18:3, 205
18:36, 205
18:42, 80
19:2, 169, 194
19:13–14, 195
41:3, 82
42:1, 172
42:2, 173
42:7–9, 60
45:1, 67
45:2, 67
45:4, 67, 68, 69
45:15–18, 195
51:1, 87
68:2, 191
68:5, 191
68:5–10, 82
68:6, 192
68:20, 192
68, 29, 191
72:20, 181
78:1–2, 84
78:12, 84
87:5, 194
98:3, 90
142:1, 88
149:9, 173–174
Proverbs
1:7, 250
Song of Songs
1:2, 161
1:8, 161

2:7, 75, 178
2:8, 179, 181, 184
2:10–13, 75
8:11–14, 158, 160, 162
Qohelet
1:1, 250
4:13, 229
Daniel
8:17, 98
Ezra
2:1, 253
2 Chronicles
29:28, 187, 258
32:25, 253
Matthew
12:15–21, 225
John
19:19, 204
1 Corinthians
10:11, 37
Galatians
4:24, 83
Qur'an
3:7, 120, 132
12:81–82, 106

Index of Rabbinic Sources

Babylonian Talmud

Bava Batra
14b, 180
14b–15a, 199, 248
15a, 249, 258
39a, 216
43a, 216
51a, 216
65b, 216
69a, 216
80a, 214
104b, 216
119b, 183

Bava Meṣi'a
33a, 239, 242

Berakhot
28b, 242

Giṭṭin
60a, 269

Ḥullin
100b, 260
140a, 226

Ketubbot
83b, 44

Megillah
31b, 266

Pesaḥim
6b, 169
111a, 26
117a, 180, 194

Rosh ha-Shanah
17a, 96

Sanhedrin
34a, 43, 72, 115
59b, 224
86a, 226
99b, 266

Shabbat
55b, 183
63a, 5, 66–69, 242, 267

Soṭah
12b, 53, 154

Yevamot
11b, 5, 67
22b, 64
24a, 5, 61, 63, 67, 241

Midrash

Avot de-Rabbi Natan, 143

Genesis Rabbah
12:8, 267
21:9, 39
38:13, 56
42:2, 58
43:3, 46
44:9, 45
59:8, 235
70:8, 153
82:7, 40
89:4, 152

Leviticus Rabbah
1:3, 154

Mekhilta de-Rabbi Ishmael
Be-shallaḥ, Vayassa', §4, 110

Midrash Tehillim
Ps 5:1, 42
Ps 19:14, 195
Ps 149:9, 174
Mishnah of Rabbi Eliezer / Midrash of Thirty-Two Hermeneutic Rules, 112, 185–186
Numbers Rabbah
3:13, 143
Qohelet Rabbah
1:1, 249
Ruth Rabbah
2:1, 154
Song of Songs Rabbah
1:10, 249
Tanḥuma
Bo §7, 48
be-Ha'alotekha §3, 112
Tanḥuma ha-Qadum, *Ḥayyei Sarah* §6, 235
Yalqut Shimoni, Ps 19:14, 195

Mishnah

Bava Qamma
1:4, 234
10:2, 193
Niddah
10:8, 234
Rosh ha-Shanah
3:8, 236

CPSIA information can be obtained
at www.ICGtesting.com
Printed in the USA
LVHW111223030821
694401LV00002B/85

9 781108 470292